Russian politics under Putin

Published in our
centenary year
2004
MANCHESTER
UNIVERSITY
PRESS

Russian politics under Putin

edited by

Cameron Ross

Manchester University Press
Manchester and New York

distributed exclusively in the USA by Palgrave

Copyright © Manchester University Press 2004

While copyright in the volume as a whole is vested in Manchester
University Press, copyright in individual chapters belongs to their
respective authors, and no chapter may be reproduced wholly
or in part without the express permission in writing of
both author and publisher.

Published by Manchester University Press
Oxford Road, Manchester M13 9NR, UK
and Room 400, 175 Fifth Avenue, New York, NY 10010, USA
www.manchesteruniversitypress.co.uk

Distributed exclusively in the USA by
Palgrave, 175 Fifth Avenue, New York,
NY 10010, USA

Distributed exclusively in Canada by
UBC Press, University of British Columbia, 2029 West Mall,
Vancouver, BC, Canada V6T 1Z2

British Library Cataloguing-in-Publication Data
A catalogue record for this book is available from the British Library

Library of Congress Cataloging-in-Publication Data applied for

ISBN   0 7190 6800 2 *hardback*
        0 7190 6801 0 *paperback*

First published 2004

12 11 10 09 08 07 06 05 04   10 9 8 7 6 5 4 3 2 1

Typeset in Times
by Graphicraft Limited, Hong Kong
Printed in Great Britain
by CPI, Bath

Contents

Tables, figures and maps   *page* vii
Contributors   x
Abbreviations   xi

I Leadership and regime change

1   Vladimir Putin's leadership in comparative perspective
    Archie Brown   3

2   Regime change from Yeltsin to Putin: normality,
    normalcy or normalisation?   *Richard Sakwa*   17

II Political parties and democratisation

3   Russia's Law on Political Parties: democracy by decree?
    Edwin Bacon   39

4   The Putin paradigm and the cowering of Russia's
    communists   *Luke March*   53

5   Russia's disempowered electorate   *Stephen White*   76

III Economy and society

6   The economic legacy: what Putin had to deal with
    and the way forward   *David Lane*   95

7   The Russian economy under Vladimir Putin
    William Tompson   114

8   Politics and the mass media under Putin   *Laura Belin*   133

Contents

IV Regional politics

9	Putin's federal reforms *Cameron Ross*	155
10	Measuring and explaining variations in Russian regional democratisation *Christopher Marsh*	176
11	Regional elections and democratisation in Russia *Valentin Mikhailov*	198

V Foreign policy and Chechnya

12	Russian foreign policy under Putin *Dmitry Polikanov and Graham Timmins*	223
13	Russian foreign policy towards the European Union *Jackie Gower*	236
14	Conflict in Chechnya *Mike Bowker*	255
15	Russian foreign policy: the CIS and the Baltic states *Ella Akerman and Graeme P. Herd*	269
	Index	287

Tables, figures and maps

Tables

3.1	Voting on the Law on Political Parties, State Duma of the Russian Federation, 21 June 2001	*page* 44
3.2	Registered political parties as of 31 March 2003	45
4.1	Distribution of Duma committee chairs	64
4.2	CPRF leadership in the Duma	66
5.1	Trust in institutions, 2001	78
5.2	Measures of political efficacy, 2001	80
5.3	Party family preferences, 2001	81
5.4	'Best' and 'worst' features of communist rule, 1993 and 2001	83
5.5	The 'most characteristic' features of communist and post-communist rule	84
5.6	Freedoms under communist and post-communist rule	85
5.7	Membership of civic associations, 2000	86
5.8	Corruption and government, 2000	87
5.9	Political system preferences, 2000	88
5.10	Trust in civic institutions: Russia in comparative perspective	89
6.1	Levels of poverty (18 Central and East European countries)	100
6.2	Political and economic transformation	101
7.1	Economic and social indicators from Yeltsin to Putin	118
7.2	Fiscal performance, 1998–2002	121
9.1	Economic status of the seven federal districts	161
10.1	Comparison of regional democracy ratings	182
10.2	Regression models of civic community indicators predicting index of regional democratisation	184
10.3	Regression models of socio-economic development indicators predicting index of regional democratisation	186
10.4	Regression models of civic community and socio-economic development indicators predicting index of regional democratisation	188

Tables, figures and maps

10.5	Regression models of civic community and socio-economic development indicators predicting index of regional democratisation, controlling for ethnicity	190
11.1	Examples of 'administrative management' of the 1996 presidential elections in Tatarstan	200
11.2	Maximum turnout in selected TECs in the 1996 and 2000 presidential elections	202
11.3	Correlation coefficient between turnout and Putin's support in four subjects of the Russian Federation	203
11.4	Comparison of the maximum and the minimum share of votes cast 'against all' in various TECs of the same subject of the Federation in the 1999 State Duma elections	211
11.5	Comparison of the maximum and the minimum share of invalid votes in various TECs of the same subject of the Federation in the 1999 State Duma elections	212

Figures

5.1	Satisfaction with democracy	90
11.1	Election of Russian Federation President, 26 March 2000 (88 subjects of the Federation)	202
11.2	Lipetsk and Perm oblasts: election of Russian President, 26 March 2000; linear regression for turnout and voting for Putin	204
11.3	Tatarstan and Bashkortostan: election of Russian President, 26 March 2000; linear regression for turnout and voting for Putin	205
11.4	Lipetsk and Perm oblasts: election of Russian President, 26 March 2000; linear regression for invalid ballots and voting for Putin	206
11.5	Tatarstan and Bashkortostan: election of Russian President, 26 March 2000; linear regression for invalid ballots and voting for Putin	207
11.6	Gosduma RF election 1999, St Petersburg, 30 TECs; linear regression for turnout and voting for Edinstvo, SPS, OVR and CPRF	208
11.7	Gosduma RF election 1999, Moscow, 126 TECs; linear regression for turnout and voting for OVR, CPRF and SPS	209
11.8	Gosduma RF election 1999, Tatarstan, 62 TECs; linear regression for turnout and voting for OVR and CPRF	210
11.9	Samara Oblast: governor election 2000, 47 TECs; turnout 45%	213
11.10	Ulyanovsk Oblast: governor election, 24 December 2000, 29 TECs; turnout 56.2%	214
11.11	Republic of Tatarstan: presidential election, 25 March 2001, 63 TECs; turnout 79.3%	215

11.12 Tatarstan presidential election 2001, 6 TECs; rank correlations between invalid ballots (or voting against all) and voting for Shaimiev — 216

Maps

6.1 Inequality and poverty — 99
6.2 Successful transition to economic growth and polyarchic polity — 102

Contributors

Ella Akerman, University of Aberdeen.

Dr Edwin Bacon, University of Birmingham.

Dr Laura Belin, University of Oxford.

Mike Bowker, University of East Anglia.

Professor Archie Brown, University of Oxford.

Jackie Gower, University of Kent.

Dr Graeme P. Herd, Marshall Centre, Germany.

Professor David Lane, University of Cambridge.

Dr Luke March, University of Edinburgh.

Dr Christopher Marsh, Baylor University, USA.

Dr Valentin Mikhailov, University of Kazan, Russia.

Professor Dmitry Polikanov, NATO School (SHAPE), Germany.

Dr Cameron Ross, University of Dundee.

Professor Richard Sakwa, University of Kent.

Dr Graham Timmins, University of Stirling.

Dr William Tompson, Birkbeck College, University of London.

Professor Stephen White, University of Glasgow.

Abbreviations

ABM	Anti-Ballistic Missile Treaty
AIG	Agro-Industrial Group
BBl	Barrel
CEC	Central Electoral Commission
CEE	Central and Eastern Europe
CEES	common European economic space
CFSP	Common Foreign and Security Policy
CIS	Commonwealth of Independent States
CPRF	Communist Party of the Russian Federation
CPSU	Communist Party of the Soviet Union
CST	Collective Security Treaty
ESN	unified social tax
FAR	Fatherland–All Russia
FPG	financial-industrial group
FSB	Federal Security Bureau
GDP	gross domestic product
IMF	International Monetary Fund
IND	Independent
LDPR	Liberal Democratic Party of Russia
MPS	Ministry of Railways
NATO	North Atlantic Treaty Organisation
ND	People's Deputy
NMD	National Missile Defence
NTV	National Television
OECD	Organisation for Economic Co-operation and Development
ORT	Russian Public Television
OSCE	Organisation for Security and Co-operation in Europe
PCA	The Partnership and Co-operation Agreement
PCF	Communist Party of France
PCI	Communist Party of Italy
PECs	Precinct Election Commissions
PfP	Partnership for Peace

Abbreviations

PJC	Permanent Joint Council
R&D	research and development
RF	Russian Federation
RR	Russia's regions
RTR	Russian Television
SCO	Shanghai Co-operation Organisation
SPS	Union of Right Forces
TCA	Trade and Co-operation Agreement
TEC	Territorial Election Commission
TNK	Tyumen Oil Company
UNHCR	United Nations High Commission for Refugees
USSR	Union of Soviet Socialist Republics
VTsIOM	All-Russian Centre for the Study of Public Opinion
WEU	Western European Union
WTO	World Trade Organisation
YAB	Yabloko

I

Leadership
and regime change

1

Vladimir Putin's leadership in comparative perspective

Archie Brown

Even within the highly institutionalised Soviet system, a change of top leader generally produced some policy change and, at a minimum, a change of style. Yet, in the post-Stalin era, the Politburo and Secretariat of the Central Committee, the republican and regional party secretaries and, for much of the time, the ministries were powerful institutional actors who imposed constraints upon the freedom of action of the party General Secretary. There were norms of Soviet political life that even the *Gensek*, the person at the pinnacle of an extremely hierarchical system, could disregard only at his peril. Nikita Khrushchev rode roughshod over some of the institutions on whose functioning the system depended, but without resort to the terror that sustained Stalin's personal dictatorship. He eventually paid for this with his job when he was deposed by senior colleagues in October 1964. Mikhail Gorbachev was a still bolder reformer who, following an unsuccessful attempt to improve the working of existing structures, set about more comprehensively dismantling his institutional inheritance. Yet, transformative change of the Soviet *system* produced the quite unintended consequence of disintegration of the Soviet *Union*, ultimately leaving Gorbachev isolated as leader of a state that had ceased to exist.[1]

The leadership with which the comparative perspective of this chapter will be concerned before it focuses more specifically on the role being played by Vladimir Putin is that provided by chief executives within states, whether general secretaries, prime ministers, or presidents. Within the limiting framework of formal powers and constraints upon the powers of chief executives, there are, of course, huge variations in what the power-holders *do* with those powers. If we make a distinction, as James MacGregor Burns did in his well-known book on leadership published a quarter of a century ago,[2] between *transforming* and *transactional* leaders, we shall be concerned with the issue of whether particular leaders are able radically to *transform* policy or whether they are able to make only incremental policy change.

Burns gives a moral dimension to what he calls 'transforming leadership'. For him '*transforming* leadership . . . occurs when one or more persons *engage* with others in such a way that leaders and followers raise one another to higher levels of motivation and morality'.[3] Burns's favourite example is Franklin D. Roosevelt. Gandhi is another. As more recent examples, we might wish to add Nelson Mandela and – as a leader, though (like Gandhi) not a chief executive – Aung San Suu Kyi. Differing substantially as well as, to a minor degree, linguistically from Burns, I use here and elsewhere the term, '*transformational* leader', instead of transforming leader and do not make any assumption about the moral and political desirability of the transformation. Rather, the term 'transformational leader' indicates that transformation occurs and that the leader is, to a significant extent, the agent of that transformation. On such a basis, Stalin – even more than Roosevelt – was a transformational leader, although one should add that, by definition, a totalitarian or authoritarian system, in comparison with a democratic polity, gives the top leader possibilities of introducing more drastic changes, backed up by qualitatively different levels of coercion.

A still stronger criterion for transformational leadership is that it should denote not merely radical change of policy but *systemic* transformation, whether we are talking about the political system, the economic system, or the international system. Both Mikhail Gorbachev and Boris Yeltsin – the former more than the latter – were, in that sense, transformational leaders. Within less than a decade Russia moved from having a highly authoritarian system (Gorbachev is among those who calls the unreformed Soviet Union 'totalitarian'[4]) to political pluralism; from a command economy to a partly market and capitalist economy; from political and military hegemony over Eastern Europe to acquiescence in East-Central European autonomy, accompanied by dissolution of the Warsaw Pact and Comecon; from Cold War to East–West co-operation; and from being a state whose territory embraced the Baltic republics, Ukraine, the Caucasus, and vast tracts of Central Asia, to a country shorn of fourteen of its fifteen republics, one in which now some 80 per cent of the population are Russians (as compared to just over 50 per cent prior to the disintegration of the greater Russia that was the Soviet Union). Gorbachev played a crucial part in all five of those remarkable transformations, although the last was a wholly unintended consequence of other changes. Yeltsin was a key political actor in the building of 'capitalism Russian-style'[5] and, earlier, in the break-up of the Soviet state when he played the Russian card against the Union.[6]

Burns's *transactional* leader, in contrast, works within existing norms and does not challenge either the conventional wisdom or major institutional interests. Such leaders, it goes without saying, are more common in democracies than transforming or transformational leaders. Indeed, responsiveness to other major players within the system and political reciprocity are part of the normal leadership style of a democratic chief executive. In the British context, Harold Wilson, Jim Callaghan and John Major fit easily enough into this category. But the Soviet Union also had its transactional leaders, under whom the *society* might be changing in important ways but who themselves pursued only incremental policy change and for whom a prime concern was not to rock the boat. Leonid Brezhnev was quintessentially such a leader, as was Konstantin Chernenko in his brief period at the helm. While far from unconcerned about the opinions of a broader Soviet public – hence, for example, the huge subsidies on basic foodstuffs as well as the most rigorous controls over the mass media and the educational curriculum – their wheeling and dealing took place essentially within the confines of the political elite.

The dichotomous classification of leadership – transforming/transformational or transactional – cannot be wholly satisfactory. It certainly leaves tricky borderline cases. Where, for instance, would we fit in Clement Attlee and Lyndon Johnson? Attlee presided over dramatic policy change in Britain in the first six years after the Second World War. He was a strong leader, in the sense that he could not be intimidated, was not afraid to dismiss people he felt were not up to the job, and had firm views on certain subjects. These included defence policy, on which he was at odds with many in his party. Yet, at the same time, Attlee was someone who led, as a rule, from the centre of the Labour Party rather than from either of its wings. He was willing to give Cabinet colleagues a lot of leeway to make decisions within the competence of their departments and he was in many ways a consensus-seeker. Or what of Lyndon Johnson? As Senate Leader, he had been the archetypal wheeler-dealer, doing favours here, smoothing the path of a colleague's pork barrel legislation there, and building up a lot of bankable credit in the reciprocity ledger. But he also had some ideals, and more than a streak of ruthlessness, and he was able as president to get through Congress radical civil rights and social legislation which John F. Kennedy had been unable or unwilling to advance. Of course, it was not *only* a matter of leadership. The political climate had also changed, partly as a result of the shock of Kennedy's assassination. As Thomas Cronin has observed, 'leadership is highly situational and contextual'.[7]

Yet, if we look for *innovative* leadership, a less demanding attribute than *transforming* or *transformational* leadership, we will find that an essential prelude to it is generally *perception of failure* on the part of the leader-to-be. The failure he or she identifies can be in his or her party, in the economy or even in the political and social system. In retrospect many people assume that the Soviet Union was in deep crisis in 1985, but that is not how it seemed to most Soviet citizens or to the greater part of the Soviet elite at the time. Gorbachev was unusual in seeing in the mid-1980s 'pre-crisis phenomena' and in having a far stronger perception than his Politburo colleagues of Soviet failure in comparison with the more economically advanced countries of Western Europe. Yeltsin, too, could perceive what happened subsequently, during the years of Gorbachev's leadership, as failure. *Glasnost'* quite rapidly developed into freedom of speech and publication. However, the liberalisation of the early years of *perestroika*, which gave way from the summer of 1988 to democratisation, brought all manner of latent discontents to the surface – above all, the nationalities question which threatened, and ultimately destroyed, the integrity of the Soviet state. Similarly, partial economic reform had left the Soviet economy in limbo – no longer a functioning command economy (which, to say the least, had never worked well, but worked after a fashion so long as it was backed by discipline, fear, and a Communist Party wielding real power), but not yet a market economy, notwithstanding various important concessions to the market.

For Vladimir Putin, although he refrains from direct criticism of either of his predecessors and has quite cordial relations with both of them, the decade and a half from the launch of *perestroika* in 1985 was essentially a time of failure. Adaptation to the dismantling of the Soviet system and the disintegration of the Soviet state was not easy for Putin. On his own admission, he dreamed from the time he was a schoolboy of joining the KGB, duly entered that organisation without giving a thought to its repressive role and the history of the purges, and subsequently described himself as a 'pure and utterly successful product of Soviet patriotic education'.[8] In the late 1990s, after he had joined the Yeltsin administration, Putin's main concern was that the *vertical chain of government* (which in pre-*perestroika* Soviet times was very much a chain of *command*) had been lost.[9] Yet, even though Putin had been an uncritical supporter of the Soviet political order until very late indeed in the 1980s, at the crucial moment of August 1991 he supported Anatoly Sobchak, the Democratic mayor of St Petersburg, and opposed the putschists, although that did not prevent him, as a post-Soviet head of the Federal Security Service (FSB) and, later, as president having amicable relations with one of the leading figures in the August putsch, Vladimir Kruychkov, his former KGB chief.

Putin came to power, highly conscious of Russia's relative economic decline and loss of standing as a world power compared with a decade and a half earlier (see Chapters 6 and 7). It is unsurprising that, while taking a critical view also of the decline of central political authority during the Yeltsin years, Putin did not criticise his immediate predecessor personally, since he was hugely indebted to him. It was Yeltsin who had paved the way for Putin's convincing electoral victory in March 2000 by making him prime minister in August 1999. The prime ministership had already by that time become a likely stepping-stone to the presidency inasmuch as it greatly raised the political profile of the holder of that office and had led to several of Putin's prime ministerial predecessors, most notably Viktor Chernomyrdin in the mid-1990s and Yevgeny Primakov in 1998–99, being considered serious candidates for the succession to Yeltsin. Moreover, by resigning six months ahead of his allotted time in order to foreshorten the campaigning period and to give Vladimir Putin the inestimable advantage of being acting president between January and March 2000, Yeltsin put all potential rivals of Putin at a disadvantage. This was not, as is sometimes suggested, an example of democratic alternation, the kind of transfer of power indicative of growing consolidation of Russian democracy. It was, rather, the bequeathal of power from an outgoing president to his latest favourite and the bending of a Constitution which laid down the length of the term a president should serve. Yeltsin made no bones about the fact his was not a resignation on grounds of ill-health, but a departure timed to give maximum electoral advantage to his chosen successor. None of this guaranteed Putin an election victory, though the role of the mass media was a great additional help to him.[10] Moreover, Yeltsin was in the last years of his presidency so unpopular that it was as well for Putin that his political style was very different from Yeltsin's and that he had comparative youth and vigour on his side. Having been a relatively unknown figure to the Soviet public prior to his appointment as prime minister in the late summer of 1999, Putin combined the advantages of freshness with those of incumbency.

The style of Putin's rule has remained very different from that of Yeltsin. The first Russian post-Soviet president had a natural authority which had been enhanced by his years of being the person who ran things, the ultimate decision-maker within his own domain, whether as Communist Party First Secretary in the Sverdlovsk region, more briefly as Moscow Party First Secretary, as Chairman of the Russian Supreme Soviet (1990–91) or as president of Russia from 1991. Putin's career had seen him consistently in subordinate positions, whether within the KGB, the city government of Leningrad (which, following the failed August 1991 coup, became once again St Petersburg) under Sobchak, or the Kremlin administration. His first taste of being number one within an organisation did not come until July 1998 when he was appointed to head the FSB, the security-service successor to the KGB. During the earlier years, however, he acquired a disciplined working style and the habit of being a good listener, an essential attribute in his first career as a foreign intelligence officer. Although there have been exceptional occasions when he has acted boldly, Putin has been, in comparison with Yeltsin, a cautious decision-maker, and has not shared his predecessor's penchant for impulsive, often theatrical, announcements of dismissals, appointments, or supposed new initiatives. That aversion to grandstanding is scarcely a fault, and though there are many in the Russian political elite who regard Putin as indecisive, an alternative interpretation is that he is exercising a very necessary caution. That is the viewpoint, for example, of a State Duma Deputy with a record of independence (going back to his participation in an underground Marxist group in the mid-1960s and his arrest as a dissident in 1975),[11] Vyacheslav Igrunov. He argues that Putin's caution is entirely appropriate, since there are many points of potential conflict within the under-institutionalised Russian political system. Destabilisation, Igrunov argues, would put paid to any serious reform and he welcomes the fact that the Russian president shows awareness of the need for evolutionary change, not confrontation. He likens Putin's approach to that of Tolstoy's Kutuzov in that he knows the value of 'not hindering natural processes'.[12]

A change of style, even when in many respects positive, does not, however, amount to transformation of policy, still less of the system. Putin, in certain areas, has been an innovative leader, but in general has shown himself to be an arch-pragmatist and realist. In foreign policy (see Chapters 12–15) he does not suffer from Yeltsin's illusion that his meetings with the American president were somehow akin to the 'summit meetings' of Soviet times. He has adjusted to the indisputable fact of great disparity of power between Russia and the United States and, in one of his bolder strategic moves, Putin identified himself immediately with the 'war on terror' which followed the September 11 2001 destruction of the twin towers in New York, even to the extent of welcoming (to the chagrin of the Russian military establishment)[13] closer American ties with other Soviet successor states in the pursuit of what he was quick to identify as a common enemy. Indeed, as early as September 1999, when he had been prime minister for only a month, Putin told President Clinton (when they met in New Zealand at the Asia–Pacific Economic Co-operation forum) that he hoped the United States understood that 'Russia and the West were on the same side in a fight against global terrorism'.[14] Yeltsin craved (without ever receiving) the wide international recognition that Gorbachev had attracted. He made great play of essentially cosmetic changes such as the meetings of world leaders known as the 'G7 + 1' becoming the G8. It was particularly important psychologically for Yeltsin to be treated as an apparent equal by the American president – 'my friend Bill', as he liked to call him.[15] Putin has been less effusive, but he has accepted even highly uncongenial American policies, such as NATO enlargement, phlegmatically (see Chapters 12 and 13).

One other major factor, in addition to those mentioned earlier in this chapter, which helped to propel Putin into the Kremlin in March 2000 was the incursion of Chechen forces commanded by Shamil Basayev into the neighbouring North Caucasian republic of Dagestan in August 1999 and the blowing-up of apartment blocks in Moscow and Volgodonsk in the autumn of that same year, acts of terrorism which were blamed on Chechens, although no convincing proof as to the identity of their perpetrators has been forthcoming. These outrages provided the trigger for the second post-Soviet Chechen war. The first, launched by Boris Yeltsin in 1994, had ended in stalemate in 1996 and a ceasefire of sorts brokered by General Alexander Lebed' who briefly headed the Security Council in that electoral year. (In 1998 Lebed' was elected governor of Krasnoyarsk *krai*; he died in an air accident in 2002.) When thousands of Russian troops re-entered Chechnya in October 1999, Yeltsin was still president and so carries ultimate responsibility for this second war, as for the first. Putin, however, strongly identified himself with it from the outset (see Chapter 14).

Initially, the second war attracted much stronger support from the Russian public than the first, for the spillover of the chaos and violence that had prevailed in Chechnya (even between 1996 and 1999) into other parts of the Federation, including Moscow (if the authorities were right in blaming Chechens for the apartment block deaths) hardened attitudes against those deemed responsible for such atrocities. By strongly identifying himself with the military campaign to stamp out 'Wahhabi' terrorism emanating from Chechnya, Putin initially enhanced his popularity by demonstrating toughness and a determination to restore order. However, like Yeltsin, he appeared to have little or no idea of how to resolve the chaos of Chechnya other than by the indiscriminate use of force. A civil war waged with brutality on both sides had not, despite the federal forces' advantages in terms of numbers and firepower, come even close to being resolved by the end of 2002. In October that year, the conflict was brought to Moscow (this time indisputably by Chechens) with the theatre hostage siege that led to the deaths of some one hundred and thirty people and in December 2002 the headquarters of the pro-Moscow administration in Chechnya were blown up in a suicide mission that led to at least eighty deaths. Thus, the renewal of hostilities on the part of federal forces in 1999, which provided short-term electoral benefit to Putin, looked increasingly like a political dead-end. Putin, in contrast with Yeltsin, has generally demonstrated strict control over his emotions, but he has become notably testy when questioned by Western journalists about the wisdom and morality of the methods chosen to combat warlordism and disaffection in Chechnya. Post-September 11, however, by skilfully laying increased emphasis on how Russia's struggle in Chechnya was part and parcel of President Bush's 'war on terror', Putin succeeded in largely stilling criticism from West European and Washington *governmental* circles of Russia's military operations in the North Caucasus. His policy, in essence a continuation of that conducted unsuccessfully in the mid-1990s, had manifestly failed, however, to win the hearts and minds of Chechens.

In economic policy, too, there is considerable continuity of policy (see Chapters 6 and 7), although liberal economic reformers (including such newcomers to the top tier of the federal government as Minister of Finance Aleksei Kudrin, Minister of Economic Development and Trade German Gref, Putin's own economic adviser, Andrei Illarionov, and the supervisor of Russia's security market with ministerial rank, Igor Kostikov, all of them from St Petersburg) have been more influential than they were during long periods of the Yeltsin administration. The implementation of a reduction of income and business tax, with a concomitant reduction in tax evasion and increase in tax revenues, are cases in point. Putin's popularity has also been bolstered by inherited economic factors beyond his control. Russia – and Putin – has benefited in recent years from high oil prices and also from the involuntary devaluation which followed the economic crash of 1998. That made imports more expensive and gave a much-needed boost to Russian domestic industry, including the food industry.[16] The role of the 'oligarchs' – those business tycoons who infiltrated the corridors of power during the Yeltsin presidency, in some cases combining governmental office with the pursuit of private gain, in others making sure that their placemen were in key positions to advance their economic interests – has altered.[17] The change, however, is more of form than of content. No prudent big businessman in Putin's Russia would try publicly to tell the president whom to appoint and what to do in the manner of Boris Berezovsky or use (or be allowed to use) a television channel, as Vladimir Gusinsky used NTV during the 1999–2000 electoral cycle, to stand alone among the major media conglomerates and take a critical look at the Kremlin's favoured candidates.[18]

By selective application of the law Gusinsky and then Berezovsky were deprived of their proximity to power and the most important of their media holdings and then threatened with criminal proceedings. Both now are living abroad. Other business tycoons, who have accepted the rules of the game established during the Putin presidency (above all, that they should not *publicly* interfere in high politics) have prospered more than ever. They include Roman Abramovich, Oleg Deripaska, Mikhail Fridman, Mikhail Khodorkovsky, Aleksandr Mamut and Sergei Pugachev. The Constitution gives the Russian president a formidable array of powers. It does not accord him the right to apply the law selectively, but one of his more significant *de facto* powers is precisely that.[19] It would be hard to find a major figure in Russian financial circles who has never contravened the law. What marked out Berezovsky and Gusinsky from those who have subsequently prospered is that they failed to demonstrate loyalty to the president. Berezovsky, unlike Gusinsky, had played a prominent, supportive role in Putin's campaign for the presidency. The mass media he controlled were especially abrasive in their dismissal of Putin's potential rivals. Berezovsky, however, evidently expected to have earned thereby as much access and favour as he enjoyed in Yeltsin's Kremlin, and he became increasingly critical of Russia's new president when it began to be clear that Putin had other ideas. Given the extent to which Berezovsky had been demonised in Russia as the archetypal beneficiary of what Stefan Hedlund has called 'predatory capitalism',[20] he made a useful scapegoat.[21]

Business tycoons who have passed the loyalty test are still, however, wielding more political and economic power than is compatible either with democratic norms or genuine market relations. A test case arrived in December 2002 when the long-awaited sale of the state-owned major oil company, Slavneft, took place. There was much fanfare ahead of the sale that this time there would be genuine competition among buyers, producing an optimal return for the state exchequer. In other words, there was to be a marked contrast with the rigged auctions of the 1990s when Russia's tycoons gained huge energy resources at a fraction of their true market value. Presumably, such a break with the past was, indeed, the intention of some within the presidential administration and government. If all the principal political actors had harboured the aim of making this another manipulated sale to a pre-selected buyer, it would have been unwise to raise expectations that a new chapter was being opened. Yet what was predicted would be a model of fairness and genuine competition turned out to be a closed and rigged auction, all too reminiscent of Yeltsin's Russia.

The outcome suggests that even if no tycoon can get away with telling Putin publicly what to do, the influence over the president and government that can be exercised behind the scenes is no less telling. One by one potential buyers were warned off from bidding. They included the Chinese state oil company who had earlier been encouraged to compete. The list of bidders changed at the last minute, among those withdrawing being LUKoil. The seven 'competitors' who participated in the auction on 18 December 2002, which lasted just five minutes, turned out all to have links to Sibneft, the company controlled by Roman Abramovich (who is also the governor of Chukhotka). Hardly surprisingly, then, Slavneft passed to Sibneft for a sum much lower than it could have commanded had market competition prevailed. The government had set a minimum price of $1.7 billion and the company went to Sibneft for $1.86 billion, even though Russia's Audit Chamber had 'estimated the value of the Slavneft stake at least $3 billion'.[22] It could be argued that if the company fetched something between half and two-thirds of its market value, this was a quantitative advance on the 1990s when Russia's mineral wealth was sold for a much smaller fraction of its worth to similarly pre-chosen buyers. It did not, however, mark a qualitative change away from the politically irresponsible power wielded by Russia's new ultra-rich.

The contradiction between Putin's overt support for marketisation and the reality of a manipulated auction points not only to the continued influence of a favoured group of business tycoons but also to the fact that his administration, like Yeltsin's (and, for that matter, Gorbachev's) before him, contains very different groupings. Those who have been called the 'oligarchs' still have their close ties with many of the holdovers from the Yeltsin administration. The inherited bureaucracy, in which a key role is still played by Aleksandr Voloshin, as chief-of-staff of the presidential administration, remains an enormously powerful player in Russian politics.[23] The economic liberals – several of whom holding ministerial office are (as noted earlier) like Putin, from St Petersburg – constitute an important grouping, and the *siloviki*, the people from the power ministries (which, in the case of Putin's team, means especially from the KGB) are a third significant contingent. Both the second and the third of these groupings have a higher status today than they had during most of the Yeltsin period. But what remains the same is that the president is still the arbiter and conciliator of different interests and orientations within the administration. Continuity is to be found also in the extent to which Russian big business (not the mass media which have lost, as Laura Belin's chapter in this volume makes clear, some of their earlier independence) constitutes a 'fourth estate' (see Chapter 8).

As has been noted already, a key concern for Vladimir Putin has been to change the relations that developed between the centre, on the one hand, and the republics and regions, on the other, during the Yeltsin years (see Chapter 9). What Jeffrey Kahn has called the 'parade of treaties' consisted of bilateral agreements between the federal authorities in Moscow and Russian republics and regions, resulting in the extra-constitutional and asymmetrical devolution of a variety of powers to many of the component parts of the federation.[24] These treaties, as Kahn observes, lacked transparency and were of dubious legal standing. Neither the federal nor the republican legislative branches were allowed to take part in the negotiations, nor did the agreements require or receive legislative ratification. They were heavily 'executive-driven'.[25] They could, indeed, be regarded as private deals between Yeltsin and his team, on the one hand, and the particular presidents or governors with whom the agreement was hammered out, on the other. Putin's desire to re-establish a chain of government which will supplant such extra-constitutional arrangements is welcomed by most Moscow-based politicians for a variety of reasons.

One of the better arguments is that a rule of law requires openness and legal ratification of any new division of power and responsibilities between the federal centre and the constituent units of the federation. A second and related point is that there should be a state-wide 'common legal space'.[26] A third is that Russia's business tycoons, including some of the leading 'oligarchs', have increasingly turned their attention to the regions and have bought political influence and positions of power locally. Thus, restoring a vertical chain of government could be seen as an essential means of combating local plutocracy rather than local democracy. A contrary view, which also has merit, is that generalisations about the republics and regions are meaningless. There is great diversity among them, including the extent to which business interests have or have not established *de facto* hegemony over elected officials.[27] Moreover, since in some respects there is less political pluralism under Putin than under Yeltsin – the State Duma is less critical of the executive, the Federation Council has lost standing following the removal from its composition of governors and republican presidents, and important sections of the mass media have rediscovered self-censorship – the relative autonomy of the republics and regions can be seen as a bulwark of the pluralism that remains. Supporters of regional autonomy can point not only to the absurdity of attempting to decide in Moscow everything that matters for such a vast country but also to the part such institutional resources can play in combating a creeping authoritarianism within the Russian polity as a whole. (The paradox of that position is that, whatever their value as countervailing powers, Russian republican and regional government is quite frequently more authoritarian than politics at the federal level. In particular, party organisation and competition tend to be more of a reality at the centre.)

If Putin does not like the extra-constitutional character of the bilateral treaties, he has not been averse to undertaking extra-constitutional administrative reorganisations of his own. One of the most important was his establishment by presidential decree in May 2000 of seven super-districts which were superimposed on the existing, constitutionally recognised administrative units. His appointment of presidential plenipotentiaries or governors-general (*polpredy*) in these districts, whose boundaries correspond to those of the Ministry of Interior military divisions, was an attempt, in the first place, to re-establish central control over federal employees in the regions (including law-enforcement officers and tax inspectors) who, in many cases, had become highly dependent on local political bosses. While it remains to be seen how long-lasting these political structures will be, they are part of Putin's attempted reaffirmation of central state power. The danger of an *excessive* centralisation is less than it was in Soviet times, for as long as governors are elected (notwithstanding Kremlin manipulation of the process in line with their understanding of 'guided democracy'), and to the extent that a market economy continues to develop, the centre will have nothing like the levers of power which used to rest in the hands of the Central Committee apparatus and Gosplan (see Chapter 9).

It is evident that for Putin strengthening the state has been a higher priority than strengthening democracy. But the Yeltsin years demonstrated clearly enough that a weak state is not a desideratum of democratic development or, indeed, of a viable market economy. William Tompson has rightly pointed to what he calls 'one of the paradoxes of post-Soviet Russia'. The country has 'a weak state but strong officials'.[28] It has lacked cohesion and co-ordination and these are among the ingredients that Putin, with the help of the Kozak reforms, is attempting to introduce. Striking the right balance between strengthening institutions and not getting in the way of what Igrunov terms 'natural processes' will call for fine judgement.

Putin's caution and pragmatism may serve him well. Yeltsin would dismiss people in a fit of rage without necessarily having an immediate successor clearly in mind. Putin is prepared to see his choices for particular posts serve an apprenticeship. Thus, Sergei Ivanov was Secretary of the Security Council before he became the first ex-KGB officer to be put in charge of the army as Minister of Defence. It is fully possible that Dmitri Kozak, like the Russian president (although fifteen years younger) a graduate of Leningrad University Law Faculty, and a subordinate of Putin in the Petersburg city administration in the 1990s, will succeed Aleksandr Voloshin as chief-of-staff of the presidential administration. (Voloshin was appointed to that post by Yeltsin in March 1999; Kozak was appointed deputy head by Putin in May 2000.) Putin's confidence in Kozak was demonstrated by his putting him in charge of implementing reform not only of the civil service but also of the judiciary and local government. In contradistinction to Yeltsin, Putin has kept the same prime minister, Mikhail Kas'yanov, throughout his presidency thus far. Kas'yanov, accordingly, has been able to play a key adjudicatory and co-ordinating role in economic policy.

Putin, during his presidential first term, has been no transformational leader, but he has been moderately innovative. He has introduced a change of administrative style and has succeeded in maintaining a high level of popular approval. The latter could, however, be endangered by a lowering of the oil price and any deterioration of economic conditions which are already quite harsh enough for a substantial part of the Russian population. Putin has been learning the art of leadership, bolstered by great constitutional powers, but constrained by other elite groups – more than by formal institutions. When Yeltsin and his associates chose Putin as the presidential successor and provided him with the most favourable conditions for electoral success, they were looking for someone who would not rock the boat, who would not threaten the material and personal well-being of 'the Family', and who would consolidate the building of capitalism in Russia. On the whole, they have reason to be satisfied that their protégé has fulfilled this mission. If, however, Putin is to occupy a worthy place in Russian history he will, at some point, have to take the risk of confronting vested interests, giving a lead in the construction not merely of 'capitalism Russian-style' but of a law-governed market economy – and according no less weight to the building of democracy.

Notes

1 See A. Brown, *The Gorbachev Factor* (Oxford and New York: Oxford University Press, 1996); S. Kotkin, *Armageddon Averted: The Soviet Collapse 1970–2000* (Oxford and New York: Oxford University Press, 2001); C. Read, *The Making and Breaking of the Soviet System: An Interpretation* (London and New York: Palgrave, 2001); and S. Whitefield, *Industrial Power and the Soviet State* (Oxford: Clarendon Press, 1993).
2 J. MacGregor Burns, *Leadership* (New York: Harper & Row, 1978).
3 *Ibid.*, p. 20.
4 See M. Gorbachev and Z. Mlynář, *Conversations with Gorbachev: On Perestroika, the Prague Spring, and the Crossroads of Socialism* (New York: Columbia University Press, 2002), pp. 104, 105–106, and 200.
5 See T. Gustafson, *Capitalism Russian-Style* (Cambridge and New York: Cambridge University Press, 1999). For differing interpretations of this process, see

also A. Aslund, *How Russia Became a Market Economy* (Washington, DC: The Brookings Institution, 1995); S. Hedlund, *Russia's 'Market' Economy: A Bad Case of Predatory Capitalism* (London: UCL Press, 1999); and P. Reddaway and D. Glinski, *The Tragedy of Russia's Reforms: Market Bolshevism against Democracy* (Washington, DC: United States Institute of Peace Press, 2001).

6 For elaboration of this point, see my chapter, 'Transformational leaders compared: Mikhail Gorbachev and Boris Yeltsin', in A. Brown and L. Shevtsova (eds.), *Gorbachev, Yeltsin, and Putin: Political Leadership in Russia's Transition* (Washington, DC: Carnegie Endowment for International Peace, 2001), pp. 11–43. See also G. W. Breslauer's perceptive book, *Gorbachev and Yeltsin as Leaders* (New York and Cambridge: Cambridge University Press, 2002).

7 T. E. Cronin, 'Reflections on leadership', in W. E. Rosenbach and R. L. Taylor (eds.), *Contemporary Issues in Leadership* (Boulder: Westview Press, 3rd edn, 1993), p. 9.

8 V. Putin, *First Person: An Astonishingly Frank Self Portrait by Russia's President* (London: Hutchinson, 2000), pp. 40–42.

9 *Ibid.*, p. 129.

10 See L. Belin, 'Political bias and self-censorship in the Russian media', pp. 323–342; and Y. M. Brudny, 'Continuity or change in Russian electoral patterns? The December 1999–March 2000 electoral cycle', pp. 154–178, of A. Brown (ed.), *Contemporary Russian Politics: A Reader* (Oxford: Oxford University Press, 2001).

11 A. A. Mukhin (ed.), *Federal'naya i regional'naya elita Rossii 2002* (Moscow: GNOM i D, 2002), pp. 203–204.

12 V. A. Kuvaldin (ed.), *Kruglyy stol 'Ekspertiza': Nadezhdy i razocharovaniya prezidentstva Putina* (Moscow: The Gorbachev Foundation, 2002), pp. 126–128.

13 Initially given a cautious welcome in military circles, Putin came to be seen as pursuing an excessively conciliatory policy towards the West in general and the United States in particular. He was, for example, strongly attacked by a group of twenty retired admirals and generals, including former Defence Minister (under Yeltsin), General Igor Rodionov, for betraying Russian interests through such actions as his endorsement of American bases in Central Asia. See *Sovetskaya Rossiya* (21 February 2002), p. 1.

14 S. Talbott, *The Russia Hand: A Memoir of Presidential Diplomacy* (New York: Random House, 2002), p. 359.

15 How extremely solicitous President Clinton was of Yeltsin's political and psychological needs comes out clearly in the illuminating insider's account of those years by Strobe Talbott, *The Russia Hand*.

16 Although, as Vladimir Putin himself pointed out, when answering questions live on Russian television in December 2002, there remains an urgent need for more capital investment to modernise Russian industry to produce more 'good-quality cheap goods' (*BBC Monitoring Service*, 19 December, 2002).

17 For much fascinating information on the links between new wealth and political power in Russia, and on the individuals who became known as the 'oligarchs', see C. Freeland, *Sale of the Century: The Inside Story of the Second Russian Revolution* (London: Little, Brown, 2000); P. Klebnikov, *Godfather of the Kremlin: Boris Berezovsky and the Looting of Russia* (New York: Harcourt, 2000); and D. Hoffman, *The Oligarchs: Wealth and Power in the New Russia* (New York: Public Affairs, 2002).

18 See L. Belin, 'The rise and fall of Russia's NTV', *Stanford Journal of International Law*, 38:1 (2002), 19–42; and Belin, 'Political bias and self-censorship in the Russian media', in Brown (ed.), *Contemporary Russian Politics*.
19 For elaboration of this point, see A. Brown, 'Vladimir Putin and the reaffirmation of central state power', *Post-Soviet Affairs*, 17:1 (January–March 2001), 45–55, esp. 48–49; and for a more comprehensive analysis: R. Sharlet, 'Putin and the politics of law', *Post-Soviet Affairs*, 17:3 (July–September 2001), 195–234.
20 Hedlund, *Russia's 'Market' Economy: A Bad Case of Predatory Capitalism*.
21 P. Klebnikov has described Berezovsky's technique for 'the primary accumulation of capital'. He found that it was not necessary to buy an enterprise to control it: 'The company could remain in state hands. All one had to do was co-opt the management and then funnel the company's revenues through your own middlemen, thus "privatising the profits" without spending time and money privatising the enterprise itself' (Klebnikov, *Godfather of the Kremlin*, p. 170).
22 *RFE/RL Security and Terrorism Watch*, 3: 45 (24 December 2002).
23 A reform of the Russian civil service is under way, spearheaded by the deputy head of the Kremlin administration, a close Putin ally from St Petersburg, Dmitriy Kozak. Critics, however, fear that the laws likely to be enacted will be more concerned with strengthening the power *vertikal* and consolidating central control over the regions than with introducing a higher degree of professionalism, transparency and accountability into the state bureaucracy, turning it into a *civil* service. Kozak himself, though, is regarded as someone who believes that a rule of law and independent judiciary are desirable not only in themselves but are necessary for the development of a market economy. See A. Lukin, 'Putin's regime: restoration or revolution?', *Problems of Post-Communism*, 48:4 (July–August 2001), 38–48; A. V. Obolonskiy, *Byurokratiya dlya XXI veka? Modeli gosudarstvennoy sluzhby: Rossiya, Ssha, Angliya, Avstraliya* (Moscow: Delo, 2002); and Obolonsky, 'Competing models of Russian bureaucratic reform', paper presented to 34th National Convention of the American Association for the Advancement of Slavic Studies, Pittsburgh, 21–24 November 2002. A more far-reaching reform of the Russian state bureaucracy has, Obolonsky notes, more support within the presidential administration than within the governmental apparatus. Indeed, he suggests, there is less support for Putin generally in the Russian White House (the headquarters of the government) than among the population at large.
24 See J. Kahn, *Federalism, Democratisation, and the Rule of Law in Russia* (Oxford: Oxford University Press, 2002), esp. pp. 142–188.
25 *Ibid.*, p. 171.
26 See A. Stepan, 'Russian federalism in comparative perspective', *Post-Soviet Affairs*, 16:2 (April–June 2000), pp. 133–176.
27 See N. Lapina and A. Chirikova, *Strategii regional'nykh elit: ekonomika, modeli vlasti, politicheskiy vybor* (Moscow: INION, 2000); and M. Mendras, 'How regional elites preserve their power', *Post-Soviet Affairs*, 15:4 (October–December 1999). For an interesting attempt to construct a typology of regional political regimes, see A. S. Kuz'min, N. J. Melvin and V. D. Nechaev, 'Regional'nye politicheskie rezhimy v postsovetskoy Rossii: opyt tipologizatsii', *Polis: Politicheskie Issledovaniya*, 3 (2002), pp. 142–155.
28 W. Tompson, 'Putin's challenge: the politics of structural reform in Russia', *Europe–Asia Studies*, 54:6 (September 2002), 933–957, at 937.

2

Regime change from Yeltsin to Putin: normality, normalcy or normalisation?

Richard Sakwa

Introduction

This chapter will examine the changing nature of relations within the political system provoked by the coming to power of Vladimir Putin, and try to identify some of the shifts in relations between the regime and society. The basic argument will be that Yeltsin's regime remained a 'regime of transition' devoted to the systemic transformation of the society. By contrast, Putin's regime is one of consolidation, suggesting that as far as he is concerned the transition is over, although there remains much to be changed. The consolidation, however, is not necessarily that of democracy but of the regime (that is, the governing power bloc). The relationship, on the one hand, between the power system of the governing regime and, on the other hand, the independent institutions of the state, based on the autonomous operation of the rule of law, the impartial observance of the constitution, and the free and fair running of the electoral and representative systems, remains ambiguous. The operation of the governing system based on the presidency and the autonomous operation of the state, in Russia as in other countries, are entwined in ways that are not only confused but also prone to political corruption. In the non-Baltic former Soviet states the balance is definitely tilted towards the former.

As for the changes pursued by Putin, they are no longer couched in revolutionary terms. The approach to reform has moved away from one of systemic transformation towards system management. This suggests that politics has now become 'normal', in the sense that larger constitutional questions over the shape of the polity have now given way to governmental management of more mundane policy questions. This alone, if nothing else, provides a platform for the development of state autonomy. The period of constitutional politics, predicted by Ralf Dahrendorf to last 'at least six months',[1] in Russia effectively lasted about a decade but has now given way to the hard work of 'normal politics'.[2] The question of regime type has been resolved and the basic choices between institutions of government have been decided. For Schumpeter a transition ends when the initial period of uncertainty associated with regime change comes to an end,[3] and in Russia it appears that we have reached this point.

This return to 'normality', a theme (as we shall see below) that has been explicitly taken up by Putin, is tempered, however, by at least two other processes. The first is the strong and explicit project of a 'return to normalcy'. The notion of a return to normalcy was the slogan popular in the United States after the First World War and reflected the desire for peace of a nation tired of military exertions. In the Russian context today the politics of normalcy reflect a country that endured over a century of revolutionary, military and secret police depredations. The attempt to link up with the past, to restore the torn fabric of society, to draw on intellectual traditions and cultural values of yesteryear, all reflect this post-traumatic pursuit of the past as the grounding of the present. Putin's pragmatic approach is rooted in the explicit attempt to base Russia's politics of the twenty-first century in the repudiation of 'revolutionary' and 'shock therapy' politics of the twentieth. Putin's identification with the politics of normalcy is one of the most potent sources of his enduring popularity.

Putin's politics of normality and a 'return to normalcy', moreover, are accompanied by disturbing overtones of 'normalisation'. The concepts of 'managed' and 'guided' democracy are openly proclaimed by some of Putin's advisors as preferable to the unpredictability and disintegrative trends so evident under Yeltsin's leadership in the 1990s. A whole raft of terms has been devised to describe the state of affairs in countries like Russia where the formal institutions of democracy are vitiated by informal practices that subvert their impartial operation. O'Donnell's concept of 'delegative democracy',[4] Zakaria's notion of 'illiberal democracy'[5] and Diamond's idea of 'electoral democracy'[6] are among the best known. This post-communist normalisation is very different to that imposed on Czechoslovakia by Gustav Husak in the wake of the Soviet invasion of August 1968, yet in certain respects the attempt to subvert the free operation of politics and the accompanying dialectic of coercion, consent and consumerism of the earlier period find some echoes today.

Putin's approach, which is overall characterised by the pursuit of a politics of stability, is thus riven by contradictory processes. These contradictions, moreover, are accompanied by a number of constraints, above all on Putin's ability to create his own leadership team and to ensure the implementation of the policies that he espouses. Putin, however, has been able to forge an administration that has to a remarkable extent been able to transcend these contradictions and constraints. The sharp polarisation that attended Yeltsin's rule has given way to an explicitly consensual and 'centrist' approach. The nature of this centrism is not simply an avoidance of the extremes of left and right but is based on a radical centrism of the type espoused by 'third way' thinkers like Giddens,[7] although Putin's third way is tailored to Russian circumstances. This chapter will examine the extent to which a relatively coherent and enduring new political order has emerged and will indicate some of the features of the system. Are we seeing no more than the temporary consolidation of a regime based primarily on the personality of the president, or does the present relationship between the state, governing regime and society suggest the emergence of an enduring new political order that could outlast Putin's presidency?

From a 'regime of transition' to a 'regime of consolidation': the politics of normality, normalcy and normalisation

Yeltsin's regime was a 'regime of transition' devoted to the systemic transformation of the society. This characteristic is highlighted, for example, by Reddaway and Glinski, who subtitled their major analysis of the Yeltsin years 'market Bolshevism against democracy'.[8] By contrast, Putin's regime is one of consolidation, suggesting that as far as he is concerned the transition is over, although he does not deny that there remains much to be changed, above all in the economic sphere and in the area of federal relations (see Chapters 6, 7 and 9). The profound structural problems of the economy are being tackled,[9] while in the sphere of federal relations Putin has committed himself to reversing the leakage of sovereignty from the centre to Russia's sub-national units.[10] Although the degree to which Putin's attempts to restore the 'vertical of power' has been successful remains contested, at the level of political theory Putin's 'new statism' is rooted in the neo-Jacobin republican state-building tradition, where citizenship is considered individual, universal and homogeneous. The degree to which the French republican tradition is compatible with federalism's promise of shared sovereignty remains to be seen. In addition, the assimilationist aspect of French (unitary) nation building threatens the accrued rights of the ethnofederal formations on Russia's territory, and in particular the privileges of the 'ethnocratic' elites based on the titular nationalities at their heart.

While Putin is undoubtedly a reformer, his approach to change is no longer one of systemic transformation but of system management. His speeches and interventions are peppered with the concept of 'normality'. For example, in his greeting to the delegates to the constituent congress of the Unity party in February 2000, Putin argued that it would be 'normal' for Russia to have a three- or four-party system, instead of the 150-odd registered at that time.[11] The 'normalisation' of Russia was also a process proceeding at the international level (for more details, see Chapters 12–15), with the US State Department, for example, in February 2001 abolishing its special section on Russia and reducing it to a sub-unit of the European department. On a more general level, what are the key features of Putin's politics of stability, what we label the search for normality and the return to normalcy?

The first feature is the refusal to accept changes to the Constitution. This was highlighted in his very first policy statements, although repeated rather less frequently thereafter. Instead, institutional development, as with the establishment of the seven Federal Districts, has assumed para-constitutional forms. Although the system of federalism, as outlined in the Constitution, has been modified by the establishment of these districts, the change is portrayed as affecting the organisation of executive power and thus not requiring constitutional amendment (see Chapter 9). Another case of para-constitutional change is the adoption of the law on the merging of subjects of the federation and the incorporation of new subjects. It should be noted that the constitutional order in all democratic societies evolves as a result of legislative activity and changes in political practices, but there comes a point when quantitative changes, to use Marxist terminology, require a qualitative readjustment of constitutional doctrine. In the Russian case this would probably be necessitated by attempts to extend the presidential term to seven years, or to make the government and prime minister directly responsible to a parliamentary majority. However, in Putin's first term there was no indication that he favoured such changes.

The second feature of Putin's politics of stability is the refusal to reverse the results of the privatisations of the Yeltsin years, above all in the mid-1990s. Current privatisations have been achieved on a competitive open tendering basis, and even at their current relatively low level have yielded more for the state exchequer than all of Yeltsin's mass privatisations combined. The refusal to re-open the question of the legality of earlier privatisations is often interpreted as a token of Putin's pusillanimity in the face of the entrenched interests of 'the family', the colloquial term for the combination of favoured oligarchs, insider politicians and political advisors, and some of Yeltsin's blood family members, above all his daughter Tatyana Dyachenko. It can also be seen as a refusal to engage in another social revolution. Putin accepts that Yeltsin's 'revolution from above' laid the foundations of a market economy and established the basis of a bourgeois social class in which democracy could be rooted. Putin also accepts that a wholesale review of the corruption and outright theft that accompanied this process would be socially divisive and disruptive. Only clearly provable criminal cases, he insists, will be investigated. Putin thus exposes himself to the charge of prosecuting those who made their fortunes in the era of wild capitalism, the so-called oligarchs, on a selective and politically biased way. It also made him extremely cautious in pursuing privatisations, as in the repeated back-pedalling over attempts to privatise parts of United Energy Systems (RAO UES), the electricity monopoly.

The third feature is Putin's insistence in the foreign policy sphere that Russia should be treated as a 'normal' great power (see Chapters 12–15).

This was most vividly seen at the G8 summit in July 2000 in Okinawa and Miyazaki, when Putin successfully convinced the other seven world leaders that Russia should be treated as just another country, asking neither for exceptions nor expecting any favours. On numerous occasions thereafter Putin argued that Russia's foreign policy should serve the country's economic interests, a policy that was evident in debates over the union of Russia and Belarus. In general, while regretting the disintegration of the Soviet Union, Putin accepted that the break-up was irrevocable and thus jettisoned illusions about the recreation of some sort of unified successor state based on the Commonwealth of Independent States (CIS).

The fourth feature, following on from the above, is the explicit repudiation of revolution as an effective form of achieving positive political change. In his question and answer session with the Russian people in December 2001 Putin noted: 'As one of my acquaintances said, "Russia in the past century over-fulfilled its plan for revolutions" I hope that in the twenty-first century there will be no revolutions, that things will only be positive.'[12] This echoes Putin's sentiments already voiced in his *Millennium Manifesto* in December 1999, where he noted that the communist revolutionary model of development not only had not delivered the goods, but could not have done so.[13] Putin once again returned to this theme in an interview shown on Russian Television (RTR) on 7 October 2002, his fiftieth birthday: 'I would like to remind you that I am a lawyer and I think that one's actions should be based on law, and not revolutionary expediency.'[14] It is this nuance that represents an epistemological break of enormous proportions between Gorbachev and Putin, and reflects the gulf that separates their respective generations. If Gorbachev in power reflected the preoccupations of the *shestdesyatniki*, the children of the Twentieth Party Congress, the thaw, Khrushchev's destalinisation and its associated aspirations for reform communism, then Putin is a *semidesyatnik*, a product of the 1970s and Brezhnev's stagnation, a peculiar type of late Soviet politics of stability and normality that proved to be far from stable and a 'normality' that turned out to be unsustainable, hence clearly abnormal.

There are many other features of Putin's politics of normalcy that could be identified. Let us note in conclusion to this section perhaps the most important and the source of all the others: Putin's attempt to reconcile the various phases of Russian history, especially over the last century. In his New Year message to the Russian people on 31 December 2000 Putin noted that it had been 'a year of cheerful and tragic events' but above all had seen the emergence of 'distinct elements of stability'.[15] The day before at a Kremlin reception he noted that the adoption of the new Russian anthem, combining a peculiar hybrid of Soviet and Russian themes,[16] represented 'an important indication that we have finally managed to bridge the disparity between past and present', adding that 'one cannot be in permanent contradiction with one's own history and the destiny of one's own country'.[17] Putin sought to put an end to this 'permanent contradiction', one that some see as having been imposed on Russia at the dawn of the modern era by Peter the Great's attempts to impose modernity by unmodern means. Since then, it could be argued, Russia had been living in a type of 'permanent transition' (with transition here defined as the attempt to impose models of modernisation devised elsewhere). This long transition, Putin suggests, has now come to an end.[18]

At the same time, the 'what country are we living in?' question appeared also to be resolved. Gleb Pavlovsky, the *éminence grise* if not Svengali of the new regime, argued that Putin had put an end to the question of the USSR. 'Today the army in Chechnya', he insisted, 'is victorious under the Russian flag, whereas in the previous war the Soviet army lost.'[19] Russia still hesitated to allow the formal demarcation of borders with countries like Ukraine, but under Putin the Yeltsinite 'smaller Russia' policy triumphed, although this did not mean the relinquishment of the new country's assertion of its alleged great power interests in the former imperial sphere. It did mean, however, that these national interests were now defined in terms of Russia's own needs, above all the pursuit of economic advantage. Although never losing sight of larger security and other interests, Putin has explicitly espoused the 'economisation' of Russian foreign policy.[20]

All of the above suggests that politics have now become 'normal', in the sense that larger constitutional questions over the shape of the polity have now given way to governmental administration of more mundane policy questions and the management of a functioning market economy based on private property and international economic integration. However, while a sense of normality has undoubtedly returned to Russia after nearly fifteen years of post-communist revolutionary upheaval, quite apart from the preceding century of revolutionary 'extraordinary' measures, there are also some disturbing overtones of 'normalisation'. It is to these 'normalising' features that we now turn.

Democratic consolidation and regime type

The question 'When does a transition end?' has about it something of the medieval scholasticism that is typical of the study of comparative democratisation.[21] The immediate answer, if we pose the question in this way, is to say that a transition ends when democracy is consolidated. There has been a vigorous debate about what constitutes democratic consolidation.[22] Whatever definition we chose to apply, from Linz and Stepan's argument that consolidation has been achieved when all significant political groups accept that democracy is the 'only game in town',[23] to Higley *et al.*'s emphasis on elite consensus,[24] and on to Samuel Huntington's two turnover test,[25] I think we can reasonably suggest that Russian politics are not characterised by democratic consolidation. As Stephen E. Hanson notes, 'the institutionalisation of democratic institutions in Russia has been very weak', although he also suggests that the ability of anti-democratic groups to attract followers has if anything been even weaker.[26] Although there is a large degree of elite consensus that the formal observance of democratic forms of conflict adjudication and the observance of legal and constitutional norms is the only acceptable way of conducting political affairs, the tendency for the electoral process to be subsumed into the power system and the lack of convincing mechanisms of executive accountability at the central and regional levels suggests that the impartial application of normative standards is incomplete. There remain large questions over the independence of the judiciary. This is not to deny the undoubted achievements since 1993 toward the establishment of the institutions of a modern democratic state based on constitutional norms and the separation of powers, but only to suggest that this process has been partial and incomplete.[27]

Rather than democratic consolidation, we see instead regime consolidation. I have argued elsewhere (and mentioned above) that between the fully-fledged development of autonomous state institutions typical of developed liberal democracies and the forms of modern political democracy (parties and social movements as representative of civil society) there emerged a power bloc or regime system based on the institutions of the presidency, but not coterminous with those institutions.[28] Systemic integration is achieved not so much by law as by personal ties; but at the same time these ties reflect a regularised pattern of relationships between major stakeholders in the system. Thus we need to distinguish, on the one hand, between a regime type, designating the categorisation of a relatively differentiated legal system and mechanism of social regulation; and, on the other hand, a governing political regime based on a particular elite configuration operating in the interstices of state institutions and social power. Legal proceduralism in the former and democratic institutionalisation of the latter are subverted by the relative autonomy of the power system from both the state and society. The problem is the classic one of differentiating between state and government in the passage from absolutism to modern representative democracy.[29] The term 'regime' is classically applied to a government that is not adequately, from the perspective of democratic theory, separated from direct access to the instruments of state power (legal, coercive and ideological). It shares many features with the crypto-politics that T. H. Rigby identified as one of the key features of the Soviet system. Rigby describes crypto-politics as

> not overt and channelled through specialised 'political' institutions, but covert, masquerading as the faithful performance of assigned organisational roles. It involves competition between constituent organisations and their formal subdivisions, biased reporting of information relevant to the formation or vetting of policy, informal networks or cliques, the use of personal powers to reward friends and punish enemies, and bias in the execution of policy so as to facilitate or prejudice its success or to favour certain affected interests rather than others.[30]

While the institutional framework of the Soviet and Russian systems have changed dramatically, certain political practices have been perpetuated in new forms.

This crypto-democratic regime system is not unique to Russia but shares a pathology with other newly democratised states like post-war Japan under the Liberal Democratic Party, Italy until the collapse of the *partitocrazia* system in 1992, and are widespread in Latin America, notably in Brazil. These systems have corporatist features, but lack many of the defining features of either statist or societal corporatist regimes. Instead, these are extended patronage systems that, while formally democratic, subvert the free operation of democratic pluralism by tying key interests and political elites into the crypto-democratic regime by the application of the gamut of tried and tested methods of political co-optation and subordination, ranging from open bribery to clientelism and, when all else fails, selective coercion. We use the prefix *crypto-* in this context to indicate the hidden, informal and secretive nature of political processes in such regimes. By the same token, the premium is on personal ties and the subversion of the autonomous operation of independent political institutions.[31]

Understanding the relationship between regime consolidation and state development is the key to revealing the nature of the political order emerging in Russia. Without an effective differentiated state there can be no democracy, but in conditions of the development of a crypto-democratic regime state autonomy is compromised, not so much by the invasion of societal interests but by parasitic colonisation by the governing (managing) mechanism itself. There are elements of rule by law (*Rechtsstaat*) rather than the rule of law involved, reminiscent of the Bismarckian Second Reich, where neither law nor societal representation could hold the executive to account. It may well be argued that the achievement of positive law in Russian conditions would be no mean feat, denoting at a minimal level the achievement of what Zakaria, as noted above, has called 'illiberal democracy'.[32] However, the historical process cannot be hermeneutically asynchronic, as modernisation theory has always asserted, and instead the whole tenor of transition studies suggests that there is a unified developmental process in which relatively more under-developed societies remain 'backward' relative to the more advanced societies and cannot be isolated in some sort of holding pen for catch-up societies. This was part of the ruthless logic that brought down Soviet communism, and it is a logic that is accepted by Putin in his advocacy of the 'politics of normality' and international economic integration. The politics of normality thus stand in stark contrast to the politics of exceptionalism that have so haunted Russian history. A stable political order based on positive law, international integration and constitutional liberal rights, if only in the first stages a simulacrum of democracy, makes possible the later achievement of democratic consolidation.

Regime change from Yeltsin to Putin

A crypto-democratic system took shape during Yeltsin's presidency, but in what ways has this changed under Putin? Is Liliya Shevtsova right to argue that Putin's rule was little more than 'Yeltsinism without Yeltsin'? Can we still argue that the regime as described above continues to exist? My argument is that crypto-democracy remains prevalent as a characterisation of the state regime, but that the system of relations within the governmental regime, its mode of operation and relations with society, have undergone considerable evolution. Let us examine some of these changes in turn.

1 The first and most important change is the new relationship between the economy and politics. If under Yeltsin there had been a thorough interpenetration of these two spheres, to the extent that access to government became one of the cardinal economic resources, under Putin the declared aim has been to keep economic interests at equal arms' length from the state. This could be taken to indicate that Italian or Japanese style political economies have been repudiated, but this would probably be premature at this stage. A new model of relations between politics and economics has emerged, some of whose features will be discussed below.

2 The far-reaching scope of legal reforms in Putin's first term, symbolised by the coming into effect of the new Criminal Procedural Code on 1 July 2002, should not be under-estimated. The commission planning the legal reforms under Putin's ally Dmitrii Kozak saw fundamental change to Russia's legal culture, including the extension of trial by jury, greater independence for judges and some limits to the powers of the procuracy.

3 The reorganisation of patronage and political mechanisms is at the heart of Putin's reconfiguration of power relations. If under Yeltsin key insiders gathered at his table on social occasions at which the familial and the political were thoroughly entwined, with little differentiation between family matters and affairs of the state, under Putin formal mechanisms, in this sphere at least, predominate. The reorganisation of the party system is at the heart of the long-term development of a mechanism formally to propagate the regime's policy and to establish a national system of patronage disbursement that would challenge regionally based alternative networks (see Chapters 3 and 4).

4 Michel Debray, founder of the Fifth Republic in France, talked in terms of establishing a 'Republican monarchy', a phrase that De Gaulle was fond of repeating. In Russia's three-quarter presidential system the 'monarchical' elements are even more accentuated than in France. It is this that prompted Klyamkin and Shevtsova to talk in terms of an 'elected monarchy' in Russia.[33] Monarchy, however, suggests that it is the office rather than the incumbent that is central, yet in a presidential system the need to face the electorate and to root political legitimacy in public responsiveness means that the analogy is rather far-fetched. In France and to a lesser extent in

Russia there are real limits to presidential power. In addition, the succession operation in the passage from Yeltsin to Putin was by no means assured of success and its achievement owed not a little to Putin's personal qualities and the absence of real alternatives.[34]

5 There were a number of qualities associated with Yeltsin's image: firmness, a man of the people, rebel and revolutionary. Putin, however, stresses other qualities: an iron will, health, youth and decisiveness, tempered by popular support. The development of a Putin mini cult of personality was based on a formidable personality at its heart. Although charisma may well to a large degree derive from the office rather than the personal characteristics of the office holder, the nature of leadership has clearly changed in the passage from Yeltsin to Putin. Yeltsin's was a towering personality that dominated through sheer force of character, whereas Putin's leadership cult has combined both spontaneous and administrative facets. Elements of a 'cult of personality' emerged remarkably quickly, with official portraits going up in official buildings and the like. This reached its apogee with the celebration of Putin's fiftieth birthday in October 2002, when he was showered by gifts from the people including, most symbolically, a replica of the Cap of Monomakh, the ceremonial crown used in the coronation of the Tsars.

6 Public opinion has been a political resource used with great skill by Putin. The elements of enlightened authoritarianism are qualified by their rootedness in popular support, a crop that is tended and watered as the shepherd tends his flock. This is not to say that Putin's popular support is not genuine or that it is artificially manufactured; but only to say that it is maintained and monitored. Public opinion, moreover, is not always followed, as in Putin's commitment to the abolition of the death penalty despite polls showing 80 per cent support for its retention. Putin on numerous occasions has proved himself to be a president willing to take risks with his popularity. This is evident above all in the foreign policy sphere after 9/11, and will no doubt become more in evidence in his second term. From the very first, in dealing with the Chechen incursion into Dagestan in August–September 1999, Putin showed himself to be a leader capable of transcending short-term interest, and is a characteristic of any leader with ambitions to achieve major and lasting deeds. In other words, power for Putin was not simply a commodity to be hoarded but a resource to be used judiciously and for a purpose.[35]

7 There has been a renewed emphasis on institutional consolidation under Putin. This has taken the guise of state reassertion, above all in the federal, economic and legal spheres. However, the struggle to achieve greater autonomy for the state is also accompanied by the consolidation of the regime, processes that are not so much contradictory as mutually self-reinforcing. The results appeared to include the elimination of alternative autonomous sources of power. The dual nature of state reassertion, both

constitutional and coercive, allows the process both to facilitate the development of democracy while encouraging some illiberal practices. In short, it promotes both normality and normalisation.

8   The nature of the political process itself has changed. Initially, this took the form of a dangerous homogenisation of the political arena, most evident during the 2000 presidential election. Even Pavlovsky warned about the lack of a serious opposition in the elections themselves, and warned that 'If there will continue to be no strong, intelligent opposition to the new president, a second or third Putin so to speak, power will find itself in political isolation and the country in a dangerous situation.'[36] Pavlovsky did, however, stress that 'The time when electoral deals became administrative ones, and consequently financial ones, have passed with Yeltsin's era.'[37] Putin's refusal to make extravagant promises in the 2000 presidential election contrasted strongly with Yeltsin in 1996, who promised everything to all and sundry and above all indebted himself to the oligarchs. While Yeltsin after the election repudiated most of his spending promises to the public, he delivered the goods to those who had provided financial support for his campaign, and thus opened the way to the 'golden age' of the oligarchs, a period that lasted until the financial crash of August 1998. Putin, however, insisted on the autonomy of the political, and this clearly distinguished his leadership from Yeltsin's. Yeltsin struggled to maintain his personal autonomy but was willing to compromise the integrity of the regime to ensure the perpetuation of his leadership. Putin has been more willing to lay his personal leadership on the line in pursuit of systemic goals.

This section has argued that the general characterisation of Russia's post-communist political system (the nature of the regime itself) retains significant continuity between the Yeltsin and Putin eras, but the governmental regime has undergone significant evolution. In addition to the points mentioned above, we could add that relations between the media and the regime have changed in subtle and not-so-subtle ways, while the emergence of a quasi-established religion in the form of Russian Orthodoxy has gone even further than under Yeltsin. The next section will focus on para-political aspects of the governmental system and tie this in with programmatic shifts. In other words, the consolidation and evolution of the governing regime has not only an institutional but also a personal and ideological basis, and it is these that we now explore.

Putin's 'third way' and the post-transition consolidation of the centre

In keeping with the political terminology of a world where ideology and class no longer exert their traditional influence, we can identify a Putinite 'project'. The polarisation accompanying Yeltsin's leadership, above all the periodic whipping up of fears of a communist *revanche* that would seek to change the constitutional order, has given way, as noted, to a consensual and 'centrist' approach. Let us examine each of these in turn.

Consensualism or weakness?

Is Putin weak or strong? The whole tenor of this chapter is to argue that to pose the question in this way is a misleading simplification. Nevertheless, let us pause to examine the issue. Sergei Glaz'ev, the economist who advised the Communist Party and who stood in Krasnoyarsk in October 2002 to replace Alexander Lebed as governor, was unequivocal: 'His [Putin's] independence and freedom are severely restricted by Voloshin and Kasyanov – plus the oligarchic clans these gentlemen serve.'[38] A report by the presidential administration's own Main Control Directorate (the agency responsible for the implementation of policy) suggested that Putin's tough talking was not effectively translated into action and the fulfilment of presidential orders. Only 48 per cent of the 543 orders given to officials in 2001 were promptly fulfilled, with 328 direct orders remaining unfulfilled. Putin in that year signed 1,013 presidential decrees, of which 787 were fulfilled. Eighty-three per cent had been carried out in a timely manner. In sum, 81 per cent of Putin's orders had been fulfilled, representing a sharp increase from the 54 per cent in 1999, in Yeltsin's last year in power. In general, the level of efficiency had declined from the Soviet period, with fewer than 5 per cent of orders remaining unfulfilled before Gorbachev's ascent to power. The decline reflected not just the general debilitation of the state apparatus and the lack of experience of many officials, but above all the confused and contradictory competencies of many agencies. The classic example was that of pensions, handled by three agencies: the Ministry of Economic Development and Trade, the Labour Ministry and the Pension Fund, leading to major problems of co-ordination.[39]

Putin's style is undoubtedly consensual, to the point even that some have noted the gradual 'Gorbachevisation' of his leadership: the failure to take resolute and consistent policy decisions. Tsipko diagnosed Putin as suffering from a 'Hamlet syndrome'. 'With few exceptions', Tsipko argues, 'he [Putin] is currently incapable of saying a definite "yes" or "no" on any single question concerning his personnel. Stories of Putin's iron will and his determined pursuit of his objectives were clearly exaggerated'.[40] In his interview with Boris Berezovsky, the patriot and editor of the opposition paper *Zavtra*, Alexander Prokhanov, argued that 'growing dissatisfaction with Putin is becoming a consolidating factor ... Putin has pretended to be in the driver's seat for two years now. He creates the illusion of activity, appears everywhere, makes energetic speeches – but in reality he remains in place. Stagnation is setting in; social and historical time is being wasted'. Berezovsky concurred, noting

Putin fears losing his approval rating. He carefully maintains his image through PR campaigns and political consultants. He has the rating but not the respect. A popularity rating actually boils down to a set of expectations. Putin has a high rating but low respect. He has not done what had to be done. This situation has lasted for over two years already, and people are sensing the emptiness. He is empty. The people like him for speaking the correct Russian. They assumed that behind correct language there must be correct ideas and will, an ability to work on their behalf. It never happened. I was one of the first to perceive this emptiness in Putin. It happened when we were meeting regularly. More and more Russians are becoming convinced that he is an empty shell, a mannequin.[41]

Tsipko argues that the return of Yevgenii Kiselev to prominence in TV-6, albeit part of a consortium of former communist *nomenklatura* figures (the head of the Russian Chamber of Commerce Yevgenii Primakov and the head of the Russian Union of Industrialists and Entrepreneurs Arkadii Volskii), revealed that Putin was 'simply not in a position to clear the TV screen of all of his detractors'.[42] Another interpretation would be that Putin was less concerned about Kiselev and more worried about ensuring that Boris Berezovsky (and Vladimir Gusinskii in the case of NTV earlier) lost their access to the airwaves. Above all, according to Tsipko, Kiselev was supported by the liberal community in the West, in particular in the United States, that Putin did not wish to offend as he tried to establish 'normal' relations with G7. In addition, the consortium behind Kiselev had the backing of the oligarchs led by Anatoly Chubais and comprised several members of 'the family': Roman Abramovich, Oleg Deripaska (whose father-in-law is now Valentin Yumashev (a presidential chief of staff under Yeltsin); thus he has now literally become a member of Yeltsin's family); Alexander Mamut and others. According to Tsipko, the TV-6 episode showed that Putin had 'no administrative, political, or financial resources with which to stand up to the family, especially when it is acting in concert with the liberal elite and big business. The old Kremlin elite, combined with the Liberal Party led by Anatoly Chubais, is now simply beyond Putin's grasp'.[43] Tsipko's argument suggests that there is robustness, indeed independence, to the governmental regime that transcends the powers of the individual president. We could go further and suggest that at a certain point the interest groups and individuals behind the regime may find it expedient to jettison a particular incumbent. The presidency may well be the heart of the governmental regime, but an individual president may well be expendable.

But to what degree is Putin a prisoner of the regime? On personnel issues there is no doubt that Putin is far from ruthless. There is a recurrent pattern of sacked officials being reappointed to new posts; perhaps the most spectacular being the former governor of Primorsk Krai, Alexander Nazdratenko, to the fisheries ministry. The former head of the disbanded presidential clemency commission, the human rights activist Anatolii Pristavkin, was immediately re-appointed as one of Putin's advisors. The marginalisation of some members of the 'family' suggests some freedom of manoeuvre (above all with Vladimir Berezovsky going into 'exile' in London and Vladimir Gusinskii in Spain), but the extreme caution with which Putin moves (as in the attack on the former railways minister, Nikolai Aksenenko) also indicates limits to his powers. In addition, while Putin may well have been a scion of the security services and relied on the FSB for some of his personnel, it was clear that he had to be careful not to alienate his former colleagues. He allowed them a relatively free hand in Chechnya and in the persecution of a new wave of 'dissidents', notably Alexander Nikitin, Sutyagin, Grigorii Pasko and others.

However, when it comes to policy Putin has been capable of decisive action. At certain moments he has been able to take decisions that break with the consensus. An example of this is his speech of 24 September 2001 and the consistent way that he then pursued the consequences of membership of the 'coalition against terrorism' after 9/11. This does not, of course, demonstrate complete political autonomy but it does reveal that in certain policy areas (and foreign policy is of course a presidential prerogative) there is scope for independent leadership.

It is clear that the governing elite and Putin need each other, and their power is mutually reinforcing, but we should be careful not to collapse the one into the other. This perhaps is the greatest difference in the regime system between Yeltsin and Putin: the potential contradiction between the incumbent and the regime. Indeed, one could go further and argue that in trying to buttress the autonomous powers of the state, Putin is thereby finding a way of liberating himself from the clutches of the regime. Another way of doing this is by devising an independent political platform, and it is to this that we now turn.

Putin's centrism: what is 'thirdist' about Putin's third way?

Putin's centrism is not simply an avoidance of the extremes of left and right, of backward-looking traditionalists and nationalists or teleologically inspired Western-oriented modernisers, but represents a radical centrism of the type espoused by 'third way' thinkers like Giddens, although Putin's third way is tailored to Russian circumstances.[44] This argument runs counter to much conventional wisdom about Putin's allegedly inchoate political programme.

Victor Sheinis, for example, argued that victory in the December 1999 Duma elections went to the 'quasi-centre'.[45] The basic policy orientation of this quasi-centre, insofar as it has one, he argued, is right-wing economics and left-wing politics: economic liberalism accompanied by statist great-power politics. This meant, he argued, a continuation of privatisation and other economic reforms, but also the continued iron grip of the bureaucracy over the 'market'. According to him, the 2000 presidential elections revealed 'the minimal movement towards a self-sustaining civil society' and 'the separation of the political class from the deep layers of society'. This gulf between the power system and society was something noted by many other commentators. This is why Sheinis' notion of a quasi-centre is so suggestive. It does not come from a historical convergence on the centre ground of policy, but from the opportunistic co-optation of political actors and ideas to ensure regime survival.

This is, however, only half the story and fails to take into account tensions within the regime itself (above all between the presidency and the power elite), and between the governing regime and the putative autonomy of the state. It is not enough to talk about a manipulated and opportunistic quasi-centre, and that Putin's centrism does indeed represent a distinctive type of Russian 'third way'. A genuine third way, *à la* Giddens, is derived not simply from the repudiation of idealised notions of left and right, reflected in traditional class politics, but from attempts to create a genuinely radical politics of the centre. This is not a trivial political project, although much of the writing and commentary about the subject is indeed trite. The argument here can be reduced to the following: while the 'third way' in the West is an attempt to come to terms with the apparent exhaustion of traditional social democracy and represents an attempt to renew it, Russia's third way, or genuine politics of the centre, is drawn from an older tradition, namely liberal conservatism. Writers like Peter Struve and Semyon Frank are drawn on to sustain the emerging consensus over a Russian 'third way' based on support for the reconstitution of state authority while continuing market reforms and international economic integration. It draws in particular on the figure of Peter Stolypin, perhaps Russia's most effective prime minister (1906–11) in the dying days of Tsarism.

Although Von Mises always argued that there was no 'third way' or 'third system' between the Soviet and the American forms of social organisation, today with the end of the Cold War and the ideological confrontation between East and West, the possibility of testing out a variety of paths is now more relevant than ever. We do not need to think in terms of only a 'third' way, of course, since there is no reason not to think in terms of a fourth, fifth and ever more ways. However, in our conception the notion of a third way is specific to the attempt to overcome the traditionally polarised nature of Western European and Russian politics: between socialism and capitalism, between market and non-market, between individualistic and collectivist approaches to social development; and between universalistic models of modernity and particular national histories. In that sense, a third way represents not an abstraction but a very specific response to Russia's confused and multi-layered self-identity and problems of development today. It means finally coming to terms with modernity as something emanating from Russia itself rather than as something alien and imposed.[46]

Jowitt has argued that in the context of the strong 'Leninist legacies' in Eastern Europe traditional attempts to strike a balance between economic development and democratic participation may not be effective. Liberal authoritarianism may well be a more 'desirable alternative' and a 'more practical response than the utopian wish for immediate mass democracy in Eastern Europe'.[47] It is precisely this tension between the authoritarian reimposition of order and democratic anarchism that Putin sought to finesse. Behind the talk of 'guided democracy' and 'manipulated democracy' (to use Sergei Markov's term) there lies the classical problem identified by Huntington in his seminal work: how to maintain political order in changing societies.[48] Putin provides a new approach to the problem of institutionalising order between the old-fashioned establishment of a repressive order and the anarchisation of social relations that characterised early post-communist Russia. The key point is precisely the institutionalising of order, to make it not something external but vital to the very operation of the system. In short, by radicalising and mobilising the centre, the aim was to achieve the internalisation of authority where power moved from being despotic and arbitrary to becoming infrastructural and legitimate. The aim was to shift from power to authority. Between radical liberalism and restorationist authoritarianism there perhaps lies another way, and this was now sought by Putin.

Conclusions

To what extent was Putin the continuer of Yeltsinism, or did he represent its repudiation? To what extent has there been regime change, in both senses of the term? To use the word 'regime' to describe the nature of the state system as a whole, have we seen a change from Yeltsin's relatively democratic yet disordered to a more ordered but semi-authoritarian system? And as for reconfiguration within the governmental regime itself, in what ways has the relationship between state and society changed?

In terms of style of governance, it is clear that Putin broke with the inclusive regime politics typical of Yeltsin, where oligarchs, technocrats, regional bosses and officialdom were also included in a broad coalescence of rule. Putin managed to ensure that oligarchs like Berezovsky were distanced from the sources of power, but this did not mean that the political basis of Putin's rule was reduced to the military and security services. It is clear that Putin's rule cannot be reduced to a simplistic formula, for example that he was an instrument of the old KGB. While Putin's government built on the broad framework of Yeltsin's policies, a number of important shifts have taken place. Above all, the presidency gained a degree of autonomy from the governing regime, and in seeking to strengthen the autonomous institutions of the state was able to achieve greater freedom for itself from powerful social interests. For Putin the question of what is normal for Russia was misleading. As far as he was concerned, normality for Russia was much the same as it was in the rest of the world. This, of course, was not a wholly satisfactory formulation, but it did represent an epistemological break of fundamental proportions with those who still sought some sort of special path (*Sonderweg*) for Russia. The fundamental difference between Putin and Yeltsin ultimately was the repudiation of mythologised representations of Russia's path.

The regime of transition has given way to one of 'normality' and 'normalcy', although both are coloured by elements of normalisation. Under Putin both the governing regime and the state became more ordered, but the tension between the two precluded full-scale democratic consolidation. The governmental regime was increasingly differentiated from the state, but the representative system and links in the chain of accountability remained in a subaltern position. A new series of contradictions emerged, and it is by exploiting the power of these that Putin managed to maintain his own power. In this lies the danger of new disorders and also the opportunity for renewed democratisation. The greatest contradiction of all, however, may be that Putin has finally drawn the country out of crisis, but at the same time he has ended the period of *krizis*, in the Greek sense of a time of reflection in the life of the community (*polis*), and Russia is all the poorer for that. Russia gradually became more normal, but it also became less interesting.

Notes

1 R. Dahrendorf, *Reflections on the Revolution in Europe* (London: Chatto & Windus, 1990), pp. 92–93.
2 *Ibid.*, pp. 60, 85 and *passim*.
3 J. A. Schumpeter, *Capitalism, Socialism and Democracy* (London & New York: Routledge, 1943/1976).
4 G. O'Donnell, 'Delegative democracy', *Journal of Democracy*, 5:1 (January 1994), 55–69.
5 F. Zakaria, 'The rise of illiberal democracy', *Foreign Affairs*, 76:6 (November–December 1997), 22–43.
6 L. Diamond, *Developing Democracy: Towards Consolidation* (Baltimore and London: The Johns Hopkins University Press, 1999).
7 A. Giddens, *The Third Way: The Renewal of Social Democracy* (Cambridge: Polity Press, 1998). See also A. Giddens, *The Third Way and its Critics* (Cambridge: Polity Press, 2000); A. Giddens (ed.), *The Global Third Way Debate* (Cambridge: Polity Press, 2001).
8 P. Reddaway and D. Glinski, *The Tragedy of Russia's Reforms: Market Bolshevism against Democracy* (Washington, DC: The United States Institute of Peace Press, 2001).

9 For an evaluation, see W. Tompson, 'Putin's challenge: the politics of structural reform in Russia', *Europe-Asia Studies*, 54:6 (September 2002), 933–958.
10 For an analysis of the problems, and Putin's attempt to deal with them, see J. Kahn, *Federalism, Democratisation, and the Rule of Law in Russia* (Oxford: Oxford University Press, 2002).
11 R. Medvedev, *Vladimir Putin – deistvuyushchii prezident* (Moscow: Vremya, 2002), p. 410.
12 'Stenogramma "Pryamoi linii" Prezidenta Rossiiskoi Federatsii V. V. Putina', 24 December 2001, www.president.kremlin.ru/events/423.html.
13 V. Putin, 'Rossiya na rubezhe tysyacheletii', *Nezavisimaya gazeta* (30 December 1999), p. 4; www.pravitelstvo.gov.ru. The *Manifesto* 'Russia at the turn of the millenium' is reproduced in V. Putin, *First Person: An Astonishingly Frank Self-Portrait by Russia's President Vladimir Putin*, with N. Gevorkyan, N. Timakova, and A. Kolesnikov, translated by C. A. Fitzpatrick (London: Hutchinson, 2000), pp. 209–219, at p. 212. Putin talked in terms of the 'historic futility' of the communist system, insisting 'It was a blind alley, far away from the mainstream of world civilisation.' The phrase 'blind alley' is clearly an allusion to Alexander Solzhenitsyn's depiction of Soviet communism as 'a mad dash down a blind alley'.
14 Interview in a TV film made by Igor Shadkhan called *Vladimir Putin: A Conversation in the Evening*, BBC Monitoring, *Johnson's Russia List*, 6483:6 (2002).
15 www.president.kremlin.ru/events/131.html.
16 The 'new' national anthem adopted in December 2000 was the old anthem composed in 1943 by Aleksandr Alexandrov, with new words written by the author of the original lyrics, Sergei Mikhalkov (the father of film director Nikita Mikhalkov). Continuity in both form and content was thus accentuated.
17 *Moskovskii komsomolets* (30 December 2000); The Jamestown Foundation, *Monitor*, 2 January 2001.
18 The 'contradiction' between Russia and Western-generated models of development was symbolised by the shift of the capital from Russia's Muscovite heartland to St Petersburg as a 'window to the West'; and it perhaps was not accidental that a citizen of St Petersburg sought to resolve this contradiction.
19 'V Kreml' "cherez postel'" ne popadesh', *Argumenty i fakty*, 12 (2000), 9.
20 B. Lo, *Vladimir Putin and the Evolution of Russian Foreign Policy* (London: Blackwell, Royal Institute for International Affairs, 2003), Chapter 4.
21 T. Carothers, 'The end of the (democratic) transition paradigm', *The Journal of Democracy*, 13:1 (January 2002), 5–21.
22 For a sceptical appraisal of the concept, see A. Schedler, 'What is democratic consolidation?', *Journal of Democracy*, 9:2 (1998), 91–107.
23 J. J. Linz and A. Stepan, *Problems of Democratic Transition and Consolidation: Southern Europe, South America, and Post-Communist Europe* (Baltimore: The Johns Hopkins University Press, 1996), p. 5.
24 J. Higley and R. Gunther, *Elites and Democratic Consolidation in Latin America and Southern Europe* (Cambridge: Cambridge University Press, 1992); J. Higley, J. Pakulski and W. Wesolowski, *Postcommunist Elites and Democracy in Eastern Europe* (Basingstoke: Macmillan, 1998).
25 S. P. Huntington, *The Third Wave: Democratisation in the Late Twentieth Century* (Norman, OK: University of Oklahoma Press, 1991).

26 S. E. Hanson, 'Defining democratic consolidation', in R. D. Anderson, Jr., M. S. Fish, S. E. Hanson and P. G. Roeder, with an Introduction by G. W. Breslauer, *Postcommunism and the Theory of Democracy* (Princeton and Oxford: Princeton University Press, 2001), p. 150.
27 For a discussion of the incomplete nature of Russia's democratic transition, see M. McFaul, *Russia's Unfinished Revolution: Political Change from Gorbachev to Putin* (Ithaca and London: Cornell University Press, 2001).
28 R. Sakwa, 'The regime system in Russia', *Contemporary Politics*, 3:1 (1992), 7–25; in Russian as 'Rezhimnaya systema i grazhdanskoe obshchestvo v Rossii' ('The regime system and civil society in Russia'), *Polis*, 1 (1997), 61–82.
29 For an interesting discussion of this question, see J. Hoffman, *Beyond the State: An Introductory Critique* (Cambridge: Polity Press, 1995), Part I.
30 T. H. Rigby, 'Stalinism and the mono-organisational society', in R. C. Tucker (ed.), *Stalinism: Essays in Historical Interpretation* (New York: Norton, 1977), pp. 58–59.
31 Andrew Wilson in the Ukrainian context calls this 'virtual politics', but whether he is focusing on the enhanced role of the media, the extensive use of 'black PR' techniques, or the manufacture of a 'virtual' reality through the manipulation of discursive space is not clear. A. Wilson, 'Ukraine: virtual politics, real corruption', *The World Today*, 57:6 (June 2001), 14–16.
32 Zakaria, 'The rise of illiberal democracy'.
33 I. Klyamkin and L. Shevtsova, *Vnesistemnyi Rezhim Borisa II: Nekotorye Osobennosti Politicheskogo Razvitiya Postsovetskoi Rossii* (Moscow: Carnegie Centre, 1999).
34 The battle for the succession was hard fought and dirty, with the incumbent governmental regime using every technique in the book to assure victory for its candidate, yet ultimately the election on 26 March 2000, despite some evidence of fraud, by and large reflected public sentiments.
35 A similar argument is made about Tony Blair by Andrew Rawnsley, 'How the Prime Minister lost his alter ego', *The Observer* (6 October 2002), p. 29.
36 'V Kreml' "cherez postel'" ne popadesh', *Argumenty i fakty*, 12 (2000), 9.
37 *Ibid.*
38 *Gazeta*, 11 October 2002, interview with Olga Redichkina, *Johnson's Russia List*, 6487/8. Alexander Voloshin was head of the presidential administration and a holdover from Yeltsin's presidency, while Mikhail Kasyanov was prime minister and had formerly been close to 'the family'.
39 N. Abdullaev, 'Not all listen to Putin's orders', *Moscow Times* (18 September 2002).
40 A. Tsipko, 'Putin's tactics for compromise with the liberals', The Jamestown Foundation, *Prism*, Vol. 8, 4:2 (April 2002).
41 Prokhanov A., interview with Boris Berezovsky in London, *Zavtra*, 41 (October 2002), pp. 1–2.
42 Tsipko, 'Putin's tactics for compromise'. Kiselev represented the liberal face of Gusinskii's NTV, presenting one of the main current affairs programmes, *Itogi*. When Gazprom called in its half billion dollar loan in 2001, NTV came under new management and Kiselev resigned from the station.
43 *Ibid.*

44 Dahrendorf warns that 'the notion of a third, or middle, way is not only wrong in theory because it arouses the totalitarian potential of all Utopias; it is also wrong in practice. In constitutional terms, there are only two ways: we have to choose between systems and the open society', *Reflections on the Revolution in Europe*, p. 61. Putin's third way, from this perspective, does indeed entail connotations of normalisation's 'systemic' thinking.
45 V. Sheinis, 'Posle bitvy: itogi parlamentskikh vyborov i novaya Gosudarstvennaya Duma', *Nezavisimaya gazeta* (29 December 1999), p. 8.
46 The works of A. S. Panarin, for example, deal with this problem, *Rossiya v tsiklakh mirovoi istorii* (Moscow: Izd-vo MGU, 1999).
47 K. Jowitt, 'The Leninist legacy', in *New World Disorder: The Leninist Extinction* (Berkeley: University of California Press, 1992), p. 293.
48 S. P. Huntington, *Political Order in Changing Societies* (New Haven, CT: Yale University Press, 1968).

II

Political parties and democratisation

3

Russia's Law on Political Parties: democracy by decree?

Edwin Bacon

Introduction

The transition towards a multi-party democracy in post-communist Russia encountered an ironic obstacle throughout its first decade; if the democratic deficit of the Soviet Union was founded on the fact that only one party existed, post-Soviet Russia's electoral system foundered on an excess of parties. On the party list ballot in Russia's parliamentary elections of 1995 there were forty-three parties. In an established democracy this multiplicity of parties need not present any problems, as the distinction between established mainstream parties, fringe parties, and 'silly' parties is apparent from the historico-cultural tradition of a state. In the Russia of the mid-1990s, however, the difficulty of excessive electoral choice was compounded by the youthfulness of the party system, which contributed to volatility amongst parties and voters. With the Soviet system having collapsed only in 1991, there was of course no settled group of established parties and, with the exception of certain communist voters, no solid and traditional electoral constituency for those parties which did exist.

The Yeltsin regime attempted, in the spring of 1995, some seven months before the parliamentary elections in which forty-three parties were to compete, to create from above a neater, more ordered party system by establishing two parties, one centre-right and one centre-left. The hope was that these parties, formed with the approval of the head of state, and led by numbers two and three in the constitutional hierarchy, the prime minister and speaker of the parliament respectively, would emerge as the clear front runners in the election and, between them, as the natural home for most voters. The centre-left party, the Bloc of Ivan Rybkin, would supposedly take support away from the Communist Party of the Russian Federation (see Chapter 4). The centre-right party – Our Home Is Russia, led by Prime Minister Viktor Chernomyrdin – would attract the liberal, reformist voter and bring into the fold the disparate democratic forces which had appeared out of the wreckage of the 1993 election's pro-Yeltsin party, Russia's Choice. This ill-thought-out attempt at party and electoral management enjoyed only limited success. Although Our Home Is Russia performed creditably in the 1995 election, becoming the second largest party in the parliament, though a long way behind the communists, the Bloc of Ivan Rybkin gained just three seats and slightly over 1 per cent of the vote. Perhaps more importantly though, the naïve attempt to conceive a neat, controlled party system and to create it from above met with failure.

Putin's party law

President Yeltsin attempted in the mid-1990s to create a predictable and limited party system. His half-hearted attempt failed in 1995, and although by 1999 there were fewer parties on the ballot paper – twenty-six to be precise – plenty of scope for consolidation of parties remained. Like his predecessor, President Vladimir Putin made no secret of the fact that he would prefer to see fewer political parties operating in Russia. Speaking in May 2000 Putin indicated the type of party system which he favoured:

> No pocketsize parties should appear, but parties actively involved in forming the authorities and nominating from their ranks outstanding leaders, outstanding people, capable of setting up teams which operate effectively and which are responsible to society and to the state . . . only a party choosing this difficult path can count on a future.[1]

Later in the same speech, Putin more explicitly outlined his views on the ideal party system: 'Only a small number of parties can have real influence in society. In practice, it is just not possible any other way. A functioning party system has two or three parties.'[2]

Acting on this conviction, President Putin submitted a bill to parliament, and in June 2001 the Russian parliament passed a Law on Political Parties in an attempt to consolidate an ordered multi-party system in Russia. According to Putin, this was the centrepiece of his first full year as president. For him it was 'the most significant event in the political arena for the past year':[3] more significant then than the other events and initiatives which gained more headlines in Putin's first full year in office. More significant than the introduction of seven federal districts with presidential representatives to cover the eighty-nine regions of Russia; more significant than the removal of the regional heads of executives and legislatures from the upper house of the Russian parliament; and more significant than the adoption of a 'new' national anthem and accompanying symbols by the Russian state. And yet at the same time, the adoption of the Law on Political Parties, was of a piece with these reforms, just as it was with Putin's much vaunted attempt at 'the liquidation of the oligarchs as a class' and the takeover of the NTV television network by the state.

All of these major reforms initiated under President Putin share two characteristics. First, they can be seen as part of the 'state strengthening' agenda proclaimed by the Putin administration, and acknowledged by many Western 'Russia watchers' as a much-needed corrective to the pseudo-strength of the Yeltsin years, when a constitutionally powerful president 'ruled' a state where observance and enforcement of the law came a distant second to the rule of connections, corruption, and *kompromat*. Second, they contain a duality personified in the contradictory figure of Putin himself; few had much argument with the stated ends of these reforms – a more settled party system, a more effective means for a unified state to be governed in conformity with the Constitution – many feared, however, that their means were undemocratic and represented the true intentions of the regime. In this negative interpretation, the regional reforms were not merely about strengthening power vertically but about delivering to the president the power to sack governors and appoint members of the upper house of parliament. Similarly, the reining in of the oligarchs Berezovsky and Gusinsky was not so much about financial probity and distancing the government from the idea that money and connections could buy influence, but was more about the state's desire to control the independent and often critical media holdings of these two men. In terms of the party law, critics saw the laudable aim of consolidating a multi-party system across the Russian Federation as vitiated by the opportunity which the law gives the state to oversee, influence and ban parties.[4]

This chapter is structured around the duality outlined above. We will consider the case for and against the Law on Political Parties, looking at the background to the law, its content and its consequences.

The case for the Law on Political Parties

In the decade following the collapse of the Soviet Union in 1991, Russia's nascent party system was characterised by a number of features deemed negative by the Russian authorities and by many observers adhering to a normative model of a 'Western-type' party system. These negative features are familiar to those who have observed Russia over this period, and have been rehearsed in depth with sufficient regularity elsewhere for this chapter to content itself with a summary.[5]

After the collapse of the Soviet system the very concept of 'party' was ambivalent, and tainted in the eyes of many activists and voters by being redolent of the one Party of the Communist era. Amongst the reformists in particular there was a marked preference for loose blocs and movements, rather than a disciplined party machine. In terms of public opinion, political parties were the least trusted institutions in Russian society throughout the 1990s,[6] and, given the lack of established parties noted above, there was an understandable absence of party identification.[7]

Compounding these barriers to the establishment of an ordered party system, the institutional arrangements of Russia's Constitution, passed in December 1993, did little to encourage disciplined, consolidated parties. The central institutional problem in this regard is the distance between political power and the political space occupied by parties. The Russian Constitution is heavily presidential. President Yeltsin had risen to his position of power without a party organisation behind him, he saw himself, however erroneously, as representative of the Russian people as a whole. For him to join a party offered no advantage from this symbolic point of view, and his personal power would be diluted were he to subject himself to party discipline. The institutional arrangements of the Russian Constitution mean that the only major role played by parties is in the lower house of parliament, the Duma, where half of the deputies are elected by a party list system. In all of the remaining important representative spaces – the constituency-based side of the Duma election, the upper house of the Russian parliament (Federation Council), regional government and local government – the role of parties is minimal.

To argue the case in favour of the Law on Political Parties then, the background to the law would be presented broadly in terms of the following discourse. The Russian 'party system', such as it was in the 1990s, experienced considerable volatility with a multiplicity of small parties springing up, disappearing and 're-badging' with regularity. The democratic and centrist sectors of the political spectrum in particular have been subject to regular splits, feuds and realignments, caused partly by ideological differences and partly by personality clashes.

The centre was dominated in the first post-communist decade by 'parties of power', in other words, parties which gain their position from support for the president, turning on its head the normative notion of the president gaining his position via the support of a party. Such parties have consequently neither acquired nor required sufficient independent strength to cut their political umbilical cord to the presidency. Since 1991 there have been at least four parties of power.[8]

Ironically for the post-communist democracy-building project, two of the most stable parties in 1990s Russia came from the anti-reform wing, namely the Liberal Democratic Party of Russia and the Communist Party of the Russian Federation (see Chapter 4). The latter party is often cited as the only party in Russia which can lay some claim to having mass membership.[9] In the first decade since the Soviet collapse, there has been little depth to Russia's party system in terms of regional penetration, party loyalty amongst the electorate, and party discipline within the parliament.

By the end of 2000, there were 57 political parties, 100 political social associations, and 33 political social organisations officially registered in

Russia, to use the terminology of the 1995 Law on Social Associations under which these registrations were made.[10]

It is the discourse of party development presented above which created the background against which President Putin made the case for action to be taken on the party front. In his State of the Nation address of July 2000, Putin emphasised the role parties should play in Russian society:

> Political parties ensure uninterrupted connection between the people and the authorities in a democratic society. The elections created the best conditions for the development of this vital instrument now. The policy of the majority cannot be pursued and the positions of the minority cannot be protected without parties.[11]

He went on to argue that the drawbacks of the Russian party system were apparent when compared with the background of century-long parliamentary traditions and the multiparty systems of other countries. Concluding that 'a weak power needs weak parties' and that 'a strong power wants strong rivals', Putin stated that 'Russia needs parties that enjoy mass support and stable prestige'.[12]

This desire to restructure the Russian party system provided the context in which the Law on Political Parties was drafted by the Central Electoral Commission and then adopted by the Russian parliament in June 2001. The law states that:

- Parties must have regional branches in no fewer than half of the 89 constituent members of the Russian Federation, and there must be no fewer than 100 registered members in each of these (Article 3/2).
- The minimum national party membership is 10,000 (Article 3/2).
- The formation of parties based on profession, race, ethnicity or religion is prohibited (Article 9/3).
- On election a president may choose to suspend any party membership which (s)he may hold (Article 10/4).
- The leadership of a party must be elected by the party's members (Article 23/5).
- A party's candidate list for elections must be confirmed by a party congress (Article 25/1).
- Private financial contributions to parties are limited (Article 30/9).
- Parties gaining more than 3 per cent of the vote in parliamentary or presidential elections will receive state-funding in proportion to the number of votes gained (Article 33/5a).
- Parties may refuse state funding (Article 33/10).
- Parties are the only social organisation allowed to independently nominate candidates in elections (Article 36/1).
- If a party is banned for violation of the party law, it is also banned from holding public meetings and demonstrations (Article 40/1).

Table 3.1 Voting on the Law on Political Parties, State Duma of the Russian Federation, 21 June 2001

	For	Against	Did not vote
Agro-industrial group	0	41	1
Communist Party of the Russian Federation	0	78	7
Fatherland–All Russia	43	0	1
Independent Deputies	8	8	2
Liberal Democratic Party of Russia	12	0	0
People's Deputies Group	57	1	2
Russia's Regions Group	20	1	24
Unity	80	0	1
Union of Right Forces	1	35	1
Yabloko	17	0	2
Total	238	164	41

Source: *Gosudartsvennaya Duma Stenogramma Zasedanii*, 103, 551, 21 June 2001, pp. 21–22.

The Law on Political Parties was submitted to the Duma by President Putin on 28 December 2000, and considered in its first reading on 7 February 2001. Much of the details of the law were drafted in the Central Electoral Commission, by commission member Elena Dubrovina who suggested that between 20 and 30 parties would renew registration under the new terms.[13] Despite opposition from the Communists in particular, the bill passed rapidly through its various stages, with the crucial second reading on 24 May and a final reading on 21 June. It was signed into law by President Putin on 12 July 2001. The voting on the final reading (see Table 3.1) only just received the necessary majority of half the Duma's deputies. In fact, even this majority was achieved only after one failed attempt. In the first vote on the law's third reading 46 per cent of deputies supported it. A second vote was then called for by Yekaterina Lakhova, a member of the Fatherland–All Russia (FAR) faction and the deputy chair of the Duma Committee for Social Associations and Religious Organisations, under whose remit the committee stage of the bill had come. It was this second vote which achieved the necessary majority.[14]

What then are the likely consequences of the Law on Political Parties? Supporters of the new law draw the following conclusions. First, the multiplicity of parties which has sprung up before previous elections and disappeared equally quickly afterwards will no longer be able to appear with such rapidity. Instead there will be an established and stable set of parties. Supporters of the law hoped that this set of parties would number around twenty to thirty. By the end of March 2003 – nine months before the scheduled parliamentary elections – fifty parties had registered with the Ministry of Justice (Table 3.2), though whether all of these will be able and willing to sustain an electoral campaign is not yet certain. Furthermore, there is a four-month period between initial registration and the requirement to

Table 3.2 *Registered political parties as of 31 March 2003 (in order of registration)*

	Name of party	Leader
1	People's Party	Gennadii Raikov
2	Democratic Party of Russia	Mikhail Prusak
3	All Russian Party 'Unity' and 'Fatherland'–United Russia	Aleksandr Bespalov
4	Conservative Party of Russia	Lev Ubozhko
5	Party of Peace and Unity	Sazhki Umalatova
6	National Patriotic Forces of the Russian Federation	Shmidt Dzoblaev
7	Development of Entrepreneurship	Ivan Grachev
8	Communist Party of the Russian Federation	Gennadii Zyuganov
9	Russian Party of Peace	Iosif Kobzon
10	Union of Rightist Forces	Boris Nemtsov
11	Liberal-Democratic Party of Russia	Vladimir Zhirinovsky
12	All-National Russian Party, 'Union'	Aleksandr Pronin
13	Yabloko	Grigorii Yavlinsky
14	Russian Party of Workers' Self-Government	Levon Chakhmakhch-yan
15	Russian Party of Labor	Sergei Khramov
16	Russian Party of Stability	Vladimir Sokolov
17	Russian Party of Pensioners	Sergei Atroshenko
18	Social-Democratic Party of Russia	Mikhail Gorbachev
19	Russian Ecological Party 'The Greens'	Anatolii Panfilov
20	Russian Agrarian Party	Mikhail Lapshin
21	'Freedom and Sovereignty of the People'	Viktor Cherepkov
22	Eurasia	Aleksandr Dugin
23	Party of National Revival 'The People's Will'	Sergei Baburin

Political parties and democratisation

Table 3.2 (*cont'd*)

	Name of party	Leader
24	Republican Party of Russia	Boris Fedorov
25	Unified Socialist Party 'Spiritual Heritage'	Aleksei Podberezkin
26	Russian Communist Labour Party–Russian Party of Communists	Viktor Tiul'kin
27	Russian Party of Life	Rafgat Altynbaev
28	National-Patriotic Party of Russia	Igor Rodionov
29	Creation	Mikhail Moiseev
30	National Power Party of Russia	Boris Mironov
31	Russian Network Party in Support of Small and Medium Business	Aleksandr Riavkin
32	Party of Russian Citizens	Zaur Abdula-Zade
33	Republican People's Party of Russia	Vladimir Kushnerenko
34	Conceptual Party 'Unity' [Edinenie]	Konstantin Petrov
35	Unified Russian Industrial Party	Elena Panina
36	Eurasian Party – Union of Russian Patriots	Abdul-Bakhed Niiazov
37	'International Russia'	Omar Begov
38	'For Holy Russia'	Sergei Popov
39	Party for Social Equality	Larisa Babukh
40	Liberal Russia	Sergei Iushenkov
41	All-Russian Great Power Party	Aleksandr Chuev
42	True Patriots of Russia	Zaur Radzhabov
43	Party of Russia's Revival	Gennadii Seleznev
44	Civic Party of Russia	Damir Serazhetdinov
45	Communists of Working Russia	Viktor Anpilov
46	Russian Conservative Party of Entrepreneurs	Mikhail Toporkov
47	Russian Constitutional Democratic Party	Viacheslav Volkov
48	New Communist Party	Andrei Brezhnev
49	Party of Russia's Regions	Oleg Denisov
50	Socialist People's Party of Russia	Nikolai Gul'binskii

Source: Central Electoral Commission website: www.cikrf.ru.

prove the existence of regional branches in over half of Russia's regions, and so some of these parties' registrations are as yet provisional.[15] The registered parties are from across the political spectrum, and it is likely that three or four of these parties – likewise from across the spectrum – will consolidate a position as the major contenders for votes in Russia's elections.

The parties which are registered by the time of the next election will be by definition national parties, and will not represent narrow sectoral interests such as a particular ethnic group, religion or profession. Financial contributions from private donors are limited, and the state will fund political parties in proportion to their support amongst the electorate. Parties must have transparent financial accounting, and a transparent democratic structure. Consequently corruption will be more easily exposed, and individuals will find it more difficult to use parties merely as vehicles for their own political ambitions. In other words, what will emerge will be a multi-party system, which will look like that to be found in most Western democracies. The facts that the parties will not be based to any great extent on socio-economic cleavages, and that the party of government looks likely to come from a large, somewhat non-ideological centre, merely serve to emphasise the match with most Western party systems.

The case against the Law on Political Parties

The arguments in favour of the Law on Political Parties are clearly substantive, and were sufficiently convincing to gain majority support in the Russian parliament. Nonetheless, parties as diverse as the Communists and the pro-market Union of Right Forces voted against the law. What then are the central criticisms of a law which on the face of it appears to create the sort of party system which advocates of democracy in Russia have been seeking since the collapse of the Soviet Union?

Let us start with the background. Few would deny that the litany of problems with the party system outlined above broadly represents the situation in Russia for much of the 1990s. However, to concentrate on these is to overlook the developmental nature of the Russian party system in the first postcommunist decade, and indeed the developmental nature of party systems in general. The establishment of a stable democratic party system takes time, and there is a case to be made that the Law on Political Parties is a typical Soviet-style attempt to decree from above what should have been left to develop from below.

Perhaps the low point for the Russian party system was the 1995 Duma election when there were forty-three 'parties' on the party list ballot and only four of these managed to pass the 5 per cent threshold for gaining seats. Of all the votes cast in the party list ballot, approximately half went to parties which then failed to gain seats through this ballot as they fell short of the threshold. As negative as this election might have been though in terms of illustrating the shallow and fractious nature of the Russian party system in the mid-1990s, and proving to be remarkably unproportional in the allocation of seats,[16] nonetheless it did contribute towards the establishment of a more stable party system. The four parties which passed the threshold clearly gained not only in seats, but also with regard to their establishment as the core of the Russian party system. Furthermore, the experiences of 1995 meant that smaller parties began to consider more urgently the advantages of amalgamation into larger blocs or even new parties. The liberal right parties formed the Union of Right Forces in 1999, and a number of smaller groupings and independent candidates came together in the same year as the FAR bloc. In terms of the party law then, the argument can be made that Russia's party system was not quite the basket-case which proponents of the law suggested. The developing party system was running its race adequately before the law cut in.

Moving on from the background to the law, the substance of the Law on Political Parties contains a number of features of concern to those who see it as undemocratic. Critics of the law insist that this is a measure which enables the state to control political parties by means of financial contributions and detailed oversight of the parties. Independent Duma deputy, Vladimir Ryzhkov argued during the bill's progress through parliament that: 'This is a draft law on how toughly to control parties, how to have a file on every member of a political party, how to check every kopek that is received or spent by a political party.'[17] Similarly, Communist deputy, Aleksandr Kuvayev, while accepting the need for a Law on Political Parties, urged that 'it should not be an instrument for the president to manage parties'.[18]

Already in Russia's post-communist political history, attempts have been made by the Central Electoral Commission to bar major political parties from the ballot before each general election (the Communist Party of the Russian Federation in 1993, Yabloko in 1995, and the Liberal Democratic Party of Russia in 1999). In the latter two cases at least, the move to bar these major parties from the election was based on technical infringement of registration criteria. The raft of regulations required for a party to register under the 2001 law is such that arguably it would be relatively easy for a state organ, should it so wish, to find reason to remove the registration of any party. The Law on Political Parties can be put into the context of similar laws – for example, on religion, on social organisations, or the summer 2002 Law on Counteracting Extremist Activities – which introduce state oversight of civil society in Russia. In all of these laws stringent registration criteria, which are assessed by state organs, are required before organisations (be they churches, NGOs or political parties) have the right to exist. In 2000 the Ministry of Justice checked about four thousand public associations and found fault with half of them.[19] What we see is by no means widespread repression – there is broad freedom of religion in

Russia, NGOs act with government approval, and there is a clear plurality within the party system. However, it could be argued that there remains the possibility of 'snatch squad authoritarianism', where the state retains the means to move into targeted political spaces when required.

A major criticism of the Law on Political Parties as it passed through the Russian parliament was that the provision of state funding links parties to the state rather than to the people. The fear that a state which pays the party piper will want to call the political tune was repeatedly expressed, particularly by the liberal parties Yabloko and the Union of Right Forces. It was only a last-minute amendment to the law, stipulating that parties would be free to refuse state funding (Article 33/10), which secured the support of Yabloko deputies for the final reading of the bill.

Finally, the party law can be seen as an attempt at 'freezing' Russia's party system, by making it too difficult for new parties to emerge without state support in one form or another. Such a freezing of the system as it now is has been voted for by the parliament, made up of parties which might perceive themselves as benefiting from the restrictions on emergent competition inherent in the new law. Furthermore, the attempt to freeze the system is occurring at a time which is particularly beneficial for the Putin presidency, which has a broadly supportive parliament. However, if the party law was intended to freeze Russia's party system, it has not yet had much success in achieving this aim (see below).

Conclusions

Whether the Law on Political Parties matches the hopes of its supporters, the fears of its opponents, a mixture of the two or something completely different is at the time of writing a matter of some conjecture. Nonetheless provisional conclusions can be reached, which suggest that although not all of the concerns expressed by opponents to the party law are likely to materialise, there are indications that the law does contain sufficient excuse for registration to be refused to particular parties should the authorities believe this

What is certain is that by definition any party which participates in the next general election, due in Russia in December 2003, will have a presence across the Russian Federation, and a reasonably large nominal membership. It is certain too that the registration requirements in terms of party organisation will mean that organisational distinctions between the parties will decrease. In other words, parties will begin to look like each other, in terms of their constitutions, funding arrangements, and relations with the state.

Equally certain is the fact that the Law on Political Parties has not served to freeze the Russian party system in terms of registered political parties.

If anything it has provided a fresh impetus to party formation. In fact in the calendar year after the passing of the party law there were fifty-six founding congresses of political parties and forty-nine organising committees were established. If the intention of the party law was to decrease the number of parties on the ballot, then it appears to have failed; the early prediction of the Central Electoral Commission (CEC) was that between twenty and thirty parties would register, and in mid-2002 the head of the CEC, Vladimir Veshnyakov, believed that around thirty would be the final number of parties participating in the next Duma election. By the spring of 2003 fifty parties were provisionally registered, of whom most are new parties in the sense that they did not participate in the 1999 Duma election. It may be the case that not all of these parties will participate individually in the election, with some possibly forming into larger blocs to pool resources and voters.

Even if the number of parties on the ballot paper does not decline dramatically, the central criticism of opponents of the law was that it provided the state with the mechanism for tighter control of parties, and for preventing particular parties from registering. Over the period in which twenty-four parties were granted initial registration, seven parties were refused registration. The registration refusals were for various violations of the new law; some fairly straightforward – for example, the Russian Christian Democratic Party fell foul of the ban on parties representing particular religious groups – and some more technical. In particular, the banning of Sergei Yushenkov's, Liberal Russia party raised questions about the even-handedness of the law's application by officials in the Justice Ministry. According to Robert Coalson, 'the Justice Ministry's explanations for refusing to register the party border on the ludicrous. For example, the ministry took exception to several passages in the party's charter that were taken word-for-word from the charter of the already-approved pro-Kremlin Unity party'.[20] The clear implication of critics of this initial rejection of registration was that the party's application had been disallowed because of the Kremlin's ongoing battle with Liberal Russia's exiled co-chairman and chief financial backer, Boris Berezovsky.

A final possibility to consider with regard to the consequences of the party law is that it will begin to increase the 'partyness' of government in Russia. So far the Russian government has evaded the principle of party, with party politics being confined largely to the lower house of parliament, whose only role in relation to the executive is to confirm – or reject – the president's nominee for prime minister. This separation of parties from executive power is partly constitutional, but more to do with the fact that neither of Russia's post-communist presidents have been members of political parties. Consequently, they have been elected as individuals, not as the candidates of political parties. It is conceivable, however, that the Law on Political Parties will reassure President Putin that the once dangerously volatile arena of party politics is now sufficiently regulated to enable him to have a far closer involvement with what is clearly his party, the newly created United Russia. Such involvement might usefully start with his membership of the party. Any progression to leadership and the democratic nomination of a presidential candidate from within the party would represent a major increase in the role of parties in Russia. A party would be the route to real executive power for the first time since the Communist Party of the Soviet Union. That Putin is thinking in these terms was revealed at the founding congress of United Russia, when he talked about the new party having to earn the right to be called the 'party of power'.[21] Party leader and Minister for Emergency Situations, Sergei Shoigu, similarly stated that the new party must earn the right to have Putin as leader.[22] After ten years as a tainted concept in the eyes of people and president, the idea of party may be regaining the political high ground in Russia.

Notes

1 www.president.kremlin.ru/events/35.html.
2 *Ibid.*
3 www.democracy.ru/english/library/laws/parties_fz95_eng/index.html.
4 See, for example, O. Lyakhovich, 'Oni v svoikh koridorakh. Konets khoda', *Obshchaya gazeta* (30 August 2001), p. 7.
5 For a more detailed treatment of these issues see, E. Bacon 'Party formation in Russia', in P. Davies and J. White (eds.), *Political Parties and the Collapse of Old Orders* (New York: SUNY Press, 1999).
6 R. Rose, *New Russian Barometer Trends Since 1992* (Centre for the Study of Public Policy, University of Strathclyde: Studies in Public Policy No. 320, 1999), p. 21.
7 S. White, R. Rose and I. McAllister, *How Russia Votes* (New Jersey: Chatham House Publishers, 1997), pp. 134–141.
8 Russia's Choice, Our Home Is Russia, Unity, and United Russia.
9 L. March, *The Communist Party in Post-Soviet Russia* (Manchester: Manchester University Press, 2002), pp. 2, 142.
10 T. Shkel', 'Partii budut schitat'golosa i rubli', *Rossiiskaya gazeta* (7 February 2001).
11 Vladimir Putin's State of the Nation Address to the Federal Assembly, 8 July, *RIA Novosti.*
12 *Ibid.*
13 V. Vorobev, 'Bol'shoi filtr dlya mini-partii', *Trud* (1 December 2000).
14 *Gosudartsvennaya Duma Stenogramma Zasedanii*, 103, 551 (21 June 2001), pp. 21–22.
15 At the time of writing (April 2003) thirty-four of the fifty parties have received complete registration, with the number of their regional branches confirmed as being higher than forty-four. Interestingly, only one party has succeeded in establishing regional branches in all eighty-nine of Russia's regions. That party is United Russia, the current 'party of power', supported by President Putin.

16 According to White, Rose and McAllister, 'The 1995 Duma election produced the most disproportional election result of any free and fair proportional representation election ... The average first-past-the-post system in Anglo-American democracies falls 21 percentage points short of pure proportionality; the Duma result was more than twice as disproportional.' White, Rose and McAllister, *How Russia Votes*, p. 227.
17 S. B. Glasser and P. Baker, 'Putin plans to eliminate most Russian political parties', *Washington Post* (24 January 2001).
18 'Communists will vote against presidential draft bill', http://russia.strana.ru/981464843.html, 7 February 2001.
19 Uryvayeva, M., 'The Minister of Justice of the Russian Federation highly assesses the prospect of the adoption by the State Duma of the draft Law on Political Parties', *RIA Novosti* (24 January 2001).
20 R. Coalson, 'The Kremlin throws a party', *RFE/RL Russian Political Weekly*, 2:24 (24 July 2002). It must be assumed that Coalson is here confusing the party Unity, with the registered party United Russia.
21 Vladimir Putin, 'The right to be called "The Party of Power" must be deserved', www.russianobserver.com (3 December 2001).
22 '"Unity", "Fatherland" and "All Russia" parties converge to form formidable pro-Putin bloc in the State Duma', www.russianobserver.com (3 December 2001).

4

The Putin paradigm and the cowering of Russia's communists

Luke March

> When we not merely match up to ... best world practice, but create it ourselves, only then will we genuinely have an opportunity to become rich and strong.[1]

For many, one key measure of Russia's ability to match best world practice has been the state of its chief political party, the Communist Party of the Russian Federation (CPRF). After all, the standard story had it, this was the party filled with 'obvious hatred ... toward reform and change',[2] the most obvious symbol of Russia's imperfect democratic transition and relic of a bygone epoch, whose imminent march into obscurity was feted at every, even temporary reverse.[3]

Although such Cassandras often made these predictions more in hope than expectation, by 2002 they appeared vindicated. The CPRF apparently remained Russia's largest party more by default than dexterity; it maintained the slimmest lead over the newly created *Edinstvo* (Unity) bloc in the Duma elections of December 1999, yet lost much influence in the new parliament. If the Sixth Duma of 1996–99 had often been seen as the 'communist' Duma, then in the Seventh Duma of 2000–3 the party proved unable to oppose the prevailing socio-economic agenda, demonstrated graphically by an impotent vote of no confidence in the government in early 2001. As if to underline this, the purging of much of the CPRF's parliamentary portfolios in April–May 2002 and an all-too public rupture within the party leadership led the party's demise to be predicted with renewed vigour.

This chapter has two aims: we evaluate the CPRF's development in the Putin era in the light of its long-term dynamics, examining in particular the causes and consequences of this latest crisis. Secondly, as Blondel argues, 'the character of the opposition is tied to the character of the government'.[4] Therefore we examine the implications of the CPRF's activity for the Putin regime, in particular for the development of party politics and political opposition.

While the development of a stable multi-party system is considered of vital importance to the legitimacy, stability, and representativeness of a consolidated liberal democracy, the absence of a powerful opposition representing an 'explicit authoritarian alternative' and the emergence of within-system opposition that aims for a change of government not regime are recognised as similarly vital for entrenching the principle of a democratic electoral alternation of power.[5] Although the active formation of a developed party system and civil society have now caught the attention of the political class in a way unimaginable under Yeltsin, developing a strong political opposition has been less evidently one of the key aims of the Putin regime. It is the attempt to provide an incentive for developed, structured political parties, while apparently draining this forum of content through the intolerance of substantive social dissent that has been one of the most apparent paradoxes of the Putin regime. In this process, studying the CPRF, both Russia's largest party and its self-proclaimed 'opposition', is an important test case.

As the ensuing chapter will show, the CPRF approached the 2003–4 election round with its national political position under serious threat. Whereas it remains premature to pronounce the party's demise, signs of re-alignment on Russia's left increasingly demand analytical attention. While the process of 'managing' the party system is an important part of Putin's Westernisation, it remains fraught with dangers to the political and social stability of the Putin regime. Before analysing the political earthquake confronting the CPRF under Putin, we will briefly take stock of its political role 'on the eve', when many of its later predicaments were already foreshadowed.

Communists in post-communist Russia: from revanche to retreat

Although on its foundation in 1993 the CPRF became Russia's largest and best-organised political party, this was a dubious honour. If in Rose and Mackie's view the big trade-off facing a political party is between introverted needs of the party *qua* organisation and an extroverted concern with the broader political environment, the CPRF's extreme introversion, a trait of highly ideological parties, gradually became clear as the external monolith fragmented into increasing organisational, ideological and strategic incoherence.[6] Though the chief opposition to the Yeltsin regime, the party's integration within it was incomplete and ineffective: it remained in limbo between the irreconcilable opposition most of its supporters wished, and a responsible opposition with a coherent and popular programme able to win an electoral mandate. Why was this, and what was its effect on Russian politics?

The most obvious point was the *crisis of movement*. Simply put, communism as an idea lacked an electoral attraction to the majority of Russian citizens, even in the homeland of Soviet socialism in the depth of socio-economic cataclysm, and in a presidential system that majority was vital. To a much greater extent than commonly realised, the CPRF leaders were pragmatic moderates who had wrested control from the reactionaries during reconstitution of the party after its ban, and who were committed to re-orienting the party towards post-Soviet conditions (such as the mixed economy and political pluralism), without divorcing it from its name, ideology or heritage. As early as December 1991 party leader Gennadii Zyuganov had insisted on the need for communists to learn new approaches from both patriots and democrats.[7] Yet, as for so many electoral communists before them, the attempt to evolutionise revolution was fraught with irreconcilable contradictions, and the closer they came to effecting their aims through the 'bourgeois' system the more they had to lose by destroying that system.

Tannahill defines two electoral communist party ideal-types with different responses to the crisis of movement: the 'Eurocommunist party' and the 'neo-Stalinist party'.[8] A Eurocommunist party such as the Communist Party of Italy (PCI) arises from weaker class and value cleavages, co-operative relations with labour unions and a party system that allows some proximity to power. Such variables are a powerful incentive to political moderation, alliance-seeking strategies and the flexibility which allowed the PCI both to maintain reserves of intellectual and youth support and to prolong its political survival (as the current Democrats of the Left) by a pre-emptive refoundation. In contrast, a neo-Stalinist party like the Communist Party of France (PCF) may emerge from relatively intense social and political cleavages, a polarised political system, and prolonged illegality, which increase its propensity towards doctrinaire politics. The relative ideological and organisational *immobilisme* of the PCF left it unable to reform or revive, marginalised in stagnant and secular sclerosis as it lost first its role as left vanguard to Mitterrand's Socialist Party and second its protest role to the National Front.

In comparative terms the CPRF is a hybrid: the open political space of the post-communist political system, the party's weak working-class roots and the presence of a significant number of crypto-Eurocommunist 'Marxist reformers' among pragmatists in the leadership gave the potential for 'pragmatic reform' in the direction of the Eastern European social democracy practised by parties such as the Polish Democratic Left Alliance. However, the genetic similarities to the PCF became ever more apparent: the polarised transition and the CPRF's ban from 1991 helped the heirs of the Communist Party of the Soviet Union (CPSU)'s conservative wing, already 'steeped in the mythology of Soviet development',[9] remain excluded from the post-1991 political settlement, and only after election defeat in 1996 did they confront the unfeasibility of revanche.

Indeed, the CPRF appeared as Bolshevised as the PCF. While the party lacked the PCF's bedrock in blue-collar unions and sought electoral alliance from its inception, any additional manoeuvre was limited by its electoral and organisational dependence on the most Sovietised, economically depressed, politically passive strata, including pensioners and peasants from central and southern Russia. For many supporters, its whole *raison d'etre* was as a neo-Soviet 'counter-society', a fragment of the CPSU in the 'bourgeois' system. When reinforced by the party's founding myth as an anti-bureaucratic mass democratic party, and a cumbersome internal balance towards its more unreconstructed activists, the vast majority of whom were sociologised in Brezhnevite conformity, such introversion was always a barrier to electoral expansion and left the CPRF exceedingly vulnerable to generational turnover in its social base.

If such travails have more clearly structural reasons, then the party leadership have received ample blame. Some accusations concentrate more on leadership style, the leaders seen as woefully uncharismatic, 'pathologically cautious', inert and inept in the public sphere. Internal party critics focus on Zyuganov and his deputy Kuptsov's intolerant and unreflective authoritarianism and secretive style.[10] Other serious allegations focus on leadership aims, from specific tactical mistakes (such as the 1996 election failure in the most propitious socio-economic conditions), to overall strategy.[11] In this regard, the most serious allegations were that the party's policies 'appeared to place its own institutional comfort ... above principle'.[12] On this telling the communist leadership, comfortably ensconced in the Russian parliament and enjoying the perks of the Russian elite, was content with being the 'bridesmaid but never the bride', enjoying closeness to power but never the responsibility of exercising it.[13]

In the communists' defence, even grounded allegations often ignore the structure of incentives. The allegation of the communists' 'parliamentary cretinism' is somewhat harsh given the limited prerogatives of the Duma, to which we return below, which made parties dependent upon it as their only means of national presence and institutional leverage. Yet irrespective of intentions, manoeuvring between opposition and conformism risked constant disappointment both to the party's many ideological supporters, and to pragmatic governors such as Tuleev of Kemerovo who increasingly distanced themselves from a party unable to translate opposition rhetoric into action. Zyuganov's lack of obvious public persona was in a large part a function of his party role: within the party he was ideal – a balancer able to express the collective position of a highly divided party through a mixture of personal skills, consensus-building, conflict management and outright intrigue, while the authoritarianism of party leadership has structural origins in the constricting effects of democratic centralism.[14] Moreover, the incentives to reform the party structure were more mixed than often acknowledged: against the ageing of the communist electorate and the docility of the post-Soviet trade unions, the continued poor performance of competitor parties until the arrival of *Edinstvo* (not least those professing a more modern 'democratic left'), and contemporary Russia's lack of resemblance to an advanced democracy, weakened would-be party reformers.[15]

Nevertheless, while describing the CPRF as 'flexible and moderate only in its approach to electoral politics and parliamentary maneuvering'[16] is perhaps a harsh assessment of its survival instincts, the leadership's consistent inability to transcend its introverted party aims provoked quasi-Brezhnevite stagnation. Zyuganov was unable to evolve from party patrician to presidential probable, with his 'democratically centralised' persona remaining a millstone in a personality-based presidential system, as the PCF had found to its cost. The *nomenklatura* background of the party hierarchy contributed to a conformist political culture, and by 2002 Zyuganov's quasi-Yeltsinite heavy-handedness towards potential leadership challengers had led to a serious 'personnel famine' in the party. His eclectic ideological position, melding late Stalinist national-Bolshevism, Slavophile Orthodox conservatism with smatterings of social democracy and ecologically tinged 'new left Marxism' in an anti-liberal rejectionist front lost its logic with the end of electoral polarisation from 1996, and left the party's views of democracy, the Soviet past, and its attitude to parliamentary and non-parliamentary struggle less clear than ever in 2002. Ultimately, the leadership's tactical ability was not matched by strategic vision, while nothing in the CPRF's communism implied that it possessed any 'third way' between a split and transcendence and self-interested retrenchment.

Given such problems, it is perhaps surprising how the party managed to exceed most observers' expectations in the election round of 1999–2000, preserving its status as premier opposition party, and despite serious attrition in 'red-belt' strongholds, actually improving its vote in regions such as urban centres in south and east Siberia.

Most obviously, and in direct contrast to the West European communist experience, was the simple fact that, whatever its own weaknesses, the CPRF remained far more consolidated than its competitors. Western analysts point out the obsolescence of mass-type parties in post-communist societies, in particular the constraints of an unwieldy membership and party structure, yet what such parties lack in flexibility they make up for in stability and longevity, a clear consideration in the repeated re-election of Zyuganov as the only leader capable of preserving the balance of interests within the party. It is no accident that competitors such as 'United Russia' have sought disciplined and hierarchical organisations to overcome the democratic anarchy of many post-communist organisations.

Moreover, the communists skilfully exploited their party monopoly, absorbing or sidelining opposition challengers such as Sergei Baburin to maximise their role as an alternative opposition 'party of power'. Sakwa's notion that the CPRF 'is not the source of patronage or advancement, even where its governors identify with it' is overstated.[17] It was never a 'party of power' in the sense of a party created directly by government for government, and clearly lacked the financial and elite resources provided to parties like *Edinstvo*. Yet the notion reflects a role as an *ad hoc* instrument 'to gain, maintain or extend personal/state power', which garners 'bandwagon' support around the expectation of success.[18] While unquestionably ideologically driven, the CPRF also represented the careerist wishes of the ousted Soviet elite who used party structures to return to mainstream politics, particularly after Yeltsin abolished local-level Soviets in 1993, while the CPRF's status as 'the opposition' garnered it bandwagon support from non-communists such as its economic advisor Sergei Glaz'ev, and executive chairman of the communist-allied National-Patriotic Union of Russia, Gennadii Semigin.[19] Though the limits of all parties' links with regional representatives were everywhere apparent, the CPRF's role as the most stable regional and local level grassroots party often allowed it a role in governors' ascent to power, even as a rung in a ladder which they would thereafter kick away.[20]

This local party monopoly had another effect: given the parlous state of Russia's civil society the CPRF was often one of the only functioning local non-governmental organisations. It cultivated this position assiduously, with its slogan 'for every *raion* there is a *raikom*'[21] and with a gradual movement to a more pragmatic, non-ideological stance. Although many communist grassroots organisations were weak, the more organised ones managed to recreate at least a semblance of 'womb-to-tomb' welfare and social service provision, albeit sporadically.

The role of opposition 'party of power' co-existed and often conflicted with its role as the 'opposition party of protest'. Brudny notes with apparent surprise that some 47 per cent of those who voted for Zyuganov in 2000 may have done so as an anti-Putin protest.[22] Indeed, much of the CPRF's rhetoric emphasises its role as the only serious alternative, and this, plus the decline of the LDPR, helped the CPRF's electoral gains in 1999–2000. Too much is made of the party's role as a 'mummified organisation' of programmed pensioners who have always voted communist and always will.[23] Recent statistical studies buttress anecdotal evidence that the CPRF has become the 'party of the relatively deprived', augmenting its vote with enough younger strata, particularly in the 35–50 range in industrial and university centres, to prevent the predicted generational attrition.[24] The increasing problem, to which we return below, has been to manage the transition from 'a party of old die-hard officialdom into a party of offended yet socially-active people', particularly with such officialdom at the apex.[25]

Finally, an important part of the CPRF's longevity has been its absorption as a 'junior partner' into the elite 'balance of interests', apparent first in the *de facto* alliance between Chernomyrdin and the CPRF moderates in 1996–98. Such a balance of interests, according to Sakwa and Shevtsova, reflects a political elite who 'failed to institutionalise either the political influence of social movements through party forms of representative government, or its own responsibility to society through . . . elements of a pluralistic civil society'.[26] Huskey's description of the Russian transformation as a 'permanently negotiated transition'[27] also reflects the achievement of short-term social peace through elite bargaining and bureaucratic co-optation rather than normative social consensus or institutionalised rules. Such negotiation was mutually beneficial – providing the party with important resources and the elite with a 'blocked opposition' whose 'revolutionary' nature consolidated the political elite against them when they threatened to come to power, but whose essential political conservatism meant that they channelled and managed rather than provoked social protest.[28] Yet this was an inherently unstable substitution for coherent party–state institutionalisation and open electoral turnover: the pacification of the party hierarchy always threatened its social pacification function by opening up an unsustainable gap between the party's rhetoric and action, whilst the regime oscillated between co-opting the communists and revolutionary mobilisation against them. Neither regime nor opposition answered this quandary in the Yeltsin era.

The Putin paradigm

So if expressions such the 'floating party system' have been coined to reflect the lack of stable party identification in Russia politics,[29] then Russia's political system as a whole can be described as a 'floating political system', where formal institutions remain under-developed, weakly grounded in civil society and heavily moulded by the personalities of their incumbents. Nowhere is this more apparent than the speedy reconfiguration of relations between the executive, parties, and parliament ushered in by Putin's presidency, where the relative popularity and vigour of the new president explain much of the apparent strengthening of state power. We can identify several features of this paradigm-shift in Russian politics relevant to our discussion.

Putin is Russia's first post-communist leader: unlike Yeltsin, whose personality and politics were clearly bound up in the transitional period, Putin has made it explicit that he considers the 'transition' to be over, and in terms that Zyuganov could have used, that the time for revolutions is at an end. He is also Russia's first post-modern leader, in that he espouses a non-ideological pragmatism and inclusive consensus-oriented style, where economic competence, 'modernisation' and stability are key aims.[30] One can agree with Sakwa that Putin's 'politics of the radical centre' may have the intention and potential to generate a distinct ideological tradition of liberal-patriotic conservatism, yet note also that specifics of the Russian institutional context and the methods by which this centre is forged may provide for a less optimistic outcome. The much noted 'left-patriotic consensus' (Byzov) or 'quasi-centre' (Sheinis) evident since 1998 and fostered by Putin involves less a normative project than an exhausted society's rejection of radicalism and the risky delegation of authority to a leader prepared to do what it takes to avoid it, while the exact blend of left and right politics is not definitively fixed.[31] The term 'managed democracy' popularly associated with Putinism may describe an unattainable outcome, but it certainly encapsulates the revived technocratism, manipulative social engineering and restrictive attitude to social debate as compared with Yeltsin, who, though more by accident than design, was far more inconsistent and *laissez-faire* in his use of the presidency as the aggregator of national interest.

Indeed Putinism elided the differences between consensus, centrism and conformity, and implied real limits on social pluralism, despite reinvigorated rhetoric about developing civil society and the party system. Party leaders were quick to point out how disorientating Putinism was; with a politics which was 'amorphous and omnivorous',[32] Putin's combination of 'communist' great power politics (in his centralising statism in domestic politics), and a liberal economic emphasis, with the presidency's ability to act as a supra-political arbiter, made him a moving target for opposition.[33]

Such problems were particularly acute for the CPRF. Putin's much-noted lack of ideological anti-communism is deceptive: consistent with his call for pragmatic modernisation he was clear that, although the party's electoral weight precluded a ban, he regarded communism as an obsolete 'blind alley' with repellent 'ideological cockroaches'.[34] This pragmatic anti-communism actually made him a more formidable opponent than Yeltsin's knee-jerk version, by moving political combat from an ideological battle of regimes to the politics of results, and challenging the communists to put pragmatism before principle. The essence of Putin's contract with the communists was that they 'reform or die': co-operate, adapt ideologically to become a 'modern left party' earning a role in the party system, or meet a well-overdue demise. Putin's ability to adopt, adapt and effect the communists' 'patriotic' positions 'pulled the carpet from under Zyuganov within his own party', and sparked an internal battle within the CPRF which Zyuganov only quelled by adopting the stance of a reformed Marxist.[35] Putin also found a common working language with party moderates such as Seleznev, unlike Yeltsin, who dealt with all communists with distaste, if at all. All of this upset the delicate intra-party balance and promised a far more nuanced version of presidential 'divide and rule' than under Yeltsin, as Putin threatened to 'kill the communists with compromise'.[36]

The party in the new Duma

It was in the Duma where the implications of the new paradigm for political parties were most apparent. Analysts remain divided over the Duma's political role. The conventional view is of a subordinate institution in a strongly 'super-presidential system' whose importance is more as a staging post in the presidential electoral cycle than as a source of independent authority.[37] This is challenged by those who have argued that the Duma has developed significant legislative and policy autonomy as a counterweight to the presidency.[38]

The CPRF's activity, as the Duma's largest faction in 1996–99, has been intimately bound up with its institutional evolution, and shows that while the Duma is much more than a 'rubber stamp', its role is still heavily circumscribed. The CPRF's Duma performance was more effective than popularly acknowledged: although it failed with bids for constitutional change, it succeeded in halting some of the most liberal or pro-Western legislation (for example land privatisation and the ratification of START-II). It propagandised the image of a Duma as an opponent of presidential arbitrariness, while becoming an increasingly important participant in the budgetary process. Meanwhile, the most important concomitant was the 'parliamentarisation' of the party elite. As the Duma became the party's *de facto* nerve centre, its resources (parliamentary aides, communications and finances) were gainfully employed in national party building.[39] However self-interested the party's defence of the Duma in the crises of 1997–99, it played a key role in the consolidation of that institution against the unpredictability of dissolution, and in its emergence as Russia's sole 'oasis of party development' in a nascent cadre party system.[40]

Yet ambiguities remained. Critics were swift to accuse the CPRF fraction of a neo-Leninist 'colonisation' of the Duma for narrow party ends.[41] Certainly, accusations of party venality were heard from too many disparate sources to be easily dismissed.[42] The extent of the party's 'parliamentarism' is often overstated, with many Duma communists apparently not internalising parliamentary values. Despite rejecting its members' most maximalist demands, the CPRF's inability totally to transcend Lenin's dictum 'the worse [for the bourgeois], the better [for the communists]' was reflected in its most apparently self-defeating manoeuvres, particularly its abrupt withdrawal from power-sharing negotiations with Yeltsin in autumn 1999 and its failure effectively to capitalise on the popularity of the Primakov government.[43]

Certainly, the CPRF's 'colonisation' interacted with the Duma's ambiguous internal democracy. The parliament's internal procedures were based on decentralised power-sharing principles that fostered inter-party consensus, but often caused excessive bargaining, incoherent or chaotic policy-making, and deadlock.[44] Symptomatic was the rather toothless steering committee, the Council of the Duma, on which all parliamentary fractions had equal representation regardless of size, and the informal 'package agreement' which distributed committee chairs and vice-chairs in rough proportion to party size, but often created overlapping, redundant and internally divided bodies. As Ostrow argues, this was usually 'nothing to do with legislative necessity and everything to do with partisan politics',[45] and represented in microcosm the balance of interests between mutually suspicious forces schooled in zero-sum politics, where coherent formal procedures took second place to informal short-term and self-interested bargaining. Within this context, the self-interested behaviour of the CPRF as the Duma's largest faction becomes more understandable.

Moreover, however great a niche parties carved out within the Duma, the broader role of parties and parliament remains very curtailed. As the communists found out to their cost in 1996–99, with no institutional linkage with the government, and severe penalties for expressing no-confidence, the majority faction in the Duma finds itself with few options between obstruction of and complete compliance with the executive. Sharing responsibility with the government over many legislative initiatives (such as the budget) leaves the Duma very much a junior partner, unable to achieve concrete control over or credit for policy outcomes, and risking serious displeasure before a demanding electorate. Political-institutional factors such as the super-presidency (in the sense that it arbitrates *above* particularistic interest in an echo of the CPSU), and the non-partisan basis for the upper house further limit the space for organised opposition. As Bacon states, Russia may be dubbed an 'anti-oppositional regime', whereby the heavily presidential provisions clearly and intentionally 'vitiate opportunities for organised opposition'.[46] Moreover, the precise balance of legislative-executive relations is heavily influenced by how personality and patronage affect the elite balance of interests. In the Duma of 1996–99, the CPRF's often-formidable poll-ratings and the presidents' faltering health balanced the 'executives ability to use monetary rewards to generate a legislative majority'.[47] This was buttressed by the often ignored threat of 'psychological pressure' to garner legislative compliance.[48]

All these factors indicated that the parliament's nascent role as a counterweight would be severely tested after the election result of 1999, with a re-invigorated executive, and several 'firsts' for the post-Soviet era: the first parliamentary reverse for the left opposition (with their overall share of seats in parliament declining from 47 to 29 per cent) the first truly popular government (Duma elections usually having a role as a referendum on the government's performance) with a potential first pro-government parliament majority. All of this clearly tipped the 'balance of interests' away from an autonomous parliament.

Putin's policies soon indicated that a co-operative parliament could indeed mean a more co-opted parliament. The January 2000 deal between *Edinstvo* and the communists which ruptured the 'package agreement' by sharing the lion's share of committee chairs and leaving Gennadii Seleznev as speaker was highly significant: it allowed the CPRF to save face just prior to the presidential elections, yet co-opted them by making them highly dependent on presidential patronage and psychological pressure. The intention to redress an imbalance that the presidential administration had itself helped create was raised repeatedly throughout the state Duma, particularly when parliamentary compliance was demanded.[49] Seleznev, who could be removed by a simple parliamentary majority, was made particularly vulnerable as a pro-government majority of 280 was fashioned through a mixture of such co-optation, coercion (the marginalisation of Primakov and absorption of FAR), and consent (by previously unheard-of regular consultations with the heads of Duma fractions).

The extent of the CPRF's marginalisation within the new Duma was quickly revealed. In the previous Duma, the 211 votes of the agrarian-left coalition had considerable blocking potential, but now the pro-government majority was increasingly able to deliver two-thirds majorities to pass the liberal agenda of the Kasyanov government in the teeth of agrarian-left opposition.[50] Particularly bitter were the rapid ratification of START-II and the movement towards land privatisation, the latter of which was described by Zyuganov as his 'Stalingrad' and was a major threat to the party's rural electoral strongholds. Liberal socio-economic legislation like the flat tax law and labour law liberalisation also demonstrated the party's loss of leverage, as was witnessed in the re-orientation of the party towards extra-parliamentary opposition throughout 2001.

The party's attitude to the executive's domestic political agenda was more ambiguous: although it had long supported the rhetoric of state centralisation, it grew suspicious of possible authoritarian outcomes – increasingly notable was rhetoric about 'liberal fascism', while the party ended up voting against laws it had earlier supported (notably Putin's law on reforming the seven federal districts). Its attitude to the 'Law on Political Parties' was also complex. As Russia's best-organised party it was an obvious beneficiary of raising the 'entry fee' for political parties, originally supporting strict requirements which would have immediately penalised its left competitors, and registered easily. While it also used the registration process to re-affirm internal discipline, it argued against attempts to expose its finances and membership procedures to greater external control, eventually voting against.[51] Although this militancy reflected increased internal party tensions, it also showed real problems of opposition, with the party concerned to demonstrate their right to dissent from the quasi-centrist consensus, however ineffectually.

The 'portfolio purge'

Communist over-representation in the Duma hierarchy was compounded by their alliance with the nominally independent agro-industrial bloc, giving them three seats on the ten-member Duma council, three speakers (of eight) and eleven of twenty-eight committee chairs in total (see Table 4.1). Their increasing opposition thus made it unsurprising in April 2002 when the centrist parliamentary fractions stripped the CPRF of its most important committee chairs, leaving them with a mere two. The party Central Committee responded

Table 4.1 *Distribution of Duma committee chairs*

	January 2000		August 2002	
Fraction	No. of seats (%)	Committee chairs (%)	No. of seats (%)	Committee chairs (%)
CPRF	89 (20.2)	10 (35.7)	82 (18.2)	1 (3.6)
AIG	41 (9.3)	2 (7.1)	43 (9.5)	1 (3.6)
Edinstvo	81 (18.4)	7 (25.0)	83 (18.4)	7 (25.0)
ND	58 (13.2)	5 (17.9)	55 (12.2)	5 (17.9)
FAR	45 (10.2)	1 (3.6)	52 (11.6)	5 (17.9)
LDPR	17 (3.9)	1 (3.6)	12 (2.7)	1 (3.6)
SPS	32 (7.3)	1 (3.6)	32 (7.1)	3 (10.7)
Yab	21 (4.8)	0	17 (3.8)	1 (3.6)
RR	38 (8.6)	1 (3.6)	47 (10.4)	2 (7.1)
Ind.	19 (4.3)	0	22 (4.9)	2 (7.1)
Total	441 (100)	28 (100)	445 (100)	28 (100)

Source: www.duma.gov.ru.
Notes: CPRF (Communist Party of Russian Federation); AIG (Agro-Industrial Group); FAR (Fatherland–All Russia); ND (People's Deputy); LDPR (Liberal Democratic Party of Russia); Yab (*Yabloko*); RR (Russia's Regions); Ind. (Independent).

by demanding Seleznev and the remaining committee heads resign forthwith in protest. The refusal of Seleznev, Nikolai Gubenko and Svetlana Goryacheva to comply prompted their eventual expulsion from party and fraction. The evolution of what was dubbed by some as the most important event in the Duma of 2000–3 was rarely less than opaque, with several conflicting motives appearing to have prompted it.

Most obvious was the demand by fractions originally sidelined in January 2000 (like SPS), to re-establish the system of Duma proportionality and consensus.[52] An added impetus to this was given by the gradual consolidation of the Duma majority around the Fatherland–All Russia (FAR) and *Edinstvo* fractions in the 'United Russia' bloc, which removed one original reason for the deal (to marginalise FAR in the electoral race). FAR deputies, who did best from the new deal, had allegedly pressurised *Edinstvo* leaders for dividends to match the concessions they had acceded to.[53]

Yet of arguably greater weight were the presidential administrations' attempts to hasten party consolidation as upcoming elections approached. Recent opinion polls had demonstrated the communists still comfortably ahead of 'United Russia', while the problems of party construction and internal criticism of the pro-Western direction of Putin's foreign policy (voiced particularly vigorously by the CPRF) seemed to incur increasing irritation with the communist opposition. Concerns at a possible downturn in the economy and the close sequencing of the next parliamentary and presidential elections also provoked debate on United Russia's future prospects.

Although some such as Gleb Pavlovskii and FAR deputy Fedulov (who called for banning the CPRF) seemed motivated by a desire to obliterate the CPRF for good,[54] that the electoral consideration of damaging the CPRF's ability to use the Duma for its propaganda and patronage purposes before the upcoming elections was paramount was shown by the nature of the attack on Gennadii Seleznev. Seleznev's removal was apparently only raised by accident, with the removal of his casting vote in the council of the Duma and the CPRF's patronage ability through head of the Duma apparatus Nikolai Troshkin being the key aims.[55] Similarly, the portfolio purge focused on those with a socio-economic bent (Glaz'ev, Maslyukov and Saikin), undermining key party leaders such as Lukyanov, Melnikov and Ivanchenko. Once sufficient disarray had been fostered in the communist camp, the Duma seemed disinclined to force the issue – allowing Seleznev, Gubenko and Goryacheva to remain in post in a way that would maximally embarrass the communist leadership.

Too many actions can be ascribed to the hidden hand of the Kremlin: the contradictory conduct of the *Edinstvo* fraction in the previous years' failed vote of no-confidence indicates that the centrist factions are often less disciplined than they aim to be.[56] However, the aims of the Duma purge clearly accorded with the presidential administration's long-term interest in maintaining pressure on the communists to 'reform or die', while keeping Seleznev in his Duma seat in order to maximise the possibilities of creating an alternative centre-left movement.[57] An added factor was Zyuganov's precarious leadership position in the electoral run-up: party critics noticed that if he had adopted a more moderate position earlier he might have been able to negotiate over portfolio redistribution.[58] Instead he insisted on absolute subordination to party discipline, less as a matter of principle than as a test of loyalty of those party colleagues, particularly Seleznev, who had been openly or covertly supportive of party social democratisation.[59] Certainly, despite its rhetoric about the impossibility of serving in a 'servile' Duma the CPRF tacitly permitted some committee heads to bargain with the centrists to stay in position (see Table 4.2).[60]

Consequences of the portfolio putsch

The seriousness of this body blow was immediately obvious: such a public loss of such authoritative leaders really looked like beginning the long-predicted party split, as some of the party's key notables rapidly either dissociated themselves from the party or expressed their need for a new leader.[61] Accelerated crisis was apparent in the regions, where the trend

Table 4.2 *CPRF leadership in the Duma*

Post	January 2000	After April crisis 2002
Speaker	Gennadii Seleznev	Gennadii Seleznev (Ind)
Deputy Speaker (of 8)	Petr Romanov	Petr Romanov
Deputy Speaker	Gennadii Semigin (AIG)	Gennadii Semigin (AIG)
Committee for:		
State construction	Anatolii Lukyanov	Valerii Grebennikov (FAR)
Industry, construction etc.	Yurii Maslyukov	Martin Shakkum (RR)
Labour and social policy	Valerii Saikin	Andrei Selivanov (SPS)
Economic policy	Sergei Glaz'ev	Grigorii Tomchin (SPS)
Federation affairs and regional policy	Leonid Ivanchenko	Viktor Grishin (FAR)
Education and science	Ivan Melnikov	Aleksandr Shishlov (Yab)
Women's, family and youth affairs	Svetlana Goryacheva	Svetlana Goryacheva (Ind)
Affairs of social and religious organisations	Viktor Zorkaltsev	Viktor Zorkaltsev
Culture and tourism	Nikolai Gorbenko	Nikolai Gorbenko (Ind)
Agrarian questions	Valerii Plotnikov (AIG)	Gennadii Kulik (FAR)
Nationalities affairs	Aleksandr Tkachev (AIG)	Valentin Nikitin (AIG)

Source: Adapted from Duma web rage: www.duma.gov.ru.

since 1999 (despite notable gubernatorial successes in 2000–1) was further loosening of the red belt.[62] Fraught relations with the official trade unions had finally broken down in 2001.[63] For many observers, the blow to prestige and lobbying potential, combined with active attempts to reconfigure the left of the political spectrum could find the party competing against revived centre-left competitors and its role as alternative party of power undermined further by administrative pressure.[64] One had only to look at the March 2002 election result for Ukraine's Communist Party, where loss of lobbying potential combined with the effects of loyalist governors had caused considerable electoral erosion.

Yet several observers argued that the portfolio putsch was a big miscalculation, facilitating a sense of grievance and the communist party's return to extremist opposition.[65] It was noticeable that the CPRF's moderate wing was critical whereas troublesome party radicals appeared content to rally round Zyuganov in response to a long-awaited move.[66] The Law on Political Parties could prove significant (see Chapter 3), because although it did not appear to impose strict quantitative limits on parties (twenty-four had registered by August 2002), critics' assertions that it allowed greater state control of the type of parties were borne out by the apparently political refusal to register parties like 'Liberal Russia'. The attempt to manipulate the party system could clearly misfire, leaving aggrieved voters little choice but to vote for the CPRF as the only *de facto* opposition on the ballot, a tendency which played a key role in the strong electoral performance of Czech communists in 2002. The real potential for the implementation of Putin's socio-economic programme (particularly in the areas of land reform, labour law and social service privatisation) to puncture the broad but shallow social consensus was something the communists vowed to exploit.[67]

It would indeed be premature to write off the CPRF: its subcultural and consolidated vote means that the party might rely on at least 15 per cent of the vote in the future if, and *because* it does not change its programmatic positions.[68] External factors such as the economic situation, the performance of its competitors, or the administrative resources used against it remained variables, while the portfolio putsch's effect on party resources can be exaggerated: money alone has never guaranteed electoral victory.[69] Nevertheless, the CPRF's own ability to expand significantly beyond the subculture remains doubtful.[71] Urban offers two options for the revival of the Russian left: the first a militant quasi-Marxist 'New Left' exploiting the tremors of both globalising capitalism and its Russian variant, the second moderate social democracy.[70] With the events of April 2002 finally achieving the emasculation of the party's social democratic wing its recent internal paralysis had suggested, the party's emphasis on renewed populist social-class protest and anti-globalisation clearly indicated its preference.[72] However such a path remains challenged by the party's organisational inflexibility, political-cultural and generational conservatism, not to mention its unvanquished Russophilism and continued internal divisions.[73]

What were the broader consequences of the CPRF's travails? Given its previously pivotal parliamentary role, the communists' marginalisation therein inevitably affects parliamentarism. As well as addressing an imbalance of resources within the Duma, it clearly smoothed the path for the government's liberal agenda, while the trimming of the speaker's role resolved Seleznev's clash of interests between his party and parliamentary personality that had long irked other fractions.[74] However, the portfolio putsch indicates the continuation of 'Market bolshevik' tendencies: for Putin, marketisation appears to take priority to democratisation, and the two processes can be antithetical. Although a less partisan speakership and return to non-majoritarian intra-Duma processes might emerge, these were hardly the primary aims. Indeed, the usual anti-party sentiment and the presidency's ability to manipulate institutions and dependent political forces in a highly secretive way for short-term political gain were most apparent.[75] The new distribution of seats was scarcely more proportionate (see Table 4.2), while the suggestion that the manoeuvres of the centrists had powerful backing elsewhere was reinforced by rumours of money going from the state coffers to 'United Russia' giving it a head-start in the parliamentary race. If the classic trade-off for parliaments is between efficiency and representativeness, the unseemly haste with which governmental projects were increasingly able to get endorsement indicated that the cowering of the communists had significantly weakened the Duma's role in providing a representative balance-of-powers.[76]

Within the electoral realm, the CPRF's failure to respond to Putin's call to recognise its own obsolescence provoked the hope that increasing ghettoisation in the manner of the PCF might unfreeze the left of the political spectrum and allow a potent left-opposition to outflank the CPRF.[77] Although the communists forecast that the nascent centre-left was doomed to repeat the 'Rybkinisation' and irrelevance of the 1990s, there were indeed strong contra-indications. Analysis has long shown that the average Russian voter is a 'textbook social democrat' with a preference for state paternalist values that have provided the bedrock for the re-emergence of successor parties in Eastern Europe.[78] While Russia's polarised transition long meant that social democracy was too socialist for democrats and too democratic for the socialists, the emergent 'left-patriotic consensus' showed both FAR and *Edinstvo* borrowing from the communist arsenal, while socialism is once again a suitable subject for public rumination by leading politicians such as Luzhkov and Tuleev. If Zyuganov always insisted that social democracy was a Western import to which Russia was culturally unsuited (ignoring Marxism's intellectual heritage), then as Urban argues, perhaps the demographics, economic dependency, international ties and information technologies that draw Russia Westwards make the Westernisation of the Russian left increasingly likely.[79]

However, even granted that scenario, the centre-left remains divided, strategically, ideologically and socio-culturally: its future depends on felicitous alliances and, given the centre's amorphousness, the emergence of prominent personalities and the support of wavering governors like Tuleev and Khodyrev. Its most prominent party vehicles include elements of *Yabloko* and FAR, Titov, Gorbachev's Social Democratic Party of Russia, and now Seleznev's *Rossiya*. Its ideological spectrum ranges from the radical Marxist Oleg Shein and Boris Kagarlitskii to many moderate pragmatists.[80] The key schism remains the gulf between *nomenklatura* representatives and the grassroots in the absence of the strong middle class, historically the bedrock of moderate leftism. Seleznev's *Rossiya* is indicative: while its leader's name recognition, elite connections and appeal to CPRF defectors are to its benefit, wider appeal might be limited by the bureaucratism and conformism of its founder, as well as the existence of ever stronger competition.[81]

However, the emergence of a democratic but *dirigiste* Russian political culture as envisaged by Urban is problematic. Deeply ingrained traits such as the endemic corruption and bureaucratisation of the state, the gulf between regime and society and post-imperial nostalgia remain fertile ground for extremist reaction. While such trends might sustain the CPRF for a time, the eventual unblocking of a political system where civil and political society remain so poorly integrated in the regime has unpredictable outcomes. There are clear dangers for socio-political stability, since the ghettoisation and radicalisation of the CPRF potentially deprives it of its social pacification and (albeit limited) system-integrative role. Declining turnout and 'against all' voting in several elections certainly indicated continued disillusion with the democratic process.[82]

Against this background the Law on Political Parties, which attempts to stem the symptoms of party weakness (quantity of members and coherence of structures) without addressing its causes (absence of institutionalised link with the executive) appear attempts to 'cartelise' political competition within the political establishment.[83] Such 'cartelisation', alongside the weakening of traditional social ties, has been a notable contributory factor in the success of several radical anti-establishment parties in Europe. It is hardly too fanciful to imagine that heavy-handed efforts to manage the transition of Russia's left might also provoke the long-term reconfiguration of the diminished Russian right from dispossessed protest constituencies in a way reminiscent of the rise of Le Pen, as hasty government initiatives against extremism implicitly recognise.

Conclusion

Whereas Yeltsin had always promised to be the gravedigger of communism, it appeared that it was left to Putin to achieve this task. What then was the future for the CPRF, and what did this reveal about Putinism?

The CPRF's change of fortune under Putin was rapid: from the leading electoral party in December 1999 the CPRF fast lost parliamentary and elite influence, while electoral trends threatened a similar demise. In part this was simply the maturation of embedded crisis tendencies of a party which was firmly entrenched in the pro-Soviet subculture, and whose ideological glue was anti-system opposition to all things Yeltsin. Generational turnover and the decline of revolutionary polarisation were always likely to expose such a party to severe strain.

Putinism quite deliberately exacerbated these strains. If one feature of Yeltsinism was the mobilisation of regime and society around the image of the negative 'other', be it the communists in 1996 or Chechens in 1999, then Putin sought a more positive consolidation of state–society linkages through inclusive 'centrism' and active management of civil society. The cowering of the communists demonstrates the paradoxes of this managed democracy in microcosm. It is a confirmation of Putin's belief that transition has given way to state consolidation on the basis of a managerial and pragmatic modernisation, buttressed by a more intrusive style. This deprived the communists of their remaining ideological vigour, and whole *raison d'etre* as a revolutionary party believing that the post-1991 system was indeed transitional. Yeltsin's ideological anti-communism at least granted the party a semantic niche, whereas Putin's 'politics of normalcy' gives the communists no quarter: no end goal, no fear factor, just results that they are ill equipped to give.

The decline of significant anti-system oppositions is seen as an important stage in democratic consolidation, and clearly was important for Putin symbolically (indicating modernisation), pragmatically (in removing an often obstructive and unco-operative opposition) and strategically (in furthering an inclusive party system). It clears the way for an 'unblocked' political system in which a revived centre-left may emerge from the communists' shadow. Yet the administrative way in which it was attempted was fraught with risks to the very aims that Putin wished to achieve: the sidelining of the communists did not remove those who voted for them, while depriving them of the crucial social consolidation role which their partial pacification in power had enabled. That under Putin the regime depends less on abstract ideological stereotypes is to its credit, but the emphasis on results makes the need to transcend the latent instability of the 'floating political system' ever more urgent.

Notes

1 Putin's state-of-the-nation address to the Russian parliament 18 April 2002.
2 B. Yeltsin, *Midnight Diaries* (London: Weidenfield and Nicolson, 2000), p. 353.
3 See the comments of Baburin, amongst others, *Kommersant* (14 March 2001).
4 J. Blondel, 'Political opposition in the contemporary world', *Government and Opposition*, 32:4 (1997), 463.
5 See N. Yanai, 'Why do political parties survive? An analytical discussion', *Party Politics*, 5:1 (1999), 5–17; and S. Huntington, *The Third Wave: Democratization in the Late Twentieth Century*, (Norman, OK: University of Oklahoma Press, 1991), p. 263.
6 R. Rose and T. F. Mackie, 'Do parties persist or fail? The big trade-off facing organisations', in K. Lawson and P. H. Merkl (eds.), *When Parties Fail: Emerging Alternative Organisations* (Princeton: Princeton University Press, 1988), pp. 533–558. I have dealt with communist crises extensively in L. March, *The Communist Party in Post-Soviet Russia* (Manchester: Manchester University Press, 2002), as well as in 'The pragmatic radicalism of Russia's communists', in J. B. Urban and J. Curry (eds.), *The Left Transformed in Post-Communist Societies: The Case of East-Central Europe, Russia and Ukraine* (Lanham MD: Rowman and Littlefield, 2003).
7 *Sovetskaya Rossiya* (19 December 1991).
8 R. N. Tannahill, *The Communist Parties of Western Europe: A Comparative Study* (Westport, CT: Greenwood Press, 1978), pp. 214–224. See also J. B. Urban, 'The Russian left and the French paradigm', *Demokratizatsiya*, 11:1 (winter 2003).

The Putin paradigm and Russia's communists

9. A. Wilson, 'Reinventing the Ukrainian left: assessing adaptability and change', *Slavonic and East European Review*, 80:1 (2002), 23.
10. E. Martynov, member of Moscow *gorkom* of CPRF, in a letter he alleges the party press would not publish, *Patriot* (24 June 2002).
11. For example, Y. Brudny 'In pursuit of the Russian presidency: why and how Yeltsin won the 1996 presidential election', *Communist and Post-Communist Studies*, 30:3 (1997), 255–75.
12. Richard Sakwa, *Russian Politics and Society* (London: Routledge, 2002), p. 186.
13. One of the most savage and articulate demolitions of Zyuganov's communists is in B. Kagarlitsky, *Russia under Yeltsin and Putin* (London: Pluto Press, 2002).
14. This outstanding mediocrity makes Zyuganov even more of a non-charismatic conflict broker than described in C. K. Ansell and M. Steven Fish, 'The art of being indispensable: noncharismatic personalism in contemporary political parties', *Comparative Political Studies*, 32:3 (1999), 283–312.
15. Hence the communists' increasing reference to the party name as a trusted 'trade-mark'.
16. Urban, 'The Russian left'.
17. Sakwa, *Russian Politics and Society*, p. 195.
18. H. Oversloot and R. Verheul, 'The party of power in Russian politics', *Acta Politica*, 35 (2000), 123–145.
19. One might also add Pavel Borodin, reputedly now a member of the Yakutsk *oblast'* committee of the CPRF (*Nezavisimaya gazeta*, 18 January 2002).
20. For example in Volgograd, communists in the *oblast'* Duma and regional electoral commission stacked electoral conditions in incumbent governor Maksyuta's favour (by removing the requirement of a second round run-off election (which Maksyuta might have lost), and by censuring media opposition to the governor during the election (*Obschaya gazeta*, 21 December 2000).
21. *Raion* means district and *raikom* is the word used for *raion* Communist Party committee.
22. Y. M. Brudny, 'Russian electoral patterns: 1999–2000', in A. Brown (ed.), *Contemporary Russian Politics: A Reader,* (Oxford: Oxford University Press, 2000), p. 170.
23. For example, Kagarlitskii, *Russia under Yeltsin and Putin*, p. 182.
24. Although they focus on those approaching retirement, see D. R. Kiewet and M. Myagkov, 'Are the communists dying out in Russia?', *Communist and Post-Communist studies*, 35 (2002), 39–50 and regional patterns in *Novaya gazeta* (21 January 2002).
25. D. Oreshkin, *Johnson's Russia List*, 6189 (17 April 2002).
26. R. Sakwa, 'The regime system in Russia', *Contemporary Politics*, 3:1 (1997), 8–9; I. Klyamkin and L. Shevtsova, *This Omnipotent and Impotent Government: The Evolution of the Political System in Post-Communist Russia* (Moscow: Carnegie Moscow Center, 1999).
27. E. Huskey, *Presidential Power in Russia* (Armonk and London: M. E. Sharpe, 1999), p. 213.
28. Anatolii Baranov has described the CPRF as the 'joint-stock monopolist for the provision of opposition services to the population', *Novaya gazeta* (3 June 2002).
29. R. Rose. N. Munro and S. White, *The 1999 Duma Vote: A Floating Party System,* (Glasgow: University of Strathclyde, 2000).

30 V. Putin, 'Russia at the turn of the millennium', appendix to V. Putin (with N. Gevorkyan, N. Timakova and A. Kolesnikov), *First Person: An Astonishingly Frank Self-Portrait by Russia's President Vladimir Putin* (London: Hutchison, 2000).

31 L. Byzov, 'Presidentskaya kampaniya-2000 i novyi electoralnyi zapros' in M. McFaul, N. Petrov and A. Ryabov (eds.), *Rossiya v izbiratelnom tsikle 1999–2000 godov* (Moscow: Moscow Carnegie Center, 2000), pp. 484–496. Sheinis' concept of quasi-centre is explored by Richard Sakwa in *Russian Politics and Society*, p. 460. Both concepts stress the centre's combination of statist politics and liberal economics. The concepts are not identical and potentially contradictory: left-patriotic consensus addresses the more Russocentric and left-paternalist slant evident in the electorate; 'quasi-centre' better describes the more Eurocentric and economically liberal elements of Putin's post-9/11 westwards tilt.

32 G. Diligenskii, '*Putin i rossiiskaya demokratiya (razmyshleniya po rezultatam oprosov 2000g.*) from www.fom.ru, 18 January 2001.

33 As Andrei Kolganov argues, 'What can an opposition do if the president himself combines all possible political oppositions within himself?' *Jamestown Foundation Prism*, 7:9 (September 2001).

34 Putin, *First Person*, pp. 180, 212.

35 J. B. Urban, 'Russia's communists after Zyuganov: forward toward Europe or back to the "bright future?"', *The New Leader* (Sept.–Oct. 2000). For a detailed exposition of the party debate see also March, *The Communist Party in Post-Soviet Russia*.

36 *Johnson's Russia List*, 5411 (27 August 2001).

37 William V. Smirnov goes so far as to say elections to the Duma are 'largely worthless' due to its inability to shape policy in 'Democratization in Russia: achievements and problems' in Brown, *Contemporary Russian Politics*, p. 527.

38 T. F. Remington, *The Russian Parliament: Institutional Evolution in a Transitional Regime, 1989–1999* (New Haven: Yale University Press, 2001); P. Chaisty and P. Schleiter, 'Productive but not valued: the Russian State Duma, 1994–2001', *Europe–Asia Studies*, 54:5 (2002), 701–724.

39 J. B. Urban and V. D. Solovei, *Russia's Communists at the Crossroads* (Boulder: Westview, 1997), p. 138. See also *Komsomolskayaa pravda* (26 March 1996).

40 The phrase is from Michael McFaul, 'Explaining party formation and nonformation in Russia: actors, institutions, and chance', *Comparative Political Studies*, 34:10 (2001), 1160.

41 For example, *Izvestiya* (7 February 1996).

42 An interesting account of communist corruption, though mixing allegation with fact, is R. C. Otto, 'Gennadii Zyuganov: the reluctant candidate', *Problems of Post-Communism*, 46: 5 (1999), 37–47.

43 The CPRF undermined the Primakov government by insisting on impeachment of Yeltsin to appease its radical wing – see *Parliamentskaya gazeta* (8 June 2000).

44 S. S. Smith and T. F. Remington, *The Politics of Institutional Choice: The formation of the Russian State Duma*, (Princeton: Princeton University Press, 2001), J. M. Ostrow, 'Procedural breakdown and deadlock in the Russian State Duma: the problems of an unlinked dual-channel institutional design', *Europe–Asia Studies*, 50:5 (1998), 793–816.

45 Ostrow, 'Procedural breakdown and deadlock in the Russian State Duma', 796.

46 E. T. Bacon, 'Is there any opposition in Russia? Analysis of the influences on and prospects for political opposition in Russia', paper presented to CREES Annual Conference, Cumberland Lodge, Windsor, 16–18 June 2000, p. 5.
47 Huskey, *Presidential Power*, p. 172.
48 Such 'psychological pressure' included consistent rumours of Duma dissolution, suggested amendments to electoral law to reduce the role of PR and political parties, the constant suggestion of legal moves against communists on the grounds of 'extremism', and unimplemented inducements such as the promise of round-table talks.
49 For example *Nezavisimaya gazeta* (14 December 2000). The abortive attempt by Unity to call the communists' bluff by demanding a vote of no confidence in February 2001 is another such example (G. Pavlovskii, www.strana.ru, 21 February 2001).
50 The communist and agro-industrial factions supported the government on only 16 per cent and 19 per cent respectively of key votes held between June 2000 and February 2001. The next most anti-government group were the independents, which supported the government on 60 per cent of the key votes at this time. See T. F. Remington, 'Putin and the Duma', *Post-Soviet Affairs*, 17:4 (2001), 285–308.
51 A state subsidy which would have equalled approximately $95,000 in 1999 (plus a private contributions limit of approximately $100) would hardly cover campaign costs, when the CPRF's 1999 campaign fund had stood at $1.2 million. There were also suggestions that the law could reveal CPRF membership to be much lower than claimed.
52 *Kommersant vlast'* (9 April 2002).
53 See comments by T. Remington, in *RFE/RL Russian Political Weekly*, 2:11 (9 April 2002).
54 For example, Gleb Pavlovskii in *Nezavisimaya gazeta* (26 June 2002).
55 Zhirinovskii put the question on the agenda after AIG leader Nikolai Kharitonov had blurted it out. Troshkin was a protégé of Seleznev and Zyuganov, who had on occasion been accused (especially by *Edinstvo*) of diverting Duma resources (allegedly some $65 million per annum, plus property and communication allocation) to the CPRF.
56 P. Rutland, 'Putin's path to power', *Post-Soviet Affairs*, 16:4 (2000), 313–354.
57 There were rumours of a written Kremlin blueprint for the creation of a social democratic party on the basis of the CPRF, *Izvestiya* (16 May 2002). Deputy head of the presidential administration Vladislav Surkov was rumoured to have insisted on strict limits to the extent of the attack on the CPRF, *Moskovkie novosti*, 18 (2002).
58 E. Martynov, *Patriot* (24 June 2002).
59 Goryacheva had built up close links with Seleznev as vice-chair in the previous Duma, while both Seleznev and Gorbenko had served in the moderate patriotic Spiritual Heritage movement. For Goryacheva's drift towards social democracy, see Urban, 'Russia's communists after Zyuganov'.
60 *Nezavisimaya gazeta* (25 June 2002).
61 At the central committee plenum of 25 May 2002, approximately 25 per cent voted not to exclude Seleznev versus almost 40 per cent for Gorbenko and Goryacheva. Key leaders expressing extreme dissatisfaction with the leadership

Political parties and democratisation

included Starodubtsev of Tula, Mashkovtsev of Kamchatka, Mikhailov of Kursk and Viktor Ilyukhin, while Gennadii Khodyrev of Nizhnii Novgorod ostentatiously resigned.

62 CPRF-backed gubernatorial candidates in Smolensk and Penza failed to win in May 2002, in part because of serious competition on the left, while late 2001 and early 2002 saw poor CPRF performances in Tula, Novosibirsk Krasnoyarsk, Sverdlovsk, Belgorod, Omsk and Orel legislative elections.

63 This was prompted by CPRF support for an alternative leader for the Federation of Independent Trade Unions of Russia, and disagreements over the new labour code.

64 SPS member Aleksei Kara-Murza has talked of the regime's ability to 'come to old women, give them firewood and take their votes', gazeta.ru (25 July 2002).

65 Sadchikov, A., *Izvestiya* (16 May 2002, Kagarlitskii, B., *Novaya gazeta* (3 June 2002).

66 Seventy-three per cent of party members supported Seleznev's expulsion according to a poll by the CPRF-allied Centre for Researching Russian Political Culture, *Massovye nastroeniya* 2:9 (2002).

67 As Regina Smyth asserts, 'Putin's support is conditioned on not inflicting economic, social and military hardship on the beleaguered Russian population'. See R. Smyth, 'Putin's tightrope: maintaining support in the face of domestic and international policy demands', *PONARS Policy Memo*, 242 (2002).

68 Fifty-three per cent of Zyuganov's supporters (approximately 11 million people or 15 per cent of the popular vote) still claimed to be 'communist' in 2000 (*New Russia Barometer*, 11, 14–18 April 2000 from www.russiavotes.org).

69 On one hand the party lost its most important chairs, who have a propaganda, gatekeeper and patronage role, directing working groups and consultants to work on legislation and control the committee budgets. Yurii Maslyukov, in particular, was one of the Duma's most successful lobbyists. On the other, Gennadii Semigin, apparently close to Putin, remained in position, while the party had already lost the most prestigious committees (security and legislative) in January 2000.

70 Most opinion polls in the wake of the April events show a decline in support for the CPRF and Zyuganov personally.

71 Urban, 'The Russian left'.

72 See 'Ocherednye zadachi KPRF' in *Sovetskaya Rossiya* (7 December 2000) for the party's current ideological preferences.

73 Those vying for influence within the party include the radical head of the Moscow *gorkom* Aleksandr Kuvaev, and supporters of the ascetic, isolationist and authoritarian Russophilism of writers like Sergei Kara-Murza and Andrei Parshev, for whom see A Makarkin, 'Kompartiya i novaya oppozitsiya', accessed from www.politcom.ru (2 February 2002).

74 Yet, although Seleznev had refused to give up his party membership and had retained a seat on the CPRF's presidium, he claimed rarely to have used his Duma council votes, while his Duma voting record reveals many moments where he either did not vote or deviated from the party position. Indeed, many in the CPRF hierarchy saw his speakership as insufficiently responsive to party aims, while even non-communists such as Boris Nemtsov rejected his dismissal.

75 As FAR fraction leader Vyacheslav Volodin remarked regarding Seleznev: 'the interests of the state must be higher than those of the party', *Vremya novostei* (5 May 2002).
76 *Vremya MN* (28 June 2002).
77 Kagarlitsky, *Russia under Yeltsin and Putin*, pp. 159–187; Urban, 'The Russian left'.
78 Fedor Gavrilov in Sakwa, *Russian Politics and Society*, p. 197.
79 For Zyuganov's unambiguous refutation of social democracy see *Pravda Rossii*, 20–26 (February 2002).
80 Oleg Shein is an anti-communist trade unionist Duma deputy (RR), who heads the nascent Workers' party. Among the most loyalist groups is the Socialist United Party of Ivan Rybkin, Yurii Petrov and Aleksei Podberezkin.
81 Seleznev claimed that some 26 CPRF regional organisations did not support his expulsion, and some (such as the Tyumen *obkom*) soon joined *Rossiya*. It could also claim the support of left-wing groupuscules such as the Ural-based *Mir, Trud, Mai*, and the Party of Worker's Self-Management, regional Agrarian Party organisations, and claimed (without proof) organisations in 88 regions and 600,000 members, *Obshchaya gazeta* (18 January 2001), *Nezavisimaya gazeta* (11 January 2001). A potential rival/ally of *Rossiya* that has already invited Seleznev to join it, is Gennadii Raikov's 'People's Party', created on the basis of the ND state Duma faction and given state backing as another 'spoiler' for the CPRF.
82 This trend was evident in several regional elections in Sverdlovsk, Pskov and Krasnoyarsk in the winter of 2001–2, as well as in the Nizhnii Novgorod gubernatorial elections of August 2001. See *Novaya gazeta* (13 May 2002).
83 Against this, electoral law 67-F3 of 12 June 2002, which stipulates that half of the deputies of regional legislative assemblies must be elected according to party lists may go some way towards addressing the lack of incentives for party formation in Russia.

5

Russia's disempowered electorate

Stephen White

Formally, Russia's post-communist institutions provide every opportunity for its citizens to choose the government they want and to influence its actions. There are secret and competitive elections, held at regular intervals. The new constitution, adopted by referendum in 1993, prescribes the absence of any official ideology, political diversity, and multiparty politics. There is a separation of powers, and an independent judiciary. The classic liberal freedoms are all secured: freedom of speech, movement and assembly, freedom of conscience, and equality before the law. In the event of any disagreement, international norms take precedence over the laws of the state itself. There are freedoms that go beyond the practice of many liberal democracies, including the requirement that official bodies make available any information they hold on private individuals unless national security considerations are involved. And there are freedoms that have a particular resonance in post-communist conditions: freedom of entrepreneurship, and the right of private as well as other forms of ownership. The new constitution even begins, in words that are hardly accidental, 'We the multinational people . . .'

Russians themselves have taken a less positive view. Asked to consider the changes that have taken place since 1991, a large proportion of ordinary Russians think it has become much easier to speak their mind, to join any organisation they wish, and to choose whether or not they will take part in political life. But (as we shall see), the same people, compared with the late Soviet period, think they are no less likely to be arrested improperly. And remarkably, more think it is less easy than it was in the late Soviet period for ordinary people to influence the government that rules in their name, and less likely that government will treat them fairly and equally. Communist rule, it emerges, was 'close to the people', 'legal', even 'honest and open'. Post-communist rule, by contrast, is most closely associated with criminality and corruption, but also with being remote and irresolute, and hardly less bureaucratic than the communist system it has replaced. Meanwhile the

USSR, as a concept, remains as popular as it was in the spring of 1991 when it secured the support of more than three-quarters of the Soviet electorate.

This chapter examines these contrasting judgements. In particular, it explores the paradox by which ordinary Russians have acquired all the mechanisms that in other countries are thought to give ordinary citizens an effective means of holding their government to account – independent courts, a free press, political parties and competitive elections – but believe themselves they have less influence than in the years before *perestroika*, when the political system began to undergo a limited democratisation. The discussion is largely based on a representative national survey that was fielded in the spring of 2001 (fuller details are provided in Appendix 5.1); comparisons are drawn between these results and those that emerged from a similar survey by the present author and associates in 1993, and between the results that emerge from Russian surveys and those conducted in Ukraine, Belarus and the European Union member states.[1] We consider, first of all, some of the major findings relating to Russia itself; we look, secondly, at comparisons across time, and then at comparisons across space. A fuller study, obviously, would range more widely, including some of the social correlates of the attitudinal distributions with which we are primarily concerned.

Russians and their political system

Among the most fundamental attributes of a pluralist political order is trust in civic institutions, and indeed in other citizens. In one of the most influential of scholarly writings on regime and society, Almond and Verba in the early 1960s pointed to the close association between the establishment and consolidation of liberal democracy, and popular attitudes that were supportive of a political system of this kind.[2] There has been little consensus, over the intervening years, about causality: did the attitudes account for the institutions, or were they shaped by them? But either way, it was clear that pluralist politics were stronger where popular attitudes were supportive, and that supportive attitudes helped to sustain a corresponding set of political institutions. Within this complex of attitudes, trust was one of the most important: trust, for instance, can 'indicate the extent of diffuse political support', and a high level of trust in some institutions can 'compensate for low or declining confidence in others, or cushion and blunt the effect of their temporarily deficient credibility'.[3]

One of the clearest conclusions of survey research in post-communist Russia is that ordinary citizens have low levels of trust in their civic institutions, and particularly in their political institutions. This is not an exclusively Russian phenomenon (even scepticism, as Rose and Mishler have pointed out, 'is in short supply' across the post-communist nations[4]); nor was it unknown during the years of Soviet rule. It is, however, one of the

Political parties and democratisation

Table 5.1 *Trust in institutions, 2001 (%)*

	Full confidence	Some confidence	Not much confidence	No confidence
The churches	19	28	26	16
Armed forces	14	36	29	13
State television	13	44	31	8
Radio	12	41	26	7
The press	7	40	34	8
Independent television	7	31	28	12
Government	7	24	46	19
Parliament	2	14	47	28
Political parties	2	9	42	37

Source: Author's survey (see Appendix 5.1).
Note: Don't knows and non-responses were included but are not shown here.

defining features of the contemporary Russian system. Russians, according to the survey evidence, are actually quite ready to trust their fellow citizens – it was through social networks of this kind that they survived the communist period, and through such networks that they continue to make good the shortcomings of the consumer market.[5] But there are much lower levels of trust in civic institutions of all kinds: from the churches to organs of government, including structures such as trade unions and political parties that nominally represent the interests of newly enfranchised citizens. Indeed, there is less trust in the new and independent trade unions than in their Soviet-period equivalents.[6] Levels of trust, moreover, have generally been declining, even for the churches and armed forces, which had traditionally enjoyed the greatest public confidence.[7]

Russians took broadly the same view in our own survey, which was fielded in the spring of 2001. As before, there was most confidence in the church and the armed forces (see Table 5.1), which have articulated the interests of the whole nation for hundreds of years. There were comparable levels of confidence in the mass media, particularly state television and radio (which is also, overwhelmingly, a state service). Independent television enjoyed less support, but its reach does not extend to the entire country and more than a fifth of our respondents felt unable to offer any opinion about the extent to which it could be trusted. The press had a slightly higher rating, especially at intermediate levels of confidence. The institutions of government themselves, however, enjoyed little support, with low levels of confidence and particularly high levels of mistrust. Just 16 per cent had some confidence in their elected parliament, and only 11 per cent expressed some confidence in political parties, with 79 per cent taking the opposite view (the only institutions that have been found to enjoy less support than political parties were the investment funds set up after privatisation, many of which defrauded citizens of their vouchers).[8] It was notable, moreover, that even institutions with relatively high levels of support inspired far from unqualified confidence: the churches, in particular, were distrusted almost as much as they were trusted.

Russians have not been reluctant to use many of the rights with which they have been formally entrusted. For a start, they have been willing to vote: 61.8 per cent took part in the Duma election of December 1999 and 68.7 per cent in the presidential election of March 2000, both well in line with levels of turnout in the Western democracies. But earlier studies had already suggested that Russians set little store by the electoral mechanism as a means of influencing the government that rules in their name. Russians, for instance, were much less likely than their British or even Ukrainian counterparts to believe that elections played a part in 'holding governments accountable for their past actions'. Russians were also less likely to think that elections allowed people to 'choose among particular policies' and to 'comment on the state of the country'. About a third of Russians, in fact, thought that elections 'deceived the people', evidence that beliefs about elections as a mechanism of accountability and policy formation had 'not replaced the basic cynicism displayed by many people toward electoral manipulation'.[9]

Competitive elections, ten years after the end of communist rule, were certainly welcome in principle. More than a third of our respondents 'entirely approved' of them and another quarter did so to some extent, although a substantial minority (21 per cent) took a different view. When elections took place, a clear majority of our respondents (66 per cent) thought they should definitely take part, and another 14 per cent were inclined to do so provided it did not involve undue inconvenience. Was voting, however, likely to make any difference to public policy? And was it of particular significance within the repertoire of political action that was available to ordinary citizens? Opinion was in fact quite evenly divided on the extent to which elections could 'change the future course of events' (42 per cent agreed, 49 per cent disagreed). And there was considerable scepticism about the extent to which elections offered ordinary people an opportunity to influence the way in which the country was governed. Only 5 per cent agreed strongly that they offered an opportunity of this kind and another 24 per cent agreed to some extent, but 62 per cent took the opposite view.

Elections, moreover, counted for relatively little among the mechanisms that were available to ordinary people to influence national decisions on matters they thought important. About a third (32 per cent) thought voting in local and national elections was the most effective way in which they could seek to exercise political influence; a few mentioned demonstrations (7 per cent), or letters to government bodies or the newspapers (2 per cent

Table 5.2 *Measures of political efficacy, 2001 (%)*

	Entirely agree	Partly agree	Partly disagree	Entirely disagree
'It is difficult for ordinary people to secure their legal rights'	60	28	6	3
'Politicians don't care what ordinary people think'	60	26	8	2
'Duma deputies soon lose contact with their electors'	63	25	6	1

Source: Author's survey (see Appendix 5.1).

each). The largest proportion of all, however (43 per cent), thought there was simply no effective way in which they could seek to influence decisions on matters of national policy. Similarly, there was substantial support for the proposition that a 'strong, powerful leader [could] achieve more than any laws': fully 60 per cent agreed in varying degrees, compared with 19 per cent who took the opposite view.

We asked several other questions that related to political efficacy, or the extent to which ordinary citizens believe they can exercise real influence over the process of government (see Table 5.2). What opportunity, for instance, did ordinary Russians have to make use of the rights with which they had nominally been endowed under the post-communist constitution? The overwhelming majority (88 per cent) agreed largely or entirely that it was difficult for them to do so. At least in part, this was because politicians had little interest in the views of the citizens they represented: politicians '[didn't] care what ordinary people think', and Duma deputies in particular 'soon [lost] contact with their electors'. We asked a more general question – familiar in crossnational investigations – about the extent to which 'people like you can have a direct influence on the actions of central government'. Overwhelmingly, our respondents took the view that ordinary people could have 'not the slightest' influence upon such actions (60 per cent), or very little (another 24 per cent); only 12 per cent took a more positive view.

Classically, citizens have organised to express their preferences through political parties. But parties, as we have seen, enjoy particularly low levels of public confidence – and lower levels in Russia than in the other post-communist countries.[10] In part, this appeared to be attributable to the long monopoly of the Communist Party of the Soviet Union, which had discredited the very concept of 'party'. Membership levels, certainly, were very low. In our survey, just 0.9 per cent of adults were members (or considered themselves to be members) of a political party, compared with 1.4 per cent who took part in neighbourhood associations, 1.9 per cent who took part in a cultural association of some kind, and 7.6 per cent who took part in the work of a sports or health society. Levels of party membership are much lower in all the post-communist countries than in the liberal democracies; but among the post-communist countries, numbers are particularly low in Russia.[11]

Russians, of course, could relate to parties in other ways. One of the oldest traditions in voting studies focuses on party identification – whether individuals identify with a party in a manner that can help to sustain a consistent electoral preference. We asked, accordingly, if there was a political party that was 'closer to you than others in its policies'. For nearly three-quarters, there was no such party. We found, similarly, that a large majority agreed that 'None of the political parties reflects the interests of people like me' (65 per cent shared this view, and just 23 per cent disagreed). Questions about previous voting choice of a kind that identify patterns of electoral support are difficult to conduct so long as Russia has a 'floating party system', with parties that have so far shown little ability to sustain a presence from election to election.[12] We asked, accordingly, not only about choices in the parliamentary and presidential elections, but also about a broader form of orientation, towards a 'party family' – communist, socialist, pro-market, nationalist, national minority or environmental. The largest proportion favoured a communist party, and substantial numbers a pro-market party (see Table 5.3). But still larger proportions were not prepared to commit themselves to any of the party families, or found it difficult to say.

We also asked a larger question about the role of political parties in contemporary Russian society. Two of our options reflected a broadly 'positive' view of political parties. Did they, for instance, represent the views of ordinary people? And did they influence the formation of national policy?

Table 5.3 *Party family preferences, 2001 (%)*

None	25
Hard to say	21
A communist party	19
A pro-market economy party	17
A socialist party	6
A Green party	5
A nationalist party	2
A national minorities party	1

Source: Author's survey (see Appendix 5.1).
Note: Three per cent opted for a different party than those proposed, and 2 per cent offered no reply.

Two other options were broadly 'negative'. Were parties, for instance, simply a vehicle for satisfying the material interests of their leaders? Or did they pander to the vanity and personal ambitions of their leaders? Broadly, a quarter agreed with the two positive assessments, but twice as many supported the two negative judgements. This, moreover, was the balance of opinion in every section of the society, although there was some tendency for younger respondents to take an even more negative view than other respondents, while older respondents – to whom competitive politics were much more of a novelty – were less likely to offer an opinion of any kind.

Looking back

Russians have shown little inclination to return to the Soviet system when they have been given the electoral opportunity to do so. But this is not to say that they reject all aspects of their communist past. In earlier research, the present author and associates found that 'job security' was the most widely valued feature of Soviet rule (29 per cent); but there was also praise for the way in which 'peace between nationalities' (24 per cent) and 'economic stability' (22 per cent) had been maintained. Very few (just 7 per cent) thought the communist system had no positive features of any kind. What, on the other hand, were the worst features of communist rule? Clearly, there was 'too much bureaucracy' (32 per cent). In addition, 17 per cent thought communist rule had 'oppressed human rights', and 15 per cent that there had been too much corruption; another 13 per cent, however, thought it had no negative features at all. There was less concern about human rights in Russia than in Ukraine, or – still more so – the countries of East Central Europe; the main shortcoming of the old system, for ordinary Russians, was that it had been 'tediously inefficient rather than monstrously oppressive'. And fewer had felt personally oppressed in Russia (11 per cent) than in East Central Europe (23 per cent).[13]

Ten years on, was there a similar distribution of opinion about the communist past? And were there respects in which attitudes had become more or less favourable? The evidence is set out in Table 5.4, comparing the responses we obtained in 2001 with those that were given in 1993. As we can see, the pattern of responses reflects the same priorities. Once again, job security was seen as the main positive feature of communist rule, followed by peace between the various nationalities and economic stability. Slightly more, in 2001, drew attention to the equality that at least nominally characterised the communist period, and slightly fewer thought it had no positive features. On the negative side, bureaucracy was once again the main perceived shortcoming of communist rule, but its human rights record was less important, in 2001, than the economic stagnation that had become increasingly apparent during the late Brezhnev period. Strikingly, the formal

Table 5.4 *'Best' and 'worst' features of communist rule, 1993 and 2001 (%)*

Best features	1993	2001	Worst features	1993	2001
Job security	29	28	Too much bureaucracy	32	31
Interethnic peace	24	25	Oppressed human rights	17	11
Economic stability	22	21	Corruption	15	14
Law and order	12	11	None	13	14
More equality	7	12	Pollution	12	9
None	7	2	Economic stagnation	11	21

Source: Author's survey (see Appendix 5.1); and a national representative survey conducted by ROMIR in December 1993–January 1994 (n = 2141) reported more fully in William L. Miller, Stephen White and P. Heywood, *Values and Political Change in Postcommunist Europe* (London: Macmillan and New York: St Martin's, 1998).
Note: Don't knows and similar responses are excluded in both cases.

attributes of democracy played a rather minor part in both positive and negative assessments: it was social and economic achievements that accounted for most of the favourable judgements, and social and economic shortcomings that – at least by 2001 – accounted for most of the criticisms.

As well as their assessments of the present and the previous system, Russians have been asked for their view of the 'reforms that were begun in April 1985'. For more than half (55 per cent), the main consequence of the Gorbachev reforms was their loss of certainty in the future. Similar proportions identified 'chaos and disorganisation in government' and a 'crisis of interethnic relations' (both 45 per cent). Further substantial proportions pointed to the 'deepening of the economic crisis' (39 per cent) and a 'weakening of the country's defensive capacity' (37 per cent); others, but much smaller numbers, spoke of an 'increase in political and economic activism' (19 per cent) or a 'broadening of political rights and freedoms' (17 per cent). Judgements about those who had initiated the reforms were equally uncompromising. For the largest proportion (48 per cent), the Gorbachev leadership had 'begun to reform the country without thinking of the consequences'; for 40 per cent, they had 'taken no account of what ordinary people needed'; and for 37 per cent, they had 'acted only in their own interests'. Older respondents were particularly likely to complain about the economy and defence, younger respondents to note some positive changes in the political sphere; but the broad structure of responses was similar across the age-groups, the genders and the occupations.[14]

Russians have also been asked to suggest the characteristics that they associate with their current regime, and with the Soviet system of the 1970s and 1980s (see Table 5.5). Communist rule, in spite of its lack of fully or

Table 5.5 *The 'most characteristic' features of communist and post-communist rule (%)*

Soviet rule, 1970s–1980s		Post-communist rule, 1990s	
Close to the people	36	Criminal, corrupt	63
Legal	32	Remote, alien	41
'Our own', familiar	32	Irresolute	32
Bureaucratic	30	Weak, powerless	30
Strong, firm	27	Short-sighted	28
Short-sighted	23	Bureaucratic	22
Authoritative, respected	21	Parasitic	18
Secretive, closed	17	Illegal	12
Just	16	Unprofessional	12
Honest, open	14	Incompetent	11

Source: Adapted from *Ekonomicheskie i sotsial'nye peremeny*, 3 (1998), 57 (national representative survey, February–March 1998, n = 1500).

– until its final years – even partly competitive elections, had many shortcomings: it was bureaucratic, short-sighted and secretive. But its virtues were more apparent. It was 'close to the people', 'legal', and 'our own' – in other words, accessible, indigenous, and (for ordinary Russians) legitimate. Post-communist rule, by contrast, was most closely associated with criminality and corruption; but it was also remote, irresolute, weak, short-sighted, and hardly less bureaucratic than the communist system it had replaced. Indeed, the post-communist system had no positive features at all, in this inquiry; it was also parasitic, illegal (in spite of its independent courts and competitive elections), and incompetent.

In our 2001 survey we asked a series of more specific questions about particular freedoms (see Table 5.6). Questions of this kind have regularly been asked in other Western inquiries; they have consistently found that ordinary Russians think their individual liberties have improved markedly since the communist period, but that there has been no comparable improvement in the extent to which they think they can influence government, or expect fair treatment (in some respects, in the view of ordinary citizens, there has been a move in the opposite direction).[15] Our own results bear out these earlier findings. There is no doubt, for ordinary Russians, that they have more opportunity to practise a religion than in the communist period, or to express their opinions. Similarly, they think it is easier to choose whether to join an organisation, and to decide whether or not to take part in politics (in the communist period, some had suggested, everything that was not banned had been compulsory). But they think there is less opportunity for ordinary Russians to travel or live wherever they wish, and they think

Table 5.6 *Freedoms under communist and post-communist rule (%)*

	Much better	Somewhat better	Stayed the same	A bit worse	Much worse
Religious life	56	29	13	1	1
Join any organisation	51	35	11	2	1
Take part in politics	49	28	19	2	2
Freedom of speech	47	34	13	3	3
Travel and residence	30	24	12	9	25
Freedom from illegal arrest	14	17	44	11	13
Influence public policy	5	12	53	11	20

Source: Author's survey (see Appendix 5.1).
Note: Don't knows and non-responses have been excluded.

there has been little improvement in the protection of citizens from the threat of illegal arrest. Most strikingly of all, ordinary people have (in their own view) much less influence over the making of public policy than in the communist period, although the largest proportion of all think there has simply been no change.

A comparative perspective

Russians may be distrustful, distanced from their politicians and sceptical about the extent to which the end of communist rule has represented a 'transition to democracy'. But Russians are not unique in their scepticism: Western societies have also experienced a form of 'civic disengagement', with falling turnouts, a withdrawal from party politics and declining levels of civic activism.[16] Are Russians, at least, distinctive in their orientations to the political process? Are they not simply disenchanted and disempowered, but more so than in other post-communist countries, or in the liberal democracies?

Russians, in fact, are often very similar in their responses to their counterparts in Ukraine and Belarus. They are somewhat more likely to think of themselves as a supporter of a political party (27 per cent, compared with 21 per cent in Ukraine and just 10 per cent in Belarus); they are much more typical in other respects, including their feelings of disengagement and powerlessness. Was it 'hard for ordinary people in our country to secure their legal rights', for instance? Overwhelmingly, they agreed (88 per cent); but so did Ukrainians (with an identical score), and Belarusians (77 per cent). Did state officials 'treat everyone equally and fairly'? Overwhelmingly, Russians thought they did not (85 per cent); but similar proportions took the same

Political parties and democratisation

Table 5.7 *Membership of civic associations, 2000 (%)*

	Russia	Ukraine	Belarus
Political party	1	1	2
Charitable association	1	3	3
Housing association	2	2	3
Musical society	2	3	4
Sports society	8	6	10
Trade union	19	24	38

Source: Author's survey (see Appendix 5.1).

view in Ukraine (93 per cent) and in Belarus (82 per cent). To what extent were 'human rights observed?' Hardly at all (9 per cent) in Russia or Ukraine, although they were thought to be more widely respected (28 per cent) in Belarus.

Levels of membership of civic associations reflect these sceptical responses (Table 5.7). Russians, in most cases, have the lowest levels of all; but it is much clearer that membership of secondary associations throughout the region is at a low level, with membership of political parties at the lowest point of all. Only trade union membership has held up reasonably well from the all but universal levels of the communist period; and most of all in Belarus, where traditional Soviet workplace practices have survived to the greatest extent. In other respects Russia emerges reasonably clearly as a 'nation of non-joiners', with very few mechanisms that can still connect ordinary people with the society in which they live and not simply with its political system. These, moreover, are levels of membership that are low in comparative, as well as absolute terms. Russia, in fact, has one of the lowest levels of organisational membership among the postcommunist countries, which in turn have levels below those of postauthoritarian countries as well as those of the older democracies.[17]

In other respects, Russians were even more disenchanted than their counterparts in Ukraine and Belarus – let alone the liberal democracies. They were the most likely to believe they had no real influence on the conduct of national affairs, which is a classic measure of political efficacy: no more than 12 per cent thought they had some influence of this kind, compared with 16 per cent in Ukraine and 23 per cent in Belarus. Russians were as likely as their counterparts elsewhere to believe in the principle of competitive elections, but they were less likely to believe their own elections could actually make a difference: 42 per cent thought they could make at least a minor difference to the 'course of events in our country', substantially fewer than the 53 per cent in Ukraine and 65 per cent in Belarus who took the same view.

Russians were also less likely than their counterparts in the other Slavic countries to believe that voting gave them an opportunity to 'influence the management of the country': just 29 per cent agreed, compared with 40 per cent in Ukraine and 51 per cent in Belarus (these Belarusian responses, it should be noted, are very much at odds with conventional assessments of the nature of its political system). Russians, compared with the Slavic colleagues, were also more likely to believe that a 'strong, powerful leader [could] do more for our country than any laws': 60 per cent agreed with this view, compared with just 32 per cent in Ukraine and 39 per cent in Belarus.

One reason for the greater pessimism of ordinary Russians about their ability to influence the political process was the extent to which they believed that process had become corrupt and criminalised. There was understandable concern in other European Union countries about the extent to which parliamentary parties, legislation and parliamentary seats were being bought and sold across the post-communist countries that were negotiating for membership. Corruption was endemic, according to independent analysts, in government, public administration, the judiciary, media and business.[18] The same conclusion emerged from the annual surveys of Transparency International, which bases itself on the personal experience of foreign businessmen. The 2002 survey put Russia in 77th place among the 102 nations that were included, beside India and Zimbabwe, with just 2.7 points out of 10. Russia was also one of the top countries in the Bribe Payers Index, which measures the propensity of companies from the top exporting countries to pay bribes in emerging markets.[19]

Russians themselves had few illusions. No more than a small minority thought their country was close to the idea of a 'law-governed state' that had originally been proclaimed by Mikhail Gorbachev (Table 5.8). A very large majority thought bribery and corruption were widespread, and an overwhelming majority thought the problem was worse than it had been in Soviet times. Not surprisingly, it was a view that had direct implications for their assessment of the responsiveness of government. For instance, of those who thought corruption was widespread, 11 per cent thought they

Table 5.8 *Corruption and government, 2000*

	Russia	Belarus	Ukraine
We live in a law-governed state	30	46	36
Bribery and corruption are widespread	77	57	77
These problems are worse than in Soviet times	89	59	78

Source: Author's survey (see Appendix 5.1).
Note: Figures show % agreement.

Political parties and democratisation

Table 5.9 *Political system preferences, 2000*

	Russia	Ukraine	Belarus
Better to restore the communist system	40	30	26
Army rule	11	7	8
Get rid of elections and have dictatorship	29	8	22
Monarchy	10	8	11

Source: Author's survey (see Appendix 5.1).
Note: Figures show % agreement.

could exercise some influence on the process of government but 63 per cent thought they could have no influence of this kind. But among those who did not think corruption was widespread, 29 per cent thought they could exercise some influence on government and only 43 per cent thought they could exercise no influence of this kind. The higher the level of perceived corruption, the lower the level of perceived influence on the political process.

Russians, for these and other reasons, were more disposed than their counterparts in Ukraine and Belarus to favour an authoritarian regime rather than the one they actually had (Table 5.9). There was little support, anywhere in the region, for the restoration of a monarchy, or for a military dictatorship. But there was substantial support, in Belarus and even more in Russia, for a dictatorship of a different kind. And there was still more support – most of all in Russia – for the restoration of communist rule. Support has typically been high for other nondemocratic options in other recent investigations. For instance, more Russians agreed that an 'authoritarian government can be preferable to a democratic government' than believed democracy was 'preferable to any other form of government' (still larger numbers were indifferent), and more than half (51 per cent) would approve to some degree if the Russian parliament was suspended.[20]

Many of these dimensions can be considered in a still broader perspective, comparing responses in Russia, Ukraine and Belarus with those in the member countries of the European Union. The evidence leaves little doubt that Russians are more distrustful of their civic institutions than ordinary citizens in Ukraine and Belarus, and much more distrustful than their counterparts in other European countries (Table 5.10). Certainly, there are some universals. Russians, for instance, are reasonably typical in their attitudes to organised religion, with high levels of distrust as well as confidence. But with very few exceptions, Russians have less confidence in their civic institutions than their counterparts in the other Slavic republics, and far less confidence than citizens in the EU member states: by a substantial margin in the case of business and the institutions of government, and by a spectacular margin in the case of law enforcement. Political parties are, everywhere, the

Russia's disempowered electorate

Table 5.10 Trust in civic institutions: Russia in comparative perspective

	Russia	Ukraine	Belarus	EU15
Army	49	49	50	70
Church	48	35	56	44
President	22	30	41	48
Trade unions	21	19	25	39
Courts	18	20	28	51
Police	18	16	20	67
Private enterprises	16	20	27	33
Parliament	12	10	23	51
Political parties	9	7	12	18

Source: Author's survey (see Appendix 5.1).
Note: Figures show % who chose 5, 6 or 7 on a 7-point scale. Data for the EU15 are derived from Eurobarometer 56, fieldwork November 2001, accessed at http://europa.eu.int/comm/public_opinion/archives/eb/eb56/eb56_en.htm. The figure for 'president' relates to 'national government' and for 'private enterprises' to 'big companies'.

least trusted of all civic institutions; but here again, Russians are much less supportive than their counterparts in the European Union.

• The evidence is equally that ordinary Russians are particularly likely to be dissatisfied with the state of human rights in their own country, and with the state of their 'democracy'. Across the European Union as a whole, more were satisfied than dissatisfied with the situation in their own country in these respects. Candidate countries, by contrast, were more likely to be dissatisfied than satisfied. But *every one* of the CIS member countries included in the Eurobarometer was more dissatisfied than *every one* of the EU members or candidates; and among the CIS countries themselves, Russia was the most dissatisfied of all (see Figure 5.1). The same was true when the questions related to the state of individual human rights. And Russians, according to the same evidence, were becoming increasingly dissatisfied. In 1991, 15 per cent had been satisfied with the 'development of democracy' in their country, and 67 per cent were dissatisfied; by 1997, when the last of these surveys was conducted, satisfaction was down to 8 per cent and dissatisfaction had reached 82 per cent.

Conclusion

According to an older body of theory, authoritarian political systems would gradually disappear as the forces of modernisation advanced across their societies – communist or noncommunist. On this basis, more developed parts of the post-communist universe would be the first to democratise, but

Figure 5.1 *Satisfaction with democracy (%)*

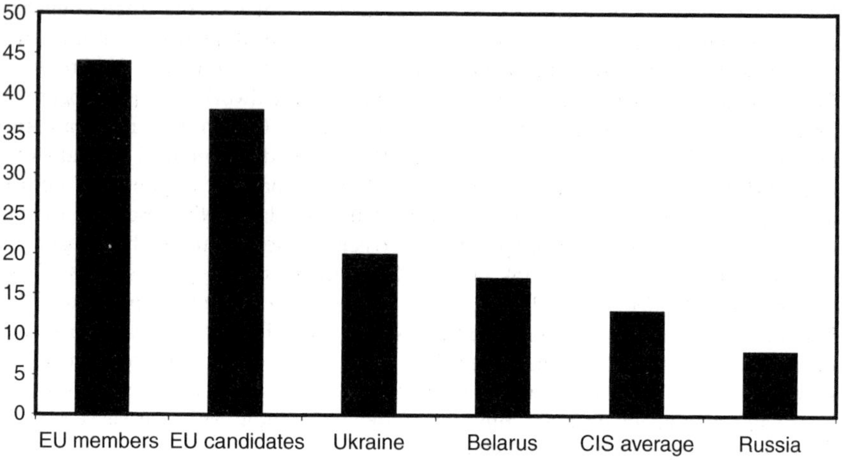

Source: Derived from the *Central and Eastern Eurobarometer* (Brussels: European Commission, 1997), Annex Figure 4; the figure for the fifteen EU member states is taken from *Eurobarometer 56* (see Table 5.10).

they would be followed in due course by their less developed neighbours. An optimistic school of thought held similarly that as communist forms of rule were succeeded by the institutions of liberal democracy, parties and social movements would emerge (or re-emerge) and a form of pluralist politics would develop (the 'transition to democracy') and then establish itself ('consolidation'). All that remained was local variation, or 'path dependency', but even that would be obliterated in due course by larger processes of globalisation and, indeed, formal political union.

Russia's post-communist experience cautions against some of these early, mechanistic approaches. Authoritarian forms of politics did not automatically give way to pluralism, and new constitutions did not automatically mean new politics. Indeed, there was no single process, as the very different destinies of the fifteen former Soviet republics made clear, but a variety of trajectories reflecting a wide range of factors and circumstances – culture, location and level of development as well as institutional choice and elite behaviour. In these circumstances, attitudes and institutions could become mutually reinforcing: a cynical electorate mirrored in a corrupt and largely self-recruiting elite, which itself repelled the investment that might otherwise have brought about development. Russia was too large to be restructured by international finance, and (with Ukraine, Belarus and Moldova) it was likely to be denied membership of the European Union, which was a major agency of change in the other post-communist countries. In these circumstances, its electorate was likely to remain disempowered for a considerable time to come.

Appendix 5.1

Nationally representative surveys were conducted in each of the three countries using a common questionnaire and a well-established local agency. In Russia our surveys were conducted respectively by the All-Russian Centre for the Study of Public Opinion (VTsIOM) and by Russian Research. Fieldwork took place between 19 and 29 January 2000 and between 17 June and 3 July 2001. In the former case, the universe was the resident population of the Russian Federation aged 16 and over, and 2003 interviews were conducted on a face-to-face basis in respondents' homes (our results are based on the 1940 interviews that took place with those aged 18 and over). A four-stage stratified sample was constructed in accordance with the agency's normal practices. Interviews took place in 107 primary sampling units in 38 of the 89 subjects of the Federation; 193 interviewers were employed, and 16 per cent of the interviews themselves were monitored by agency supervisors. In the latter case the universe consisted of Russian Federation residents aged 18 and over, excluding soldiers, convicts and those of no fixed address. Interviews took place in 195 primary sampling units in 42 different subjects of the Federation; 197 interviewers were employed, yielding a total N of 2000.

Our survey in Belarus was conducted by Novak under the direction of Andrei Vardomatsky. Fieldwork took place between 13 and 27 April 2000. There were 62 sampling points, and 90 interviewers conducted face-to-face interviews in respondents' homes. The total number of interviews was 1090, using the agency's normal three-stage stratified sampling model to secure representation of the resident population aged 18 and over. All seven of the country's regions were included. In Ukraine our survey was conducted by the Kyiv International Institute of Sociology under the direction of Vladimir Paniotto and Valeriya Karuk. The questionnaire was piloted between 28 and 31 January and fieldwork took place between 18 February and 3 March 2000. A four-stage stratified sample was constructed, and 110 primary sampling units were employed. A total of 125 interviewers took part, who conducted 1600 interviews on a face-to-face basis in respondents' homes of which 10 per cent were subject to a check by supervisors, yielding a valid total of 1590.

Notes

1 The research reported in this chapter was funded by the UK Economic and Social Research Council under grants L213252007 to Stephen White, Margot Light and John Löwenhardt, and R223133 to Sarah Oates, Stephen White and John Dunn.
2 See G. A. Almond and S. Verba, *The Civic Culture: Political Attitudes and Democracy in Five Nations* (Princeton, NJ: Princeton University Press, 1963).
3 F. Plasser, P. A. Ulram and H. Waldrauch, *Democratic Consolidation in East-Central Europe* (London: Macmillan and New York: St Martin's Press, 1998), p. 111.
4 W. Mishler and R. Rose, 'What are the origins of political trust?', *Comparative Political Studies*, 34:1 (February 2001), 41.
5 W. L. Miller, S. White and P. M. Heywood, *Values and Political Change in Postcommunist Europe* (London: Macmillan and New York: St Martin's Press, 1998), p. 100.

6 *Ibid.*, p. 102, and (for trade unions) R. Rose and C. Haerpfer, *New Russia Barometer III: The Results* (Glasgow: Centre for the Study of Public Policy, 1994), p. 32.
7 For VTsIOM time-series data see S. White, *Russia's New Politics* (Cambridge: Cambridge University Press, 2000), p. 270.
8 Cited in *ibid.*
9 J. H. Pammett, 'Elections and democracy in Russia', *Communist and Post-Communist Studies*, 32:1 (March 1999), 45–60 (53, 55).
10 R. Rose, *Russians under Putin: New Russia Barometer 10* (Glasgow: Centre for the Study of Public Policy, 2001), p. 34 (indicating 7 per cent support in Russia), compared with R. Rose and C. Haerpfer, *New Democracies Barometer IV: A 10-Nation Survey* (Glasgow: Centre for the Study of Public Policy, University of Strathclyde, 1996), p. 79 (trust in parties averaged 14 per cent across Central and Eastern Europe).
11 M. Wyman, S. White, B. Miller and P. Heywood, 'The place of "party" in post-communist Europe', *Party Politics*, 1:4 (October 1995), 535–548 (538–539).
12 See R. Rose, N. Munro and S. White, 'Voting in a floating party system', *Europe-Asia Studies*, 53:3 (May 2001), 419–443.
13 Miller, White and Heywood, *Values and Political Change*, pp. 86–88.
14 *Monitoring Obshchestvennogo Mneniya*, 2 (2001), 85.
15 For data, see the New Russia Barometer and the New Democracies Barometer, both maintained by the Centre for the Study of Public Policy at the University of Strathclyde (www.cspp.strath.ac.uk).
16 The most influential single statement within a burgeoning literature is R. D. Putnam, *Bowling Alone: The Collapse and Revival of American Community* (New York and London: Simon and Schuster, 2000).
17 M. M. Howard, 'The weaknesses of postcommunist civil society', *Journal of Democracy*, 13:1 (January 2002), 159.
18 *Guardian* (9 November 2002), p. 16. A more comprehensive study is available in W. L. Miller, A. B. Grodeland and T. Y. Koshechkina, *A Culture of Corruption? Coping with Government in Post-Communist Europe* (Budapest: Central European University Press, 2001).
19 See *Transparency International Corruption Perception Index 2002*, accessed at www.transparency.org, November 2002.
20 Rose, *Russians under Putin*, pp. 23, 25.

III
Economy and society

6

The economic legacy: what Putin had to deal with and the way forward

David Lane

With the advent of President Putin, the reconstruction of the former state socialist societies under post-communist governments has proceeded for over ten years and the period of transition has turned to one of consolidation. During this period, the command economy has been destroyed and in its place a market mechanism has been installed, prices of commodities and labour are determined by the market, the currency is negotiable on world markets enabling the economy to become a constituent part of the global economy, privatisation of previous state assets has led to over 60 per cent of property being privatised. The economy is set in a mould of capitalism, the president, however, has to construct policies to make capitalism work. The argument of this chapter is that the economic formation inherited by Putin has been shaped by the legacy of communism and the peculiar form that the privatisation of assets has taken. Policy, it is contended, should move towards a more explicit form of organised market state capitalism.

The most general definition of modern capitalism has been given by Max Weber. For him, modern bourgeois capitalism is 'identical with the pursuit of profit and forever renewed profit, by means of continuous, rational, capitalistic enterprise'.[1] There are of course, other types of capitalism – for Marxists, monopoly and finance capitalism and imperialism. The major distinction for Weber was between 'political capitalism' and modern capitalism. In the former, opportunities for profit are derived from 'the exploitation of warfare, conquest and the prerogative of political administration'[2] – profits are made from various forms of political domination. Modern bourgeois capitalism is based on the private ownership of the means of production and the continuous *accumulation* of capital derived from profits received through the market. For both Weber and Marx, capitalism was a function of class interests derived from ownership which had developed over centuries, culminating for Marx in the class conflict which brought in bourgeois society. Since the time of Weber and Marx, moreover, different structural types of capitalism have been defined, the three major types being: competitive market-led capitalism (Anglo-American), nationally co-ordinated negotiated social-democratic economies (Denmark, Sweden), and negotiated corporatist market economies (German–Japanese). These will be discussed in more detail below.

In the case of the post-communist countries, capitalism had to be introduced from above. The revolutions which had brought the new elites to power were essentially 'rejective revolutions'[3] which had 'rejected communism and Soviet power' but were not predicated on class or social forces with a vision of an alternative social system. The early political leadership of the post-communist states had no idea of the type of political and economic system which should be constructed on the 'ashes of communism'.

In the early years of transformation in Russia, radical reformers like Chubais and Yavlinski wanted to reconstruct the economy on the model of the USA. They turned therefore to the West and asked for policy advice on how to construct a capitalist economy and democratic type of society. The most favoured model was what has become known as the 'Washington consensus'.[4] Advisors from the West advocated a transition to an Anglo-American type of capitalism. This involved the introduction of markets for commodities, assets and labour, a low level of government intervention in the economy, exposure to foreign competition, monetary stability and a free exchange rate. Privatisation of economic assets was to be introduced to create a self-motivated business class. The stock exchange would become a crucial institution channelling investment to companies to meet consumer market demand. These policies would preclude the reproduction of the Communist administrative class which, it was claimed, would replicate the institutional features of state socialism.

The adoption of Anglo-American neo-liberalism was a rational strategy for the new radical reform leadership: it legitimated destroying the political and economic base of the old ruling classes as well as the formation of competing units on the domestic market; global competition would promote economic efficiency and industrial restructuring on the basis of comparative advantage.

State activity was to be minimal, its role was to set the rules in which neo-liberalism was to operate. This particularly meant divesting state ownership and a lack of intervention in the market with respect to the protection of national economic interests. The ruble had to be negotiable on world currency markets, and tariffs had to be minimal to allow foreign competition. Such an 'institutional design', moreover, ruled out other forms of capitalism such as that which had developed in Germany, Korea, Japan and Scandinavia.

There were three major policy objectives:
1 To put in place irreversible changes. Any hardships would have to be introduced at the beginning when support for change was greatest. The changes would be such that, if disillusion with reform set in, the costs of

moving back to the old system would greatly outweigh any possible short-term improvements.
2 To open windows of opportunity. These would give rise to role-models, and expectations of what capitalist and democratic society would bring. This is particularly where open economic markets to the West came in.
3 Reform policies should be put into effect quickly and simultaneously. The most favoured policy was for a Big Bang. The idea being that it would be better to have all the negative effects of change occur at one time when support for reform was greatest.

Essentially, privatisation of assets, the opening up of the economy to foreign competition (thereby enriching consumer society), the creation of competitive political parties and civil society would make the political ballast in support of the new system. If you could create economic prosperity in terms of a market society, then stability, prosperity and political democracy would follow. The intended model is summarised below.

The intention: competitive market-led capitalism

Key components

- *Driving forces*: internal political elites, foreign advisers and institutions (IMF), (intended) competitive market-led forces.
- *Institutions*: initially state committees, (intended) private business, stock exchange.
- *Ideology*: consumerism (lacking).
- *Basis of solidarity*: new civil society (lacking).
- *Culture*: new competitive electoral process, new supportive capitalist culture (business class, consumer society).

In the period 1990 to 1993, in all the post-communist countries' significant reforms took place along these lines. The major elements of neo-liberal policy have been adopted: free exchange rates, relatively low tariffs, price liberalisation, opening up of internal markets, privatisation of assets, an emphasis on monetary regulation and a considerable weakening of the state's economic activity.

The outcomes

How successful have the former communist countries of Eastern Europe and the USSR been in creating modern capitalism? What were the outcomes of these policies? Let me briefly consider the economic outcomes in the former communist countries of Eastern Europe and the USSR.

The first five years of transition (1989–95) were characterised in all the post-communist countries by severe transformation recession.[5] Only Poland, which had declined to 80 per cent of its 1989 figure in 1991, had recovered to nearly 100 per cent by 1995. Hungary came next, with a maximum decline to 80 per cent of the 1989 level and by 1995 had recovered to 82 per cent. Severe depressions had occurred in Russia: GDP declined to 58 per cent of its 1989 level by 1995 and Ukraine had fallen to 40 per cent. By way of comparison, the decline of GDP in the Great Depression in the USA in 1933 (1929 = 100) was only to 70 per cent and in the Second World War GDP declined in the USSR to 75 per cent (1942 compared to 1940).[6]

Even ten years of transition had not significantly improved the situation for most of the post-communist countries. By 1998 only Poland and Slovenia had surpassed the 1989 levels and not by much – only 18 per cent higher in Poland. They were followed by three other countries which had recovery rates of over 90 per cent (of the 1989 level): Slovakia, Hungary and the Czech Republic. Much less successful are the countries of the former USSR – nearly all having GDPs of less than 60 per cent of the 1989 level and Russia and the Ukraine with massive falls to 55 per cent and 38 per cent.[7]

Not only has gross domestic product declined, but also the inequality of income distribution has increased markedly and there has been a significant rise in levels of poverty. The gini coefficient is a measure of income inequality, the higher the coefficient, the greater the inequality; a coefficient of 0 would show a completely equal distribution of income. Before transformation, income inequality was fairly modest and relatively constant between all the countries. After the collapse of state socialism, however, inequality became more regressive in all countries (except Slovakia) and the differential between countries increased significantly.

For Russia, in 1987–88 the index was 22 whereas in 1993–95, it had grown to 48. Similarly in Ukraine, the growth was from 21 to 47; at the other end of the scale more modest rises were experienced by Hungary – from 21 to 24 and Czech Republic from 19 to 28.[8] In all the unequal societies, real income decreased, between the two time periods, by between a third and a half, and inequality rose: in Russia the top quintile increased its share of income from 19.45 per cent in 1988 to 39.52 per cent in 1993.[9]

There has been a steep increase in poverty (see Table 6.1). According to data collected by Milanovic, in eighteen Central and East European countries, before the transition, there were 14 million people in poverty (4 per cent of the population), this figure rose to 168 million or 45 per cent of the population in 1993–95.[10]

Map 6.1 shows those countries combining high inequality and high levels of poverty on the one hand and those with low levels of both on the other. These countries are also the ones which had relatively unsuccessful levels of recovery and are also characterised by higher levels of unemployment and crime.

The economic legacy

Map 6.1 *Inequality and poverty*

Economy and society

Table 6.1 *Levels of poverty (18 Central and East European countries)*

	Before 1987–88	After 1993–95
Less than $120 per month	14 million people	168 million people
% of population	4	45

Source: Branco Milanovic, *Income, Inequality and Poverty during Transition from Planned to Market Economy* (World Bank: Washington, DC, 1998), p. 45.

Structural changes in polity and economy

How then are these outcomes related to the move to capitalism and to democracy or polyarchy? Transformation was to herald a shift in organising principles: politically, from hegemonic party control to political pluralism and polyarchy and economically, from central planning and state owned assets to the economic market and private property. In scope, this was a revolutionary transformation.

To measure the success of building capitalism in terms of the movement to a market and to a pluralist or polyarchic type political system, I have utilised data from two sources which claim to monitor economic and political developments. These are biased towards the values of Anglo-American societies. While they might be criticised as a measurement of 'real democracy' they are good enough for our purposes. They tell us how far neo-liberal ideals have been reached.

The Fraser Institute's *Economic Freedom of the World 2000 Index*[11] ranks countries on a 10-point scale (0 the least free, 10 the most free).[12] This index is quite sensitive to different elements in the development of market capitalism.[13] It measures the magnitude of price controls, exchange rate controls and the size of the private sector. The extent of private sector share of GDP is regularly monitored by the EBRD.[14] On the development of political pluralism, the Freedom House Index has devised two measures of 'freedom' in terms of levels of political rights and civil liberties. Political rights include the prerogative of adults to vote and compete for public office and for 'elected representatives to have a decisive vote on public policies'. Civil liberties include the rights to 'develop views, institutions and personal autonomy' independently of the state.[15] The results are shown in Table 6.2 which combines countries by extent of political transformation and economic transformation.

To facilitate discussion, I distinguish three different sets of countries. First, the top right-hand corner: Poland, Hungary, Czech Republic, Slovenia, Lithuania, Latvia and Estonia which have relatively successfully extricated themselves from state socialism. These countries have founded pluralistic political regimes, have restructured their economies in the direction of private

The economic legacy

Table 6.2 *Political and economic transformation*

Extent of political transformation	Extent of economic transformation			
	No data	*Little*	*Partial*	*Great*
Great			Romania	Hungary Czech Republic Estonia Latvia Lithuania Slovenia Poland Slovakia
Partial	Mongolia Macedon		Bulgaria Ukraine Georgia Russia Croatia Armenia Moldavia	
Little	Bosnia Yugoslavia Cuba Vietnam	North Korea Turkmen Belarus	Tadjikistan Kyrgyz Uzbekistan Kazakhstan Azerbaijan	China

ownership and marketisation and, in doing so, have achieved modest though positive rates of growth. Second, is a group of countries which have extricated themselves from state socialism but only share some, but not all, of the features of Western-type societies. They have been relatively unsuccessful in achieving a transition to capitalism. They have encountered severe economic and social deterioration. These include the countries of the former USSR which have experienced high levels of poverty, excessive income differentials and low levels of per capita income. Russia is typical of this group. They also have weak pluralistic political structures. We may also note that some have managed partial and great economic transformation (e.g. China) with very little political transformation.

Map 6.2 shows a distinctive geographical pattern to these changes. The more successful countries all border on the NATO and European states of West Europe.

Economy and society

Map 6.2 *Successful transition to economic growth and polyarchic polity*

How then can we explain these differences? Why have some countries done relatively well and others disastrously badly? And finally, what policy could be adopted to improve the conditions in the transition failures, particularly Russia?

There are three major explanations of these differences:
1 faulty implementation of system change;
2 initial conditions and political geography;
3 failure of system transfer.

Faulty implementation of system change

The first argument is put by those who supported the neo-liberal policy in the first place. Their argument is that the policy was basically correct but that the implementation of system change was faulty. Consider Russia as an example of transition failure. The main arguments here are those put forward by Anders Aslund (a former economic advisor) and Joseph Stiglitz (formerly chief economist at the World Bank).

Aslund's argument is that in the transition failures, such as Russia and Ukraine, liberalisation was only partial. In the successful Eastern European countries, 'The credo of radical reformers appears empirically robust'.[16] Aslund argues that price decontrol was only partial and allowed managers to extract rents from the difference between controlled internal and free export prices. Economic policy then promoted rent seeking. Enterprise managers in the Soviet system were able to secure privilege for themselves and, following 'elite enrichment from the Soviet collapse, made it extremely difficult to impose a radical market reform.'[17] 'Corruption or state failure, as opposed to market failure, appears to be the fundamental problem of the transition countries.'[18] Rent seeking then dominated the transition period in these transition failures, and rent seeking institutions were able to buy politicians. 'Crony networks' between business and the state prevented the development of a proper market system.

Stiglitz's position is that the form and extent of privatisation were premature. His prognoses was that the method of privatisation of property was a major cause of transition failure in Russia. Stiglitz's argument is that 'if privatisation is conducted in ways that are widely regarded as illegitimate and in an environment which lacks the necessary institutional infrastructure, the longer-run prospects of a market economy may actually be undermined. Worse still, the private property interests that are created contribute to the weakening of the state and the undermining of the social order, through corruption and regulatory capture'.[19] As there were no legitimate sources of private wealth to accomplish privatisation, the government allowed private entrepreneurs to create banks which then lent private parties money with which to buy enterprises. 'Robber baron' privatisation consequently took place.

The allocation of property did not lead to the development of a capital market which in turn did not allow allocation of assets to proceed in an efficient manner. Managers remained in control and impeded capital-market regulation and competition. The new controllers rationally stripped assets of companies rather than 'redeploying assets in a way that would provide the foundations of wealth creation'.[20]

Enlarging on Stiglitz's approach, the ownership share of financial companies in Russian industry in 1999 amounted to only 10.4 per cent.[21] Non-financial companies owned the assets of commercial banks, rather than the other way around. An implication here is that non-financial companies, with a stake in or owning a bank ('pocket' banks), could transfer profits abroad leading to significant national capital loss. While the banks provided money changing facilities, they did not create deposits for the accumulation of capital in Russia. On the contrary, they facilitated capital flight. Official estimates of capital exports (for 1998) are 3,999 million dollars inward investment, compared to 15,194 million dollars outward payments.[22] Western estimates confidently claim that foreign capital outflows are much larger than those declared: Fitch IBCA in 1999 estimated that 136 billion dollars of capital was exported from Russia between 1993 and 1998.[23] Another (conservative) estimate by the Central Bank of Russia is that capital flight came to 14.1 billion dollars per annum during 1994 to 1998.[24]

While the reasons for transition failure differ, the conclusions are similar: mistaken and badly managed policies led to rent seeking. A kind of 'political capitalism' suggested by Weber occurred precluding continual investment and accumulation, thus a successful transition to modern capitalism has not occurred.

My own view is that this explanation is too narrow. The reform leaders in Russia attempted to carry out the neo-liberal policy and did so as far as was possible under the circumstances. The measures of reform were successful in some respects: they secured a high level of irreversibility. The planning mechanism, the dominant communist party, and the ideology of statism have all been destroyed. The costs of going back will outweigh any short-term benefits. Russia cannot move out of the constraints of the international capitalist system. The problems of transition were well known: it is not surprising that price reform and privatisation failed and led to political opposition. A successful economic policy cannot be constructed independently of the political and economic interests in a country.

Consider the effects of the introduction of Aslund's hard budget constraints (bankruptcies) to create efficiency. Loss-making factories and organisations (excluding small businesses) came to 41.6 per cent of the total number of factories in 2000.[25] They made a loss of 131,336 million rubles.[26] Over 50 per cent of coal and agricultural enterprises, and 64 per cent of personal services enterprises made losses.[27] Bankruptcy, the neo-liberal

The economic legacy

option, on the scale involved in Russia is not a political option. It would create social instability which in turn would undermine the regime.

Initial conditions and political geography

The second explanation considers individual acts of policy to be inadequate, and asks how policy-makers took these decisions in the first place. They see policy as the result of different constellations of factors in different countries. This argument emphasises the initial conditions and political geography to explain the phenomena. Those Central European countries which are adjacent to the West and are small – Hungary, Slovenia, the Czech Republic – have all done relatively well.

First, geographical proximity to the West enabled institutional diffusion to spread more rapidly to the Central and Eastern European countries. They are able to readjust their economies to a capitalist market and consequently they received the highest shares of Western direct investment which, in turn, compensates for the decline of their own economic base. Geography is an important explanatory factor. They have also been drawn to NATO and European Union membership. There is a greater reciprocity of interests between them and the West. The conditionality requirements necessary to join these political and military blocs acted as incentives to change and to accept a more stringent neo-liberal economic policy.

Second, there is the affinity between their previous history and political culture. These East European countries were previously more bourgeois and anti-communist – the communists had a much smaller social base before Sovietisation. They had a self-defined history of being part of the West. The value systems were more conducive to the implant of capitalism and liberal democracy. Hungary and Poland had a tradition and political culture opposed to communism and Russian hegemony. Surveys show that support for state involvement in the control of economic institutions was much less than in Russia and Ukraine. With far greater support for the transition than in Russia and Ukraine – communist parties (or their surrogates) in Hungary and Poland did much worse in the first elections after the collapse than in the other countries. Third, economically, state socialism was unsuccessful in Hungary in the period immediately prior to reform and support for communism was weak: in both Hungary and Poland there had been significant political demonstrations against the Communist governments.[28] Hungary and Poland had both begun economic reform well before the collapse of communism. In Hungary, from 1968, the New Economic Mechanism increased the autonomy of enterprises and, as early as 1974, legislation allowed joint ventures to be established. The Law on Enterprise Councils of 1984 decentralised the public sector and delegated property rights to the enterprise level.[29] By 1987, 35.8 per cent of Hungary's exports (value terms) were with developed capitalist countries – the highest of any of the state socialist societies, and the same was true of imports of which 41 per cent originated from developed capitalist countries.[30] An economic reform had already preceded a political reform. Poland also had developed trading and commerce with the West as far back as the Kania regime. Poland also had never collectivised agriculture and this left in place a larger number of people with an entrepreneurial outlook. The population was therefore more prone to accept radical changes.

In the successful countries, the initial conditions then were more conducive to a move to capitalism whatever paradigm of change was adopted. They also had the incentive to join NATO and the EU – which the heartland states of the former Soviet Union had not. It is not obviously the case that the Washington Consensus would have worked any better than any other paradigm. The conditions however in these countries were better adapted to this policy. It may be that success was despite, rather than because of, the neo-liberal model which was adopted.

The transition failures had many institutional features which impeded a swift, successful transition to capitalism. First, communism was more strongly embedded in the Slavic republics of the former USSR. They had had their own indigenous socialist revolutions and had experienced over eighty years of state planning and party control. In Eastern Europe, traditionally the communist parties were weak and the communist system arose out of the conditions following the military presence of the USSR after the Second World War.

Second, Russia and Ukraine are very large countries – Russia is still the largest country by area in the world, and under state socialism had an integrated and comprehensive economy. It is much more difficult to adjust and integrate their moribund economies into the world order on conditions defined by the world market without significant dislocations. The new capitalist institutional structures, such as the legal system and the stock exchange, were not in place and could not have been adequately formed in such a short period. During the early period of radical reform, the role of the state was severely weakened as a consequence of policy to promote individualistic capitalism. It is true that China has adapted, but China has kept in place important elements of the socialist command economy as well as the dominant ideology and hegemonic party.

Third, transformation created a vicious circle. The expected window of opportunity did not open. Transformation has turned out for the worst, therefore people do not see a positive capitalist alternative. They too are excluded from NATO and had no chance of joining the European Union. Hence the stimulation effect does not apply. Social factors differed greatly compared to the Eastern European countries. There had been no bourgeoisie within living memory and one had to be formed from heterogeneous social groups. Public distrust of this alien class was exacerbated by the form of privatisation. The new bourgeoisie was not widely viewed as legitimate (Stiglitz's point). Consequently, prior to the collapse of communism, elites exhibited great internal conflict. There was much disagreement about the values and institutions of the communist system.

These differences became manifest when transition failed. Lack of economic growth, decline in welfare, large scale unemployment have led to disenchantment of a large proportion of population. Consequently, capitalism lacks social support among important segments of the population. The legacy of state socialism is an important variable. Where it had been more successful (or seemed retrospectively to have been more successful), it had greater support which continued into the transition period, especially when transition failed.

A failure of system transfer

The policy failed because it did not take account of major political, economic and social conditions in the countries of the former USSR. The third explanation is one of general policy failure rather than ineffective implementation. It is here that the initial conditions come into play. The institutional structure of capitalism – the banking system, financial institutions, legal framework could not be built at the breakneck speed which was attempted. The readjustment to the world economy led to grave internal dislocations.

Policy informed by the Washington consensus was far too narrow and ethnocentric a policy. In adopting a neo-liberal market system it has exacerbated the tendency of competitive capitalism to disorganisation. The economic effects of neo-liberalism have been quite catastrophic in terms of wealth creation. These cannot be explained merely in terms of wrong-footed processes of privatisation and insufficient marketisation. Neither can the excuse of inadequate institutions and political opposition be accepted. The difficulties of instituting privatisation and a securities market were well known before transformation and should have been taken into account in policy. Policy was at fault.[31] Privatisation, it is contended, was largely politically and ideologically motivated – to put in place a capitalist class and to make going back to a statist system impossible.

Anders Aslund's recommendation for greater marketisation and greater exposure to world market pressures would lead to a further decline of Russian industrial production. International competition is good for strong economies, but not for weak ones. The history of all developing countries, including the present developed ones, shows that without considerable state support and encouragement they will not grow. This applied particularly to the leading exponents of neo-liberalism, the USA and UK, the early economic histories of which both included an active tariff system against superior outsiders, the theft of patents and invention and the instigation of unequal treaties against third parties to support their own industries.[32]

The neo-liberal model ignored the legacy of Russian state enterprises. Enterprises are embedded in the former system of welfare. They provide unwaged employment due to political and economic constraints. They are also a source of welfare support, the loss of which would have serious social and political repercussions. The policy of a minimalist state has led to the incapacity of the federal government to collect taxes and enforce laws in the republics and regions of the country.

The upshot of this policy is that a system which systematically and continuously promotes the accumulation of capital has not been established. Indeed, export of capital has characterised the economy. It is a form of political capitalism, rather than a modern wealth-creating one.

The future capitalism in Russia: a state-led scenario

In seeking greater stability for the future, the footprint of state socialism may 'fit' into a pattern of co-operative state-led capitalism. In the discussion of transformation to capitalism in the post-communist countries, it is surprising that so little mention has been made of non Anglo-American forms of capitalism. The major contenders are the systems characterising Germany, Japan, and the Scandinavian countries. It is to the formation of capitalism in these countries that I think President Putin must look for solutions to Russia's problems.

Consider the peculiarities of evolving capitalism in Russia. First is the role of financial institutions and the interlocking ownership of holding and subsidiary companies. Interlocking companies rather than individualistic shareholdings are dominant economic (and political) forces. Second is the power of management in the control of companies. Management not only owns considerable assets but is strategically positioned in companies to provide leadership. The management interest, inherited from the state socialist system, is far more confident in pursuing a hegemonic role. This is the major political interest in Aslund's account, but is conceived of negatively. Third, one must consider the political and ideological factor – the orientation inherited from state socialism is a corporate one. The state is assumed to have a legitimate role in promoting employment and comprehensive welfare. The legacy of communist public provision is an important factor giving rise to expectations of state provision of welfare and employment. The attempt to graft the economic processes of neo-liberalism onto these structural legacies of communism has led to economic failure.

There are great similarities here with aspects of the corporatist systems of capitalism in Germany and the social democratic ones in Scandinavia. Under Swedish–Danish capitalism there is strong cohesion between state,

The economic legacy

company and society. Companies have a clear 'obligation' to stakeholders – to existing shareholders, to management, employees, and the state is a major partner. There is a weaker dominant class consciousness; trade unions have greater salience in the society. The state has a paternalist role and comprehensive welfare state services are provided, many directly by public services. Employment is high and inclusive with the state having an active role in job creation[33] and achieving a high proportion of women in the labour force. Politically there is little political contestation and the highly de-ideologised social democratic party is hegemonic. Equality is a strong value and economic freedom is severely constrained.

Key components of social-democratic capitalism

- *Driving forces*: state/trade union led.
- *Institutions*: social-democratic parties.
- *Culture*: equalitarian welfare-state, full-employment society.
- *Solidarity*: social compact between stake-holders.

Under German–Japanese capitalism, there is firm cohesion between company and society. There is high interdependence between owners, state, management and employees. Labour has rights and short term dismissal is unlikely. Business is competitive, though there are strong employers associations and interlinked company ownership particularly by banks. Class consciousness among the dominant class is strong. The state is an important provider of welfare. Politically, in Germany, there is contestation between social democratic and Christian democratic parties but they are de-ideologised and accept the parameters of competitive capitalism. Economic freedom is mediated by wider welfare concerns.

Key components of 'co-operative' capitalism

- *Driving forces*: bank/business led.
- *Institutions*: state/business labour consensus.
- *Culture*: national stake-holders.
- *Solidarity*: stake-holder society, welfare provision.

In the conditions of post-communist societies, these are not templates which can be automatically transferred. However, they are building bricks from the old regime and do suggest alternative and more appropriate forms of capitalist organisation. Rather than building anew on the ashes of the old regime, I contend that one has to build anew utilising as best one can assets of the old regime. These countries point to a model of 'co-operative' capitalism, with financial institutions and other companies having considerable stakes in the holding companies, and management having power over strategic decisions. The state, moreover, has *potentially* a greater role in co-ordination. President Putin's policy, as discussed in other chapters in this book, is moving very much in this direction. To overcome the tendency towards rent-taking and to increase levels of accumulation, the state has to take a greater role in the direction of corporate investment and the economic risks involved.

Co-ordination in all modern economies is based on a combination of market, state, competitive and co-operative economic institutions. A possible scenario for the stability of Russia is an economy with a limited market economy, a regulative state and co-operative economic institutions in which management has an important place and in which ownership is in the hands of interconnected state and private businesses and financial institutions. This kind of state-led capitalism might ensure accumulation. Not only will the state directly channel economic rents earned from export-oriented industries such as armaments, precious metals and energy, but also private and semi-private companies will indirectly be financed through state institutions and banks. A state-led development policy would involve support for space and nuclear industries, computer software, arms production, aircraft. The state could also support low labour cost industries such as textiles, which would supply the home market.

Key components of [proposed] corporatist Russia

- *Driving forces*: state.
- *Institutions*: stake-holders: industrial management, leading capitalists, political elites, workers' collective.
- *Culture*: nationalist.
- *Solidarity*: social compact, welfare state.

Such a policy is not without critics. Internally, a free market ideology and policy is advocated by the Ministry of Finance, the Ministry of Economy, the Ministry for the Management of State Property and is supported by the IMF and other leading Western governments, particularly the USA. Also successful companies in export industries, such as oil, are associated with radical market reformers in the government. Their interest lies with a global economy, foreign markets and external capital investment. In this context, outside political actors become a major determinant of the direction of economic change.[34] The 'conditionality' of support by international agencies such as the IMF and the European Union is usually in terms of a neo-liberal form of economy.

At a more theoretical and general level, major criticisms of this approach come from those who hold that a one-way convergence is taking place between the different types of capitalism considered. The direction of convergence is towards the competitive Anglo-American system. The globalisation of capitalism is inimical to a state-led negotiated form of capitalism. It is claimed that co-operative-type economies of the German model do not lead to innovation. The growth of countries such as Germany and

Japan declined in the 1980s and 1990s and at the beginning of the twenty-first century they are restructuring in the direction of competitive capitalism. Moreover, co-operative capitalism, it is contended, is a sure way to promote economic decline. The Thatcher reforms have not only been copied on a transcontinental scale, but have been continued by the Blairite Labour government in the UK.[35] Global convergence to a market-led capitalism, it is argued, is now under way and cannot be stopped without substantial costs to domestic economies. The political and economic space for state-led as well as 'co-operative' systems is limited. The international financial organisations and international political gatekeepers, such as the International Monetary Fund (IMF), Organisation for Economic Co-operation and Development (OECD), World Bank and European Union, are able to impose their conditions on emerging countries. The argument here is that state-led corporatism is not efficient and is severely constrained by the forces of globalisation.

These arguments, I believe, are 'overdetermined'. While there certainly are trends towards convergence, there are also divergences.[36] Production in an economy as large as Russia is local in character and regional companies and political actors have considerable scope for action independently of the global economy. With the exception of the extractive industries, the globalisation of finance has had little effect on Russian. Governments may oppose free trade if it is not in their economic interests and maintain tariffs in support of home industries. As Joseph Stiglitz has pointed out, the developed countries demand trade liberalisation and the elimination of subsidies while maintaining trade barriers and subsidies for their own products.[37]

The main advantages for adopting a model of organised market capitalism in Russia is that it may be able better to cope with competition on a world scale. Greater regulation (such as in the recent history of France) may lead to more effectively organised restructuring. A positive legacy of communism is high investment in human capital which is a considerable asset in transformation. The recent history of existing welfare states, such as Sweden and Denmark, is mixed with regard to development and competition. It certainly is not a foregone conclusion that their days are numbered.

My own conclusion is that a state-led corporatist economy is by no means perfect but is the best system for Russia. As Winston Churchill put it about democracy: It is 'the worst form of government, except for all those other forms that have been tried'. Similarly, state-led corporatism in Russia is the worst form of economy, except for all those that have been tried.

Notes

1 M. Weber, *The Protestant Ethic and the Spirit of Capitalism* (London: Unwin Books, 1970), p. 17.

Economy and society

2   H. H. Gerth and C. W. Mills, *From Max Weber* (London: Routledge, 1949), p. 66.
3   This phrase has been popularised by Leslie Holmes, *Post-Communism: An Introduction* (Cambridge: Polity Press, 1997), pp. 13–14.
4   J. Williamson, 'What Washington means by policy reform', in J. Williamson (ed.), *Latin American Adjustment. How Much has Happened?* (Washington, DC: Institute for International Economics, 1990).
5   Source: World Bank, *World Bank World Development Report* (Oxford: Oxford University Press, 1996), p. 26.
6   *Ibid.*
7   *Transition Report 1999* (London: EBRD, 1999), p. 23.
8   B. Milanovic, *Income, Inequality and Poverty during the Transition from Planned to Market Economy* (Washington, DC: World Bank, 1998), p. 41.
9   *Ibid.*, p. 160.
10 *Ibid.*, p. 67.
11 www.fraserinstitute.ca. Another index, using a five-point scale is that of the Heritage Foundation: see G. P. O'Driscoll, Jr., K. R. Holmes and M. Kirkpatrick, *2000 Index of Economic Freedom* (Wall St Journal, Heritage Foundation, 2000).
12 This index considers government consumption as a proportion of total consumption, the ratio of transfers and subsidies to GDP, the number, composition and share of output by state-operated enterprises, government investment as a share of total investment, the use of price controls, the rates of top marginal tax thresholds, duration and use of military conscription, growth rate of money supply, level of inflation, access to foreign currency bank accounts, exchange rate controls, risk of property confiscation, risk of government cancelling contracts, revenue derived from taxes on international trade, variation on tariff rates, share of trade sector covered by non-tariff restrictions, size of the trade sector, percentage of bank deposits held in privately owned banks, share of total domestic credit allocated to the private sector, determination of interest rates by market forces, access to country's capital markets by foreign capital. Summarised from Appendix 2, Explanatory Notes and Data Sources.
13 P. G. Roeder has also constructed an index of national, democratic and capitalist transformations, 1999 see, P. G. Roeder, 'The revolution of 1989: postcommunism and the social sciences', *Slavic Review*, 58:4 (1999), 743–755. His economic data are derived from The Heritage foundation and Wall Street Journal index, Bryan T. Johnson, Kim R. Holmes and M. Kirkpatrick, *The 1999 Index of Economic Freedom* (Washington, D.C.: Wall St Journal, Heritage Foundation, 1999).
14 EBRD, *Transition Report 1999* (London: EBRD, 1999), p. 24. In interpreting these data, one should note that in some countries, privately owned companies may still have considerable state ownership, especially in large-scale industry.
15 Freedom House, *Freedom in the World 1998/99*, www.freedomhouse.org. I have reversed the rankings given by Freedom House to make symmetric with the economic ratings: hence the higher the rank the higher the level of freedom.
16 A. Aslund, *Building Capitalism: The Transformation of the Former Soviet Bloc* (Cambridge: Cambridge University Press, 2002), p. 4.
17 *Ibid.*, p. 69.
18 *Ibid.*, p. 443.

19 J. Stiglitz, 'Whither reform? – ten years of the transition', reprinted in Ha-Joon Chang, *The Rebel Within* (London: Anthem Press, 2001), p. 132.
20 *Ibid.*, p. 134.
21 See D. Lane, 'The evolution of post-communist banking', in D. Lane (ed.), *Russian Banking: Evolution, Problems, Prospects* (Cheltenham, UK, and Northampton, MA: Edward Elgar, 2002), p. 18.
22 *Sotsial'no-ekonomicheskoe polizhenie Rossii (jan–apr 1999g)* (Moscow: Goskomstat, 1999), p. 153.
23 J. Thornhill and C. Clover, 'Robbery of nations', *Financial Times* (21 August 1999), p. 6.
24 See C. M. Buch *et al.*, 'The political economy of banking reform and foreign debt', in Lane, *Russian Banking*, p. 211, fn. 5.
25 *Goskomstat Rossii, Rossiya v tsifrakh 2001* (Moscow: Goskomstat, 2001), p. 295.
26 *Ibid.*, p. 295.
27 *Ibid.*
28 Taking the index of real wages of manual and non-manual workers, it fell from 100 in 1980 to 96 in Hungary in 1985 and to 81 in Poland; in Czechoslovakia there was only a slight rise to 101. *Statisticheski ezhegodnik . . . 1988*, p. 81.
29 L. Urban, 'Hungarian transition from a public choice perspective', in A. Bozoki, A. Korosenyi and G. Schopflin (eds.), *Post Communist Transition: Emerging Pluralism in Hungary* (New York: St Martin's Press, 1992), p. 92.
30 *Statisticheski ezhegodnik stran-chlenov soveta ekonomicheskoy vzaimopomoshchi 1988* (Moscow: Goskomstat, 1988), p. 342.
31 See the documented analysis of policy failure in G. W. Kolodko, *From Shock to Therapy* (New York: Oxford University Press, 2000).
32 Ha-Joon Chang, *Kicking Away the Ladder* (London: Anthem Press, 2002), especially Chapter 2.
33 For a more detailed discussion see D. Coates, *Models of Capitalism* (Cambridge: Polity Press, 2000), p. 96.
34 As Michel Camdessus has put it: 'I cannot emphasise strongly enough that Russia cannot afford to take this [corporatist] route.'
35 D. Coates, 'Models of capitalism in the new world order: the UK case', *Political Studies*, 47 (1999), 658.
36 Further discussion see H. Kitschelt, P. Lange, G. Marks and J. D. Stephens, 'Convergence and divergence in advanced capitalist democracies', in H. Kitschelt, P. Lange, G. Marks and J. D. Stephens (eds.), *Continuity and Change in Contemporary Capitalism* (Cambridge: Cambridge University Press, 1999), pp. 427–460.
37 J. E. Stiglitz, *Globalisation and its Discontents* (New York: W. Norton, 2002).

7

The Russian economy under Vladimir Putin

William Tompson

The story of the Russian economy in the 1990s is the story of an ambitious attempt at rapid, wholesale system replacement by a government – or, to be more precise, a series of governments – enjoying limited political support and presiding over an extremely weak state structure. This political and administrative weakness is central to understanding the uneven progress of market reforms in the 1990s. Reforms that enjoyed the support of influential vested interests and made limited demands on the administrative capacities of the state proceeded rapidly. Thus, substantial, though by no means complete, liberalisation of both domestic prices and foreign trade were implemented fairly swiftly, and privatisation proceeded rapidly, if chaotically. In each case, the extent of the reforms was limited by the need to appease various domestic interests: rapid privatisation, as is well known, became possible only after substantial concessions were made to enterprise insiders (managers and workforces) and a range of controls on both foreign trade and the domestic prices of sensitive goods (above all, fuels) remained in place. The story of macroeconomic policy was broadly similar. Bolstered by substantial external financial support, the government was able, for a time, to bring down inflation by relying chiefly on exchange-rate management – an approach that made few demands on state capacities, as long as the Bank of Russia was prepared to sell dollars and buy rubles at its target exchange rate.[1]

By contrast, reforms stalled when they brought the government into conflict with powerful entrenched interests or made excessive demands on the administrative capacities of the state itself. Russia fell into the trap identified by Hellman, as incomplete early reforms created winners who resisted further reform efforts. These early winners stood to gain more from the 'transition rents' generated by partial reform than from the full implementation of the reform programme.[2] Price and trade liberalisation, for example, stalled after the initial 'big bang', in large measure because distortions introduced by the remaining controls generated arbitrage opportunities for well-connected agents to reap enormous profits. Similarly, the initial insider-oriented voucher privatisation process established a pattern of strong insider control that distorted subsequent privatisation policies and created impediments to enterprise restructuring and the creation of an effective market in corporate control.[3] Political and administrative weakness also ensured that a host of other structural reforms, in spheres ranging from electricity to banking, stalled. This weakness also undermined efforts at macroeconomic stabilisation, since the government proved unable to put its own finances in order: fiscal consolidation would have required the co-operation of all parts of the state, as well as a major overhaul of both tax legislation and the tax and customs services themselves. These tasks were simply beyond the governments that held office from 1992 to 1998.

Ultimately, this uneven pattern of reform proved unsustainable: the attempt to sustain exchange-rate-based stabilisation in the absence of structural reform or fiscal consolidation led directly to the financial collapse of 1998.[4] While memories of the collapse faded during the surprisingly robust recovery that followed, it would be difficult to exaggerate the importance of this crisis for understanding economic policy in the Putin era. The perceived lessons of August 1998 continued to shape the Russian authorities' approach to economic policy throughout Putin's first term. Thus, economic policy came to rest on three key pillars: careful exchange-rate management, fiscal consolidation and the implementation of a range of micro-level structural reforms that are needed to complete Russia's systemic transformation by creating much of the basic legal and organisational infrastructure of the new market economy. It is important to note that the two latter priorities – fiscal consolidation and structural reform – both require the reconstitution of the policy-making and administrative capacities of the state.

If the first generation of Russian reformers destroyed the socialist system and 'unleashed' market forces, then the chief concern of the second generation has so far been the reconstruction of the state. This involves more than simply the recovery of capacities eroded in the 1990s. Russia does not merely need a stronger state; it needs a state different in kind to that which it inherited from the Soviet Union. Soviet administrative bureaucracies were chiefly concerned with *directing* economic activities. The role of the state in a market economy, by contrast, is overwhelmingly *regulatory*. In most cases, the state's function is not to tell economic agents what ends to pursue but to act as an impartial referee and a provider of public goods in a marketplace full of autonomous actors choosing and pursuing their own ends.

This concern with the state-building aspects of economic reform under Putin is central to the discussion that follows, which begins with a look at the changed political environment in which economic reform was pursued, before proceeding to examine macroeconomic policy and performance, structural reform issues, and the evolving relationship between Putin and Russia's commercial elite.

Economy and society

The changing political context

Putin's accession coincided with, and to a significant extent contributed to, two major developments, which substantially altered the politics of economic reform in ways that facilitated the pursuit of this agenda. The first was the stabilisation of Russia's polity and economy after a decade of uninterrupted turbulence. Putin's rise both reflected and assisted the stabilisation of political life, while the unexpected post-devaluation recovery that began in 1999 gave Russia its fastest growth rates in a generation. This stability was a crucial precondition for any serious attempt to complete the transition begun in the 1990s, since it made it possible for agents to think about the long term and thereby altered the incentives they faced. In an environment of extreme political and economic instability, rational actors tend to discount the future heavily and therefore focus on short-term gains: asset stripping is preferable to investment, rent-seeking to entrepreneurship, and speculation to restructuring. The predatory behaviour of much of Russia's elite in the 1990s reflected these incentives. With the advent of Putin, this began to change. Those who had acquired assets after 1992 could finally be confident that they would keep them and could thus begin thinking about them as businesses to be developed rather than plunder to be stashed safely abroad. Political and economic stability thus constituted a necessary – though by no means sufficient – condition for the successful pursuit of many 'second-generation' reforms.

Closely related to this was a second development: a fundamental change in the Russian elite's attitude towards the state. There is now a broad consensus shared by the great bulk of the elite and the population that the principal political task facing Russia in the post-Yeltsin era is the reconstruction of the state. This, too, is a major change from the 1990s. During the Yeltsin years, the Russian state was weak – and remained weak despite popular demands for more effective governance – in large measure because Russian elites had no incentive to strengthen it. Indeed, they faced many incentives to weaken it. As Ganev argues:

> Post-communism is a historical period characterised by a dominant elite project most aptly described as 'extraction from the state'. Powerful elites involved in this project prey upon the wealth accumulated in the state domain. Fully capable of manipulating flows of resources within the existing institutional edifice of the state, these elites have no incentive to develop strong state structures; quite on the contrary, undermining key institutions from 'inside' is necessary for the success of their project . . . While popular demands for good governance persist, the extraction from the state dictates that powerful elites weaken the institutional basis of effective political action.[5]

Ganev's generalisations certainly apply to the scramble for assets that unfolded in Russia in the 1990s. However, with the advent of Vladimir Putin, this largely changed.

By late 1999, both the winners and the losers of the 1990s shared a common interest in rebuilding the state. The victors, having acquired vast wealth amid the chaos of the Yeltsin era now need to consolidate their position. They need an effective state to protect their new property rights and to provide an environment in which they can develop and enjoy the assets they have acquired. The mass of ordinary citizens simply need a state capable of providing basic public goods, paying budget-sector wages and pensions, and fostering economic growth. To be sure, the political elite and society as a whole are still divided about virtually every major question concerning Russia's future, but there is a general consensus on the fundamental issue of the need to reconstitute state authority, which is integrally linked to the 'second-generation' reforms mentioned above.

Macroeconomic performance

In terms of economic performance, Vladimir Putin could scarcely have come to power at a more opportune time. When he was appointed Prime Minister in 1999, less than a year after the August financial collapse, a surprisingly robust economic recovery was already under way, driven by a combination of ruble devaluation, very low real wages and domestic energy prices, and exceptionally high world prices for oil and other export commodities. As import-competing domestic producers took advantage of the cheap ruble to regain market share, exports of hydrocarbons, metals and other raw materials surged. Real GDP, which had fallen by a total of 37.8 per cent on the (admittedly problematic) official data in 1991–98, increased by a cumulative total of 25.8 per cent during 1999–2002 (see Table 7.1). At the same time, the burst of inflation that followed the August devaluation was contained, and while inflation at the end of 2002 was still above the pre-crisis lows of early 1998, it was falling slowly but steadily back towards single digits. At the same time, Russia's external debt burden grew significantly lighter. The ratio of total external debt to GDP fell from around 63 per cent in 1998 to just 40 per cent at the end of 2002, as a result of a combination of economic growth, ruble appreciation and debt restructuring.

Recovery brought palpable benefits to ordinary Russians, albeit not immediately. Average real wages fell by 10 per cent in 1998 and a further 17 per cent in 1999, despite the resumption of economic growth. In 2000, however, household incomes began to bounce back, with real wages rising by almost 64 per cent in 2000–2 inclusive, and the broader measure of real disposable incomes rising by around half that figure on the official data. Some of this recovery was, of course, a statistical artefact: the replacement of a fairly steep graduated income tax with a flat 13 per cent rate in 2001 appears to have encouraged Russians to declare a larger share of their total earnings to the authorities. The State Statistics Committee estimated that

Economy and society

Table 7.1 *Economic and social indicators from Yeltsin to Putin*

	1998	1999	2000	2001	2002
Real GDP growth (%)	−4.9	5.4	9.0	5.0	4.3
CPI inflation (average)	27.8	85.8	20.8	21.6	15.8
Fiscal balance (% of GDP)[a]	−7.4	−3.2	3.3	2.9	1.4
Industrial production (1991 = 100)	49.8	55.2	61.8	64.8	67.2
Current account balance ($bn)	1.0	24.7	46.4	34.8	31.7[b]
Exchange rate (average Rb/$)	9.71	24.62	28.13	29.17	31.41
Life expectancy at birth					
Male	61.30	58.83	59.92	62.12	62.29
Female	72.93	71.72	72.20	72.83	72.97
Average real wages (% change)	−10.1	−22.0	17.9	19.1	16.6
Population (millions, year-end)	146.5	146.0	145.2	144.5	145.0[c]

Sources: Goskomstat, *Rossiiskii statisticheskii ezhegodnik 2001*; World Bank, *Russian Economic Report* (March 2003); *CIA World Factbook 2002* (Washington, 2003); Central Bank of Russia (www.cbr.ru); Economist Intelligence Unit, *Country Profile: Russia* (London, 2002).
Notes: [a] General government balance, including federal, regional and local budgets and off-budget funds. [b] Preliminary estimate. [c] July 2002 estimate.

the unreported proportion of wages and salaries fell from around 35 per cent in 2000 to about 27–28 per cent in 2002, and many private analysts argued that the drop in 'shadow' earnings was even greater.[6]

Despite this impressive record, Putin and his colleagues continued to express serious concerns about the sustainability of the recovery in the short term and the prospects for healthy growth over the long run. Growth, having peaked in 2000, fell sharply in 2001–2. While growth rates remained at levels that most developed Western economies would envy, Russian policymakers were acutely aware of the need for Russia to sustain much faster growth rates over an extended period if it were to achieve relatively rapid convergence with the *per capita* output levels found in the OECD countries. Putin's liberal economic advisor, Andrei Illarionov, pointed out in 2001 that Russia would need to grow at 8 per cent per year for 15 years merely to reach the level of *per capita* GDP recorded by Portugal in 2000. There were and are a number of reasons for doubting whether Russia is really well equipped for such sustained, rapid growth. The extent to which Russia's economic fortunes remains dependent on its resource-extraction sectors – above all oil and gas, but also metals – means that short-term performance is subject to changes in volatile international commodity prices, over which Russia has little or no control. Moreover, natural resource dependence is negatively correlated with growth performance over the long term. Explanations of the so-called 'resource curse' vary widely, but the empirical link is now well established.[7]

More generally, research into the determinants of long-term growth suggests that Russia faces a number of other handicaps as well, including high levels of government consumption, weak legal regulation and enforcement, institutions that favour rent seeking over entrepreneurship, a recent history of high inflation and relatively large income differentials. Russia's infrastructure is poor and, for the most part, deteriorating, and its demographic profile combines the worst features of developed countries (an ageing population, low birth-rates, a declining total population and rising dependency ratios) and developing ones (epidemic diseases, high levels of infant mortality and low – and falling – life-expectancy).[8] The skill level of its workforce, though still relatively high by international standards, has been eroded since 1991, while the R&D base has all but disappeared. State funding for science, which never fell below 2 per cent of GDP in Soviet times, fell during 1992–2001 from about 1 per cent of GDP to around 0.33 per cent – a decline rendered even more dramatic by the sharp fall in GDP. The resulting brain drain saw as many as 400,000 scientists and technical specialists emigrate during the 1990s, drawn by the attractions of better pay and better working conditions – or simply 'pushed' by the collapse of state funding for their work. As many as 1.5 million science professionals remaining inside Russia shifted to work in other fields.[9]

The foregoing problems must be borne in mind when assessing economic policy under Putin. There is little that Putin or the government can do about many of them, either because they are structural (geography, resource endowments) or can only change very slowly over time (institutions, industrial structure, demographic trends). It is thus far from clear how much Putin or any other leader can do to affect long-term growth prospects beyond providing a basic framework of macroeconomic and political stability. The next two sections, therefore, will consider the government's attempts to prove the sceptics wrong and create a framework for sustained, rapid growth, via both careful macroeconomic management and the aggressive pursuit of micro-level structural reforms.

Macroeconomic management

The macroeconomic policies pursued during Putin's first term continued to reflect the lessons learned from the August 1998 collapse. Monetary policy was thus dominated by a determination to protect Russia from a recurrence of 'Dutch disease', the phenomenon whereby the strength of the country's resource-exporting sectors results in an overvaluation of the national currency, reducing the competitiveness of producers in higher-value-added sectors.[10] There was a widespread – and not entirely ill-founded – belief that the ruble had become significantly overvalued prior to 1998. This had destroyed the competitiveness of many processing sectors, fuelling the growth of payment arrears and non-monetary settlements, and had also set the stage for the exchange-rate collapse, since the rate proved unsustainable once the prices of oil and other key export commodities fell.[11] When export prices recovered in 1999–2000, Russia's trade and current account surpluses reached staggering proportions, generating massive foreign exchange inflows that put considerable upward pressure on the exchange rate. The real effective exchange rate (measured in trade-weighted terms on the basis of consumer prices) strengthened by an estimated 35 per cent during 1999–2002, despite considerable efforts by the Bank of Russia to limit ruble appreciation.[12] The problem was that the monetary authorities had few instruments for sterilising these inflows, apart from the federal budget surplus. The price of checking exchange-rate appreciation was therefore inflation, as the Central Bank accumulated reserves and expanded the ruble money supply faster than the economy could absorb it.

It did not help matters that a secondary lesson of the August collapse was that the authorities should be in a position to control capital outflows. The authorities therefore proved reluctant to relax the currency control regime, which had been extended and tightened after August 1998 in an attempt to prop up the ruble. By 2000, however, the concern was not the ruble's weakness but its strength, and the controls merely added to this problem, since they increased the demand for rubles, which was already excessive. Exporters, for example, had to sell a large proportion of their hard-currency earnings for rubles on recognised exchanges within 90 days.[13] This forex surrender requirement ensured that any rise in Russia's trade surplus would lead more or less automatically to an acceleration of money-supply growth. Only in early 2003 did the government finally put legislation liberalising this currency control regime to the State Duma.

Reducing inflation was made still more difficult by the cost–push pressures generated by the need to raise the tariffs charged by Russia's infrastructure monopolies – chiefly the gas monopolist Gazprom, the electricity giant RAO EES and the Ministry of Railways (MPS). It was generally accepted that tariff levels must rise substantially over the medium term if the sectors involved were to remain viable: domestic gas and electricity prices were well below production costs and had to be raised sufficiently to allow producers to cover their costs and to make investment in electricity and gas production economically attractive. Yet the knock-on effects of higher energy and transport tariffs on other sectors meant that every tariff adjustment represented a significant increase in inflationary pressures throughout the economy.

Despite this awkward combination of monopoly tariff hikes, currency controls and a determination to avoid Dutch disease, the results of monetary policy were not bad. The hyperinflation that many had feared after the

August crisis did not materialise and inflation was brought down gradually from year to year (see Table 7.1). In 1999–2000, rapid economic growth and the rapid increase in the share of cash settlements in transactions among Russian enterprises helped limit the inflationary consequences of this policy stance. The economy was able to absorb M2 growth more than double the Bank of Russia's stated targets, while inflation continued to fall. This was because the velocity of circulation fell – a fairly normal consequence of stabilisation after a period of very high inflation – while economic activity accelerated. In 2001–2, growth slowed and the change in velocity grew less pronounced, but inflation was by then at manageable levels.

The experience of August 1998 also had a profound impact on fiscal policy. It was widely recognised that Russia's vulnerability to the external shocks of 1997–98 was chiefly the result of its failure to put state finances in order. During 1992–98, the general government balance showed one large deficit after another, fluctuating between 6 and 10 per cent of GDP. In the years following the crisis, however, the government's financial position was transformed. Large deficits were turned into budget surpluses, enabling the state to honour its financial obligations, something it had been consistently unable to do in the 1990s. Fiscal consolidation arguably contributed more than any other single factor to restoring the authority and legitimacy of the formerly bankrupt state. High export prices and economic recovery clearly contributed enormously to this turnaround, but so, too, did improved expenditure management, the reform of tax legislation and better tax administration (see Table 7.2).

Table 7.2 *Fiscal performance, 1998–2002 (% of GDP)*

	1998	1999	2000	2001	2002
Total revenue	33.4	34.0	38.4	29.6[a]	29.2[a]
Federal	10.9	12.8	16.0	17.6	17.1
Sub-national	14.0	13.4	14.3	14.6	15.0
Off-budget funds	8.2	8.2	8.2	n/a	n/a
Total expenditure	40.8	37.2	35.1	26.6[a]	27.8[a]
Federal	16.7	17.1	15.1	14.6	15.3
Sub-national	17.1	15.1	15.1	14.5	15.4
Off-budget funds	9.4	7.0	7.1	n/a	n/a
Balance	−7.4	−3.2	3.3	2.9[a]	1.4[a]

Sources: RF Ministry of Finance; World Bank, *Russian Economic Report* (March 2003); EIU, *Russia: Country Profile* (London, 2002).

Note: [a] Data for 2001–2 exclude income and expenditure of off-budget funds.

Expenditure management is probably the least known of these successes, but it is hardly insignificant. While inefficiency, corruption and mismanagement remain commonplace, the ratio of consolidated government expenditure[14] to GDP declined by no less than ten percentage points during 1997–2000 without any obvious deterioration in the financing of budget-sector activities.[15] On the contrary, budgetary arrears fell, while budget-sector wages and pensions rose rapidly. This provides the most powerful, albeit indirect, evidence that the finance ministry's long struggle to transfer all budgetary accounts to the treasury was well worth waging. The shift to a treasury system was long resisted by both the commercial banks that held budgetary accounts and the various ministries and departments themselves.[16] The former profited from the steady supply of essentially free liabilities, while the latter exploited the freedom that decentralised fiscal management gave them to depart from budgetary targets and other directives from above.

Tax reform represents perhaps the most fundamental element of the economic reform and state-building projects of the Putin administration. Rebuilding the state's extractive capacities was an essential precondition to rebuilding other sorts of state capacities. The government's achievements in this field over 2000–2 were among its most impressive. The adoption of successive chapters of part 2 of the Russian Federation Tax Code brought about a major overhaul of Russia's major taxes and the abolition of many of the minor ones. The most important innovations included a new social tax, a re-vamped profit tax and a flat income tax. The new 'unified social tax' (ESN), introduced in 2001, replaced payments to the three major off-budget funds – the Pension Fund, the Fund for Mandatory Medical Insurance and the Social Insurance Fund. With respect to the profit and income taxes, the government adopted a common approach, abolishing numerous loopholes and exemptions but slashing rates and, in the case of income tax, moving from a progressive scale to a single flat rate of 13 per cent. In addition, considerable progress was made in revising and stabilising the tax regimes applied to such crucial sectors as natural resource extraction.

The revenue effect of these changes was striking. According to the conventional wisdom, implementation difficulties generally ensure that almost any significant change to the tax system initially results in a loss of revenue, even if its ultimate effect is to increase the tax take. In Russia, however, there was little evidence of this: new or re-vamped taxes tended, on the contrary, to yield higher revenues from the beginning. The success of the new 13 per cent income tax was especially significant. There were grave doubts about whether a lower, flat rate would in fact result in increased compliance. However, the sceptics overlooked two things. First, a simpler tax closes off many legal options for tax avoidance. Secondly, tax-avoidance strategies usually impose costs of their own. Lowering rates thus changes the calculations taxpayers make about the difference between the costs of compliance and the cost of avoidance, subject to the risk of detection.

The federal budget's sensitivity to movements in oil prices remains a concern. It has been estimated that a $1 drop in the price of a barrel of oil can reduce fiscal revenues by around $1bn.[17] However, the level of oil price that is truly threatening has been reduced. Since 1998, a combination of ruble devaluation, economic growth, tax reforms and expenditure control has lowered the average international price needed to execute the budget. In 1998, world oil prices would have had to average $26.50/barrel (bbl) in order for the federal budget to balance; the actual figure was less than half that. By contrast, the federal budget for 2003 could be executed at an average world price as low as $16/bbl.[18] Recent IMF assessments suggest that the Russian budget should be better able to weather low oil prices than it was in the 1990s.[19]

Nevertheless, significant disagreements about the medium term persist. Haunted by memories of 1998 and acutely aware of the budget's vulnerability to external shocks, the finance ministry has continued to press for an exceptionally tight medium-term stance. Prime Minister Mikhail Kasyanov, however, argued that growth, rather than accumulating funds for debt service, should be the priority after 2003, an issue on which he clashed openly with Finance Minister and First Deputy Prime Minister Aleksei Kudrin.[20] Kudrin's stance was underlined when the government in early 2003 began preparing the legislation that would create the fiscal stabilisation fund proposed by Putin in his April 2001 message to the Federal Assembly. The fund's purpose is to limit the impact of volatile world commodity prices on the budget. It is to accumulate 'surplus' revenues when oil prices are high, which can then be drawn on when oil prices fall. The question is: how large should the fund be and what should be the base-line oil price, above which revenues count as 'surplus' and are channelled into the fund? The Finance Ministry's initial proposal was to create a fund equal to 8.7 per cent of GDP, with a view to covering the fiscal gap that would result from three consecutive years with an average Urals oil price of just $12/bbl.[21] This was both politically unrealistic and economically unnecessary: the degree of fiscal tightening needed to accumulate such a reserve would be very difficult to sustain and the history of world oil markets over the post-war period suggests that such an extreme scenario is highly unlikely.

Structural reform

A further lesson of the August crisis was that macroeconomic policy on its own was not enough. There was wide agreement in Russia after 1998 that one of the main root causes of the financial collapse had been a lack of structural reform. Macroeconomic policies in the mid-1990s were not underpinned by the micro-level structural changes needed to render them sustainable and to facilitate the move from stabilisation to recovery.[22] This was largely a consequence of their political and administrative weakness described above: the governments of the 1990s lacked both the political strength to challenge powerful vested interests that were threatened by reform and the administrative capacity to implement such reforms as they adopted. The lessons of the August crisis were not lost on Putin, who, under the influence of reformist ministers and advisors, made structural reform a crucial element of his state-building project. From late 2000, he gave strong and generally consistent backing to the government's pursuit of a wide-ranging structural reform agenda that addressed such problems as corporate governance, monopolies reform, tax reform, judicial reform, banking reform, land reform, bankruptcy reform and reform of the system of housing and municipal subsidies.[23] This is an extremely ambitious programme. Institutional change is generally slow and gradual and would seem to be yet another of those factors about which a government can do little except over the very long term.[24] In general, this is the case, but Russia's reformers aim to show that determined institutional engineering can improve growth performance relatively quickly.

This is not the place for a detailed examination of so many reform initiatives, especially given that most were highly technical. However, some general points can be made about the handling of these issues, particularly in the context of building a stronger state. The first is the importance attached by the government to legislating its reforms. As Woodruff has observed, the politics of economic reform in the Yeltsin era was very much a politics of *implementation*, in which the decisions taken by ministers and senior bureaucrats mattered more importantly in practice than did the fine print of legislation. Under Putin, however, there has been a pronounced attempt to move to a politics of *law-making*.[25] Both the executive branch and big business have begun to attach much greater importance to the legislative process. Thus, in addition to a raft of new tax legislation, the Kasyanov government during 2000–2 secured passage of new land and labour codes, a trio of bills aimed at reducing bureaucratic interference in the economy, the bulk of the government's pension reform package, the major elements of its judicial reform, and new laws on money-laundering, bankruptcy and joint-stock companies. In part, this is because the election of a more cooperative Duma at the end of 1999 made it possible to adopt reform legislation that would never have passed the chamber in the 1990s. However, greater legislative activism is a result of more than just the greater ease with which bills can be passed. It also reflects a shared desire to entrench reforms. Entrepreneurs want greater transparency and stability with respect to the rules of the economic game, while government reformers wish to make the most of their current influence by using the legislative process to set out lines of policy that will prove more difficult to change later on.

However, the shift to a politics of law-making has its limits. Thus, the amendments agreed by the government in order to secure the Duma's approval of its electricity reform package in early 2003 tended to give the executive branch discretion to resolve matters that previously were to be set out in the legislation. Paradoxically, it was the *legislature*, not the government that insisted that crucial issues concerning both the scope and pace of reform was to be determined by the government rather than enshrined in law. Whereas government reformers wished to fix the reform timetable in law in order to ensure that it did not stall later on, Duma deputies preferred to avoid responsibility for such decisions by shifting them back to the executive. As a result, passage of the electricity package did not so much resolve the battles over electricity restructuring as define the framework within which those battles would continue to be fought. For lobbies opposed to reform, of course, this was a major victory, since it meant that they could continue to lobby behind the scenes to delay or amend the reforms. Electricity is not atypical: Woodruff paints a similar picture of pension reform, with the reform legislation failing to resolve the very issues that prompted its adoption in the first place and leaving ample room for arbitrary action by the executive branch in implementation.[26]

A great deal of the new legislation is aimed at 'civilising' Russian capitalism, in particular by improving the protection of property rights in general and raising standards of corporate governance. However, the aim of such efforts seems in many instances to be not so much the protection of property rights in general as the protection of the 'particular conflation of ownership and control' that emerged in Russian companies in the Yeltsin era,[27] a development entirely consonant with the shift in elite interests and priorities alluded to above. In other words, the new legislation is being used to entrench the positions of those who prevailed in the scramble for assets after 1992. State-building for Russia's new rich is very much about consolidating the victories they won in the 1990s.

The impact of these legislative changes cannot be taken for granted, for there has been rather less progress with respect to rebuilding the state's rule-enforcement powers. Well-founded doubts about the independence, competence and probity of the courts, the prosecutors and the police persist. The overhaul of procedural codes has undoubtedly improved the legal framework for business in Russia, but the administration of the new legislation is still uneven.[28] And physical force, though less common than in the 1990s, is still employed with disturbing frequency in commercial conflicts, especially when the stakes are high. Often, this involves the use of state bodies as the servants of private interests – a disturbing reminder of the extent to which private interests continue to penetrate state institutions at all levels.[29] Unable to change bureaucrats' behaviour, except perhaps over the longer term, Putin has instead tried to deprive them of some of their powers. The 'debureaucratisation' legislation of 2001–2 simplified licensing, registration and inspection regimes for businesses and deprived bureaucrats of many of their legal powers to interfere in economic activity. Survey evidence suggests that the de-bureaucratisation package did have an impact: Russian officials continue to abuse their positions and to transgress the legal limits of their authority, but the curbing of that authority did have an impact. In mid-2002, managers and entrepreneurs reported significantly less bureaucratic interference in their activities than in 2001.[30]

'Chaebolisation'?

One of the most controversial trends observed during Putin's first term was the increasing consolidation of corporate shareholdings in the hands of a small number of players. Ownership was hardly dispersed in the late 1990s, but the post-devaluation recovery triggered a wave of mergers and acquisitions, largely driven by cash-rich exporters who began acquiring under-priced industrial assets at home. At the end of 2001, Boone and Rodionov calculated that the sixty-four largest privately owned companies had generated sales of $109bn in 2000, as compared with total GDP that year of just $260bn. Moreover, they found that 85 per cent of the value of these companies was controlled by just eight shareholder groups.[31]

In the main, the new business groups, many of which self-consciously tried to model themselves on South Korean chaebols, differed from the financial-industrial groups (FPGs) of the 1990s by virtue of their sectoral/technological coherence. In the mid-1990s, banks and cash-rich resource companies simply bought up whatever they could as fast as they could. The M&A wave that began in 2000, by contrast, was characterised by a determination to create vertically integrated structures. Often companies with monopoly or near-monopoly positions in one sector sought to use their market power to extend their reach into related sectors. Surviving Yeltsin-era FPGs, like Interros, also set about rationalising their businesses, abandoning some activities to concentrate on others. Defenders of this consolidation process argued that the new conglomerates were also more inclined than the Yeltsin-era FPGs to develop the businesses they had acquired rather than merely extracting rents and stripping assets. They argued that consolidation of ownership would facilitate restructuring and the channelling of badly needed investment from export industries to sectors oriented towards the domestic market. One of Russia's major problems continues to be the lack of mechanisms for efficiently allocating investment resources across – and not merely within – economic sectors. The banking system is weak and financial markets are small and illiquid. In theory at least, the formation of chaebol-like groupings could thus provide financial intermediation not otherwise available. Advocates of 'chaebolisation' also argued that large companies with secure domestic bases would be better able to compete in international markets.

There are good reasons to be sceptical about all these claims. It is not yet clear just how integrated the new groupings will be or how stable. Their structures are loose and often opaque, and some of them rest on informal networks and personal relationships. Nor is it clear how committed their core companies are to strengthening their new acquisitions. Some of the most aggressive purchasers seem inclined to use their control over those businesses to concentrate profits at particular points in the production chain, extracting value from others – a practice all too familiar to observers of Russian corporate capitalism. Nor do they yet seem to be compensating for the financial system's weaknesses: during 2000–2, investment activity remained overwhelmingly concentrated in a few sectors (mainly hydrocarbons) and the conglomerates continued to spend more on further acquisitions than on restructuring assets already acquired. The groupings' growth appears to be driven by a desire to monopolise entire sectors, or even groups of related sectors, which, unfortunately, is relatively easy to do in Russia. Many major industrial sectors may face a future of monopoly domination or oligopolistic competition, in which the main players compete with each other – more in the political arena than the commercial – while colluding to exclude new entrants. In this situation, the extent to which producers are subject to competitive pressures will depend increasingly on the international openness of the economy. This is a major reason why Russia's entry into the World Trade Organisation (WTO) is seen as being so important to the success of economic reform: it will entrench the openness of the economy and make it harder for domestic players to suppress competition.

It would, however, be a mistake to exaggerate the extent to which trends towards consolidation threaten to suppress competition in Russian product markets. This is because these markets were not very competitive to begin with. Indeed, to a great extent, the mania for vertical integration reflects the lack of competition that *already* characterised many sectors. The impetus for metals producers to secure control of upstream coal production and downstream automobile manufacture, for example, largely reflected the extent to which many of them have little choice about sourcing their energy supplies or marketing their output. The lack of alternative suppliers and customers left them vulnerable and one response was to seek security by taking direct control of up- and downstream activities. Thus, the coal concern Kuzbassugol, a medium-sized company in a not especially promising sector, fetched more than $180m when it was privatised in the autumn of 2001. The price of Kuzbassugol was driven up by the rivalry between steel concerns Severstal and Evrazkholding, each of which feared the consequences of allowing the other to control Kuzbassugol.[32]

'Oligarch management' under Putin

The Russian authorities have not – to date – taken exception to this trend towards monopoly and oligopoly in key sectors. Some senior officials are attracted to the idea of creating 'national champions' to compete on world markets, while others simply find it easier to manage the state's relations with big business and to regulate economic activity if there are fewer players to deal with. And there are, of course, still many leading politicians and high-ranking bureaucrats who are still closely linked to private business interests and can be expected to lobby their interests, even if they now do so more discreetly than they might have done in the Yeltsin era.

That said, Putin has certainly tried to redefine the relationship between the Kremlin and the country's leading tycoons, who are colloquially, if somewhat misleadingly, known as 'the oligarchs'.[33] This process of redefinition has unfolded in stages. First, Putin made it clear that he did not intend to expropriate the oligarchs *en masse*. To have launched a frontal assault on their empires would have risked political and economic instability just at the moment when political stabilisation and economic recovery were beginning to take hold. Such an offensive would have led to falling tax revenues and rising capital flight, as well as jeopardising Putin's own attempts to consolidate his power. Nevertheless, Putin moved rapidly to signal that the terms of the relationship between big business and the Kremlin were changing. In the spring and summer of 2000, virtually all of the country's top business clans came under some sort of official pressure. The most direct was applied to media tycoon Vladimir Gusinskii, who had backed Putin's opponents in the Duma and presidential elections of 1999/2000. He and his companies were subjected to a series of criminal investigations, which were conducted in extremely heavy-handed fashion. Ironically, Boris Berezovskii, who had actively aided Putin's rise and helped engineer the Kremlin's Duma election victory in 1999, soon became another major target. Yet they were not alone: Vladimir Potanin, head of the Interros grouping, faced a suit aimed at overturning the privatisation of the metals giant Norilsk Nickel, which was controlled by Interros. Four subsidiaries of the Tyumen Oil Company (TNK), controlled by the Alfa-Renova consortium, were raided by investigators in conjunction with allegations of illegal privatisation deals. The state also reversed a decision to support the re-election of Anatolii Chubais, the CEO of the country's electricity monopoly, EES Rossii, to the board of that company.

These developments did not, however, turn out to be the beginning of an open season on the oligarchs. Instead, Putin intervened as their protector. Gusinskii was released from police custody shortly after Putin criticised his detention. The Norilsk Nickel suit was settled without litigation when federal prosecutors took the case over from the Moscow city authorities – shortly after an extended meeting between Putin and Potanin to discuss the company's future. The president publicly signalled his support for Chubais, who was duly re-elected to the EES board. Putin also met Lukoil chief Vagit Alekperov, thereby scotching rumours that Alekperov was about to be arrested. In each instance, Putin demonstrated to the tycoons that he was in a position to act as their protector, while reminding them at the same time that his protection might be withdrawn – with serious consequences for them. On 1 July 2000, even as this 'catch-and-release' campaign was unfolding, Prime Minister Kasyanov stated flatly that there would be no drive to overturn past privatisation deals. However, he then added that some deals, which had involved legal violations, might yet be overturned.[34] This statement appeared to reflect the balance of Putin's own approach, reassuring the country's commercial elite that the new administration could and would respect big business – if the businessmen behaved themselves.

In the end, only two of the so-called oligarchs truly 'fell from grace' in Putin's first term: Gusinskii and Berezovskii. Both were deprived of control over key assets within Russia by means of politically motivated legal proceedings and both ended up living in exile to avoid criminal prosecution at home. These two men appear to have been singled out for political annihilation for similar reasons. Both had accumulated extensive media holdings, which they had used to advance their political agendas and which the Kremlin now wished to control. The extent to which they openly played politics also set them apart from their fellow tycoons. Most of Russia's top businessmen engaged in high politics in order to protect and advance their business interests; Berezovskii and Gusinskii often gave the opposite impression – their business empires seemed to be instruments for advancing their political ambitions. Ironically, it mattered little what these ambitions were. Gusinskii backed Putin's opponents in the Duma and presidential elections of 1999/2000, while Berezovskii helped engineer both the strong showing of pro-Kremlin forces in the 1999 Duma election and Putin's accession to the presidency. If Gusinskii was punished for his opposition, then Berezovskii was punished for his support: Putin did not wish either to allow the ever ambitious Berezovskii an influential role or to appear beholden to the unpopular tycoon. And, having won the elections, Putin and his team no longer had need of Berezovskii's services.

The rest of the commercial elite did not fail to draw lessons from the persecution of Gusinskii and Berezovskii. Certainly, they did not withdraw from politics, but they lobbied their interests more discreetly, accepting the constraints imposed on them by the new regime. Their access to Putin himself was increasingly restricted and was institutionalised via periodic meetings between the president and the presidium of the Russian Union of Industrialists and Entrepreneurs, which consequently came to enjoy a quasi-official status as the 'oligarchs' trade union'.

Yet there was more to Putin's strategy for managing the business clans than merely persecuting the odd troublemaker *pour encourager les autres*. While backing liberal reforms in the main, Putin moved to tighten the state's grip over key industrial and financial assets such as the gas monopoly, Gazprom, the oil transport monopoly, Transneft, and the state savings bank, Sberbank. In part, at least, this appears to have been motivated by a desire to strengthen the state vis-à-vis big business. Thus, state control over the pipeline infrastructure remains the government's best lever when it comes to managing the powerful oil barons and the authorities have emphatically rejected the idea of allowing private pipelines to be built. Similarly, Putin's has explicitly rejected any break-up of Gazprom, stating that the company is a geopolitical asset for Russia internationally.[35] The president also seems concerned about the implications of gas liberalisation for Russia's independent gas producers, the most important of whom are the oil companies. Politically, Putin would be most unlikely to welcome a reform that left him with a gas industry that not only resembled the oil industry in structure but was also dominated by the same players – whatever the economic implications of the reform.[36] WTO accession is important here, too: while it would benefit some of the business groupings and threaten others, it would represent an important external constraint on the power of all of them.

It is perhaps appropriate to end with this discussion of 'oligarch management', for Putin's long-term economic legacy will depend largely on how he manages his relationship with big business. The progress made on economic reforms in 2000–3 is undoubted, but so, too, is the fact that the emerging structure of Russian capitalism continues to be characterised by highly concentrated ownership and extremely close ties between powerful business lobbies and the state. The extent to which these lobbies are able to influence the formulation of further reforms or to distort their implementation will largely determine what kind of relationship between state, society and economy Vladimir Putin bequeaths to his eventual successor.

Notes

1 I have explored this line of argument with respect to the 1990s in greater depth elsewhere. See W. Tompson, 'Economic policy under Yeltsin and Putin', in S. White, A. Pravda and Z. Gitelman (eds.), *Developments in Russian Politics 5* (Basingstoke: Palgrave, 2001); and 'Was Gaidar really necessary? Russian "shock therapy" reconsidered', *Problems of Post-Communism*, 49:4 (July–August 2002). See also V. Mau and I. Starodubrovskaya, *The Challenge of Revolution: Contemporary Russia in Historical Perspective* (Oxford: Oxford University Press, 2001).

2 J. Hellman, 'Winners take all: the politics of partial reform in post-communist countries', *World Politics*, 50:2 (January 1998).

3 G. Roland, 'On the speed and sequencing of privatisation and restructuring', *Economic Journal*, 104 (September 1994), 426.

4 B. Pinto, V. Drebentsov and A. Morozov, 'Give growth and macroeconomic stability in Russia a chance: harden budgets by eliminating non-payment's', *Economics of Transition*, 8:2 (July 2000).

5 V. Ganev, 'On state weakness in post-communism: the "reversed Tillyan perspective"', (University of Chicago Workshop on Nations, States and Politics

in Comparative Perspective, January 2000); available on the internet at http://cas.uchicago.edu/workshop/nsp/vganev.rtf.
6 *Vedomosti* (11 February 2003).
7 For two recent analyses of the 'resource' curse, see J. D. Sachs and A. M. Warner, 'The curse of natural resources', *European Economic Review*, 45:4–6 (May 2001), 827–838; and R. M. Auty, 'The political economy of resource-driven growth', *European Economic Review*, 45:4–6 (May 2001), 839–846. See also Sachs and Warner, 'Fundamental sources of long-run growth', *American Economic Review (Papers and Proceedings)*, 87:22 (May 1997).
8 On Russia, see P. Hanson, 'Barriers to long-term economic growth in Russia', *Kyoto Institute of Economic Research Discussion Paper*, 520 (2000). For a look at the broader comparative literature on long-term growth, see R. J. Barro, 'Determinants of economic growth: a cross-country empirical study', *NBER Working Paper*, 5698 (August 1996); G. Ramey and V. A. Ramey, 'Cross-country evidence on the link between volatility and growth', *NBER Working Paper*, 4959 (December 1994); T. Persson and G. Tabellini, 'Is inequality harmful for economic growth?', *American Economic Review*, 84:3 (June 1994); R. Bénabou, 'Inequality and growth', *Centre for Economic Policy Research Discussion Paper*, 1450 (1996).
9 F. Mereu, 'Russian "brain drain" leaves future in doubt', *RFE/RL Weekday Magazine* (30 July 2002).
10 The label 'Dutch disease', which refers to the experience of the Netherlands after the discovery of natural gas in the North Sea, is in fact somewhat misleading and rather unfair to that country, since the Dutch in fact managed their gas wealth rather shrewdly and adapted extremely well. In hindsight, the phenomenon might be better known as 'British disease', given the rather less successful record of the United Kingdom in dealing with this problem in the 1980s.
11 P. Hanson, 'The Russian economic crisis and the future of Russian economic reform', *Europe–Asia Studies*, 51:7 (November 1999); B. Slay, 'An interpretation of the Russian financial crisis', *Post-Soviet Geography and Economics*, 40:3 (April–May 1999).
12 Economist Intelligence Unit, *Country Forecast: Russia* (10 January 2003), p. 36.
13 The surrender quota was 75 per cent until July 2001, when it was cut to 50 per cent.
14 Comprising the expenditure of the federal and regional budgets, as well as off-budget funds.
15 I am grateful to Evsei Gurvich of the finance ministry's Economic Expert Group for drawing this point to my attention.
16 For a discussion of the role of the so-called 'authorised banks' and their management of budgetary accounts, see W. Tompson, 'Old habits die hard: fiscal imperatives, state regulation and the role of Russia's banks', *Europe–Asia Studies*, 49:7 (November 1997), 1172–1173.
17 Such estimates are commonplace See, e.g., Schroder, SalomonSmithBarney, *Why Russia is More Than an 'Oil Play': Reforms, Growth and Macroeconomic Preparedness*, 9 October 2001. For a more serious analysis, see J. Rautava, 'The role of oil prices and the real exchange rate in Russia's economy', *BOFIT Discussion Papers* 3 (2002), especially pp. 9, 18.
18 P. Aven, and C. Weafer, 'Chasing Portugal or following Venezuela?', *Moscow Times* (14 January 2003).

19 IMF, *Country Report No. 01/102: Russian Federation* (Washington, 2001).
20 *Vedomosti* (16 August 2002, 17 August 2002, 14 March 2003 and 17 March 2003).
21 'Fiscal policy – MinFin outlines its vision for stabilisation fund', United Financial Group, *Russia Morning Comment* (19 February 2003), 4.
22 For Western views, Hanson, 'The Russian economic crisis'; and Pinto, Drebentsov and Morozov, 'Give growth and macroeconomic stability in Russia a Chance'.
23 For a more detailed exploration of these structural reform during Putin's first years in power, see W. Tompson, 'Putin's challenge: the politics of structural reform in Russia', *Europe–Asia Studies*, 54:6 (September 2002).
24 R. E. Hall and C. I. Jones, 'Levels of economic activity across countries', *American Economic Review (Papers and Proceedings)*, 87:2 (May 1997).
25 D. Woodruff, 'Pension reform in Russia: from the politics of implementation to the politics of law-making?', *PONARS Policy Memo*, 234 (December 2001), 1.
26 Woodruff, 'Pension reform in Russia'.
27 On the 2002 bankruptcy law, for example, see D. M. Woodruff, 'The end of "primitive capitalist accumulation"? The new bankruptcy law and the political assertiveness of Russian big business', *PONARS Policy Memo*, 274 (October 2002), 1.
28 For analyses of various facets of commercial law reform under Putin, see Woodruff, 'The end of "primitive capitalist accumulation"?'; W. Tompson, 'Judicial reform moves forward in Russia', *International Company and Commercial Law Review*, 12:7–8 (July–August 2001); 'Russia amends law on joint-stock companies', *International Company and Commercial Law Review*, 13:1 (January 2002); and, 'Reforming Russian bankruptcy law', *International Company and Commercial Law Review*, 14:4 (April 2003).
29 For an all-too-typical recent example, see Agros's attempt to secure control over the Smolmyaso meat processing plant and the Tagansk Meat Combine (TAMP); *Vedomosti* (25 March 2003; *Moscow Times*, 27 March 2003).
30 *Monitoring of Administrative Barriers to Small Business Development in Russia: Round 2* (Moscow: Centre for Economic and Financial Research, 2003), pp. 1–23.
31 P. Boone and D. Rodionov, 'Rent seeking in Russia and the CIS' (paper presented at the tenth anniversary meeting of the EBRD, London, December 2001).
32 Oxford Analytica, *East Europe Daily Brief*, 2 (12 October 2001).
33 The term 'oligarch' is problematic in many respects, not least of which is the impression it conveys of a powerful, autonomous class of tycoons who dominate and control the state. In fact, Russia's leading businesspeople, influential though they are, are better viewed as *lobbyists* seeking support and protection from the state than oligarchs who dominate it. The history of the period since 1992 largely demonstrates that state favour is crucial to business success – and that the withdrawal of that favour can be commercially fatal.
34 *Vremya novostei* (2 July 2000).
35 *Moscow Times* (17 February 2003).
36 C. Granville, 'Gas, electricity and political will', *Russia: Strategy & Politics* (Moscow: UFG, 27 January 2003), 4–9.

8

Politics and the mass media under Putin

Laura Belin

Some commentators have argued that it is too early to determine the impact of Vladimir Putin's policies or even, in some areas, what his policy priorities will be. Where Putin imposed change swiftly, experts disagree on how much his innovations have altered the playing field (for instance, the extent to which he has enhanced the federal centre's control over the regions). Where he has declined to take sides between differing factions, as in certain aspects of economic policy, it is unclear whether Putin will continue a Boris Yeltsin-style balancing act, nurturing competing groups.

Viewing Russian politics through the prism of press freedom and editorial autonomy leads to different conclusions about Putin's presidency. Not surprisingly, given the media's contribution to Putin's rise to power,[1] the president and his appointees quickly implemented a media policy with unambiguous goals: to enhance state power over the flow of information and to deter media outlets from challenging the president. As this chapter will show, the impact of Putin's approach was apparent from the earliest months of his presidency, and the tendency toward less pluralism and more self-censorship has become more pronounced with time. In addition, the chapter will analyse how Putin's administration has managed to curb media criticism (especially on television), whereas various government officials with a similar agenda failed to do so during the second half of the 1990s.

Managing coverage of Chechnya

Controlling news coverage of sensitive subjects was a priority for Putin well before his election as president. His skyrocketing popularity was strongly linked to public support for the renewed military campaign in Chechnya (see Chapter 14) which began soon after his appointment as prime minister. During the early months of the fighting, the authorities mostly got the war coverage they wanted, in part because there were few Russian journalists in the battle zone. The hostage industry in the breakaway republic had alienated many journalists from the Chechen cause and scared off some experienced correspondents who retained good Chechen contacts.[2]

In order to bolster public support for the military campaign, Putin established a Russian Information Centre in 1999 to handle news releases about the 'anti-terrorist operation' (never a 'war' in official statements). Run by the experienced image-maker Mikhail Margelov, the centre issued timely releases with a coherent message as well as gruesome videos of Chechen captors torturing and killing Russian soldiers during the first war, from 1994 to 1996.[3] Official spokesmen advised journalists about what language to use, downplayed Russian military losses, and almost always denied reports about civilian casualties. In addition, government officials summoned lower-ranking journalists for interviews and 'reminded [them] of their patriotic duty'.[4]

Meanwhile, the Russian military restricted journalists' ability to collect information in Chechnya and neighbouring regions by establishing official press pools and denying accreditation to journalists considered unreliable.[5] Military commanders also threatened to revoke the accreditation of journalists who made unsanctioned trips in the war zone[6] and promised civilians in captured territory rewards for 'denouncing' journalists who took notes or filmed without permission.[7]

Nevertheless, media criticism of the military campaign became more prevalent during the last two months of 1999. Ekho Moskvy radio and National Television (NTV), both part of Vladimir Gusinskii's Media-Most empire, were among the first to give more exposure to the tragic deaths of civilians. Commentators on TV-Centre, controlled by the Moscow city authorities, also expressed growing scepticism about official casualty estimates and prospects for winning the war quickly. Monitoring of Russian television in November and December 1999 showed that while 51 per cent state-owned Russian Public Television (ORT) and fully state-owned Russian Television (RTR) continued to devote mostly favourable or neutral coverage to the military campaign, newscasts on NTV and TV-Centre included as many 'negative' references to the war as 'positive' ones.[8] After the December 1999 parliamentary elections, NTV and TV-Centre aired more unflattering reports and commentaries about the war, and the tone of Chechnya coverage changed in several prominent Moscow newspapers that had supported the military campaign for months, such as *Izvestiya*, *Komsomol'skaya pravda* and *Moskovskii komsomolets*.[9]

In January 2000, Putin (by now acting president) put Yeltsin's former press secretary, Sergei Yastrzhembskii, in charge of managing information about Chechnya.[10] Yastrzhembskii's office brought in new accreditation rules containing 'completely obvious' inconsistencies with Russian legislation, in the view of one specialist on media law.[11] Military officials soon barred

NTV correspondents from the press pool in Chechnya after the network broadcast an unsanctioned interview with a Russian officer.[12]

The treatment of Radio Liberty correspondent Andrei Babitskii sent an even stronger message to journalists inclined to evade restrictions on their movements.[13] When the experienced correspondent disappeared in mid-January 2000, Russian officials denied knowing his whereabouts, and Yastrzhembskii commented that Russian authorities could not vouch for Babitskii's safety, since he lacked the proper accreditation. In fact, Russian security forces had secretly detained him, giving him no opportunity to contact his family, his colleagues or an attorney. After nearly three weeks in custody, Babitskii was ostensibly 'exchanged' for Russian prisoners being held by Chechens, but in fact Russian officials handed him over to pro-Moscow Chechen fighters. He was released after spending several more weeks incommunicado, but was immediately arrested and charged with possessing false documents.

The reaction of other Russian media to Babitskii's disappearance indicated that official pressure to support the military campaign was already having a 'chilling effect' on some media. During the first war in Chechnya, from 1994 to 1996, the mainstream Russian media had virtually unanimously decried efforts to intimidate journalists or restrict reporting on the war. But when the Union of Journalists and some thirty media outlets jointly sponsored a special issue of *Obshchaya gazeta* devoted to Babitskii's unlawful detention and 'exchange',[14] certain prominent newspapers declined to co-sponsor the issue. They included *Nezavisimaya gazeta* and *Kommersant*, both controlled by the powerful businessman Boris Berezovsky;[15] *Izvestiya*, controlled by Vladimir Potanin's Interros holding company and the partly state-owned oil firm LUKoil; *Trud*, financed by the partly state-owned gas monopoly Gazprom; and *Vremya-MN*, covertly financed by the Central Bank.

Still, some media outlets continued to question the Russian military campaign or present the views of Chechen leaders. The Ministry for the Press, Television and Radio Broadcasting, and Mass Communications (hereafter the Media Ministry) sought to discourage such behaviour. First Deputy Media Minister Mikhail Seslavinskii announced in March 2000 that the ministry would consider interviews with senior Chechen officials, including President Aslan Maskhadov, to be violations of the 1997 law on terrorism.[16] Since the media outside the Russian capital rarely interviewed Chechen officials or rebel fighters,[17] Seslavinskii's threat was clearly aimed at Moscow-based outlets.

In subsequent months *Kommersant*, *Novaya gazeta*, *Nezavisimaya gazeta* and NTV were among the outlets that received warnings (citing the law on terrorism or the 1992 law on the mass media) after publishing or broadcasting interviews with senior Chechen officials.[18] Although the legal justification for applying those statutes as the Media Ministry did was questionable,[19] official warnings gave the ministry a potentially deadly weapon against the media it regulated. In February 2000 the ministry had cited official warnings as grounds for putting two television networks' broadcast licences up for auction. Nor could newspapers brush aside a warning; Media Minister Mikhail Lesin favoured introducing licensing requirements for print media, in which case interviewing Chechen leaders could threaten a publication's survival.

The aggressive efforts to restrict coverage of the 'anti-terrorist operation' continued well after Putin had been elected president in March 2000. Putin once described Babitskii's reporting from the Chechen side of the front as 'more dangerous than firing from machine guns'.[20] Though it is hardly surprising that the federal authorities would try to limit separatists' access to the media, journalists could get into trouble without transmitting the views of Chechen leaders. Military commanders threatened to revoke several journalists' accreditation and kicked two ORT correspondents out of a press pool because of unauthorised filming in August 2000.[21] Officers detained *Novaya gazeta* correspondent Anna Politkovskaya in February 2001 while she was trying to cover the war's impact on the civilian population.[22] They accused her of using falsified accreditation documents and expelled her from Chechnya. In the summer of 2001, more disturbing reports emerged of reprisals against civilians whom Politkovskaya had quoted in her dispatches regarding alleged atrocities committed by Russian troops.[23]

Controlling the flow of information

Chechnya coverage was the most obvious area in which Putin's media policy affected the content of news reports, but the president's ambitions to keep certain information out of the public domain went much further. Public Opinion Foundation president Aleksandr Oslon, who assisted Putin's presidential campaign and continued to work for the Kremlin afterwards, explained the thinking behind the strategy in late 2001: 'If the subject exists in the mass media, it exists in public opinion. If it doesn't, it doesn't exist in public opinion.'[24] A national security doctrine that Putin enacted shortly after becoming acting president outlined many security threats related to Russia's information sphere.[25] That document was the precursor to a more comprehensive Information Security Doctrine, which Russia's Security Council approved in June 2000 and Putin signed in September 2000.[26]

As Andrei Richter has observed, the main purpose of the Information Security Doctrine was to establish a legal basis for increasing governmental control over the flow of information.[27] Whereas the Russian constitution (Article 29, part four) guarantees the right to 'seek, receive, transmit, produce and distribute information by all legal means', the Information Security Doctrine calls for balancing the individual's right of access to information against the interests of society and the state, which include 'maintaining accord in society' and ensuring 'political, economic and social stability'.

The doctrine emphasises the destabilising potential of 'irresponsible' news reporting, which might discredit the government, delegitimise the state or exacerbate divisions in society. In order to counteract 'abuses' of freedom of information, the doctrine advocates legal acts to prohibit media 'distortion' and the 'deliberate circulation of false information'.

The spin control during the *Kursk* nuclear submarine disaster in August 2000 hinted at how Kremlin officials would apply the principles of the Information Security Doctrine. State-owned RTR was the only television network allowed near the site and in the room when Putin met with grieving relatives of the sailors. During that meeting, the chairman of RTR edited the feed to remove embarrassing moments for the president.[28] The RTR programme 'Press Klub', which had aired live since its inception in the early 1990s, was taped after the *Kursk* sank, so that comments by participating journalists or politicians could be edited out before the broadcast.[29]

Soon after signing the Information Security Doctrine, Putin expanded the list of federal officials who were allowed to classify information, adding the heads of several ministries dealing with economic policies.[30] The presidential administration created a 'rapid reaction force' to combat 'information threats' by way of discrediting investigative reports and prominent journalists.[31] Meanwhile, the Media Ministry prepared amendments to Russia's 1992 law on the mass media in order to bring it in line with the doctrine. For instance, in 2001 the parliament approved, and Putin signed, a law prohibiting foreigners, foreign companies and individuals with dual citizenship from owning 50 per cent or more of nationwide television companies (defined as those that broadcast to more than half the country).

The Information Security Doctrine also calls for steps to 'strengthen state mass information media and expand their possibilities for bringing reliable information to Russian and foreign citizens in a timely manner.' Influential presidential adviser Gleb Pavlovskii believed that media trends during the 1990s had deprived the government of 'its legitimate tools for spreading information'.[32] He launched the strana.ru website in September 2000 to help the authorities 'bring the [official] position and the motivation of their actions to the principal groups in society'.[33]

Meanwhile, Putin expanded federal officials' leverage over the regional and local media. Throughout Yeltsin's presidency leaders of republics, oblasts and krais tended to dominate the political and economic landscape of the media sectors in their respective regions. During the 1999 parliamentary campaign, many regional leaders used the media under their control to promote the opposition Fatherland–All Russia (FAR) alliance. Soon after signing the Information Security Doctrine, Putin granted his representatives in Russia's seven federal districts the authority to appoint the chief executives of regional state-owned radio and television companies.[34] While still acting president Putin signed a law enabling the Media Ministry – not regional political bosses – to control the allocation of federal subsidies to local print media.[35] A television and radio broadcasting system created by presidential decree in August 2001 strengthened state broadcast media financially and appeared likely to increase the state's leverage over private broadcasters.[36]

As noted above, the Information Security Doctrine calls for balancing the interests of individuals, society and the state. However, since signing that document Putin has shown little interest in helping individuals better exercise their constitutional right to gather and distribute information. Throughout the post-Soviet period the absence of a law on access to information has made it hard for Russian journalists to assert their legal right to obtain information from official sources. More than two years into Putin's presidency, Russia still lacks a law outlining mandatory procedures for releasing information upon request, and the presidential administration has not proposed any such legislation. Nor has Putin embraced a European model for public-service broadcasting, which would make nationwide television more representative of Russian society as a whole. On the contrary, Putin has strengthened the Kremlin's influence over news content on state television and has intimidated other networks that once provided viewers with alternative perspectives on the news, as the next section shows.

Preventing media 'aggression'

Having benefited from an 'information war' against his political rivals in late 1999, the new Russian president moved quickly to inoculate himself against a similar media campaign. That required taming major television networks, the public's main source of news.[37]

TV-Centre had supported the opposition FAR alliance in the autumn of 1999. Shortly before the presidential election the Media Ministry scheduled an auction for TV-Centre's broadcast licence in May 2000, when it was due to expire. Russian commentators smelled politics: Media Ministry warnings used to justify the decision not to extend TV-Centre's licence related to minor infractions, and Media Minister Lesin refused to cancel the auction even after the Moscow Arbitration Court struck down those warnings. TV-Centre managed to retain its licence following backroom negotiations between Lesin and Moscow Mayor Yurii Luzhkov, the network's chief political patron.[38] The sharp attacks on Kremlin officials that typified TV-Centre's coverage in the second half of 1999 did not return.

When Lesin and his subordinates invoked the danger posed by media 'aggression',[39] they were not primarily alluding to TV-Centre, which had low ratings and a relatively limited broadcast reach. NTV, part of Vladimir Gusinskii's Media-Most empire, posed a far greater threat. Not only did NTV have the third-largest broadcast reach in Russia (some 70 per cent of the population could watch the network), its news and analysis programmes were second only to ORT's in the ratings.

NTV had little to fear from Lesin's licensing commission, because its broadcast licence was valid until 2002. However, Media-Most had taken out massive dollar-denominated loans before the 1998 ruble crash, and the ensuing economic crisis crushed the advertising market on which NTV and related media properties depended. In addition, like all Russian 'oligarchs' in the 1990s, Gusinskii had prospered through complicated business deals that might not withstand close scrutiny from law enforcement authorities. Those factors made NTV and its parent company vulnerable to a sustained pressure campaign from creditors and the Procurator-General's Office.

Media-Most's troubles began in the summer of 1999 when state-controlled Vneshekonombank declined to extend the terms of a $42 million loan. After losing a court battle, Media-Most managed to cover that debt in early 2000 by selling small stakes in NTV and the cable network TNT. However, the partly state-owned gas monopoly Gazprom, a shareholder in NTV since 1996, soon added to Gusinskii's troubles. Shortly after meeting with Putin in February 2000, Gazprom's chief executive said NTV's Chechnya coverage 'gives the Gazprom leadership serious cause to think about how we are investing our funds'.[40] The following month, Gazprom demanded reimbursement for a $211 million loan it had guaranteed on behalf of Media-Most in 1998.

As Gusinskii struggled to cover his company's debts, police raided Media-Most's headquarters four days after Putin's inauguration in May 2000. During the year to come, investigators from various law enforcement agencies conducted more than two dozen searches of Media-Most and affiliated firms in connection with 'vague and ever-changing criminal charges'.[41] Gusinskii himself was arrested in June 2000 on embezzlement charges, but the Procurator-General's Office dropped all charges the next month after Gusinskii quietly agreed to sell a controlling stake in Media-Most to Gazprom. Two months later, it emerged that Lesin had signed a secret 'protocol number 6' to the July agreement between Media-Most and Gazprom, promising that criminal cases against Gusinskii and his associates would be closed if Gusinskii sold Media-Most.[42]

Gusinskii (by now living in self-imposed exile) renounced the deal after the terms of 'protocol number 6' became public. Media-Most then faced a confusing array of criminal charges and lawsuits. The criminal investigations contributed to an atmosphere of fear and intimidation,[43] but it was Media-Most's financial trouble that sealed NTV's fate. When Gusinskii refused to follow through on the sale of a controlling stake in Media-Most, Gazprom stepped up its efforts to secure repayment of its loans. Since Gusinskii's company lacked sufficient cash, the gas monopoly's subsidiary, Gazprom-Media, eventually was able to claim a majority stake in NTV as compensation for Media-Most's debts.[44] Gazprom-Media executives immediately replaced NTV's management, and with the help of armed guards, those managers gained control of NTV's headquarters in April 2001, following ten days of protests by the network's journalists.

Gazprom soon gained sway over the publishing arm of Media-Most, which in April 2001 ceased publication of the daily newspaper *Segodnya* and replaced the staff of the weekly magazine *Itogi*.[45] Thanks to Media-Most's unpaid debts, Gazprom-Media also gained control over the Ekho Moskvy radio station and TNT. (That cable network, which had 260 partner stations broadcasting in more than 500 Russian cities and towns, had picked up many of NTV's popular politically oriented programs after Gazprom replaced NTV's management.)

The final blow to Media-Most came from a civil suit that had attracted little attention when the Moscow Tax Inspectorate filed it in December 2000. Citing an obscure point in the Civil Code allowing a company to be liquidated if, at the end of the second or any later year of operation, its debts exceeded the minimum capital required by law, the Moscow Arbitration Court resolved that lawsuit in May 2001 by ordering Media-Most's liquidation.[46] Although Gusinskii later financed small internet publications produced by former staff of *Itogi* and *Segodnya*,[47] he had lost his once-formidable media empire.

Gazprom executives repeatedly denied that any political agenda lay behind their attempts to assert the company's rights as a creditor and shareholder.[48] But Gazprom's relaxed approach to other firms that owed it hundreds of millions of dollars contrasted sharply with its relentless pursuit of compensation from Media-Most.[49] Some of the court rulings that helped Gazprom gain a controlling stake in NTV suggested that judges faced political pressure behind the scenes.[50]

As for Putin, he characterised Media-Most's struggle with Gazprom as a simple business dispute[51] and told NTV staff seeking his help that '[t]here is nothing I can do'.[52] But Gazprom began to put pressure on NTV and Media-Most only after Putin met with the gas monopoly's chief executive in February 2000.[53] Even more telling, the president and his chief of staff, Aleksandr Voloshin, intervened to prevent Gusinskii from selling his Most Bank to a subsidiary of the Central Bank in May 2000.[54] (That deal was to have raised cash to cover Media-Most's debts.) While Media-Most's financial troubles mounted, state-controlled Vneshekonombank repeatedly extended the terms of a $100 million loan to the Channel 1 broadcaster ORT.[55]

In addition, the on-again, off-again criminal investigations surrounding Media-Most attested to the selective application of the law. Putin resisted calls to sack Lesin and Procurator-General Vladimir Ustinov, despite the clear abuse of power involved in 'protocol number six'. Prosecutors did not investigate Lesin or former managers of the state-owned network RTR, despite a secret Audit Chamber report which uncovered evidence of massive financial abuses at that politically loyal network.[56]

TV-Centre and Media-Most executives might have expected trouble from Putin's administration, having supported FAR in 1999. But steps taken to dismantle Boris Berezovsky's media empire demonstrate that Putin's media policy had less to do with revenge than with depriving anyone of the capacity to use influential media against him.

Berezovsky was one of Putin's most valuable allies during his rise to power, both financially and as unofficial boss of ORT, the network with the largest broadcast reach and highest ratings. But following Putin's inauguration, the Procurator-General's Office soon revived criminal investigations into companies linked to Berezovsky. After ORT commentators criticised Putin's handling of the crisis surrounding the sinking of the *Kursk* nuclear submarine in August 2000, pressure mounted for Berezovsky to give up control over a 49 per cent stake in ORT.[57] The next month, the network's general director fired the two Berezovsky allies in charge of ORT's news department and cancelled Sergei Dorenko's popular weekly analytical programme. Informally known as 'Berezovsky's bull terrier', Dorenko had helped destroy the reputations of Putin's rivals during the autumn of 1999 but had begun to criticise Putin in the summer of 2000.

Berezovsky finally agreed to sell his ORT shares when Russian police arrested his long-time business partner Nikolai Glushkov on embezzlement charges in December 2000. Though ORT remained a partly private company (the businessman Roman Abramovich bought Berezovsky's shares), its news and analytical programmes remained loyal to the Kremlin. In effect, the network fell fully under state control.

However, Berezovsky remained the dominant shareholder in TV-6, Russia's fourth-largest television network in terms of broadcast reach. In April 2001 he offered jobs to prominent journalists displaced by Gazprom's takeover of NTV. Unlike Gusinskii's Media-Most, TV-6 did not owe huge debts to state-controlled banks or parastatal entities. But a pension fund affiliated with the partly state-owned oil company LUKoil owned a 15 per cent stake in TV-6. Almost immediately after Berezovsky brought in the NTV refugees, the LUKoil-Garant pension fund filed two lawsuits seeking to nullify the TV-6 shareholders' meetings which approved those hirings. The Moscow Arbitration Court rejected those petitions in June 2001.

Having failed to get rid of the new TV-6 managers, LUKoil-Garant pursued a third court case, similar to the Moscow Tax Inspectorate's successful lawsuit to liquidate Media-Most. Russia's law on joint-stock companies allowed a minority shareholder to seek a company's liquidation if, at the end of the second or any later year of operation, its debts exceeded the minimum capital required by law. After a series of court rulings that went all the way to the Supreme Arbitration Court in January 2002, TV-6 was ordered to be liquidated under the provisions of the law on joint stock companies. The Media Ministry soon cancelled the network's broadcast licence and scheduled an auction for the frequency. In the meantime, the satellite sports network NTV-Plus received temporary rights to broadcast on Channel 6 for free.

As during the struggle for control over NTV, state officials argued that political considerations played no role in a commercial dispute settled within a legal framework. Few observers shared that view. Having tolerated losses at TV-6 throughout the 1990s, LUKoil-Garant filed suit to shut down the network just as its finances were improving. (TV-6's ratings rose substantially, especially in Moscow, after the network picked up many NTV programmes.) LUKoil declined Berezovsky's offer to pay $10 million for LUKoil-Garant's 15 per cent stake in TV-6.[58] At one point, LUKoil's chief executive, Vagit Alekperov, expressed interest in buying Berezovsky's controlling stake in the network,[59] and later suggested that he would like to trade LUKoil-Garant's stake in TV-6 for some of Berezovsky's assets in the Russian oil sector.[60] Yet LUKoil-Garant pressed ahead with a lawsuit that, if successful, would make shares in TV-6 worthless.

In addition, some legal experts questioned the courts' interpretation of the law and the unusual speed with which the Supreme Arbitration Court took the case and issued its ruling on TV-6. Even then, there was no legal basis for the Media Ministry's withdrawal of TV-6's licence or the decision to let NTV-Plus use the frequency, since Russia lacked a law on radio and television broadcasting.

Different techniques were used to alter editorial policy at Russia's leading television networks, but the campaigns had one thing in common: the selective application of the law against networks considered unreliable. Virtually every media company in Russia could have been liquidated during the 1990s under the obscure point of law that doomed Media-Most and TV-6, but only those companies faced such court cases, and only after Putin came to power. Virtually all of Russia's most prominent businessmen could have faced criminal investigation, but cases were pursued only against those whose media outlets were critical of the Kremlin: Gusinskii and Berezovsky.

State bodies' selective application of the law was not restricted to television networks. Tax inspectors frequently visited the editorial offices of the biweekly *Novaya gazeta*, which was sharply critical of the military campaign in Chechnya and other policies implemented by Putin. Officials in the presidential administration covertly warned some companies that they would face tax inspections if they continued to place advertisements in the newspaper.[61] (*Novaya gazeta* did not belong to any major corporate group and earned the bulk of its revenues through advertising.) In February 2002, a district court in Moscow fined *Novaya gazeta* a total of $1.5 million in connection with two libel lawsuits. The sum total of fines and damages awarded in 54 previous libel and defamation lawsuits in Russia had been just $50,000.[62]

The application of licensing rules by government ministries also raised questions about double standards. As mentioned earlier in this chapter, the

Media Ministry forced TV-Centre to fight to retain its broadcast licence. Following Gazprom's takeover of the outlets in the Media-Most group, journalists from Ekho Moskvy radio launched plans for a new talk radio station. They raised funds for the Radio Arsenal project and in February 2002 won a competition for a licence to use an FM frequency. But a licence from the Communications Ministry to use broadcasting equipment – which normally would have been issued within days[63] – was not forthcoming for months, leaving the station in limbo.[64] Radio Arsenal finally went on the air in October 2002.

Explaining Putin's success

'Information wars' during the second half of the 1990s created the impression that media owners and financiers, not government officials, controlled the news agenda. But early in Putin's presidency it became clear that the ground had shifted. Media Minister Lesin topped a list of 'enemies of the Russian press' released by the Union of Journalists in July 2000, followed by Procurator-General Ustinov and Putin himself.[65] Political bosses in the regions had repressed the media in their domains during Yeltsin's tenure, but only under Putin did federal officials come to be seen as leading antagonists of press freedom. Just a year after Putin's inauguration, the Union of Journalists warned that '[a]ttacks on freedom of speech in Russia are becoming more and more persistent and refined'.[66] Putin appeared on the US-based Committee to Protect Journalists' list of ten enemies of a free press, and Russia was among thirty countries criticised in a similar report by the European organisation, Reporters Without Borders. The media law expert Andrei Richter noted that the 'government now plays a greater role in running media affairs'.[67] Yassen Zassoursky, dean of Moscow State University's Journalism Faculty, argued that a new 'federal state-controlled media model' was replacing the 'combined free press-corporate media model' that (in his view) best described the sector during the late 1990s.[68]

Corporate shareholders and creditors such as Gazprom and LUKoil assisted Putin's campaign against the media. Criminal investigations compelled Gusinskii and Berezovsky, the leading media moguls of the Yeltsin era, to leave Russia during Putin's first year as president. No media owner or sponsor could feel sure that he would not be next. In the summer of 2000, law enforcement agencies opened criminal cases affecting companies and top personnel in nearly all of Russia's major corporate groups. (For instance, LUKoil's chief executive was investigated, though never charged, with tax evasion.) The 'oligarchs' learned that using media assets to promote one's business interests was acceptable, as long as news coverage did not cross the limits of political correctness.[69]

Many journalists learned lessons as well. Consider the behaviour of Yevgenii Kiselev, NTV's star commentator, who rose to the position of general director. During the final days of Media-Most's showdown with Gazprom in April 2001, defiant protests against Gazprom dominated NTV newscasts. After losing that battle, Kiselev quickly became general director of TV-6, and that network's staff adopted a far more cautious editorial policy under pressure in late 2001.[70] Once the Supreme Arbitration Court had approved TV-6's liquidation, Kiselev teamed up with 'oligarchs' and political heavyweights who were on good terms with the Kremlin.[71] The gambit paid off when his consortium won the March 2002 tender for the use of the Channel 6 frequency. During a radio appearance the following day, Kiselev's new political patron Yevgenii Primakov expressed the hope that Channel 6 would impose 'internal censorship'. When an interviewer suggested that self-censorship was 'dangerous', Primakov objected that 'on the contrary, [self-censorship] is a guarantee against danger'.[72]

Few journalists publicly embraced the phenomenon as did Primakov, but self-censorship became widespread during Putin's tenure.[73] Treatment of the president himself was particularly gentle. The deputy editor of one Moscow-based newspaper that had not been afraid to oppose Yeltsin explained his newspaper's guiding principle in 2001: 'Write what you want – just don't criticise Putin or what he is doing.'[74] Some of Putin's political opponents, such as Yabloko leader Grigorii Yavlinskii, found it more difficult to gain exposure on television or in large-circulation newspapers. Though state officials did not impose direct control over television, numerous media commentators and watchdogs noted that alternative views received less exposure on the air.[75] Vsevolod Vilchek, a sociologist who worked at both ORT and NTV during the 1990s, commented in the autumn of 2002 that 'Censorship has appeared on television, and what's more its most effective form: the censorship of subconscious fear.'[76]

What altered the landscape so dramatically? Putin's political priorities were different from those of Yeltsin, who 'never used his powers to punish the media outlets that attacked or ridiculed him personally'.[77] Regarding corporate-backed media, Kremlin advisor Pavlovskii characterised Yeltsin's attitude as follows: 'Do the media owners support [the president] politically? Wonderful – let them do whatever they want with the television networks.'[78] In fact, at several junctures during Yeltsin's second term, government officials such as Anatolii Chubais and Yevgenii Primakov tried to use the levers of power against corporate-backed media, only to be undercut by the president.

That is not to say that Yeltsin was indifferent to media coverage. He occasionally used his decree power to intervene in the media sector and pulled out all the stops to secure the media's backing during his 1996 re-election campaign. An unnamed official source told one Russian newspaper during the summer of 1999: 'We don't care at all what is shown on television or written in newspapers, but the authorities must have a 100-per cent guarantee that at any moment when it becomes necessary, information will be provided [by the media] as the authorities wish.'[79] In other words, Yeltsin became concerned about news coverage mainly when he faced an imminent political threat.

Putin was far less tolerant of media criticism, despite his consistently high approval ratings during his first two years as president. Having had little political experience before gaining the highest office in the land, he lacked the 'thick skin that every public politician should develop,' according to an image-maker who worked on his 2000 presidential campaign.[80] Some of Yeltsin's advisors had good contacts with journalists and editors, but Putin did not surround himself with people inclined to argue against suppressing the media.

Not only did Putin have the political will to act against the media, he faced virtually no institutional opposition to that agenda. Unlike Yeltsin, he could count on a majority in both houses of parliament to support many official policies, including bills to bring Russian media law in line with the Information Security Doctrine. The State Duma deputies who objected to the pressure campaign against NTV lacked the votes to put discussions of that controversy on the chamber's agenda. Challenging restrictions on journalists' rights in the Judicial Chamber on Information Disputes ceased to be an option when Putin disbanded that quasi-judicial body in June 2000.[81]

Putin framed his media policies as a campaign against crooks who were weakening the Russian state. In his televised address to the parliament in July 2000, Putin endorsed the idea of 'genuinely free media' but accused media owners and sponsors of turning their investments into 'vehicles of mass disinformation and vehicles for battling the state'.[82] Stung by unfavourable news coverage of the *Kursk* disaster, Putin repeatedly sought to shift the blame to the financial backers of media outlets who, he charged, used 'unscrupulous' means to turn the tragedy to their advantage.[83] That kind of rhetoric seemed to strike a chord with the Russian population. Various surveys in 2000 and 2001 showed that while a majority of respondents supported press freedom as an abstract value,[84] only a minority considered press freedom to be at the heart of the battles surrounding NTV and TV-6.[85]

Even within the journalistic community, there was little collective resistance to Putin's media policies. The blatant exploitation of private media by corporate sponsors during the late 1990s made co-operating with state officials more socially acceptable among journalists who had once prided themselves on their 'independent' stance. NTV's founding news director and long-time general director, Oleg Dobrodeev, was so admired that most observers interpreted his departure from NTV in January 2000 as a sign that Gusinskii planned to lower that network's professional standards.[86] Instead, Dobrodeev presided over a loyal editorial policy at state-owned RTR, which he defended on the grounds that 'at this stage, the interests of society and the president coincide'.[87] Having once expressed contempt for officials who spurned 'information' in favour of an 'instrument of instantaneous influence',[88] Dobrodeev himself censored footage of Putin's meeting with relatives of the *Kursk* sailors in August 2000. Several prominent NTV journalists followed Dobrodeev to RTR, including Yelena Masyuk, who stood up to official pressure during the first war in Chechnya even when faced with a criminal investigation. NTV's news director left in October 2000 to take the top job at the state-owned news agency RIA-Novosti.

Putin's administration sought to exploit the divisions in the journalistic community. In late 2000 Kremlin officials recruited several big names to found a Media-Union. Its leaders pledged to protect journalists from the 'arbitrary' decisions of employers and media owners,[89] but the organisation's primary goal was to undermine the Union of Journalists.[90] (That union had become increasingly vocal in its condemnation of official media policies during Putin's presidency.[91]) While the well-financed Media-Union assembled a regional network, the government's Property Ministry challenged the Union of Journalists' right to collect rent for office space in a federally owned Moscow building that it had used for many years, in accordance with a Yeltsin decree.[92] As of October 2002, it appeared likely that the Union of Journalists would lose that battle and thus its primary source of income.[93]

Although the government is at odds with Russia's Union of Journalists, the satisfied comments of state officials indirectly confirm that union's warnings about declining press freedom and journalists' growing reluctance to challenge the authorities. Media Minister Lesin, who complained in 1999 that the media 'have more powers and opportunities than the state,'[94] noted approvingly in May 2001 that NTV's story had reduced the 'politicking of the mass media' and made media outlets 'reassess their own positions on many questions, above all, those regarding their economic and financial independence'.[95] Presidential advisor Yastrzhembskii alluded to the media's greater deference when he commented in October 2002 that relations between the authorities and the media had become more 'civilised' in the previous two to three years. Russia had ended its 'orgy of free speech'.[96] Though it may be too early to judge some aspects of Putin's presidency, the verdict is in when it comes to the media.

Notes

1 On how sympathetic media coverage helped transform Putin from a little-known Yeltsin appointee to the front-runner for the presidency in the space of a few months, see A. Kachkaeva, 'Image factory: television as the key instrument for creation of political myths', published in January 2000 at www.internews.ru/crisis/imagefactory.html; A. Raskin, 'Television: medium to elect the President', in K. Nordenstreng, E. Vartanova and Y. Zassoursky, *Russian Media Challenge*

(Helsinki: Kikimora Publications, 2001); L. Belin, 'State TV wages unprecedented "information war"', *RFE/RL Russian Election Report* (17 December 1999); and L. Belin, 'How state TV aided Putin's campaign', *RFE/RL Russian Election Report* (7 April 2000).

2. See N. Abdulaev, 'Moscow tightly controls information on the Chechen conflict', *Jamestown Foundation Prism*, 20:1 (December 1999); Zolotov A., 'Journalists bemoan Chechen coverage', *Moscow Times* (28 October 1999).

3. On the Russian Information Centre, see O. Panfilov, 'Ot VITsa k RITsu', *Sreda*, 11 (December 1999) available at www.cjes.ru/public/panfilov1.shtml; D. Filipov, 'Moscow launches video offensive seeking support for Chechnya war', *Boston Globe*, 17 October 1999; M. R. Gordon, 'Russia copies NATO in war to win minds', *New York Times* (28 November 1999).

4. T. de Waal, 'Introduction', in A. Politkovskaya, *A Dirty War: A Russian Reporter in Chechnya* (London: Harvill Press, 2001), p. xxvi.

5. See O. Koltsova, 'Change in the coverage of the Chechen wars: reasons and consequences', *Javnost/The Public*, 7:4 (2000), 39–54; A. Zolotov Jr., 'Kremlin scores strategic victory in Chechnya – over the media', *Institute for War & Peace Reporting Caucasus Reporting Service*, 5 (9 November 1999). Distributed on the fsumedia email list.

6. See O. Panfilov's interview in *Russkaya mysl'* (8–14 June 2000).

7. While posing as a Chechen, French journalist Anne Nivat witnessed a Russian officer making one such appeal to a crowd; see A. Nivat, *Chienne de Guerre: A Woman Reporter Behind the Lines of the War in Chechnya* (New York: Public Affairs, 2001), p. 120.

8. Comparisons can be found in Semen Liberman, 'Vtoraya Chechenskaya – akt sleduyushchii', *Sreda* (December 1999), 13–16, also available at www.internews.ru/sreda/17/5.html.

9. Lev Lurie, 'The Russian media turns', *Institute for War & Peace Reporting Caucasus Reporting Service*, 14 (January 2000) available at www.soros.org/caucasus/0005.html.

10. See G. P. Herd, 'The "counter-terrorist operation" in Chechnya: "information warfare" aspects', *Journal of Slavic Military Studies*, 13:4 (December 2000), 57–83.

11. E. Kandybina, 'Publikatsii o chechenskoi voine v rossiiskoi presse: vzglyad yurista', prepared for the website 'Conflict in Chechnya: Prague Watchdog' and republished on the website of the Centre for Journalism in Extreme Situations: www.cjes.ru/public/kandyb5.shtml.

12. J. Tracy, 'Kremlin tells press to toe the line', *Moscow Times*, 25 January 2000. On the military's power to keep journalists away from the front line, see also 'Media coverage of the Chechen war: then and now', excerpt from the weekly programme *Chetvertaya Vlast'* on REN-TV, 22 January 2000, as translated and published at www.internews.ru/crisis/mediacoverage.html.

13. Comprehensive coverage of Babitskii's detention and subsequent trial on the charge of using false documents can be found at www.rferl.org/nca/special/babitsky.

14. The special issue of *Obshchaya gazeta* came out on 16 February 2000.

15. During the first war, *Nezavisimaya gazeta* had published the Glasnost Defence Foundation's monthly reports listing violations of journalists' rights in Chechnya.

16 F. Fossato, 'Russia: officials ban interviews with Chechen leaders', feature for *RFE/RL* (16 March 2000) available at www.rferl.org/nca/features/2000/03/f.ru.000316153911.html.
17 Coverage of Chechnya in the regional media tended to focus on local angles, such as how home-town boys were doing at the front; see S. Karush, 'Chechen war hits home in provinces', *Moscow Times* (7 December 1999), and F. Fossato, 'Russia: press ban doesn't bother regional media', feature for *Radio Free Europe/Radio Liberty* (21 March 2000), available at www.rferl.org/nca/features/2000/03/f.ru.000321141934.html.
18 See F. Fossato, 'Russia: prosecutors probe Maskhadov's interviews', feature for *RFE/RL* (8 May 2000), available at www.rferl.org/nca/features/2000/05/f.ru.000508140938.html.
19 See an excellent commentary produced by the Moscow Media Law and Policy Institute, published in the March 2001 issue of *Zakonodatelstvo i praktika Mass-Media* (www.medialaw.ru/publications/zip/79/ch1.htm); Kandybina, 'Publikatsii o chechenskoi voine v rossiiskoi presse'; Fossato, 'Russia: Officials Ban Interviews With Chechen Leaders', citing Mikhail Fedotov, an author of the 1992 media law.
20 As quoted in a lengthy interview published in *Kommersant*, 10 March 2000.
21 *Kommersant*, 1 September 2000.
22 For more about the Politkovskaya case, see the Committee to Protect Journalists' annual report on 'Attacks on the Press 2001', available at www.cpj.org/attacks01/europe01/russia.html.
23 See E. Borisova, 'Reporter: military killed my sources', *Moscow Times* (4 July 2001).
24 Quoted in A. Nagorski, 'Who is Vladimir Putin?', *Newsweek Poland* (20 December 2001), distributed on *Johnson's Russia List*, 5613 (23 December 2001).
25 See O. Panfilov, 'Putin and the media – no love lost', *East European Constitutional Review*, 9:1–2 (winter/spring 2000), 60–64.
26 The full text of the Information Security Doctrine appeared in *Rossiiskaya gazeta* (28 September 2000). English translations can be found in Nordenstreng, Vartanova and Zassoursky, *Russian Media Challenge*, pp. 251–292, and M. E. Price, A. Richter and P. K. Yu, *Russian Media Law and Policy in the Yeltsin Decade* (The Hague: Kluwer Law International, 2002), pp. 492–525.
27 A. Richter, 'Media regulation: foundation laid for free speech', in Nordenstreng, Vartanova and Zassoursky, *Russian Media Challenge*, p. 125.
28 Uzelac, A., 'The *Kursk* media legacy', *Moscow Times* (2 September 2000).
29 E. Albats, 'Cry for Russia's lost press liberty', *Guardian* (11 May 2001). She noted that 'Press Klub' retained production elements likely to give viewers the misleading impression that they were watching a live broadcast.
30 *RFE/RL Security Watch* (2 October 2000).
31 *Segodnya* (22 September 2000).
32 From Pavlovskii's commentary posted to the pro-Kremlin website www.strana.ru on 28 September 2000.
33 According to an official statement on the day strana.ru was launched, quoted in 'V strane nachinaetsya novyi vek novostei', www.infonet.nnov.ru/nnews/arch/mess.phtml?mess_id=35534.
34 *Nezavisimaya gazeta* (29 September 2000), and *Kommersant* (29 September 2000).

35 See *Izvestiya* (13 January 2000), and *Rossiyskaya gazeta* (13 January 2000).
36 See Zolotov A., 'President approves VGTRK overhaul', *Moscow Times* (14 August 2001); Glasnost Defence Foundation weekly digest, 20 August 2001, available at www.gdf.ru; L. Belin, 'Putin centralises management of TV and radio towers', *RFE/RL Russian Political Weekly* (12 September 2001).
37 On how nationwide television networks are the Russian public's main source of news, see E. Vartanova, 'Media structures: changed and unchanged', in Nordenstreng, Vartanova and Zassoursky, *Russian Media Challenge*, pp. 25, 49; T. J. Colton and M. McFaul, 'Are Russians undemocratic?', Working Paper (Washington: Carnegie Endowment for International Peace, 2001).
38 See Fossato and Kachkaeva, 'Russian media empires VI'; F. Fossato, 'Luzhkov's TV station back in favor', feature for *Radio Free Europe/Radio Liberty* (7 July 2000), www.rferl.org/nca/features/2000/07/f.ru.000707152617.html.
39 According to a World Press Freedom Committee press release of 14 July 2000, quoted in *RFE/RL (Un)Civil Societies* (20 July 2000).
40 *RFE/RL Newsline* (16 February 2000).
41 Bernstein, J., 'Why they're praying for Russia's NTV', *Wall Street Journal Europe* (6 April 2001).
42 Excerpts from 'protocol number 6' appeared in *Izvestiya* (19 September 2000).
43 In April 2001 a panel of Spanish judges refused to extradite Gusinskii to Russia to face charges of obtaining fraudulent loans. Media-Most chief financial officer Anton Titov, arrested in Moscow in connection with the same criminal case in January 2001, remains in pretrial detention as of October 2002.
44 The complicated negotiations and legal manoeuvrings between Gazprom and Media-Most in late 2000 and early 2001 are covered in more detail in L. Belin, 'The rise and fall of Russia's NTV', *Stanford Journal of International Law*, 38:1 (spring 2002), 19–42.
45 M. Lipman, 'Putin will get away with it', *Newsweek* (30 April 2001); M. Lipman, 'Russia's free press withers away', *New York Review of Books* (31 May 2001).
46 See *Kommersant* (30 May 2001).
47 *Yezhenedel'nyi zhurnal* published a pilot issue in November 2001 and began regular publication in early 2002; the business weekly *Delovaya khronika* published its first issue in January 2002.
48 See R. Vyakhirev's open letter to shareholders of Media-Most and NTV in *Tribuna* (9 February 2001), and A. Kokh's interview in *Moskovskii komsomolets* (1 February 2001).
49 On Gazprom's 'disparate treatment of its debtors', see P. Baker, 'Gazprom divulges finances: Russian gas monopoly's books tell tale of insider dealing', *Washington Post* (15 June 2001).
50 G. Chermenskaya, 'After the battle', *Jamestown Foundation Prism*, 7:5 (May 2001).
51 See *RFE/RL Newsline* (27 September 2000), and *RFE/RL Newsline* (10 April 2001).
52 On Putin's January 2001 meeting with NTV staff, see D. E. Hoffman, *The Oligarchs: Wealth and Power in the New Russia* (New York: Public Affairs, 2002), p. 484; *Jamestown Foundation Monitor* (30 January 200).
53 According to Moscow's rumour mill, Putin threatened Rem Vyakhirev during that meeting; see *Novye izvestiya* (4 April 2001), and Vladimir Gusinskii's interview in *Kommersant* (6 February 2001). Al'fred Kokh, the head of Gazprom-Media, indirectly acknowledged the official pressure on Gazprom when he argued that

under Putin 'the rules changed' for Gazprom as well as for Media-Most; see Kokh's interview in *Komsomol'skaya pravda* (14 April 2001).
54 Hoffman, D., 'Putin's Actions Belie Promise on Tycoons: "Strange Decisions" Reveal Favouritism Despite Vow to Bring Equality', *Washington Post* (7 May 2000); Hoffman, *The Oligarchs*, p. 477.
55 ORT repeatedly missed scheduled payments on that loan; see *Vedomosti* (25 May 2000) and *Vedomosti* (19 September 2002).
56 See *Obshchaya gazeta* (25–31 January 2001); *Obshchaya gazeta* (15–21 February 2001); *The Russia Journal* (17–23 February 2001).
57 Berezovsky claimed Putin's chief of staff threatened him with prison; see his open letter to Putin, published in *Novye izvestiya* (5 September 2000); Hoffman, *The Oligarchs*, pp. 487–488.
58 See Berezovsky's open letter published in *Kommersant* (17 October 2001).
59 *Kommersant* (24 October 2001).
60 See Alekperov's interview in *Nezavisimaya gazeta* (15 November 2001).
61 According to *Novaya gazeta* correspondent Anna Politkovskaya, speaking in London on 2 May 2001 at an event sponsored by Amnesty International, Article 19, and the Freedom Forum.
62 See the Glasnost Defence Foundation's 'Zayavlenie po povodu sudebnogo davleniya na Novuyu gazeta', 21 March 2002, archived at www.gdf.ru/digest/digest/digest081.shtml; A. Pankin, 'Media notes: a vicious circle', *Transitions Online* (22 March 2002); *Moscow Times* (19 March 2002).
63 Russia maintains a double licensing system for radio and television. The programmer needs a licence for the right to broadcast on a given frequency, and the owner of the broadcasting equipment needs a licence for the right to use that frequency for transmissions.
64 *Vremya novostei* (30 April 2002), and the interview with Aleksei Venediktov, one of the organisers of the Radio Arsenal project, in *Gazeta* (19 September 2002).
65 *RFE/RL Newsline* (7 July 2000). Experts consulted by the Union of Journalists and the Centre for Journalism in Extreme Situations compiled the list of enemies.
66 The Ekho Moskvy news agency quoted the union's statement on 3 May 2001 (World Press Freedom Day).
67 Richter, 'Media regulation', in Nordenstreng, Vartanova and Zassoursky, *Russian Media Challenge*, p. 123.
68 Ya. N. Zassoursky, 'Media and the public interest: balancing between the state, business and the public sphere', in Nordenstreng, Vartanova and Zassoursky, *Russian Media Challenge*, pp. 162–163.
69 See the revealing comments of M. Khodorkovskii in F. Fossato, 'Regional television to pioneer new relationship with investor', *RFE/RL Russian Federation Report* (10 October 2001).
70 See Pankin, A., 'Playing devil's advocate', *Moscow Times* (18 December 2001).
71 *RFE/RL Newsline* (7 March 2002, 8 March 2002 and 28 March 2002).
72 Joint appearance by Primakov, Kiselev and Arkadii Volskii on Ekho Moskvy (28 March 2002).
73 On self-censorship, see O. Latsis, '"Internal editor" at work', *The Russia Journal* (3–9 February 2001); M. Aslamazian, 'A year of hard lessons for the media', *Moscow Times* (21 December 2001); F. Mereu, 'Russia: Putin presidency at two-year mark – no favours for free press', feature for *Radio Free Europe/Radio*

Liberty (19 April 2002), available at www.rferl.org/nca/features/2002/04/19042002094007.asp; Chermenskaya, 'After the battle'.

74 Vishnevskii recounts this and several similar anecdotes in 'Prisyatni ili proigraesh'? samotsenzura kak pravilo khoroshego tona', *Obshchaya gazeta* (20–26 September 2001).
75 See Zolotov A., '6 months on, NTV still up in the air', *Moscow Times* (15 October 2001); P. Baker, 'On NTV, Kremlin is in softer focus: seized network not puppet, but tamer', *Washington Post* (27 June 2001).
76 V. Vilchek, 'Problemy okhlovideniya', *Moskovskie novosti* (24 September 2002).
77 According to Richter, 'Media regulation', in Nordenstreng, Vartanova and Zassoursky, *Russian Media Challenge*, p. 153.
78 Pavlovskii's interview in *Krasnaya zvezda* (12 August 2000).
79 As quoted in *Obshchaya gazeta* (15–21 July 1999).
80 Former ORT news director Kseniya Ponomareva was interviewed in *Kommersant* (26 March 2001); this quotation appears as translated in the *Moscow Times* (27 March 2001).
81 The Judicial Chamber on Information Disputes angered then Prime Minister Putin in 1999, when one of its rulings criticised the government for ignoring a human rights magazine's requests for information on Chechnya; see Richter, 'Media regulation', in Nordenstreng, Vartanova and Zassoursky, *Russian Media Challenge*, p. 154.
82 Putin's address was televised on RTR (8 July 2000).
83 For instance, in an interview with Channel 2 Russian Television, 23 August 2000. See also the transcript of Putin's closed meeting with the sailors' grieving *Kursk* relatives, published in *Kommersant-Vlast* (29 August 2000).
84 See the data from various VTsIOM polls posted at www.russiavotes.org/Media_cur.htm#31; also Colton and McFaul, 'Are Russians undemocratic'?
85 See the opinion poll data available at www.russiavotes.org/Media_cur.htm#31; M. Lipman and M. McFaul, '"Managed democracy" in Russia: Putin and the press,' *Harvard International Journal of Press/Politics*, 6:3 (2001), 117–128.
86 Zolotov A., 'NTV chief leaves post without explanation', *Moscow Times* (21 January 2000).
87 As quoted in *RFE/RL Newsline* (14 July 2000).
88 Dobrodeev's harsh words about those who tried to censor state television in the late 1980s and early 1990s can be found in E. Mickiewicz, *Changing Channels: Television and the Struggle for Power in Russia* (Oxford: Oxford University Press, 1997), pp. 39, 124–125.
89 Aleksandr Lyubimov, host of an ORT interview programme and head of the VID production company, described the organisation's goals in an interview with *Rossiyskaya gazeta* (5 December 2000). For other views on the Media-Union, see A. Pankin, 'Soyuz direktorov', *Vedomosti* (7 December 2000), and a 14 November 2000 commentary by Union of Journalists Secretary Pavel Gutiontov, www.gdf.ru/arh/file005.shtml.
90 On official support for Media-Union, see *Novoe vremya* (24 June 2001), and *Kommersant* (14 June 2001).
91 R. Coalson, 'Managing the messengers', commentary for the Committee to Protect Journalists, available at www.cpj.org/Briefings/2001/Russia_coalson/Russia_coalson.html.

92 See *Kommersant* (27 September 2001), and Union of Journalists Secretary P. Gutiontov's commentary in *Novaya gazeta* (1 October 2001).
93 *Novaya gazeta* (3 October 2002).
94 See *RFE/RL Newsline* (23 July 1999).
95 As quoted by *RIA-Novosti* on 8 May 2001, cited in *RFE/RL Newsline* (11 May 2001).
96 Yastrzhembskii's comments at a seminar in Yekaterinburg were reported by *RIA-Novosti* and www.regions.ru, and distributed on the email bulletin of the Centre for Journalism in Extreme Situations (www.cjes.ru).

IV
Regional politics

9
Putin's federal reforms[1]
Cameron Ross

Introduction

Since the election of Vladimir Putin as president in March 2000, Russia's nascent federal system has suffered a major setback. Putin's primary objectives are to create a unified economic, legal and security space in the federation and to tighten the federal government's controls over the regions. But the president's attempts to reign in the power of the regions and to reassert what he calls the 'power-vertical' have made a mockery of the principles of federalism, and there must now also be serious concerns about his commitment to constitutionalism and democracy. Above all, Putin has shown that he is willing to sacrifice both federalism and democracy in order to maintain the unity and sanctity of the Russian state.

Federalism and federations

Following Watts, it is important to distinguish between: 'federalism', 'federal political systems', and 'federations'. Federalism is a normative concept, an ideology which advocates, 'multi-tiered government combining elements of shared-rule and regional self-rule.[2] Federal political systems, on the other hand, are descriptive terms referring to a broad category of non-unitary states ranging from quasi-federations to confederacies. Federations are one species of the genus 'federal political system' where according to Watt's classic definition:

> 1) neither the federal nor the constituent units of government are constitutionally subordinate to the other, i.e., each has sovereign powers derived from the constitution rather than another level of government; 2) each is empowered to deal directly with its citizens in the exercise of legislative, executive and taxing powers; and 3) each is directly elected by its citizens.[3]

Structural prerequisites for federations

How can we test if a country is a federation or not? In light of the above discussion, scholars of federalism[4] have put forward the following *structural prerequisites* which states must meet before they can be classified as federations: (1) the existence of at least two tiers of government, both tiers of which have a formal constitutional distribution of legislative, executive and judicial powers and fiscal autonomy; (2) some form of voluntary covenant or contract among the components – normally a written constitution (not unilaterally amendable and requiring for amendment the consent of a significant proportion of the constituent units); (3) mechanisms to channel the participation of the federated units in decision-making processes at the federal level. This usually involves the creation of a bicameral legislature in which one chamber represents the people at large and the other the component units of the federation; (4) some kind of institutional arbiter, or umpire, usually a Supreme Court or a Constitutional Court to settle disputes between the different levels of government; (5) mechanisms to facilitate intergovernmental collaboration in those areas where governmental powers are shared or inevitably overlap.[5]

Structure, process and culture

Another important distinction to be made is that between 'structure' and 'process'. As Elazar stresses, 'the structure of federalism is meaningful only in polities whose processes of government reflect the federal principle'.[6] In other words, federal structures may be in place in a polity, and federal principles may be enshrined in a country's constitution, but there may still be no federalism in operation, as was the case, for example, in the Soviet Union. Here, we need to add a cultural dimension to the five structural definitions provided above. A democratic and legalistic culture is required for a democratic federation. As Watts notes: 'a recognition of the supremacy of the constitution over all orders of government and a political culture emphasising the fundamental importance of respect for constitutionality are therefore prerequisites for the effective operation of a federation'.[7] As I shall demonstrate below, Russia has adopted all of the key structural trappings of a federation, and the Constitution does indeed enshrine many of the key principles of federalism and democracy, but neither the federal authorities nor the federal subjects actually operate according to federal principles. According to Gadzhiev *et al.*, federal relations in Russia actually operate under a cloud of 'unitarism' and federalism has been compromised by what the authors define as 'constitutional formalism' and 'legal dualism':

> *Constitutional Formalism*: In Russia the Constitution is effective as a legal act in the legal realm, but constitutionalism as a social-political factor does not exist. Therefore constitutional institutions, including the federal structure of

the state is not bolstered, as it should be, by a corresponding social political basis and political practice; *Legal Dualism*: There is an enormous gap between the legal norms and real life and a dichotomy between formal and informal regulation. This dualism encompasses all aspects of social life, including those which in Russia are called federative relations.[8]

Putin's radical reforms

It was Putin's election victories in 1999 and 2000 which paved the way for his radical reform of the federal system. Armed with a democratic mandate from his impressive victory in the 2000 presidential elections, coupled with the surprise success of his presidential party (Unity) in the December 1999 Duma elections, Putin was able to persuade a now 'tame parliament' that a radical overhaul of the federal system was essential if Russia was not to collapse into anarchy and ethnic turmoil. Under the anarchy of the Yeltsin years the regions had almost turned into the 'personal fiefdoms' of the regional governors and there was now a general consensus that something radical had to be done to reinstate a single legal space in Russia. One of the major powers of the governors was their control over the appointment of the heads of federal bodies situated in their territories. By controlling the appointment of such powerful officials (e.g., heads of the tax inspectorate, financial oversight bodies, and customs officers, the judiciary, procuracy, central electoral commissions and others), regional executives were able to undermine the authority of the federal government and to thwart the implementation of federal policies. As Putin stated in his annual message to the Federal Assembly,

> It's a scandalous thing when a fifth of the legal acts adopted in the regions contradict the country's Basic Law, when republic constitutions and province charters are at odds with the Russian Constitution, and when trade barriers, or even worse, border demarcation posts are set up between Russia's territories and provinces.[9]

In order, to 'restore an effective vertical chain of authority' and to implement a uniform policy, Putin called for a 'dictatorship of law'. Every citizen whether in Moscow or 'the most remote backwoods of Russia', was henceforth, guaranteed the same rights, and federal legislation was to be 'understood and enforced' in a uniform manner throughout the federation.[10]

There are five major strands to Putin's federal reforms: (1) the creation of seven new federal super-districts; (2) a reform of the Federation Council; (3) the creation of a new State Council; (4) the granting of new powers to the president to dismiss regional governors and dissolve regional assemblies; and (5) a major campaign to bring regional charters and republican constitutions into line with the Russian Constitution. Below we examine each one of these reforms in turn.

Regional politics

The creation of seven federal districts

On the 13 May 2000 Putin adopted what was to be the first of a package of decrees whose key aim was to rein in the power of the governors and to 'strengthen the unity of the state'.[11] In this first major reform of the federal system, Putin divided the country into seven super-districts, each of which contained a dozen or more federal subjects, and he appointed an envoy ('plenipotentiary representative' or 'polpredy' for short) to each district. Putin deftly sidestepped calls to format the new districts in conformity with the contours of Russia's eight interregional associations or eleven socio-economic regions. Instead, the new federal districts were drawn up to closely match Russia's military districts, thus giving the envoys (most of whom had a background in the military or security organs) direct access to the command and control networks of the military garrisons situated in their districts. And in a blow against the sovereignty claims of the ethnic republics, Putin drew up the boundaries of the new federal districts in such a way that each district would include a mixture of ethnic republics and territorially defined regions. None of the capital cities of the federal districts are situated in an ethnic republic. This has led some commentators to speculate that the creation of the federal districts is but the first step in Putin's programme of levelling down the status of the republics to that of the regions.

Putin's creation of the seven federal districts and the instigation of the 'polpredy' fully comply with Article 83 of the Russian Constitution, which simply states that the president, 'appoints and removes plenipotentiary representatives of the President of the Russian Federation'. As Oracheva notes, 'the Constitution does not specify in what particular form this institution exists, what functions presidential representatives perform, and how many representatives may be appointed.'[12] Thus, Putin can argue that the changes brought about by the 13 May decree were simply changes to his presidential administration, and not constitutional changes to the federation itself. However, as discussed below, Putin's federal reforms undoubtedly represent an assault on the federal idea, and they certainly violate the spirit of the Constitution, if not the actual Constitution itself.

The administrations of the federal districts

Five of the seven envoys have a background in the army or security services. Of the two civilians, only one (Sergei Kirienko the former Russian prime minister) has experience working in politics at the national level, and the other is a former diplomat. In terms of responsibilities, their rank is somewhere between deputy chief of staff of the presidential administration and deputy prime minister.[13] The high status of the envoys is also reflected in their membership of the Russian Security Council, and their right to attend Cabinet meetings of the Federal Government. In fact, the decree setting up the federal districts was drafted by the Security Council. The status of the envoys is also reflected in their regular meetings with the president. To prevent the polpredy going 'native' the presidential administration will fund them directly.

Many of the major ministries have begun to restructure their administrations bringing them into line with the new federal districts. Thus, each of the federal districts now has a deputy prosecutor general and each district has a department for combating organized crime under the dual subordination of the polpredy and the Russian Minister of Internal Affairs. In addition the Ministry of Justice also recently created branches in each of the seven districts and the Ministry of Finance, and the Tax Inspectorate have likewise begun to restructure their administrations in line with the reforms.

Power and responsibilities of the polpredy

The powers and responsibilities of the polpredy, at least on paper, are very impressive. Their key tasks are: (1) to monitor the regions' compliance with the Russian Constitution, federal laws and presidential decrees; (2) to oversee the selection and placement of personnel in the regional branches of the federal bureaucracy; (3) to protect the national security interests of the regions; and (4) to set up and co-ordinate within their districts interregional economic programmes.[14] They also have the power to recommend to the president that he suspend specific local laws or decrees when they contradict federal laws and to call for the dismissal of governors and the dissolution of regional assemblies if they adopt decrees or laws which violate federal laws (see below).

Putin has been at pains to stress that the primary function of the polpredy is not to supplant the role of the elected governors but rather to co-ordinate the work of the federal agencies in the their districts. As Putin observed, 'The authorised representatives, needless to say, will help in effectively solving the problems in their regions. But they do not have the right to interfere in areas under the jurisdiction of the electoral heads of the regions.'[15]

One of the most important and controversial powers of the envoys is that of the selection and placement of personnel. As presidential representative to the Volga district, Kirienko notes, 'In essence, the presidential representatives will oversee personnel policy for the president and will approve all appointments and promotions. The representatives will also maintain a reserve of personnel for all federal agencies.'[16] These powers will bring the envoys into direct conflict with the governors who can cite Article 72 of the Russian Constitution to defend their right to be consulted over such appointments especially with regard to the judiciary and law enforcement bodies.

There is also some confusion over what controls the envoys will be given in the economic sphere. Whilst they will not have direct control over the purse strings they are nonetheless charged with monitoring all the federal funds which come into their districts and overseeing the collection and transfer of taxes to the federal budget. Kirienko has stated that the districts will not have their own budgets. However, he did confirm that they would have their own socio-economic development plans, and thus, the ability to exercise some influence over economic policy-making in the regions. Putin has increased the amount of money transferred to the federal coffers by changing the balance of tax revenues between the centre and the regions. 'In 2000, the split was 50:50 between the federal government and regional shares. In 2001, it widened to 56:44 and in 2002 the numbers are expected to be 62:38.'[17]

Thus, Putin's unelected polpredy, at least on paper, have been granted considerable powers over the internal politics of federal subjects and their democratically elected representatives. And it is difficult to imagine how these new federal representatives will be able to carry out their functions without infringing the constitutionally guaranteed rights of the federal subjects.

The creation of seven quasi-states

However, whilst the powers of the polpredy are impressive on paper it remains to be seen how effective they will be in practice. Given the fact that each presidential representative will have to take charge of a dozen or so regions (whose administrative centres may be hundreds of miles apart), and the fact that every region has between forty and fifty federal agencies operating on its territory, this means that each envoy will have to co-ordinate and control the work of approximately 400–600 agencies. In some of the very large districts it is difficult to see how the envoys will be able to exercise control over such vast territories and/or populations. In some regions it has been reported that the polpredy have faced difficulties in hiring and holding on to suitably qualified staff. Moreover, the formation of the new federal districts has made the federation even more asymmetrical. Thus, for example, almost half of the Russian population is situated in just two of the federal districts: the Central district and the Volga district (see Table 9.1).

Putin's reforms may simply have created seven powerful quasi-regional states. Already the envoys have begun to create the institutions necessary to turn their districts into mini-regional states. Thus, for example, we are beginning to see the development in the federal districts of councils of the heads of regional legislative and executive bodies (mini-federal councils), councils of regional governors (mini-state councils). Councils for local self-government, and expert consultative and scientific research councils.[18] Thus, for example, Poltavchenko has created a council in his federal district (the Central District) which includes all the chief executives of the eighteen regions

Table 9.1 Economic status of the seven federal districts

District	No. of subjects of RF	Russian population (%)	Gross regional product (%)	Volume of industrial production (%)	Volume of agricultural production (%)	Capital investment (%)	Share of exports (%)	RF budget (%)
Central	18	25	28	20	23	30	37	37
North western	11	10	9	12	6	9	12	10
Southern	13	15	8	6	16	8	4	6
Volga	15	22	20	24	27	19	12	17
Ural	6	9	15	19	8	17	18	15
Siberian	16	14	14	14	17	11	13	11
Far eastern	10	5	6	6	4	5	4	4
Total	89	100	100	100	100	100	100	100

Source: Natal'ya Zubarevich, Nikolai Petrov and Aleksei Titkov – 'Federal'nye okruga – 2000' in *Russia's Regions in 1999: An Annual Supplement to Russia's Political Almanac* (Moscow: Carnegie Centre, 2000), p. 176.

under his jurisdiction.[19] The council will deal with all aspects of economic development. The new council would also appear to usurp the role of the Black Earth and Central Russian interregional economic associations. In the Volga District Kirienko has created a co-ordinating council for regional legislative chairpersons. The aim of the council is to develop a united approach for drafting regional legislation and bringing regional laws into line with federal norms. These new mini-councils will soon co-exist next to a series of new district-level banks and financial bodies

Emboldened by their new powers to appoint leaders of the regional branches of the All Union Television and Radio Company the envoys have also been actively promoting the development of a 'single information space' in each of their federal districts. To this end they have also set up district-wide mass media councils. Now the press will not only come under the control of the governors, but the polpredy, hardly a recipe for the creation of a vibrant and open 'civil society' in Russia.

There is also a danger that the envoys may simply build up personal fiefdoms of their own or they may at times act in concert with regional elites creating yet another layer of bureaucracy between the president and the regions. As Badovskii notes, in some regions the polpredy have acted as a powerful force limiting the powers of the regional governors. But, in many regions, 'the apparatus of the polpredy is created from the governor's people, is quickly integrated and absorbed by the local elites, and we see the merging or joining of federal and regional bureaucracies – eventually creating a highly effective system of regional lobbying'.[20] The relations between governors, presidential representatives, and federal bureaucrats are still unclear and will undoubtedly vary from district to district. As Orttung and Reddaway note, 'Rather then creating a stronger vertical hierarchy of authority leading from the central government to the regions, Putin has created a triangle, with the ministries, the presidential representatives, and the regions making up the triangle's three points.'[21]

Reform of the Federation Council

In a second major initiative Putin stripped the governors and chairs of regional assemblies of their ex officio right to sit in the upper chamber of the parliament.[22] These were to be replaced (from January 2002), with 'delegates' chosen by the regional assemblies and chief executives. More specifically, the governors have the right to appoint and dismiss their delegates as long as their choice of candidate is not vetoed by a vote of two-thirds of the members of their regional parliaments. The regional assemblies appoint and dismiss their representatives by secret ballot. The governors and assemblies also have the right to recall their representatives if their voting record in the Federation Council is not up to scratch.

For a number of commentators, such changes will inevitably lead to a decline in the powers of the upper chamber. On the other hand, as Putin himself has stressed, the new body will now meet full time, and not as in the past just for a few days a month. This will give the new members far greater opportunities to scrutinise legislation coming from the Duma and presidency. And we will no longer have the spectacle of members of regional executive bodies sitting in a legislative chamber thereby violating the principle of the separation of executive and legislative powers. More worrying for the governors is the fact that when they are denied membership of the upper chamber they will automatically lose their right to immunity from criminal prosecution. Putin will now be able to use the threat of prosecution to keep the chief executives in line.

As regards the appointment of new delegates, although Putin has been able to influence their selection in some federal districts,[23] in a surely unforeseen scenario we have witnessed the selection of outgoing governors or former deputy governors, as representatives. Legislative chairs have also selected former high-ranking members of their assemblies as their representatives. Thus, by the end of January 2002, twenty-three former governors and fifteen former regional speakers had been appointed to the Council.[24] And in other cases, regions have chosen Moscow insiders or high-ranking entrepreneurs. As Orttung notes, as a result of these new appointments, 'About 35 per cent of the members of the Federation Council have no connection to the regions they represent, and are either Muscovites and/or representatives of big business.'[25] Such developments have undermined one of the basic prerequisites for a federation, namely what Preston King calls 'the legislative entrenchment' of federal subjects in central decision-making.[26] The formation of a powerful pro-Putin group, 'Federatsiya' in the Council, and the election on 5 December 2001 of Putin's choice of speaker (Sergei Mironov) and the Kremlin's influence over the election of the Council's deputy speakers have seriously weakened the independence of the upper chamber.[27]

However, it would appear that the current method of selecting members of the Federation Council is only temporary. According to a new draft law drawn up by Mironov, from January 2005 members of the Federation Council will be selected by a new if rather bizarre method. According to the draft law, every candidate for the post of governor will be required to run with a 'partner'. The candidate who wins the post of governor will then delegate his partner to sit in the upper chamber. And in a similar manner candidates for seats in regional assemblies also choose 'partners', and at the first session of the newly elected legislatures the deputies elect one candidate from all their 'doubles' to sit in the Federation Council. As Tsvetkova notes, 'It is obvious that the changes provided in Mironov's draft are not of a principled nature – the senators are still chosen by governors and deputies, and not by the electorate.'[28]

Regional politics

The State Council

To sweeten the pill and to partially compensate the regional elite for their loss of membership in the upper chamber, Putin on 1 September 2000 created a new presidential advisory body – the State Council.[29] The new body, which is made up of all of the chief executives from the regions, meets once every three months and is chaired by the president. There is also an inner Presidium made up of seven governors (one from each of the federal districts), whose membership rotates each six months. The members of the presidium meet with the president once every month.

However, neither the State Council nor its Presidium is likely to have real powers. The new body is purely consultative and has no law-making functions. Moreover, as it was drawn up by presidential decree, the president may similarly dissolve it if it is not to his liking. Its main aim at present is to give the regional leaders a direct channel to the president and some limited input into policy-making.

Dismissal of governors and dissolution of regional legislatures

The third major reform strikes at the very heart of the regions' power structures – a new law giving Putin powers to dismiss popularly elected governors and to dissolve regional assemblies.[30] As Putin explains such legislation now makes it possible for federal intervention 'in situations in which government bodies at the local level [have flouted] the Russian Constitution and federal laws, violating the uniform rights and freedoms of Russian citizens'.[31] The new law gives both chambers of the legislature, the general procurator and the regional legislatures the right to recommend that a governor be removed. However, as Corwin notes, the process is so long and involved that regional leaders would have to demonstrate 'unprecedented obstinacy, audacity, and even stupidity' before they could be fired. For a regional head to be dismissed,

> One, he must on two different occasions ignore presidential decrees, two, allow the passage of two bills with provisions that violate federal laws, or three, make use on two different occasions of regional acts previously denounced by the president or the courts. And, in each of these cases, a court verdict is required ruling that these actions constitute violations of federal law.[32]

The president can also temporarily remove a governor while criminal charges that have been filed against him are being studied. If the president removes a governor from office he appoints a temporary governor to replace him. However, it is interesting to note that Putin did not use his new powers against the Governor of Primorskii Krai, Yevgenii Nazdratenko. Instead, Putin simply dismissed Nazdratenko and to keep him quiet, rewarded him with a ministerial post in Moscow. Likewise, regional heads in Ingushetiya and Sakha were removed without resort to these new powers, and only after being promised important posts in Moscow. Moreover, as Orttung and Reddaway note, 'even if the president does force a governor out of office, the region will hold new elections within six months, and there is no guarantee that the new governor will be any more pleasing to the federal government than the old one'.[33]

However, in a somewhat contradictory move Putin has also promoted the passage of the so-called third-term law through the Duma. Under this law, the leaders of sixty-nine regions of the federation will now be able to run for a third term and some for a fourth even although such extensions to their tenure violate regional charters and republican constitutions.[34] Thus, for example, Kirslan Ilyumzhinov the president of Kalmykiya, if re-elected,

> could end up holding office for a total of twenty-three years ... not retiring until 2116. The President of Kabardino-Balkariya, Valerii Kokov could remain in power until 2012 (with one more election in 2007); President Mintimer Shaimiev (Tatrarstan) and Egor Stroyev (Orel) until 2011, and Leonid Potapov (Buryatiya) and Magomedali Magomedov (Dagstan) until 2010 (all four can run in one more election in 2006). Murtaza Rakhimov (Bashkortostan) can hold office until 2013 (with two more elections in 2003 and 2008). Mikhail Prusak (Novgorod) has a chance of staying in power until 2011 (if he wins re-election twice in 2003 and 2007) and Konstantin Titov (Samara) until 2010.[35]

Putin's support for such a law reveals the weakness of his position and the stark reality that he still depends on regional elites to 'bring home the votes' in the up-coming round of parliamentary and presidential elections which are scheduled for 2003–4.

The law also calls for the dissolution of regional assemblies if they violate federal legislation. According to this legislation, regional assemblies have three months to amend any legislation that violates federal laws or legal proceedings may be enacted against them. However, the president must gain the approval of the State Duma before an assembly can be dissolved. Whilst it is certainly the case that regional assemblies do pass legislation that infringes the Constitution, it is highly questionable that Putin's right to dissolve democratically elected assemblies is itself constitutional. Nonetheless, on 4 April 2002, the Constitutional Court ruled that the president does indeed have the right to fire governors and the State Duma can disband regional legislatures. However, it made the procedure for dismissing governors and dissolving legislatures even more complicated and protracted. Under this new ruling, for the removal process to begin, the law requires that the action of a governor or regional legislature must have 'caused massive and serious violations of individual and civil rights and freedoms, threatened the unity and territorial integrity or national security of the Russian Federation and its ability to defend itself, or the unity of the country's legal and economic space'.[36]

The governors' rights to dismiss lower-level officials

Putin also steered passage of a law through the Duma, which gives the governors the right to dismiss lower-level administrative heads (with the exception of the mayors of capital cities) within their regions. As Putin explained, 'If under certain conditions, the head of a region can be removed from office by the country's president, then the regional leader should have a similar right with respect to lower-ranking authorities.'[37] Again this would appear to be a sop to the regional heads in order to compensate them for loss of membership of the Federation Council. According to Malyakin, 'the reforms complete the construction of a rigid vertical of power in which regional law conforms to federal law, the president enforces federal standards on the governors through the federal districts, and the governors in turn control local government through the municipal districts'.[38]

Bringing regional legislation into line with federal laws

One of the main aims of the Putin's reforms is to create a unified legal space in the Russian Federation. To this end therefore, the polpredy have been charged with overseeing the complex process of bringing republic constitutions and regional charters (and other local laws and decrees) into line with the federal constitution and federal laws. By 2001 the number of normative legal acts adopted by the regions and republics exceeded 300,000, and of these, just under a quarter (70,000) contradicted the federal constitution and federal laws.[39]

Within a matter of just a few months after his election to the Russian presidency in March 2000, Putin issued decrees demanding that the republics of Adygeya, Altai, Bashkortostan and Ingushetiya in addition to Amur, Smolensk and Tver oblasts, bring their regional laws into accordance with the Russian Constitution and federal legislation. Putin's decrees were backed up by two landmark decisions of the Constitutional Court (adopted on 7 June and 27 June, 2000), which ruled that the republics' declarations of sovereignty were incompatible with the sovereignty of the Russian Federation.[40]

In August 2000 the Chief Procurator of the Russian Federation called for all regional laws to be brought into line with federal laws by 1 January 2001. And reporting back, in January 2001, the deputy head of the presidential administration, Dmitrii Kozak, boasted that about 80 per cent of the regional laws checked by the administration had either already been brought into compliance with federal law, or were being considered in the courts.[41] In the same month Putin declared that sixty constitutions and regional charters, as well as over 2000 regional laws had been brought into compliance with the Constitution.[42] However, there would appear to be as many different figures about the number of laws that have been brought into line, as there are members of the presidential administration. In April 2001 the Justice Ministry reported that 23 regions continued to adopt laws that contradicted federal legislation.[43] And in the same month, in his address to the Russian Parliament, Putin declared that over 3,500 normative acts adopted in the regions continued to contradict the Russian Constitution and Federal laws.[44]

Puten's efforts to rein in the regions have elicited a range of reactions, from reluctant acquiescence to outright defiance. Many republics and regions have dragged their feet in implementing the reforms and/or they have steadfastly refused to renounce their sovereignty and their control over natural resources. Indeed, it is possible that the number of laws violating federal norms may actually have grown in number! For just as quickly as old legislation is being revised to conform to federal norms, regional and republican parliaments have been able to adopt new laws with new infringements. For example, more than two dozen amendments made to the Constitution of Khakasiya (in its revised edition of 21 November 2000) are in violation of federal laws.[45] And only under considerable pressure from the presidential representative in the Siberian district and threats that federal subsidies would be cut off, did Tyva finally adopt a new version of its Constitution on 6 May 2001. The previous version of the Constitution gave the republic the right to secede from Russia and declared that only republican laws would be in effect during crises. However, there have been so many legal violations in the process of writing the new Constitution that its legitimacy is now being challenged in the courts.[46]

In Bashkortostan 51 of the 164 articles of the new Constitution, which was adopted in November 2000, violate federal law, almost as many violations as in the old Constitution. And whilst the new version,

> places limits on the republic's sovereignty, no longer declares its laws above Russian laws, removes claims that the republic is a subject of international law, and introduces procedures for appointing judges and procurators in line with federal norms, it still includes the full text of the Republic's power-sharing treaty.[47]

The Bashkortostan authorities have refused to recognise the rulings of the Russian Constitutional Court and continue to adopt new legislation that violates federal laws.[48] By the end of December 2001, 72 per cent of Bashkortostan's laws still violated federal norms, a figure that was actually higher than it was in May 2000 at the beginning of Putin's reforms.[49] In April 2002, Aleksandr Zvyagintsev, Russian Deputy Prosecutor-General complained that the Bashkir Supreme Court continued to uphold the Republic's declaration of sovereignty, the right of the president to issue decrees on emergency situations, and to appoint the members of the republican electoral commission, and the chair of the Central Bank.'[50]

In October 2002 further radical changes to Bashkortostan's Constitution were approved by a special constitutional commission. If adopted, the post of president will be abolished, and Bashkortostan will become a 'parliamentary republic'. But there is unlikely to be any real shift in power. If the changes go ahead Bashkortostan's current president is almost certainly 'guaranteed' to become the 'speaker' of the new parliament, a post that he will be entitled to hold for life.

The Tatarstan leadership has also steadfastly refused to renounce the Republic's sovereignty. Article 1 of the revised Constitution, which was adopted in April 2002, continues to uphold the 1994 bilateral treaty with Moscow, even though it contradicts both the federal and republican constitutions in several places. The Constitution also reiterates the republic's citizenship rights.[51] In November 2002 there were still as many as fifty points in the Constitution which contradicted federal legislation.[52] In reply to criticism from Moscow, President Shaimiev stated, 'we realise that some will not like the mention of sovereignty in the Constitution of Tatarstan. However, the Russian Constitution recognises republics as states. Consequently, it is impossible to reject the notion of sovereignty either hypothetically or in practice'.[53] Shamiev has also called for the Russian Constitution to be brought into line with republican constitutions rather than vice versa.

In exchange for the few concessions that were made, such as giving up its right to an independent judicial system and the right to conclude international treaties, the federal government is reported to have transferred an additional 12.8 billion roubles for Tatarstan's socio-economic development in 2002. As Corwin notes, 'In comparison, a development programme for the entire Southern Federal District was funded at the level of only 600 million roubles.'[54]

But now there are new problems with the new Constitution. At its session on 5–6 September 2002 the Tatarstan Legislature adopted a resolution refusing to bring its 2002 Constitution into line with the Federal Constitution, and later in the same month the Republican Supreme Court defended the actions of the legislature against a number of complaints made by the Russian Deputy Prosecutor-General. As Midkhat Farukshin notes,

> These actions make clear that the republican leadership is determined to defend the inviolability of the new Tatarstan constitution and is willing to risk the disbandment of the republican legislature by the State Duma to defend it ... Tatarstan's leaders are clearly employing delaying tactics in their battle to retain as much sovereignty as possible.[55]

Likewise in Sakha there has been strong opposition to Putin's reforms. Thus, for example, on 16 January 2001 the Sakha Republican legislature rejected a law proposed by the Republican Procurator that would have renounced the Republic's sovereignty. Nineteen of the legislature's thirty-two members voted against it. And in March 2001, the legislators (in the lower house of the republican parliament) refused to make amendments to Article 5 of the Republic's Constitution, which gives it ownership over its land and natural resources. The Sakha Government had signed a 25-year agreement with the Alrosa diamond company on 11 January 2001, and it was in no mood to give up its control over such a lucrative source of income. Diamond production in the republic makes up 77 per cent of the government's revenue.[56] Nonetheless, the legislators did agree to remove from the Republic's Constitution ten of the most serious violations of federal law, including a provision that allowed the republic to have its own army.[57] However, no sooner (on 4 March 2002), had legislators finally approved a law amending a further eleven articles of the Republican Constitution, when it came to light that a further five laws which had been adopted over the period 2001–02 had created new violations.[58] In 2002 Putin was able to 'persuade' the president of Sakha, Mikhail Nikolaev, to withdraw from presidential elections and take up the post of Deputy Chair of the Federation Council. It remains to be seen whether the new president will be any more compliant than the last.

In other cases, threats to dissolve recalcitrant legislatures have met with success. Thus on 14 April 2002 Buryatiya's republican parliament under threat of dissolution adopted a resolution renouncing the republic's declaration of sovereignty.

However, it is not only in the republics that such infringements of federal legislation have taken place. Thus, Latyshev, the presidential representative to the Urals Federal District, in an examination of 1,544 regional laws found that 306 violated the Russian Constitution and federal legislation. The study also revealed that 92 per cent of municipal charters and 48 of the 67 agreements signed between federal agencies and regional executive branch agencies in the federal district also violated federal laws.[59]

In the summer of 2001 Putin, realising that his reforms were being bogged down, announced a new initiative – the formation of a Commission chaired by the Deputy Head of the presidential administration (Dmitrii Kozak). The Commission was charged with re-examining the powers and authority of federal, regional and local bodies of power. We still await the full details of the Kozak Commission's Report, which was due in September 2002. However, one of the first actions of the Commission was to call for the abolition of the forty-six bilateral treaties which had been signed between the federal government and the regions during Yeltsin's presidency. By granting special privileges and powers to a select group of regions the treaties undermined Article 6 of the Russian Constitution, which proclaims that all subjects of the federation are equal. Yeltsin often signed secret agreements with powerful regions in order to secure their political support, and in many cases the treaties violated the Russian Constitution.[60] Putin to his credit has spoken out against the lack of transparency in the treaties, and he has called for any future treaties to be ratified by the Federation Council. In his annual state of the nation address to Parliament in April 2002 Putin stated that twenty-eight of the treaties had been annulled.[61] Most observers predict that by the end of 2002 all of the remaining regions, with the probable exceptions of Bashkortostan and Tatarstan, will most likely fall into line and rescind their treaties.[62]

Putin's federal reforms and democracy

As other chapters in this book have shown, there is a paradox at the heart of Putin's reforms – that is, they can be read as both promoting and restricting democracy. Bringing regional legislation into line with the Russian Constitution is absolutely essential for the consolidation of democracy, particularly in those ethnic republics, which have deprived their citizens of universal democratic norms and human rights. Indeed, as Gordon Hahn reports, according to Vladimir Lysenko, 'a third of Russia's regions are authoritarian, with constitutions and laws that violate the Russian Constitution and its provisions on democracy and civil rights'.[63] By reasserting the rule of law and due process, Putin's reforms are positive steps in creating equal rights for all citizens across the federation. However, there are real worries that Putin's quest for law and order will be bought at the expense of civil liberties and the consolidation of democracy. Putin's reorganisation of the Federation Council, his usurpation of unilateral powers to dismiss regional assemblies and chief executives, and his creation of seven unelected super-governors have been a major setback for Russia's transition to democracy.

Putin's reforms also put into doubt his adherence to the principles of federalism as enshrined in the Russian Constitution. In his book, *First Person*, Putin states that, 'from the very beginning, Russia was created as a super centralised state. That's practically laid down in its genetic code, its traditions, and the mentality of its people'.[64] In a worrying scenario for the future of Russian federalism, Putin may well opt for a policy of defederalisation and abolish the existing eighty-nine subjects of the federation to be replaced with the seven federal districts. However, in order to carry out such a radical and potentially destabilising reform major revisions would have to be made to the Russian Constitution which is very difficult to amend. I would therefore argue that this most radical of options is highly unlikely.

Decentralisation and noncentralisation

Daniel Elazar alerts us to a vitally important factor in defining federal systems, the differences between the decentralisation to be found in unitary states and the noncentralisation of federal regimes. Decentralisation 'implies a hierarchy – a pyramid of governments with gradations of power flowing down from the top'. Noncentralisation, on the other hand, 'is best conceptualised as a matrix of governments ... where there are no higher or lower power centres, only larger or smaller arenas of decision making and action'.[65] Thus, in federations, in contrast to unitary states, regional autonomy is not only devolved but also constitutionally guaranteed.[66] Federal governments cannot legally usurp powers, which have been constitutionally devolved to the federal subjects. In noncentralised systems such as the United States, Switzerland and Canada, each has

> a national government that functions powerfully in many areas for many purposes, but not a central government controlling all the lines of political communication and decision making. In each, the states, cantons, or provinces are not creatures of the federal government but, like the latter, derive their authority directly from the people. Structurally, they are substantially immune to federal interference.[67]

In other words, in federations there is a vertical separation of powers among federal and regional bodies of power, each of which have constitutionally guaranteed rights and powers. Furthermore, as Smirnyagin notes, each tier of government is 'chosen at separate elections by the state's citizens, who give each its own legitimacy and make it independent of the others'.[68] Putin cannot unilaterally centralise policy areas which have been constitutionally assigned to the regions or which come under the joint authority of the regions and the federal government. The federal government cannot simply ignore the rights of the federal subjects without itself violating the Constitution and undermining both federalism and democracy.

Article 1 of the Russian Constitution states that the Russian Federation 'is a democratic federative rule of law state with a republican form of government'. However, whilst many of the structural prerequisites of a federal state have undoubtedly been formed, a federal and democratic culture has still to emerge. Central–periphery relations in Russia continue to be determined by political and economic factors rather than constitutional norms.

As Gadzhiev et al., argue,

> For federalism, as for chess, what is important are the rules of the game, not the board or the pieces. Unfortunately in Russia everything is just the opposite. We have federative pieces on a federative board but play is according to unitary rules. The interaction of regions and the centre does not follow constitutional rules but established informal traditions ... and backroom deals.[69]

In other words, until we have a legalistic and democratic culture in Russia, the federal idea will never be put into practice, and under Putin's presidency the hidden hand of unitarism will prevail.

Notes

1. Some of the material in this chapter was published in C. Ross, *Federalism and Democratisation in Russia* (Manchester: Manchester University Press, 2002).
2. R. Watts, *Comparing Federal Systems* (Montreal and Kingston: McGill-Queen's University Press, 2nd ed., 1999), p. 6.
3. *Ibid.*, p. 7.
4. Watts, *Comparing Federal Systems*; A. Lijphart, *Patterns of Democracy: Government Forms and Performance in Thirty-Six Countries* (New Haven and London: Yale University Press, 1999); D. J. Elazar, *Exploring Federalism* (Tuscaloosa and London: University of Alabama Press, 1987); F. Requejo, 'National pluralism and federalism: four potential scenarios for Spanish plurinational democracy', *Perspectives on European Politics and Society* 2:2 (2001).
5. D. Kempton also adds five 'beneficial conditions for the maintenance of federalism': (1) symmetry among the components; (2) decentralised federal political parties; (3) a noncentralised bureaucracy; (4) democracy; and (5) economic coordination. See, D. Kempton, 'Russian federalism: continuing myth or political salvation', *Demokratizatsiya*, 9:2 (spring 2001), 231.
6. Elazar, *Exploring Federalism*, p. 67.
7. Watts, *Comparing Federal Systems*, p. 99.
8. G. A. Gadzhiev, V. L. Lazarev, B. B. Pastukov and I. G. Shablinskiy, *Establishing Constitutional Democracy in Russia, the Present Phase: An Analytical Report* (Moscow: Institute of Law and Public Policy: Lawyers Alliance for World Security, 2002), p. 47.
9. V. Putin, 'Television address by the Russian President to the Country's citizens', *Rossiiskaya gazeta* (19 May 2000), p. 3. Translated in *CDPSP*, 52:20 (2000), 5.
10. *Ibid.*
11. See, Presidential Decree, No. 849, 13 May 2000, 'O Polnomochnom Predstavitele Prezidenta Rossiiskoi Federatsii v Federal'nom Okruge', and the accompanying Resolution, 'O Polnomochnom Prestavitele Prezidenta Rossiiskoi Federatsii v Federal'nom Okruge.' Published in *Rossiskaya gazeta* (13 May, 2001).
12. O. Oracheva, 'Democracy and federalism in post-communist Russia (relations between Moscow and the regions in the Russian Federation)', paper presented at the conference, 'The fall of communism in Europe: ten years on', 14–17 May 2001, Hebrew University of Jerusalem, p. 11.
13. 'Presidential administration's Samoilov on seven representatives', *EWI Russian Regional Report*, 5:30 (2 August, 2000), 4–6.
14. See, E. Teague, 'Putin reforms the federal system', and R. Sakwa, 'Federalism, sovereignty and democracy', in C. Ross (ed.), *Regional Politics in Russia* (Manchester: Manchester University Press, 2002); M. Hyde, 'Putin's federal reforms and their implications for presidential lower in Russia', *Europe–Asia Studies*, 53:5 (2001). The duties of the 'polpredy' were further outlined in Putin's Presidential Decree of 30 January 2001, No. 97, 'O Vnesenii dopolneniya i izmeneniya v polozhenie o polnomochnom predstavitele Prezidenta Rossiiskoi Federatsii v federal'nom okruge, utverzhdennoe ukazom Prezidenta Rossiiskoi Federatsii ot 13 Maya 2000 No 849', published in *Rossiskaya gazeta* (30 January 2001). According to this decree the presidential envoys were directly subordinate to the head of the Presidential Administration.

15 Speech by V. V. Putin at the Presentation of the Annual Message from the President of the Russian Federation to the Federal Assembly of the Russian Federation, *Rossiiskaya gazeta* (11 July 2000), pp. 1, 3. Translated in *CDPSP*, 52:28 (2000), p. 7.
16 Interview with S. Kirienko, *Nezavisimaya gazeta* (25 October 2000), p. 3.
17 R. Orttung, 'Putin's governor generals – conference analyses impact of federal reforms (7–9 June 2002),' *EWI Russian Regional Report*, 7:20 (17 June 2002), p. 9.
18 D. V. Badovskii, 'Systema federal'nykh okrygov i institut polnomochnykh predstavitelei prezidenta RF: sovremennoe sostoyanie i problemy razvitiya', in *Polpredy Prezidenta: Problemy Stanovleniya Novovo Instituta* (MGU, Nauchnye Doklady, No. 3, January 2001), p. 5.
19 A. Slabov, 'Georgy Poltavchenko raises his voice', *Kommersant* (10 February 2001), 2. *CDPSP*, 53:6 (7 March 2001).
20 Badovskii, 'Sistema federali'nykh okrugov', p. 6.
21 R. Orttung and P. Reddaway, 'Russian state-building: the regional dimension', in *The Russia Initiative: Reports of the Four Task Forces* (New York: Carnegie Corporation, 2001), p. 100.
22 See, the Federal Law, No. 113-F3, 5 August 2000, 'O Poryadke Formorovaniya Soveta Federatsiya Federal'novo Sobraniya Rossiiskoi Federatsii', adopted by the State Duma 19 July 2000 and ratified by the Federation Council 26 July, 2000, *Rossiskaya gazeta* (5 August 2000).
23 According to Robert Orttung, in the Volga Federal District Kirienko has been particularly successful in promoting his choice of candidates to the Council whereas in the Urals Latyshev has had no impact on the selection of representatives. See R. Orttung, 'Putin's governor generals – conference analyses impact of federal reforms (7–9 June 2002)', *EWI Rusian Regional Report*, 7:20 (17 June, 2002), 6.
24 R. Orttung, *EWI Russian Regional Report*, 7:5 (6 February 2002), 11.
25 R. Orttung, *EWI Russian Regional Report*, 7:20 (17 June, 2002), 5.
26 P. King, 'Federation and representation', in M. Burgess and A.-G. Gagnon (eds.), *Comparative Federalism and Federation* (New York and London, Harvester-Wheatsheaf: 1993) p. 93.
27 Under new regulations factions are no longer permitted in the upper chamber. However, a number of the leaders of 'Federatsiya' have now taken up posts as deputy chairs of the Council. As Orttung notes, former officials in the seven federal districts are also well represented in the new Council. Thus, for example, the Volga district 'sent two deputies and one chief federal inspector; the Siberian Federal District, two chief federal inspectors, and the Northwest Federal District one staff member', R. Orttung, *EWI Russian Regional Report* 7:5 (6 February 2002), p. 12.
28 M. Tsvetkova, 'Head senator wants lifelong membership in upper house', Gazeta.Ru (21 October, 2002), p. 2.
29 'Ukaz Prezidenta Rossiiskoi Federatsii', No. 602, 1 September 2000, published in *Rossiiskaya Gazeta* (1 September 2000).
30 The law on the removal of the governors and disbanding of legislatures takes the form of amendments to the federal law 'Ob Obshchikh Printsipakh Organizatsii Zakonodatel'nykh (Predstavitel'nykh) i Ispolnitel'nykh Organov Gosudarstvennoi

Vlasti Sub'ektov Rossiiskoi Federatstii', which was ratified by the President on October 6, 1999 and published in *Rossiskaya gazeta* (19 October 1999).
31 'Annual message of the President to the Russian Federal Assembly', *Rossiiskaya gazeta* (11 July 2000), 3. Translated in *CDPSP* 52:28 (2000), 7.
32 J. A. Corwin, 'Vulnerability of governors to dismissal questioned', *RFE/RL Russian Federation Report*, 2:21 (7 June 2000).
33 Orttung and Reddaway, 'Russian state-building', p. 98.
34 A. Kostyukov, *Obshchaya gazeta*, 5 (1–7 February 2001), p. 1. This amends a previous law adopted in October 1999 which limited governors to two terms. The amendment counts the first term for a governor as the one starting after 16 October 1999.
35 P. Kopov, *Izvestiya* (10 July 2002), p. 2. Translated in *CDPSP* 54: 28 (2002), 10.
36 See S. Mikhailova, 'Constitutional court confirms authorities' ability to fire governors', *EWI Russian Regional Report*, 7:14 (10 April 2002), 6.
37 Putin, 'Television address', 5.
38 I. Malyakin, 'Putin against the regions: round two', *Russia and Eurasia Review*, 1:2 (June 18, 2002), 4.
39 M. I. Vil'chek, 'O klyuchevikh problemakh stanovleniya instituta polnomochnykh predstavitelei Prezidenta RF', in *Polpredy Prezidenta*, p. 20.
40 Resolutions of the Constitutional Court of 7 June and 27 June 2000 repudiated the sovereignty of the republics as not in line with the Federal Constitution. See, M. V. Baglai, *Konstitutsionnoe Pravo Rossiiskoi Federatsii* (Moscow: Norma, 2001), pp. 305, 338–339. This same resolution also noted that it was against the Constitution for regional organs of power to appoint officials of federal bureaucracies in the regions.
41 J. A. Corwin, *RFE/RL Russian Federation Report*, 3:2 (10 January 2001) as cited in *Obshchaya gazeta*, 52 (10 January 2001).
42 *Interfax* (11 January 2001), p. 3.
43 J. A. Corwin, *RFE/RL Russian Federation Report*, 3:13 (11 April 2001), 1.
44 R. Orttung, *EWI Russian Regional Report*, 6:18 (16 May 2001), 2.
45 M. Shandarov, *EWI Russian Regional Report*, 6:5 (7 February 2001), 5.
46 *Kommersant Daily* (8 May 2001), p. 2.
47 I. Rabinovich, 'Bashkortostani legal situation is worse than before campaign to bring laws into line', *EWI, Russian Regional Report*, 6:44 (12 December 2001), 10.
48 *Ibid.*, 11.
49 *Ibid.*, 10.
50 RFE/RL Tatar-Bashkir Service (3 May 2002), 2.
51 *Ibid.*, 1.
52 RC, 'Prosecutor-General still doesn't like Tatarstan's Constitution', *Political Weekly*, 2:32 (2 October, 2002), 15.
53 *Ibid.*, 4.
54 J. A. Corwin, *RFE/RL Federation Report*, 4:8 (6 March, 2002), 5.
55 M. Farukshin, *EWI Russian Regional Report*, 7:27 (18 September 2002), 4.
56 O. Yemelyanov, *EWI Russian Regional Report* 6:3 (24 January 2001), 3.
57 *EWI Russian Regional Report*, 6:10 (14 March 2001), 6.
58 J. A. Corwin, 'Sakha's harmonisation effort found faulty', *RFE/RL Federation Report*, 4:8 (6 March, 2002), 3.
59 S. Pushkarev, *EWI Russian Regional Report*, 6:9 (7 March, 2001), 4–5.

60 See C. Ross, *Federalism and Democratisation in Russia* (Manchester: Manchester University Press, 2003).
61 'Full text of Putin annual state-of-the-nation address to Russian parliament', *BBC Monitoring*, as reproduced in *Johnson's Russia List*, 6195 (19 April 2002), p. 11.
62 Kozak originally gave the regions until 28 July 2002 to bring their legislation into line.
63 G. M. Hahn, 'Putin's federal reforms: reintegrating Russia's legal space or upsetting the metastability of Russia's asymmetrical federalism', *Demokratizatsiya*, 9:4 (2001), 498.
64 V. Putin, *First Person: An Astonishingly Frank Self-Portrait by Russia's President Vladimir Putin,* with N. Gevorkyan, N. Timakova, and A. Kolesnikov, translated by C. A. Fitzpatrick (London: Hutchinson, 2000), pp. 182–183. Cited in R. Sakwa, 'Federalism, sovereignty and democracy', in C. Ross (ed.), *Regional Politics in Russia* (Manchester: Manchester University Press, 2002), p. 18.
65 Elazar, *Exploring Federalism*, pp. 34, 35–37.
66 G. Smith, *Federalism: The Multi-Ethnic Challenge* (London and New York: Longman, 1995), p. 7.
67 Elazar, *Exploring Federalism*, p. 35.
68 L. V. Smirnyagin, 'Federalizm po Putiny ili Putin po federalizmu (zheleznoi pyatoi)', *Carnegie Briefing Papers*, 3:3 (March 2001), 3.
69 Gadzhiev, Lazarev, Pastukhov, and Shablitskiy, *Establishing Constitutional Democracy*, p. 48.

10

Measuring and explaining variations in Russian regional democratisation

Christopher Marsh

Given the country's vast size and diversity, Russian democratic consolidation hinges not only upon events in the country's executive and legislative institutions, but upon events in the regions, cities and towns as well. While the picture of Russian democracy visible from Moscow is difficult enough to discern, it is a challenge in and of itself just to catch a glimpse of Russia's regional landscape and the progress of democratisation across the country. How can one gauge the progress being made in eighty-nine regions stretching from the Baltic coast to the Sea of Japan and having different institutional structures and ethnic compositions? If that task were not daunting enough, to be of any real value we must not only *measure* the levels of regional democratisation in Russia, we must also *explain* the variation in these levels.

Although many obstacles stand in the way of successfully and satisfactorily completing such tasks, the relative importance of this information justifies employing various methods of research in an attempt to answer some very important questions. In this chapter, I employ a cross-regional quantitative methodology in an attempt to measure and explain variations in Russian regional democratisation. I begin by developing a regional index of democratisation based upon levels of electoral participation and competition in regional-level executive elections held between May 1999 and April 2002. After briefly exploring the results of this index compared to others that have been developed, I examine the relative levels of democracy throughout Russia's regions and discuss some representative examples of the various types identified.

Of course, measuring regional democratisation is only half the job. I thus move on to explore various explanations for the relative levels of democracy in Russia's regions by examining the statistical relationship between the index of democratisation and various explanatory factors. The first set of factors I examine is associated with social capital and civil society, including participation in referenda and the density of associational life in the regions. I then examine indicators of socioeconomic development and marketisation, including the value of retail trade and the number of converted state farms, private enterprises, and joint stock companies. Since both civic and socio-economic factors affect daily life in political communities, I explore the explanatory power of a combined set of measures, which results in a robust and statistically powerful model. After controlling for Russia's ethnic diversity by including such measures as a region's non-Russian population and territorial status, the result is an extremely significant and powerful predictor of the variation in levels of democracy across Russia, able to explain fully 25 per cent of such variation. I conclude by discussing some of the limitations of the analyses conducted here and speculating as to what some of the other factors might be that influence democracy in Russia's regions.

Measuring regional democratisation

December 2001 was a landmark in the process of Russian democratisation, as it marked the completion of Russia's first decade of post-Soviet democratisation. This period of ten years has seen dramatic changes in all the regions, with some making great strides towards democracy while others have gained autonomy from Moscow only to come under the thumb of local authoritarian leaders. The path to democracy, of course, is slow and fraught with problems, but the regional dimension is critical not just to gain a true picture of what is happening outside of the nation's capital, but also because regional bases of democracy can serve as a bulwark against a return to authoritarian rule. But how do we get a broader picture of what is going on in the regions? Are there emerging bases of democracy in Russia's regions, or are unpopular regional governments more prevalent? Anecdotal evidence indicates that many governors are winning elections with discomfortingly low levels of turnout and no real competition, becoming what Ross has called 'elective dictatorships'.[1] Meanwhile, other regions seem to be making strides toward democracy, such as the relatively successful Novgorod Oblast.[2] We must be careful, however, not to draw generalisations from only a few cases, which may rest anywhere from one extreme to the other. A comprehensive and consistent analysis is important, therefore, to see the forest through the trees.

The fact that between 1998 and 2002 almost every region underwent elections for executive leaders gives us the opportunity to examine the results of these elections for indicators of democracy and obstacles to its development. In exploring the variation in levels of democratisation across Russia's regions, I focus specifically on the elections held in seventy-eight regions between May 1999 and April 2002.[3] While it would have been possible to include a few other regions in this analysis, I have excluded the elections held in 1998 because they were probably affected by the financial crisis of that year, thus making them incomparable with elections held prior to the crisis or after it had begun to subside. The end point of April 2002 was chosen because that is when the analyses were performed. Postponing the analysis would have included a few more cases but would have unnecessarily prolonged the completion of this study. The seventy-eight regions included here represent a sufficient number of regions to conduct analysis and are representative of the country as a whole.

Some interesting trends emerged throughout the 1999–2002 electoral cycle. Some gubernatorial races were characterised by a high degree of competition, with as many as twenty candidates on the ballot and with margins of victory as small as a few thousand votes, as in Tver where Governor Platov barely edged out Communist Party candidate Bayunov by only about three thousand votes. Other races were less competitive, as in Kabardino-Balkariya where Governor Kokov was re-elected with over 98 per cent of the vote and no competition. This was not an isolated case, as other regions had no real opposition as well, with a single 'challenger' put on the ballot simply in order to meet the legal requirement that two candidates run in the election. Examples such as these illustrate the great discrepancy that exists between regions that seem to be developing genuine democratic institutions and those that hold elections within the confines of the law simply as a means of not drawing undue attention onto themselves. It is this variation more than anything else that leads to researchers finding seemingly contradictory evidence of both democratic success and local authoritarianism among Russia's regions.

While the use of electoral data from such a large number of regions may correct the problem of drawing conclusions from only a few cases, such an abundance of data actually makes analysis difficult. Indeed, there are perhaps as many ways to analyse these data, as there are elections that have been held. In order to discern patterns across the many regions, the data from these elections must be analysed in a systematic way, one in which the amount of information becomes manageable and the relevant figures become visible. This can be achieved by employing an index based upon the levels of competition and participation in the elections.

Regional index of democratisation

In his oft-cited treatise on democracy, Robert Dahl argued that political competition and participation are key components of democracy.[4] Following this work, Tatu Vanhanen developed an interesting and widely applicable method for measuring democracy, which he labelled the Index of Democratisation.[5] Vanhanen's index is composed of two simple quantitative indicators based on a polity's level of electoral competition and participation. In an attempt to determine the prospects for democracy in countries around the world, Vanhanen used nation-states as his unit of analysis. This method of measuring democracy is also applicable to sub-state units, however, albeit necessarily in slightly modified form. An index modelled after the one developed by Vanhanen allows us to use the data from the 1999–2002 gubernatorial elections as an indicator of regional democratisation.

In developing a regional index of democratisation, the first component I include is electoral participation for regional elections. While it would be possible to include turnout rates for regional legislative elections, I have chosen not to include them here because in post-Communist Russia such elections have been held over a period of several years and according to various electoral schemes, even including multi-member districts,[6] making their use problematic. The participation indicator is therefore composed solely of turnout rates for regional executive elections.

The second component is based on the degree of competition in regional elections. Again, it would have been possible to include data from regional legislative elections, but these were excluded because Russia's regional assemblies are little more than 'ceremonial parliaments', and have virtually no ability to check the power of the executives.[7] Given this fact, it would be improper to include a measure of competition for regional legislative elections. The competition indicator is therefore composed solely of executive competition, which is calculated by subtracting the percentage of votes for the winner from 100, producing the number of votes cast in favour of candidates other than the winner (including the vote option, against all). Moreover, the range for this variable is restricted to between 0 and 50, since 50 per cent is considered the 'ultimate' level of competition, with any score higher than this simply assigned a score of 50.

After calculating these two components, I then combine them into an index of regional democratisation by multiplying the two indicators. This assignment of equal weights assumes that one is no more important an element of democracy than the other. This method of combining the two is also useful since it magnifies the range of scores and will result in high scores only if both indicators are high.

Results

Once calculated, the index of regional democratisation indicates that indeed there are vast differences in levels of democracy among Russia's seventy-eight regions included in the analysis (see Appendix 10.1 for scores). Index scores range from a low of 337 in Kemerovo, where Governor Tuleev was re-elected with 93 per cent of the vote, to 3,776 in Sakha (Yakutiya), where over 75 per cent of the electorate went to the polls to elect Governor Shtyrov. With a mean index score of almost 2,000 (1,999.24), moreover, the results indicate that there are substantial bases of democracy across Russia's regions, while the standard deviation of 808.07 indicates that it varies widely from place to place.

The levels of democratisation throughout Russia can be grouped according to a 5-point scale, with 5 representing the highest levels of democratisation, and 1 representing the least democratic.[8] According to this analysis, regions with the highest levels of democracy include Belgorod Oblast, Tver Oblast, and the Republic of Sakha. In these regions, participation in executive elections was high, ranging between 65 to 75 per cent. While many other regions had high levels of participation as well, in these regions it was coupled with serious electoral competition, with the winner unable to secure even 60 per cent of the vote. In terms of levels of citizen involvement and political contestation, the regions in this category are perhaps the most democratic in Russia.

Many more regions in the analysis scored within the range of level 4 than in level 5, indicating that there is a substantial basis of democratic support throughout the country. Regions in this category include the Republic of Komi, Yaroslavl Oblast, Novgorod Oblast, and Pskov Oblast. Levels of participation and competition ranged substantially among the regions in this group, but overall the elections were characterised by citizen involvement and legitimate electoral competition. As an example, thirteen candidates ran against incumbent governor Yevgeny Mikhailov in Pskov's November 2000 election. Another sign of the region's competition is the fact that Mikhailov was only able to secure 28 per cent of the vote, while three other candidates each secured approximately 15 per cent of the vote.

Regions which scored around the mean and thus fell into level 3 included Voronezh, Kostroma, Stavropol Krai, Arkhangelsk, and Ivanovo. In these regions, participation was between approximately 35 and 65 per cent, and competition ranged from 30 to the maximum of 50 (although exceeding it in actuality). Voronezh serves as an example of the regions in this category. Like several other regions in which an incumbent governor lost his re-election bid to a former member of the security forces, in Voronezh incumbent governor Ivan Shabanov was defeated in the December 2000 election by regional security official Vladimir Kulakov, with 15 and 59.99 per cent of the vote, respectively. With six candidates on the ballot, two of whom received over 12 per cent, Kulakov's election illustrated a high degree of competition in Voronezh and secured him a popular mandate, although starting a potentially dangerous trend of members of the security apparatus hanging up their uniforms for the mantle of political office.

The regions in level 2 exhibited low levels of participation or a lack of serious competition, including St Petersburg, Vladimir, Tula and Krasnodar Krai. The election in Krasnodar Krai provides an example of regions that are having trouble developing genuinely competitive elections. Here Aleksandr Tkachev was elected with almost 82 per cent of the vote after being endorsed by long-time regional boss Nikolai (*Batka*, or 'poppa') Kondratenko, who declined to run for re-election due to health problems, although it was argued that this was actually just a new means of the Kremlin attempting to 'dump' a governor it did not like by compelling him to withdraw from the race.[9]

Such situations were more prevalent and obvious among the regions such as Khabarovsk Krai, Chukotka and Khanty-Mansi, which scored at the bottom of the scale on the index of regional democratisation. Politics in these regions is characterised by a lack of competition, despite relatively high levels of participation in some areas. The lack of competition is so extreme, in fact, that in four of the eight lowest scoring regions, the winner received between 90 and 95 per cent of the vote, with many of the remaining votes going to the *against all* category. Moreover, in many cases this was done in order to re-elect incumbent governors. This is even more surprising when one considers the very low levels of popularity among some other incumbent politicians in Russia, such as Yeltsin throughout the 1990s. And in Chukotka, an exception to the incumbency rule, Roman Abramovich won with 90 per cent of the vote and the previous governor's (Nazarov) blessing, hardly making it an exceptional case.

The results of the above analysis[10] indicate that democratisation in Russia's regions is progressing in a slow and uneven manner. While some regions are characterised by vibrant electoral participation and competition for political office, other regions participate in elections simply to re-elect their local bosses with staggeringly high percentages of the vote. Still other regions fall somewhere in between. The good news is that the first group of regions has a real chance of being able to counter effectively the power of the national government and contribute to the development of an effective form of federalism with powers shared more evenly by the Kremlin and Russia's subjects.[11] The regions in the middle, while not bulwarks of democracy, at least should not contribute to any authoritarian tendencies in the country. It is the last group of regions that is the cause for alarm, since, by varying degrees, politics in these regions appears to resemble local authoritarianism, and they would be likely to support or succumb to any moves by the Kremlin to develop a contracted transition to a neo-authoritarian regime.

Validity of the model

While the regional index of democratisation developed here is a significant means of discerning trends in democratisation across Russia's regions, caution must still be exercised in placing too much confidence in these findings. After all, in order to make such a large amount of information manageable, the data were necessarily simplified, perhaps distorting reality in the process. It is useful, therefore, to compare the results of this study with those of other researchers who have examined regional democratisation in Russia.

Other studies have used electoral data in similar ways to make determinations about regional democratisation, such as McFaul and Petrov's analysis of the 1995 Duma and 1996 presidential elections.[12] While there are

Regional politics

Table 10.1 *Comparison of regional democracy ratings*

Region	McMann-Petrov ranking	ID ranking[a]	Participation	Competition	Democratisation index
Belgorod	33[b]	1	71.33	46.54	3320
Tver	23	2	65.45[c]	53.46	3272
Kirov	33	3	72.29	41.97	3034
Pskov	33	4	54.12	71.99	2705
Penza	52	5	53.44	55.50	2671
St Petersburg	1	42	47.74	27.31	1304
Sverdlovsk	2	29	40.00	36.91[c]	1476
Nizhnii Novgorod	3	33	37.68	40.20[c]	1514
Samara	4	24	45.34	46.75	2119
Moscow City	5	30	66.13[d]	30.11	1991

Notes: [a] In order to compare the scores of the index used here with the ranking system developed by McMann and Petrov only the regions included in the latter study were included in this ranking. Actuall scores for all of the 78 regions included in this study can be found in the appendix. [b] Tied for 33rd. [c] This is the level of competition from the run-off election. [d] Election coincided with the December 1999 Duma elections, which may have led to a higher electoral turnout.

significant differences between our findings, the two models are not comparable, since they are based on different types of electoral data and employ data from very different periods of time. Indeed, these facts make a comparison of any two different models highly problematical.

With this caveat in mind, it might be useful to compare the results of the regional index of democratisation developed here with another significant study of Russian regional democratisation, albeit one that takes a drastically different approach to addressing a similar question. In their study of democracy in Russia's regions, McMann and Petrov rely upon a survey of forty experts who ranked the top ten most and least democratic regions. While this approach is not without its own problems, as some respondents ranked as the most democratic the very same regions that other experts considered the least democratic, it does serve the useful purpose of a benchmark against which we can compare the results of the regional index of democratisation.

In comparison with McMann and Petrov's rankings, there is no significant relationship between the two measures ($r = -0.027$; $p = 0.848$). In fact, just how different these two rankings are can be seen by comparing the top five regions according to each index. While the McMann and Petrov rankings put St Petersburg, Sverdlovsk, Nizhnii Novgorod, Samara and Moscow City as the top five, these regions only attained rankings of 42, 29, 33, 24 and 30, respectively, according to the index developed here (see Table 10.1).[13] By comparison, of the regions included in the McMann and Petrov rankings, Belgorod, Tver, Kirov, Pskov and Penza would be ranked the highest according to the index of democratisation due to their high levels of electoral competition and political participation.

Given the lack of a significant correlation between the two indexes and the incongruous findings, it is very clear that two very different phenomena are being measured. This is somewhat surprising, considering that in each case it is Dahl's concept of democracy that we are attempting to operationalise. In fact, it may be the different emphases placed on Dahl's various attributes of democracy that is the cause of the divergent findings. While the index of democratisation focuses exclusively on levels of contestation and participation, the respondents in McMann and Petrov's study were asked to consider democracy in much broader terms, including issues of freedom, participation rights, and civil liberties.

Quite simply, McMann and Petrov's study analyses respondents' perceptions of freedom, rights and liberties in the regions, while the index of democratisation only considers the degree to which the two rights of electoral contestation and political participation are actually exercised. This comparison is useful, therefore, as a means of illustrating just how limited are our current measures of regional democratisation. While we may still have a way to go before we have a sufficiently robust means of measuring democracy in Russia's regions, the various approaches being developed are certainly superior to anecdotal assessments and they provide useful benchmarks for comparison.

Explaining regional democratisation

At this point we have measured regional democratisation in Russia and identified great variation among the regions, but measurement is only half the job. To be of any real value to scholars and policy-makers, we must also explain the variation in these levels in order to determine the factors that contribute to further democratisation and potential obstacles to successful democratic consolidation. In the sections that follow, I thus explore various explanations for the identified levels of democracy in Russia's regions by examining the statistical relationship between the index of democratisation and various explanatory factors, primarily those associated with social capital, civil society, and socio-economic development.

Civil society, social capital and democratisation

Increasingly, scholars are identifying a vibrant civil society and the social capital generated therein as critical to the effective functioning of democracy and as important factors in the processes of democratisation and democratic consolidation.[14] At least as far back as de Tocqueville, observers have pointed

Table 10.2 Regression models of civic community indicators predicting index of regional democratisation

Independent predictors	Model 1 Unstandard coefficient (s)	Model 1 Standard coefficient (s)	Model 2 Unstandard coefficient (s)	Model 2 Standard coefficient (s)	Model 3 Unstandard coefficient (s)	Model 3 Standard coefficient (s)	Model 4 Unstandard coefficient (s)	Model 4 Standard coefficient (s)
CONSTANT	150.050 (956.919)		562.179 (925.759)		1836.84[b] (178.495)		294.543 (950.328)	
REFEREND	16.766[b] (6.015)	0.323	15.063[a] (5.937)	0.285			16.355[b] (6.020)	0.310
SOBRANIE	−6.767 (6.848)	−0.119	−5.693 (6.456)	−0.099			−6.252 (6.456)	−0.109
CIVIC	0.321 (0.199)	0.184			0.186 (0.205)	0.106	0.228 (0.192)	0.133
NEWS	0.105 (0.133)	0.093			2.861 (0.132)	0.025		
R-square	0.138[a]		0.104[a]		0.012		0.121[a]	
R-square adj.	0.089		0.081		−0.016		0.086	

Notes: Standard errors are given in parentheses beneath coefficients. Significance levels are: [a] $p < 0.05$; [b] $p < 0.01$; ^ moderately significant at the 0.10 level. $n = 78$; cases missing data excluded.

to civil society – that relatively autonomous realm that rests between the state and the private sphere – as an integral component of a flourishing democratic polity. It is thus simple logic to infer that an efficacious civil society will play a significant role in regional democratisation in Russia as well. To test this hypothesis, I correlate the index of regional democratisation with indicators associated with civic engagement and social capital. The indicators I employ in this task include the number of civic organisations (sign of civic involvement), participation in referenda and elections (signs of civic engagement), and the availability of print media (sign of civic interest). Specifically, I use the number of registered civic organisations in 1996 (CIVIC); participation in the 1993 referenda (REFEREND); participation in regional legislative elections 1994–96 (SOBRANIE); and the number of newspapers published in 1999 (NEWS) (see Appendix 10.2 for details).

In order to determine the impact of civil society and social capital on regional democratisation in Russia, I ran several regression analyses using the index of regional democratisation as the dependent variable (see Table 10.2). In the first model, I included all of the variables associated with a civic community. The resulting regression coefficient was statistically significant and explained a sizeable proportion of the variation in levels of democracy among Russia's regions ($R^2 = 0.138$). In the second model, I included only the two indicators associated with electoral behaviour (REFEREND and SOBRANIE). The model was also statistically significant, although its explanatory power decreased slightly.

In the third model, I then focused on the two non-electoral indicators (CIVIC and NEWS). The inclusion of only these two variables in the model resulted in no significant correlations. Finally, in the fourth and final model, I included all of the variables except for the NEWS variable, which was removed to determine how powerful the model was with only three independent variables. While the first model remained the most powerful, the fourth model was nearly as powerful when considering the adjusted R-square. The modest strength of the correlations between indicators of civil society and social capital force us to conclude that other factors must play equally critical roles in the process of regional democratisation.

Socio-economic development, marketisation and democratisation

Prior to the 1990s, when scholars began focusing on the importance of civil society and social capital in the performance of democratic regimes, a country's relative level of socio-economic development was considered one of the most significant determinants of democracy. While this 'modernisation' literature dates back perhaps even to Aristotle, contemporary scholars have only refined the theory, not abandoned it. In fact, in reconsidering the relationship between socio-economic development and democracy in the 1990s,

Table 10.3 Regression models of socio-economic development indicators predicting index of regional democratisation

Independent predictors	Model 1 Unstandard coefficient (s)	Model 1 Standard coefficient (s)	Model 2 Unstandard coefficient (s)	Model 2 Standard coefficient (s)	Model 3 Unstandard coefficient (s)	Model 3 Standard coefficient (s)	Model 4 Unstandard coefficient (s)	Model 4 Standard coefficient (s)
CONSTANT	2404.38[b] (363.012)		2568.02[b] (289.237)		2107.42[b] (208.607)		2505.91[b] (351.117)	
STUDENTS	0.705 (3.583)	0.031			−0.728 (1.004)	−0.091	1.172 (3.624)	0.323
CHANGE	−127.391 (99.830)	−0.202	−57.568 (81.698)	−0.087			−119.077 (101.004)	−0.186
MARKET	−388.984[^] (231.594)	−0.293	−323.151[a] (138.107)	−0.289			−285.392[^] (161.884)	−0.227
GNP	0.404 (0.317)	0.221			−3.348 (0.227)	−0.019		
R-square	0.077		0.083[^]		0.009		0.068	
R-square adj.	0.010		0.053		−0.023		0.019	

Notes: Standard errors are given in parentheses beneath coefficients. Significance levels are: [a] $p < 0.05$; [b] $p < 0.01$; [^] moderately significant at the 0.10 level. $n = 78$; cases missing data excluded.

Variations in Russian regional democratisation

Diamond concluded that 'the more well to do the people of a country ... the more likely they will favour, achieve, and maintain a democratic system for their country'.[15]

While Russia as a whole seems to have favoured and achieved a democratic system, we are presently concerned with the country's ability to maintain this system of governance into the future. In addition, the relationship between socio-economic development and democracy in Russia is confounded by the fact that the country was developed not as a result of Western capitalism but rather through state socialism and a planned economy. This historical fact may complicate the process, for it was implicitly understood in the West that the correlation between socio-economic development and democracy was dependent upon the nature of that economic system, i.e. free-market capitalism. Indeed, the liberal notion of the free marketplace of ideas was seen as an inevitable result of the *laissez-faire* nature of economic interaction inherent in the free market. If this is true, and free-market development in fact played a role in fostering democracy across the globe, then we can assume that marketisation – the successful development of free markets – will contribute to democratisation in Russia. To test these hypotheses, I correlate the index of regional democratisation with indicators associated with socio-economic development and marketisation (see Table 10.3). The indicators I employ in this task include the level of education (indicator of social development); per capita GNP (indicator of economic development); conversion rate for state enterprises (indicator of market adjustment);[16] and the value of goods traded (indicator of market development). Specifically, I use the number of students enrolled in institutions of higher education in 1999–2000 (STUDENTS); per capita GNP in 1996 (GNP); a combined index of conversion rates for state and collective farms, private enterprises, and joint-stock companies in 1996–97 (CHANGE); and the value of retail trade in 1996 (MARKET).

In order to test the relationship between these factors, I ran all of the variables in a multiple regression using the index of democratisation as the dependent variable. Surprisingly, the model was not statistically significant. In model 2, I included only the two indicators of marketisation (CHANGE and MARKET). The correlation between these variables was only mildly significant and very weakly correlated ($R^2 = 0.083$). Running the two indicators of socio-economic development (STUDENTS and GNP) against the dependent variable in model 3 confirmed my suspicion that these variables were not significantly correlated. Finally, including all of the independent variables except for the GNP variable did not make model 4 significant. The conclusion I reach from these analyses is that, in isolation from other pertinent factors, levels of socio-economic development cannot explain the observed variation in the levels of democratisation, although indicators of market adjustment and development do seem to have some explanatory power.

Table 10.4 Regression models of civic community and socio-economic development indicators predicting index of regional democratisation

Independent predictors	Model 1 Unstandard coefficient (s)	Model 1 Standard coefficient (s)	Model 2 Unstandard coefficient (s)	Model 2 Standard coefficient (s)	Model 3 Unstandard coefficient (s)	Model 3 Standard coefficient (s)	Model 4 Unstandard coefficient (s)	Model 4 Standard coefficient (s)
CONSTANT	−373.675 (1157.405)		272.086 (955.581)		−840.545 (1060.126)		−75.212 (988.990)	
REFEREND	15.287[a] (6.378)	0.303	16.982[b] (6.118)	0.325	17.475[b] (5.995)	0.346	15.154[a] (6.333)	0.300
SOBRANIE	4.639 (9.185)	0.063	−5.063 (7.066)	−0.090	2.300 (8.886)	0.031		
CHANGE	−181.334^ (97.933)	−0.274			−179.551^ (97.925)	−0.271	−168.485^ (93.982)	−0.254
MARKET	−152.840 (152.113)	−0.136	−31.987 (85.635)	−0.049			−133.371 (146.232)	−0.119
CIVIC	0.626[a] (0.278)	0.342	0.154 (0.203)	0.090	0.712[b] (0.265)	0.389	0.620[a] (0.276)	0.339
R-square	0.202[a]		0.138[a]		0.188[a]		0.198[b]	
R-square adj.	0.134		0.090		0.134		0.145	

Notes: Standard errors are given in parentheses beneath coefficients. Significance levels are: [a] $p < 0.05$; [b] $p < 0.01$; ^ moderately significant at the 0.10 level. $n = 78$; cases missing data excluded.

Combined and intervening effects

Although many researchers tend to focus their research on the role of either civil society or socio-economic conditions in the functioning of democratic systems, both groups of researchers also recognize that no single set of factors alone can explain democratic outcomes. In fact, civil society and socio-economic development are themselves related in often complex ways, including the propensity for civil societies to emerge in societies with relatively high levels of socio-economic development and for civil society to play an important role in the functioning of economic exchange.[17] It therefore makes sense to combine the indicators of civil society and socio-economic development used above in seeking to explain the observed variations in levels of regional democratisation in Russia.

The combined effects of the civil society and socio-economic development indicators are much greater than that of either set of factors alone (see Table 10.4). Including the three most powerful civil society indicators and the two most powerful socio-economic development indicators in a single model resulted in a rather strong and robust correlation with the regional index of democratisation ($R^2 = 0.202$). Together, these five independent variables can explain fully 20 per cent of the variation in levels of democratisation among Russia's regions. Removing the indicator of market adjustment (CHANGE) resulted in a significant reduction in the explanatory power of model 2, thus confirming the importance of the free market in post-Communist democratic development. Removing only the indicator of market development (MARKET) had only a slight impact of the strength of model 3, however, indicating that the relationship between democracy and the market in Russia is a complex one, perhaps even indicating that it is not so much the performance of free markets that is crucial, but simply their establishment. Finally, in model 4, the inclusion of all the variables except for participation in local legislative elections (SOBRANIE) resulted in a very slight reduction in explanatory power and a greater adjusted R^2, a natural result of removing one of the independent variables from the model. The combined effects of civil society and socio-economic development, therefore, have a consistently powerful and robust effect on levels of democratisation across Russia's regions.

As important as civil society and socio-economic development might be, political life is also influenced by numerous other factors, including history, religion, and ethnicity. While many such factors confound quantification, some are rather easily measured by the use of proxy indicators. Given the large amount of literature documenting the importance of ethnic factors in Russian regional politics,[18] I attempt here to control the intervening effects of ethnicity with the use of two simple proxy indicators for ethnicity. Ethnicity may impact on Russian regional politics in at least two ways, culturally and institutionally. I attempt to control for the cultural differences of

Table 10.5 Regression models of civic community and socio-economic development indicators predicting index of regional democratisation, controlling for ethnicity

Independent predictors	Model 1 Unstandard coefficient (s)	Model 1 Standard coefficient (s)	Model 2 Unstandard coefficient (s)	Model 2 Standard coefficient (s)	Model 3 Unstandard coefficient (s)	Model 3 Standard coefficient (s)	Model 4 Unstandard coefficient (s)	Model 4 Standard coefficient (s)
CONSTANT	−75.212 (988.990)		−757.823 (1147.668)		−1049.605 (1083.431)		−860.325 (1131.422)	
REFEREND	15.154[a] (6.333)	0.300	17.565[a] (6.646)	0.348	20.568[b] (6.759)	0.407	20.697[b] (6.798)	0.410
CHANGE	−168.485^ (93.982)	−0.254	−134.207 (98.237)	−0.203	−99.567 (98.123)	−0.150	−100.997 (98.668)	−0.152
MARKET	−133.371 (146.232)	−0.119	−131.079 (145.818)	−0.117	−93.755 (144.172)	−0.084	−79.708 (146.706)	−0.071
CIVIC	0.620[a] (0.276)	0.339	0.638[a] (0.276)	0.349	0.629[a] (0.270)	0.344	0.617[a] (0.272)	0.337
STATUS			315.711 (271.558)	0.153			−269.599 (436.369)	−0.131
ETHNIC					13.172^ (6.641)	0.266	18.493[a] (10.897)	0.373
R-square	0.198[b]		0.216[a]		0.248[b]		0.253[b]	
R-square adj.	0.145		0.150		0.185		0.176	

Notes: Standard errors are given in parentheses beneath coefficients. Significance levels are: [a] $p < 0.05$; [b] $p < 0.01$; ^ moderately significant at the 0.10 level. $n = 78$; cases missing data excluded.

Variations in Russian regional democratisation

Russia's regions by including the proportion of a region's population that is not ethnically Russian (ETHNIC). This allows me to measure the size of a region's minority population, which is difficult to determine since many of Russia's ethnic regions are composed of several minority nationalities. Additionally, ethnicity may impact on politics through some institutional factor relating to a region's juridical status, with ethnic regions acting as some sort of vehicle for ethnic entrepreneurs, regardless of a region's actual ethnic composition.[19] To control for the impact of such a factor, I include a dichotomous variable which divides the eighty-nine regions into two groups (STATUS), the thirty-one ethno-territorial regions (the twenty-one ethnic republics and the ten autonomous okrugs) and the country's fifty-eight krais, oblasts, and 'cities of federal significance' (Moscow and St Petersburg).

In model 1 (see Table 10.5), I again present the results of the most powerful and parsimonious model for explaining levels of democratisation in Russia's regions, that first presented as model 4 in Table 10.4. Adding the ethnic state variable (STATUS) to this model results in a modest increase in explanatory power, although at the expense of a modest reduction in statistical significance. In model 3, however, in which I add the control variable of ethnic composition (ETHNIC) to the four explanatory variables, there is a significant increase in explanatory power and the model is also significant at the highest levels of confidence. Finally, the inclusion of both control variables leads to only a slight increase in explanatory power while also resulting in a slight reduction in the adjusted R^2 as a result of having such a large number of independent variables in the model. While civil society and socio-economic development indicators alone may be limited in their explanatory power, therefore, combining these variables and controlling for the intervening effects of ethnicity can explain approximately 25 per cent of the variation in levels of democratisation across Russia's regions.

Conclusion

While the results of the statistical analyses conducted here indicate first and foremost that we still have more questions about Russian regional democratisation than we have answers, a few significant conclusions can still be reached. Perhaps most significant has been the finding that democratisation across Russia's regions is progressing in a slow and uneven manner, with some regions developing vibrant political communities while citizens in other regions remain nothing more than the pawns of local bosses. While the fact that democracy is lacking in many parts of Russia is cause enough for alarm, the situation becomes even more critical when one considers the possible implications of this for the country's political development, for substantial bases of democratic support are crucial for the development of an effective form of federalism based on a separation of powers. The question remains as to whether or not a small number of regions with strong commitments to democracy will be able to endure and resist any authoritarian tendencies in the country.

The consistent relationship between civil society and regional democratisation identified here indicates that civil society plays an important role in democratisation, and that the flourishing of civil society in many regions of Russia contributes significantly to the country's democratic consolidation. It is still premature to draw any definitive conclusions, however, for the period of democratic consolidation is often one of declining civic involvement in community affairs. Indeed, this has been the case in democratising states around the world and it seems to be the case in Russia as well. One reason for this is that once a transition to democracy begins, the ranks of many civil society organisations are rapidly depleted as opposition leaders are drawn into politics, government, or business.[20] This does not necessarily mean, however, that stocks of social capital disappear never to rise up again. While the citizenry becomes more preoccupied with the concerns of daily life and less involved in civic affairs as the heady days of the fight for democracy against the Soviet system drift into the past, civil society may rise up again in times of need.

While civil society seems to contribute to regional democratisation, it is certainly not the whole story. Other factors account for a sizeable proportion of the variation as well. This should come as no surprise, given that myriad factors affect the process of democratic consolidation, from transition problems such as weeding out pro-authoritarian officials to contextual problems including socio-economic inequality and communal conflicts.[21] It is not necessary to point out that pro-authoritarian figures still exist in Russia today, or that Russia's regions do not just vary in levels of civil society, but in levels of socio-economic development and the tenor of communal relations as well. Indeed, the examination above of the relationship between socio-economic development and regional democratisation indicates that these factors also play a significant role in Russian democratic development, particularly regarding the development of free markets. The significant impact of ethnicity in the above analyses also indicates that the process of Russian democratisation is also complicated by the country's ethnic diversity, a particularly troubling finding given that this factor has played significant roles in derailing democratisation efforts in other multinational states, such as the former Yugoslavia.

Beyond these contextual issues, the actions of individuals are also important. The immediate actions of individuals not only lead a country to democratise, they also affect the process of democratic consolidation once a transition is underway. As Huntington points out, the chances of whether a democracy will fail or consolidate 'depends primarily on the extent to which political leaders wish to maintain it and are willing to pay the costs of doing so instead of giving priority to other goals.'[22] While these factors may defy

Variations in Russian regional democratisation

quantification, and thus do not fit neatly into the sort of analyses conducted here, we should not discount their significance in drawing conclusions about the future of democracy in Russia. Nevertheless, an examination of the role of civil society and socio-economic development in regional democratisation gives us a clearer picture of how democracy is progressing in Russia and the factors that both contribute to or detract from that process.

Appendix 10.1

Region	Participation	Competition	ID	Level
Sakha	75.54	40.75	3776	5
Karachaevo-Cherkesia	70.17	24.29	3508	5
Evenki	68.28	48.92	3340	5
Belgorod	71.33	46.54	3320	5
Tver	65.45	53.46	3272	5
Koryak	63.38	49.32	3126	4
Tyva	65.58	46.45	3046	4
Kirov	72.29	41.97	3034	4
Jewish Autonomous Oblast	68.70	43.24	2971	4
Mari El	57.37	41.77	2868	4
Altai Republic	56.89	31.85	2844	4
Chuvashiya	56.46	59.27	2822	4
Pskov	54.12	71.99	2705	4
Penza	53.44	55.50	2671	4
Bryansk	53.36	70.79	2667	4
Severnaya Ossetiya	60.13	43.98	2645	4
Komi-Permyak	51.86	55.75	2592	4
Tyumen'	54.25	47.22	2562	4
Novosibirsk	50.57	45.68	2528	4
Volgograd	50.40	63.28	2519	4
Udmurtiya	50.23	62.16	2511	4
Novgorod	50.16	8.44	2507	4
Ust'-Ordin Buryat	54.04	46.33	2504	4
Yaroslavl	68.53	36.22	2482	4
Ulyanovsk	56.29	43.74	2462	4
Saratov	74.99	32.74	2455	4
Komi	48.34	60.25	2417	4
Orenburg	47.87	47.98	2393	3
Perm	48.92	48.52	2374	3
Kursk	47.30	44.46	2365	3
Kaliningrad	47.02	43.53	2351	3
Nenets Autonomous Okrug	73.77	31.72	2340	3
Moscow Oblast	46.01	51.91	2300	3
Kamchatka	45.70	54.17	2285	3

Regional politics

Region	Participation	Competition	ID	Level
Tambov	44.54	49.66	2227	3
Omsk	51.25	42.97	2202	3
Taimyr	63.94	34.30	2193	3
Stavropol	43.33	43.43	2166	3
Chita	50.29	42.98	2161	3
Ivanovo	42.88	37.64	2144	3
Samara	45.34	46.75	2120	3
Leningrad Oblast	41.73	69.70	2086	3
Ryazan	41.65	34.86	2082	3
Chelyabinsk	50.25	41.32	2076	3
Kurgan	40.94	49.62	2047	3
Sverdlovsk	40.00	36.91	2000	3
Moscow city	66.13	30.11	1991	3
Kostroma	39.56	36.91	1978	3
Adygeya	62.83	31.11	1955	3
Voronezh	47.59	40.01	1904	3
Nizhnii Novgorod	37.68	40.20	1884	3
Irkutsk	37.36	52.37	1868	3
Arkhangelsk	36.50	41.50	1825	3
Primorskii Krai	36.00	61.00	1800	3
Sakhalin	39.77	43.71	1738	3
Kaluga	39.08	43.28	1691	3
Tatarstan	79.37	20.48	1625	3
Altai Krai	71.23	22.59	1609	3
Magadan	42.30	37.24	1575	2
Khakasiya	52.25	28.77	1503	2
Tomsk	48.61	27.17	1321	2
St Petersburg	47.74	27.31	1304	2
Amur	25.00	50.58	1250	2
Vladimir	34.00	34.38	1169	2
Kabardino-Balkariya	85.87	12.82	1101	2
Rostov	48.32	21.81	1054	2
Astrakhan	55.17	18.18	1003	2
Murmansk	69.11	13.29	918	2
Krasnodar	46.73	18.22	851	2
Yamal-Nenets	68.66	11.90	817	2
Tula	25.00	28.66	717	1
Agin-Buryat	65.12	10.66	694	1
Chukotka	67.59	9.39	635	1
Khanty-Mansi	67.96	9.18	624	1
Orel	69.65	8.48	591	1
Khabarovsk	46.45	12.16	565	1
Vologda	25.00	21.45	536	1
Kemerovo	52.17	6.46	337	1

Variations in Russian regional democratisation

Appendix 10.2

Dependent variable

Comprised of two indicators: level of participation in gubernatorial elections and votes for candidates other than the winner of the election. Figures calculated from data obtained from the Central Electoral Commission of the Russian Federation website, http://www.fci.ru/.

Coding key

Participation
Percentage of eligible voters that participated in the election. If the first round was declared invalid due to a low turnout (as was the case in three regions: Vologda, Tula and Amur) then participation is calculated as 25 per cent, not as the level of turnout in the subsequent election (which could have been artificially 'raised' in order to meet the minimum).

Competition
The level of competition is calculated as the total number of votes given to candidates other than the winner. In cases in which there was a run-off election due to the failure of any one candidate to gain a 50 per cent majority (as is required by law in most regions), then the level of competition is calculated at 49.99, not as the number of votes given to the loser in the run-off. This is because the level of competition is automatically high (as expressed in the first round) no matter how many votes go to the winner in the second round. The level of competition is not affected by a run-off due to low turnout.

Independent variables

CHANGE: The Index of Change was calculated using data on the number of enterprises privatised in 1996, the number of joint-stock companies formed in 1996, and the conversion rates of state and collective farms in Russia as of January 1996. Data from *Regiony Rossii 1997: Tom 2* (Moscow: Goskomstat Rossii, 1997), 450–452, 577–579, 610–612.

CIVIC: The number of clubs and cultural associations in Russia's regions in 1996 (*chislo uchrezhdenii klubnogo typa*). Data gathered by author at Goskomstat Rossii, January 1998. Data available from author upon request.

ETHNIC: The percentage of a region's population that is not Russian, calculated as the percentage of a region's population that is Russian subtracted from 100. Ethnic data obtained from *Narody Rossii: Entsiklopediya* (Moscow: Bol'shaya Rossiskaya Entsiklopediya, 1994), 443–441.

GNP: Per capita GNP, 1996. Data from *Regiony Rossii 1997: Tom 2* (Moscow: Goskomstat Rossii, 1997).

MARKET: Volume of retail trade. Data from *Regiony Rossii 1997: Tom 2* (Moscow: Goskomstat Rossii, 1997).

NEWS: The number of newspapers published in each region in 1999, adjusted for population. Data from *Regiony Rossii 2000: Tom 2* (Moscow: Goskomstat Rossii, 2001), 256.

REFEREND: Level of participation in the 1993 referenda. The turnout for the April and December referenda are summed. Data from Leonid Smyrnyagin, *Rossiiskie Regiony Nakanune Vyborov-1995* (Moscow: Iuridicheskaya Literatura, 1995), 6–184.

SOBRANIE: Level of participation in regional legislative elections, 1994–96. Data from Leonid Smyrnyagin, *Rossiiskie Regiony Nakanune Vyborov-1995* (Moscow: Iuridicheskaya Literatura, 1995), 6–184.

STATUS: A dichotomous variable for the federal status of a region, with the ethnic republics and autonomous okrugs in one group and the non-ethnic regions in another.

STUDENTS: Number of students enrolled in institutions of higher learning, 1999–2000. Data from *Regiony Rossii 2000: Tom 2* (Moscow: Goskomstat Rossii, 2001), 194–199.

Notes

The author would like to thank Laura Belin, Vladimir Gel'man, Gregory Kljutcharev, William Reisinger, and Cameron Ross for their helpful comments and assistance.

1. C. Ross, 'Federalism and democratisation in Russia', *Communist and Post-Communist Studies*, 33 (2000), 403–420.
2. N. Petro, 'The Novgorod region: a Russian success story', *Post-Soviet Affairs*, 15:3 (1999).
3. A more detailed discussion of the recent wave of gubernatorial elections, albeit one that focuses on only the sixty-five regions that held elections between May 1999 and June 2001, is contained in Christopher Marsh, 'Social capital and grassroots democracy in Russia's regions: evidence from the 1999–2001 gubernatorial elections', *Demokratizatsiya*, 10:1 (2002), 19–36.
4. R. Dahl, *Democracy and Its Critics* (New Haven: Yale University Press, 1989).
5. T. Vanhanen, *Prospects of Democracy: A Study of 172 Countries* (London: Routledge, 1997).
6. D. Slider, 'Elections to Russia's regional assemblies', *Post-Soviet Affairs,* 12 (1996), 243–64.
7. Ross, 'Federalism'; Slider, 'Elections'.
8. The scores ranged from 337.02 to 2776.24 (mean = 1999.24; SD = 808.07). The regional scores were converted into a five-level scale by placing the regions with scores within the range of one-half standard deviation above and below the mean into level 3, and setting cut-off points for the other ranges based on their being one or two standard deviations above or below level 3. The ranges developed are as follows: Level 5: 3211.35–3776.20; n = 5; Level 4: 2403.28–3211.34; n = 22; Level 3: 1595.21–2403.27; n = 31; Level 2: 787.14–1595.20; n = 12; Level 1: 337.02–787.13; n = 8.
9. 'Russian paper outlines Kremlin ways of losing unwanted governors', *BBC Monitoring*, from *Johnson's Russia List*, 4639 (16 November 2000).
10. While this analysis includes thirteen more cases than my earlier analysis of the 1999–2001 gubernatorial elections, my conclusions remain the same as published in Marsh, 'Social capital and grassroots democracy in Russia's regions'.

11 J. W. Warhola, 'Is the Russian Federation becoming more democratic? Moscow–regional relations and the development of the post-Soviet Russian state', *Democratisation*, 6:2 (1999), 42–69.
12 M. McFaul and N. Petrov, 'Russian electoral politics after transition: regional and national assessments', *Post-Soviet Geography and Economics*, 38:9 (1997), 507–549.
13 These are not the actual rankings for the index of democratisation, however, since McMann and Petrov included only fifty-seven regions in their analysis. In calculating my rankings for this comparison, I used only the fifty-seven regions included in their analysis.
14 R. Putnam, Making *Democracy Work: Civic Traditions in Modern Italy* (Princeton, NJ: Princeton University Press, 1993); C. Marsh, *Making Russian Democracy Work: Social Capital, Economic Development, and Democratisation* (Lewiston, New York: Mellen Press, 2000).
15 L. Diamond, 'Economic development and democracy reconsidered', *American Behavioral Scientist*, 35 (1992), 468.
16 For more on the reform of the Russian rural economy, see D. J. O'Brien and S. K. Wegren (eds.), *Rural Reform in Post-Soviet Russia* (Baltimore: Johns Hopkins University Press, 2002). In particular, see Chapter 10, 'The ethnic dimension of adaptation and change', by C. Marsh and J. W. Warhola, which explores the regional differences in reform using this index of change.
17 For some recent examples of research into the relationship between civil society and economic conditions, see D. Skidmore, 'Civil society, social capital and economic development', *Global Society*, 15:1 (2001), 53–72; and C. M. Tolbert, M. D. Irwin, T. A. Lyson and A. R. Nucci, 'Civic community in small-town America: how civic welfare is influenced by local capitalism and civic engagement', *Rural Sociology*, 67:1 (2002), 90–113.
18 See, among others, A. Chirikova and N. Lapina, 'Political power and political stability in the Russian regions', in A. Brown (ed.), *Contemporary Russian Politics: A Reader* (Oxford: Oxford University Press, 2001), pp. 384–397; D. Gorenburg, 'Regional separatism in Russia: ethnic mobilisation or power grab?', *Europe-Asia Studies*, 51:2 (1999), 245–274; C. Marsh and J. W. Warhola, 'Ethnicity, ethnoregionalism, and the political geography of Putin's electoral support', *Post-Soviet Geography and Economics*, 43:3 (2001), 220–233; C. Marsh and J. W. Warhola, 'Ethnicity, modernisation, and regime support in Russia's regions under Yeltsin', *Nationalism and Ethnic Politics*, 6:4 (2000), 23–47; and G. Smith, 'Russia, ethnoregionalism and the politics of federation', *Ethnic and Racial Studies*, 19:2 (1996), 391–410.
19 Marsh and Warhola, 'Ethnicity', 2001.
20 L. Diamond, M. Plattner, Y. Chu, and H. Tien (eds.), *Consolidating the Third Wave Democracies* (Baltimore, MD: Johns Hopkins University Press, 1997), pp. xxxi–xxxii.
21 S. Huntington, *The Third Wave: Democratisation in the Late Twentieth Century* (Norman, OK: University of Oklahoma Press, 1991), pp. 209–279.
22 *Ibid.*, p. 279.

11

Regional elections and democratisation in Russia[1]

Valentin Mikhailov

Introduction

The level of democracy in a country can be determined by a number of factors such as: the freedom and diversity of the media, the independence and accessibility of courts, the development of a strong and vibrant 'civil society', the creation of democratically accountable political institutions (e.g., legislative and executive bodies) whose rules and procedures conform to internationally accepted standards and, last but not least, the provision of free and fair elections. Some of these key concepts of a democratic state are closely inter-connected and, in turn, influence the development of other indicators of democratisation (see Chapter 10). Among the above parameters, the character of elections and the degree to which they are free and fair is, possibly, the most sensitive indicator of the level of democracy in a state. The way in which elections are conducted and reported allows us, for example, to determine the freedom of the media and the strength of the civil society, and hence, of democratisation in general.

Studying elections in Russia's regions

The actions of governments and the behaviour of citizens vary enormously among Russia's eighty-nine regions. Consequently, the analysis of electoral returns which are averaged for the country as a whole cannot capture important variations in regional electoral data. In this study I examine regional voting statistics at the level of Territorial Election Commissions (TECs) (*Territorial'naya Izbiratel'nykh Komissii*) and the even lower level Presinct Election Commissions (PECs) (*Uchastkovaya Izbiratel'nykh Komissii*).

As McFaul and Petrov stress, 'Russia's peculiarity is not in the fact of falsification, but in the scope of it, and also in the cultural acceptability of it for both the politicians and the society as a whole.'[2] Republican presidents and regional governors in many of Russia's federal subjects have manipulated the conduct of elections and/or falsified election results. By using the many 'administrative resources' at their command (i.e., their command of the organisational and financial powers of their local administrations and their powers over the media, courts and electoral commissions), regional leaders have been able to prolong their tenure in office and also to 'bring home' the regional votes for their choice of candidates in national parliamentary and presidential elections. As Michael McFaul notes President Putin must now 'tread especially lightly in those places where regional leaders probably falsified the results to help push ... [him] over the 50 per cent threshold. If Putin strikes out against these regional leaders, they might be tempted to expose their falsification efforts, which in turn could call into question the legitimacy of the election results more generally'.[3]

In an important study, Oreshkin provides a territorial analysis of the 1999 State Duma and 2000 presidential elections.[4] He and his colleagues analysed nine parameters where there were deviations from the statistical norm. These parameters included, for example, voter's participation and non-valid voting forms. As a result of this analysis, Oreshkin created a map of Russia which was divided into four groups of regions. Each group contains four levels of 'administrative control'. I used a similar methodology in my quantitative comparison of the voting pattern of the winners of the first and second rounds of Russia's presidential elections in 1996[5] and I expanded this major study of Russia's 2,700 TECs to include the March 2000 presidential elections.[6]

In this chapter I shall use a statistical methodology to assess the degree to which the results of elections at the TEC and PEC levels deviate from that which has been statistically predicted. The scope of the deviation will demonstrate the degree to which 'administrative resources' have been utilised to manipulate elections.

Administrative control over elections results

To dispel any illusions we might have regarding the real opportunities which regional authorities have to manipulate and falsify elections, we have compiled a short table comparing the official results of the first and second rounds of Russia's 1996 presidential elections. Table 11.1 presents the results of separate PECs.[7]

The normal values of K lie within the interval from 1.0 to 1.6. In Table 11.1 we can see that electors initially voted mainly for Zyuganov, but in the second round they made a complete reversal switching their votes to Yeltsin. The data in the last column indicates that such practices are not confined to one TEC, similar cases are to be found in many rural areas of Tatarstan. Such erratic voting patters suggest either that the results of the elections were falsified or that there was pressure on every citizen to vote as

Table 11.1 Examples of 'administrative management' of the 1996 presidential elections in Tatarstan

District (TEC) of Tatarstan	No. of PEKs	First round: 16 June 1996				Second round: 03 July 1996				Reorientation coefficient K	No. of PEKs inside TEC with K > 40
		No. of voters	Turnout	Yeltsin Y_1	Zyuganov Z_1	No. of voters	Turnout	Yeltsin Y_2	Zyuganov Z_2		
Bavly 1	435	794	791	250	354	789	789	728	22	**47**	8 out of 31
Bavly 2	438	497	497	21	442	497	497	457	16	**601**	8 out of 31
Zainsk	1692	601	511	31	431	600	560	429	110	**54**	8 out of 41
Muslyum 1	473	276	275	29	209	277	275	98	166	**4.2**	9 out of 38
Muslyum 2	474	297	292	19	242	300	298	283	7	**514**	9 out of 38

Note: Reorientation coefficient $K = Y_2 * Z_1 / Z_2 * Y_1$.

instructed from the republican leadership. In the Muslyum district we have purposefully selected two electoral committees with contrasting results. These are neighbouring committees. The first has K = 4.2, the second has K = 514. In the latter committee, in the second round of elections, out of the 242 individuals who voted for Zyuganov in the first round there were only 7 left in the second round, while the number of Yeltsin's supporters increased 15-fold (from 19 to 283).

Further analysis of the numerous deviations from the standard statistical and electoral norms is outside the scope of this work, although these deviations become obvious if we consider the results of TECs in the rural areas. We will only note that even in the most 'managed' regions there is a considerable deviation of K. For example, in Zainsk region, where there is a mean value of K = 15, one PEC demonstrated a value of K = 398, while in another PEC the value of K was within the normal range (1.6). This signifies that there is successful resistance to the falsification of electoral results in some villages. Another observation that we have made is that in large villages with several PECs of 1000 voters and more, a reorientation of voters took place, but to a much smaller extent. If we take into account the peculiarities of the situation in the Republic of Tatarstan[8] and assume that free elections could not produce such results, we come to the logical conclusion that in a large number of TECs (at least in a third, if not in a half of them) the level of falsification in this republic reached 70–80 per cent.

Comparing the results of the 2000 presidential elections in regions of the Russian Federation

It is very important to provide a comparison of election results in various regions. Let us begin with an examination of Figure 11.1 which examines the March 2000 presidential elections and provides a graph for the Russian Federation as a whole. Here we can see a number of points (regions) which lie outside the main cluster of regions. These points refer to the following outliers: Ingushetiya, Dagestan, Kabardino-Balkariya, Komi-Permyak Autonomous Okrug and Tatarstan.[9]

An examination of elections which took place over the period 1993–2000 shows that several subjects of the federation repeatedly fall into the outlier group, and six of these regions have exercised a considerable effect on the correlation between electoral turnout and electoral support for Putin. The general correlation coefficient is 0.49, but if we remove the six outlier regions then the correlation coefficient is 0.18. Naturally, this is only an initial assessment, and more detailed information is presented in Table 11.2 describing turnout in selected regions.

As we can see in Table 11.2 the number of TECs with unusually high turnouts is highest in Tatarstan, followed by Bashkortostan and far behind,

Regional politics

Figure 11.1 *Election of Russian Federation President, 26 March 2000 (88 subjects of the Federation)*

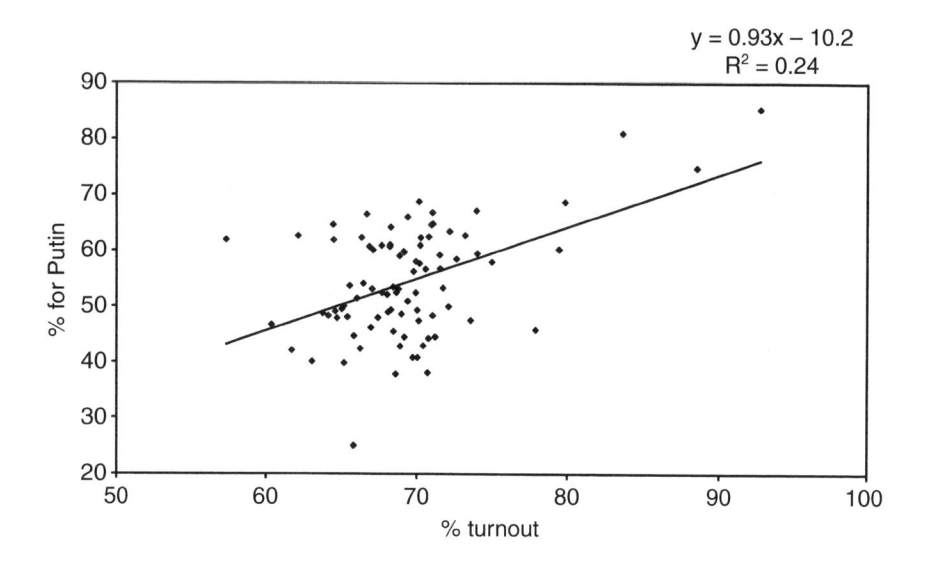

$y = 0.93x - 10.2$
$R^2 = 0.24$

Table 11.2 *Maximum turnout in selected TECs in the 1996 and 2000 presidential elections*

Presidential elections in the RF	Turnout more than (...%)	Number of the territorial election committees (TECs)			
		RF	Tatarstan	Bashkortostan	All other subjects of the RF
1996 – 1	90	55	24	24	7
	95	22	10	9	3
1996 – 2	90	78	28	34	16
	95	29	16	9	4
2000	90	121	35	31	55
	95	46	22	15	9
	98	15	8	5	2

the other subjects of the Russian Federation. If these leaders have the ability to create such obedient voters, providing 90–95 per cent turnouts (judging by official voting records), then it is not surprising that members of the republican elite have been surprisingly accurate in predicting the outcome of such elections. These unusually high electoral turnouts reflect

Regional elections and democratisation

Table 11.3 *Correlation coefficient between turnout and Putin's support in four subjects of the Russian Federation*

Region	Number of TECs	Correlation coefficient
Lipetsk oblast	23	0.04
Perm oblast	47	0.05
Tatarstan	62	0.75
Tatarstan – rural	43	0.64
Tatarstan – urban	19	0.28
Bashkortostan	70	0.73
Bashkortostan – rural	51	0.70
Bashkortostan – urban	19	0.46

the authorities' powers to mobilise the electorate and pressurise them into voting and also their ability to engage in outright falsification of official data. Some of the voters become 'virtual' voters – they have never turned out at the polling stations, but nonetheless their names still appear in official election protocols.

Now we will compare the situation in various regions. Figure 11.2 demonstrates that there is absolutely no correlation between turnout and support for Putin in Lipetsk and Perm oblasts. The same situation is found in the vast majority of regions.

Graphs for Tatarstan and Bashkortostan (Figure 11.3) on the other hand, show an obvious correlation between these variables. If it had not been for several TECs in the cities of Kazan (Tatarstan) and Ufa (Bashkortostan), and a few other urban centres, these correlations would have been even stronger.

A comparison between these two oblasts and the two republics demonstrates important differences in the methods by which the average results are obtained. This is especially obvious if we take the examples of Perm Oblast and the republic of Bashkortostan. In these two federal subjects the average value of Putin's support was similar. The difference is also confirmed by comparing the correlation coefficient for turnout in separate TECs and Putin's support as presented in Table 11.3.

Figures 11.4 and 11.5 show the correlation between invalid votes and turnout for the same four subjects of the federation. In both Tatarstan and Bashkortostan, it is obvious that all the areas with abnormally high turnout are also characterised by amazingly low levels of spoilt or invalid ballots far lower than in any other urban centre of the Russian Federation. This does not have any other plausible explanation other than the fact that some invalid wasted ballot papers must have been transferred to the pile of valid ballots, i.e., falsification.

Regional politics

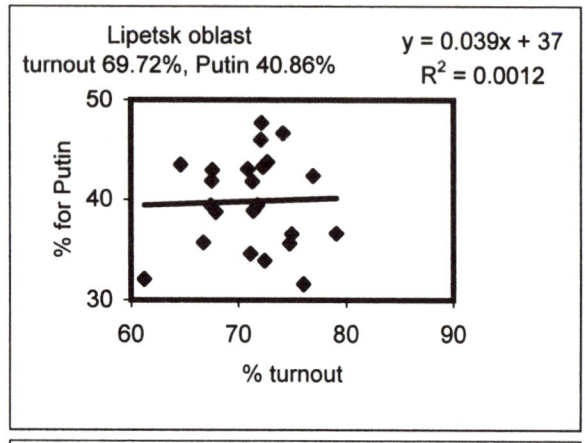

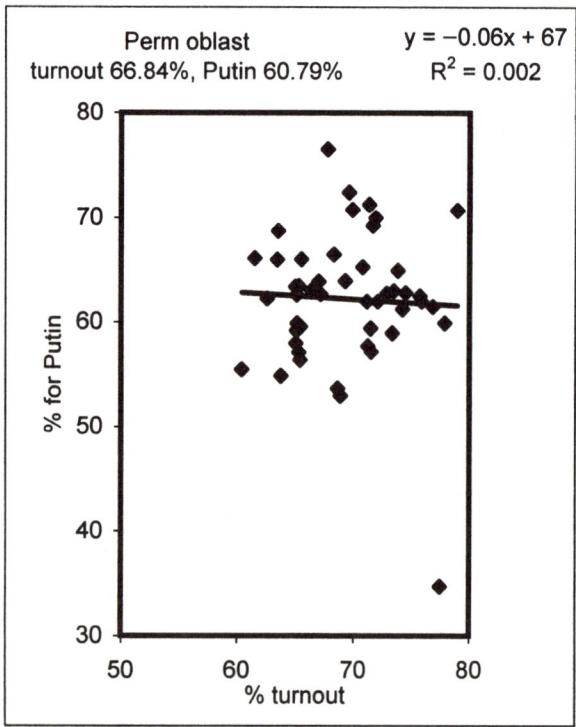

Figure 11.2 *Lipetsk and Perm oblasts: election of Russian President, 26 March 2000; linear regression for turnout and voting for Putin*

Regional elections and democratisation

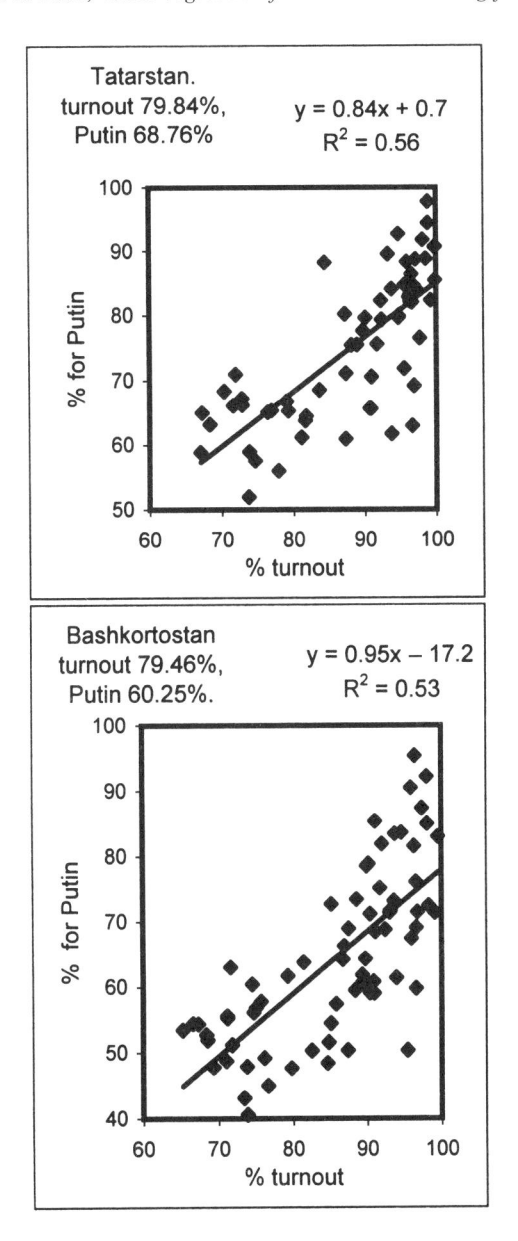

Figure 11.3 *Tatarstan and Bashkortostan: election of Russian President, 26 March 2000; linear regression for turnout and voting for Putin*

Regional politics

Figure 11.4 *Lipetsk and Perm oblasts: election of Russian President, 26 March 2000; linear regression for invalid ballots and voting for Putin*

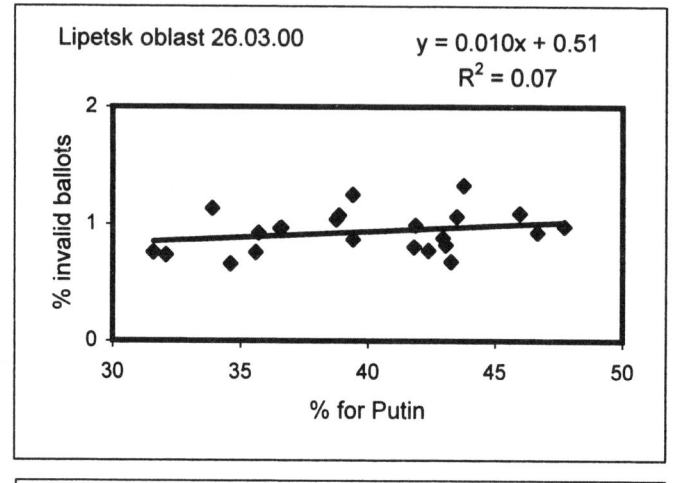

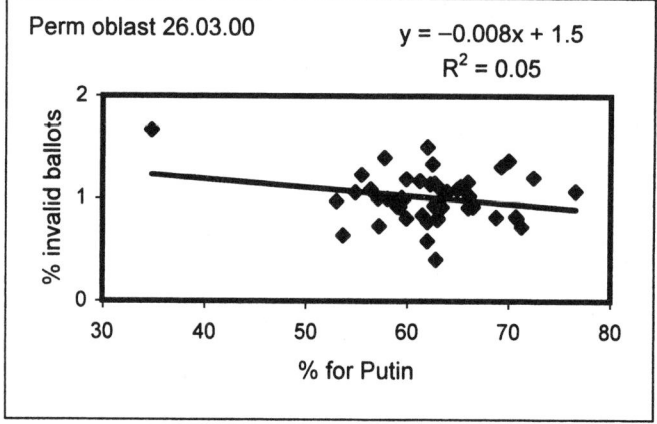

Lipetsk oblast 26.03.00
$y = 0.010x + 0.51$
$R^2 = 0.07$

Perm oblast 26.03.00
$y = -0.008x + 1.5$
$R^2 = 0.05$

The 1999 State Duma elections

Let us consider a few characteristics of the State Duma election in 1999. In most subjects of the federation the four leading parties were (in various order) the Communist Party of the Russian Federation (CPRF) which gained 24.3 per cent of the vote nationwide, Unity (Yedinstvo – 23.3 per cent), Fatherland–All Russia (FAR), 13.3 per cent, and the Union of Right Forces (SPS), 8.5 per cent. Before we continue it is important to point out that Yedinstvo is Putin's 'party of power', and one of the heads of FAR is President Shaimiev of Tatarstan.

Regional elections and democratisation

Figure 11.5 *Tatarstan and Bashkortostan: election of Russian President, 26 March 2000; linear regression for invalid ballots and voting for Putin*

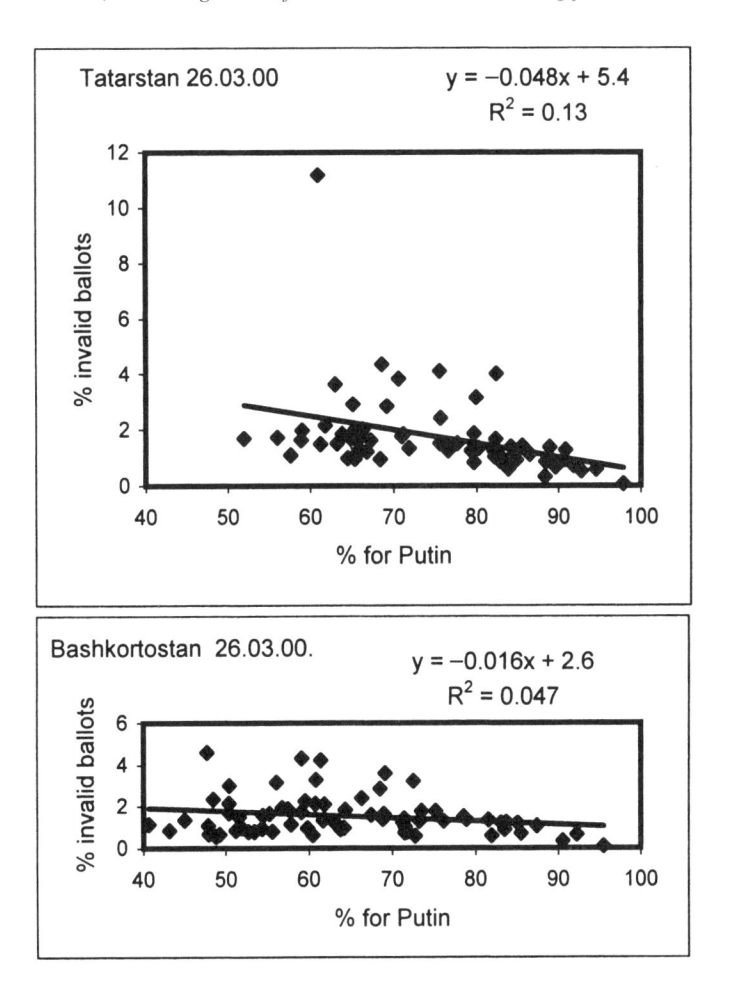

Tatarstan 26.03.00 $y = -0.048x + 5.4$ $R^2 = 0.13$

Bashkortostan 26.03.00. $y = -0.016x + 2.6$ $R^2 = 0.047$

In St Petersburg these parties were close to each other. Unity had 17.7 per cent of the vote, SPS had 17.4 per cent, FAR 15.7 per cent, and CPRF 14.2 per cent. Figure 11.6 presents a graph of the linear regression for all four political blocs. Neither Yedinstvo, nor FAR demonstrate any correlation between levels of turnout and party support. For SPS there is a weak negative correlation, and for the CPRF there is a weak positive correlation. Such correlations do not indicate any serious level of corruption.

Of the FAR voters 49.17 per cent were registered in four subjects of the federation: in Moscow (40.86 per cent), in Tatarstan (40.65 per cent), in Bashkortostan (35.20 per cent) and in Moscow Oblast (27.55 per cent).[10] According to Turovsky, 'administrative resources were crucial in determining

Regional politics

Figure 11.6 *Gosduma RF election 1999, St Petersburg, 30 TECs; linear regression for turnout and voting for Edinstvo, SPS, OVR and CPRF*

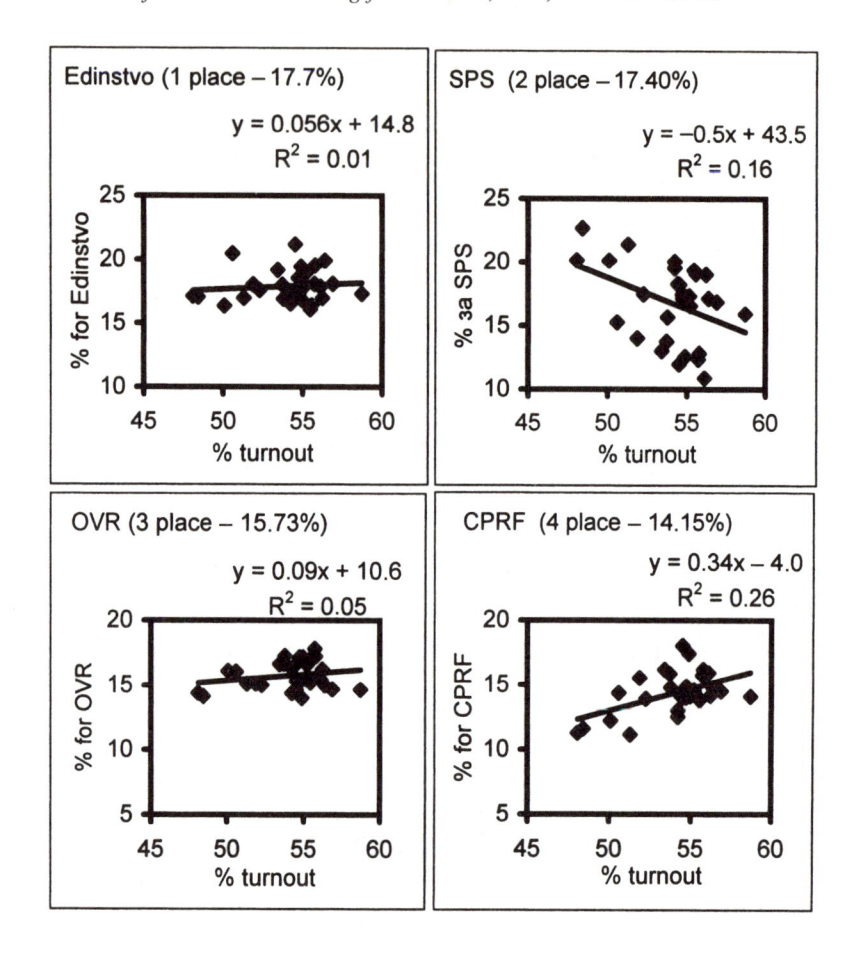

the variations in FAR's support throughout Russia.'[11] There is an even more radical outlier – Ingushetiya, where FAR support was 88.0 per cent, but that has to be considered separately.

Moscow is an interesting case. Here, in 126 TECs the results for FAR are rather similar (see Figure 11.7). They vary between 32 and 49 per cent. The turnout results are also similar and vary between 60 and 70 per cent. The correlation between turnout and voting results is negligible. Figures for the CPRF show similar results. If we exclude four outlying values, the graph for the SPS shows a correlation similar to that for the CPRF in St Petersburg.

The picture in Tatarstan, where president Shaimiev is a leading member of FAR is radically different from the other regions (see Figure 11.8). There are major variations in the support for FAR – from 16 per cent to 93.4 per

Figure 11.7 *Gosduma RF election 1999, Moscow, 126 TECs; linear regression for turnout and voting for OVR, CPRF and SPS*

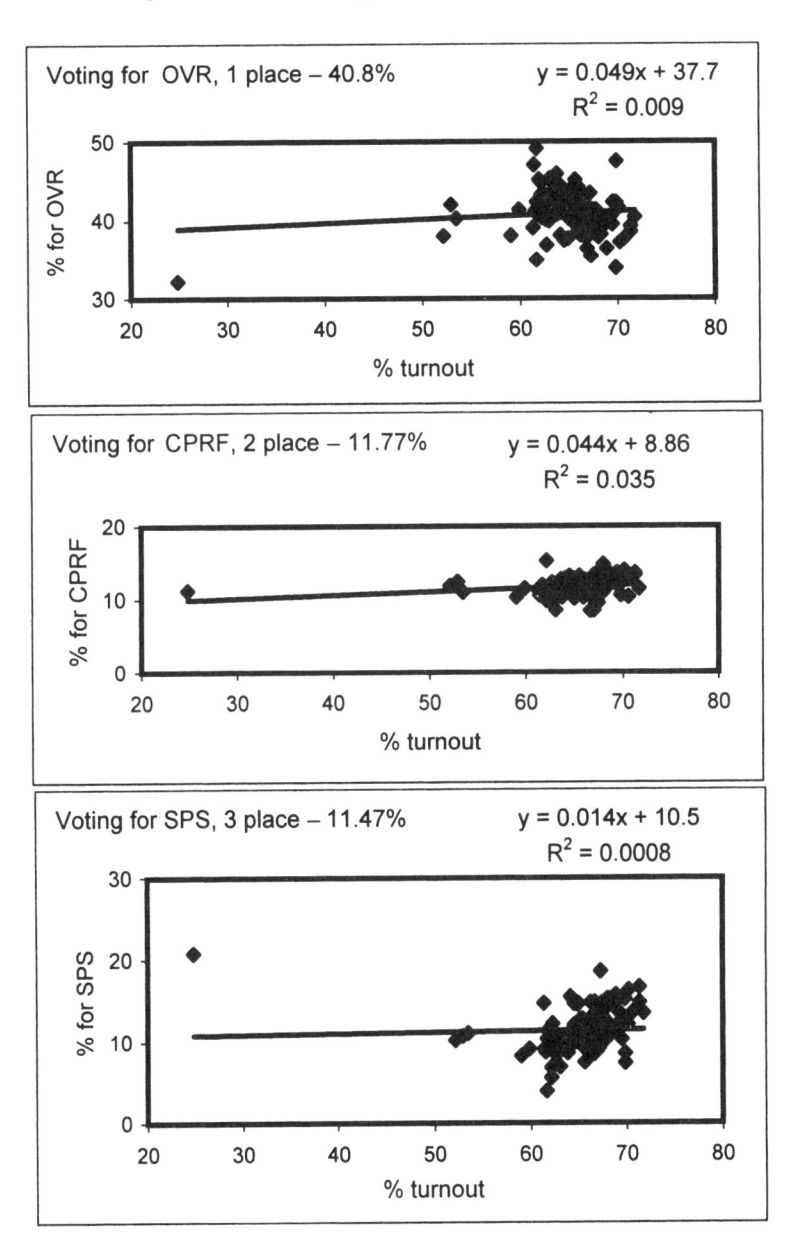

Figure 11.8 *Gosduma RF election 1999, Tatarstan, 62 TECs; linear regression for turnout and voting for OVR and CPRF*

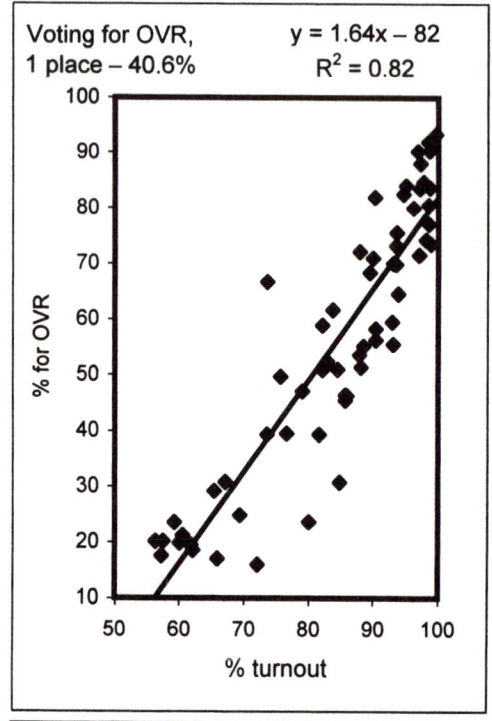

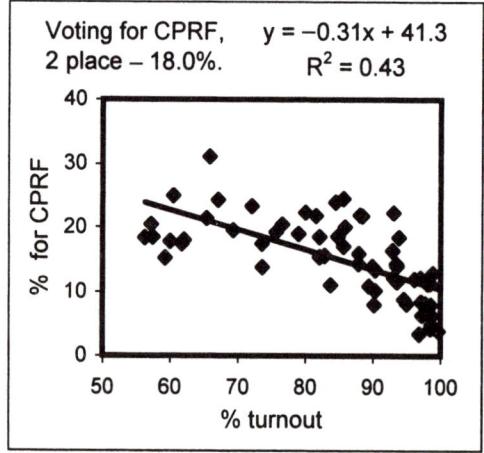

cent. Even if we take just the rural areas of Tatarstan, support for FAR oscillates from 29 per cent to 93.4 per cent. At the same time there is a strong correlation between turnout and support for FAR.

A very similar picture is found in Bashkortostan, where variations in levels of support for FAR are even greater – from 11.3 per cent to 92.8 per cent in the republic as a whole, and from 23.7 per cent to 92.8 per cent in the rural areas. Bashkortostan has a similar regression line: $y = 1.7x - 93.6$ and $R^2 = 0.58$. One important difference though is that in Tatarstan turnout is higher and there are more electoral districts with more extreme levels of support for FAR.

Comparing these results with those in Moscow, St Petersburg and other subjects of the federation demonstrates that elites in these republics use their 'administrative resources' in different ways. In Moscow, where there are few statistical anomalies in our data, the 'influence' of the leadership is more uniform across the territory of the city and does not include falsification of election results. In sharp contrast, in a number of other regions, and in particular, the republics of Bashkortostan and Tatarstan our statistical data shows evidence of serious electoral violations and falsification of election results.

There are two more telling characteristics, which become obvious when we compare the results of the 1999 Duma election in different regions. Table 11.4 presents coefficient Q for nine subjects of the federation. The coefficient, Q, is the ratio of the maximum number of votes cast 'against all' (i.e., by voting this way citizen rejects all the candidates) to the minimum share of votes cast for this category. Subjects with highly differing political regimes and geo-economic statuses may nonetheless have similar values of

Table 11.4 *Comparison of the maximum and the minimum share of votes cast 'against all' in various TECs of the same subject of the Federation in the 1999 State Duma elections*

Subject of the RF (no. of TECs)	Against all (%) Min.	Against all (%) Max.	Coefficient $Q = Max./min.$	Less than 1%
St Petersburg (30)	3.51	5.41	1.5	0
Moscow (126)	2.86	7.07	2.5	0
Nizhny Novgorod (59)	1.34	6.16	4.6	0
Samara (47)	1.00	4.35	4.3	0
Perm (47)	2.50	6.91	2.8	0
Tomsk (23)	1.95	6.23	3.2	0
Chuvashiya (28)	0.91	2.94	3.2	1
Tatarstan (62)	0.11	4.21	38.3	In 21 TECs
Bashkortostan (71)	0.17	3.36	19.8	In 17 TECs

Regional politics

Table 11.5 *Comparison of the maximum and the minimum share of invalid votes in various TECs of the same subject of the Federation in the 1999 State Duma elections*

Subject of the RF (no. of TECs)	Invalid ballots (%) Min.	Max.	Coefficient $Q = Max./min.$	Less than 1%
St Petersburg (30)	0.68	1.65	2.4	In 18 TECs
Moscow (126)	0.67	2.91	4.3	In 4 TECs
Nizhny Novgorod (59)	1.29	6.36	4.9	0
Samara (47)	1.36	4.42	3.2	0
Perm (47)	1.06	5.52	5.2	0
Tomsk (23)	0.82	3.12	3.8	1
Chuvashiya (28)	1.39	10	7.2	0
Tatarstan (62)	0.22	8.26	37.6	In 10 TECs
Bashkortostan (71)	0.68	7.58	11.2	In 4 TECs

Q from 1.5 to 4.6. However, once again Bashkortostan and Tatarstan stand out from the norm with much higher values for Q. Such high values can only have one explanation, the considerably lower share of the vote cast by citizens in these two republics for the category – 'against all'.

Table 11.5 tells us more or less the same about the share of invalid ballots. The difference is that Chuvashiya also has a higher than normal value of coefficient Q, but Tatarstan leads in this respect by a considerable amount.

During the 2000 presidential elections in the vast majority of the subjects of the Russian Federation the value of Q did not exceed 7.5. Only eleven subjects had a higher value of Q, with Tatarstan boasting a maximum value (Q = 140), followed by Dagestan (Q = 111) and Bashkortostan (Q = 38).[12]

Gubernatorial elections in 2000–01

Here we compare three elections to the position of head of executive power in three subjects of the Russian Federation, which took place in 2000 and 2001. We start with an examination of Samara Oblast (Figure 11.9). The incumbent governor, Titov, who received 53 per cent of the votes had a fairly strong opponent Tarkhov, who gained 29 per cent of the votes. The correlation between support for candidates and turnout is positive for Titov and negative for Tarkhov, but in both cases it is very weak. For the twenty rural TECs this correlation is non-existent. There is also a rather obvious negative correlation between voting in support of Titov and voting 'against all'. A similar positive correlation is observed in voting for Tarkhov. However,

Regional elections and democratisation

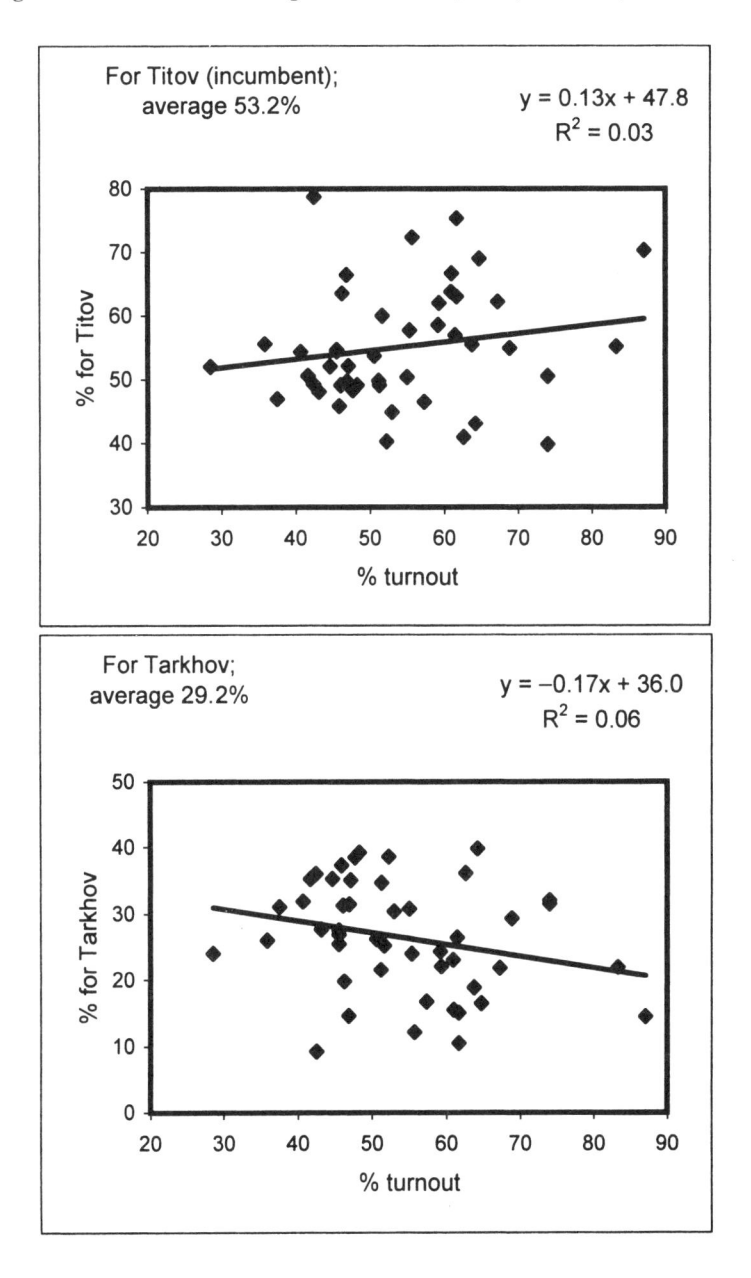

Figure 11.9 *Samara Oblast: governor election, 2000, 47 TECs; turnout 45%*

Regional politics

Figure 11.10 *Ulyanovsk Oblast: governor election, 24 December 2000, 29 TECs; turnout 56.2%*

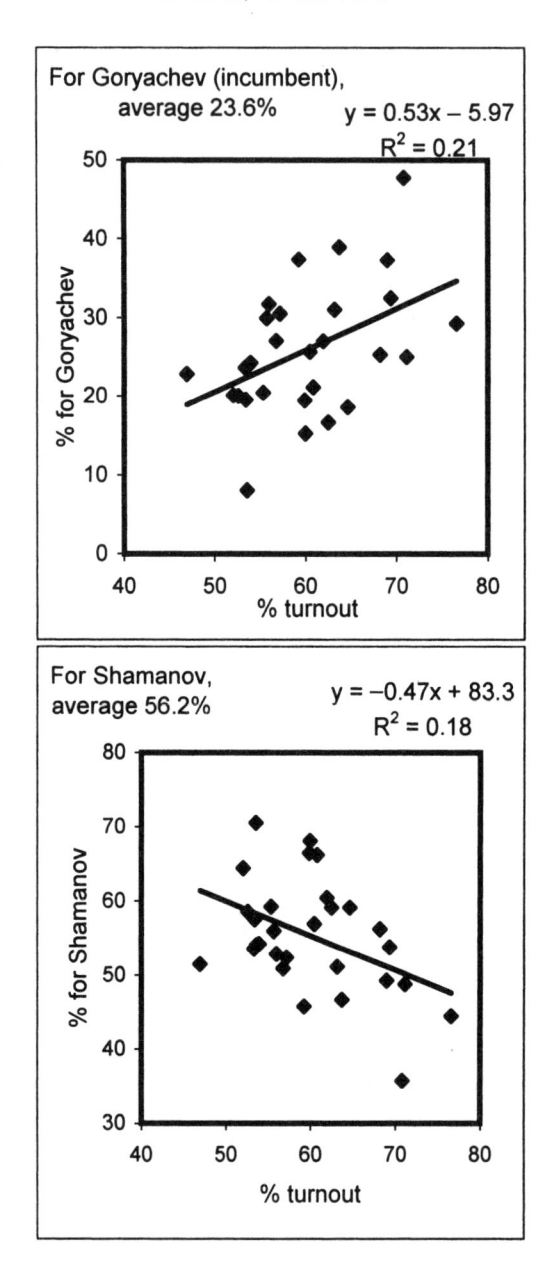

Regional elections and democratisation

Figure 11.11 *Republic of Tatarstan: presidential election, 25 March 2001, 63 TECs; turnout 79.3%*

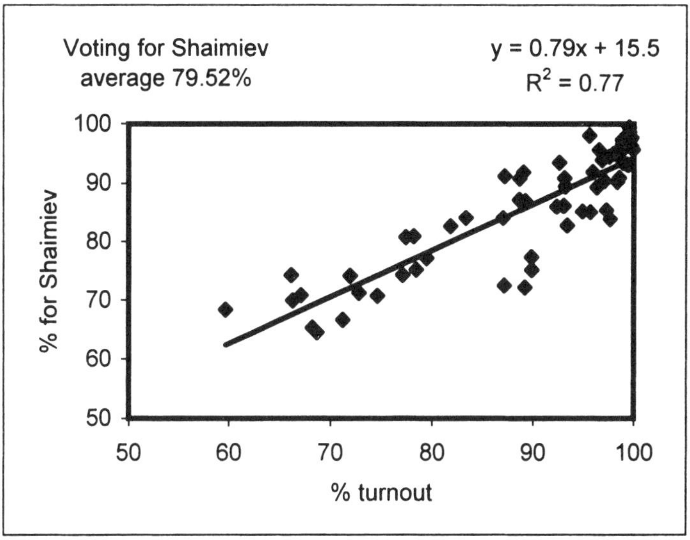

[Scatter plot: Voting for Shaimiev, average 79.52%; $y = 0.79x + 15.5$; $R^2 = 0.77$; x-axis: % turnout (50–100); y-axis: % for Shaimiev (50–100)]

all suspicion of illegal use of voting 'against all' in this case is lifted when we consider the graphs for the rural areas. There is absolutely no correlation.

The situation in Uyanovsk oblast was more competitive. The incumbent governor Goryachev was challenged by General Shamanov, who enjoyed the support of the Kremlin. Despite making use of his opportunity to influence the elections (see Figure 11.10), Goryachev lost the elections, and Shamanov's majority over Goryachev was even greater than Titov's majority over Tarkhov in Samara Oblast.

The presidential elections in the Republic of Tatarstan, which took place on 25 March 2001, were the first competitive elections in the republic. However, the other candidates did not present any serious threat to the incumbent holder of the office, Mintimer Shaimiev. Shaimiev received almost 79.5 per cent vote (with a total electoral turnout of 79.3 per cent), which far exceeds the results in Samara and Ulyanovsk oblasts. The regression line for all the 63 TECs (See Figure 11.11) demonstrates a clear correlation between electoral turnout and Shaimiev's support. An almost identical correlation is seen in the graph for the rural areas where $Y = 0.84x + 10.7$; $R^2 = 0.47$. The share of invalid ballots is close to the normal in those TECs where turnout was below 80 per cent. However, in those TECs where turnout is higher than 90 per cent the share of invalid ballots varies from very low (below 1 per cent in 20 TECs), to the more normal value of 3 per cent.

We can use another illustrative approach to the analysis of spoiled ballots and the share of vote 'against all'. The top graph in Figure 11.12

Regional politics

Figure 11.12 *Tatarstan presidential election 2001, 6 TECs; rank correlations between invalid ballots (or voting against all) and voting for Shaimiev*

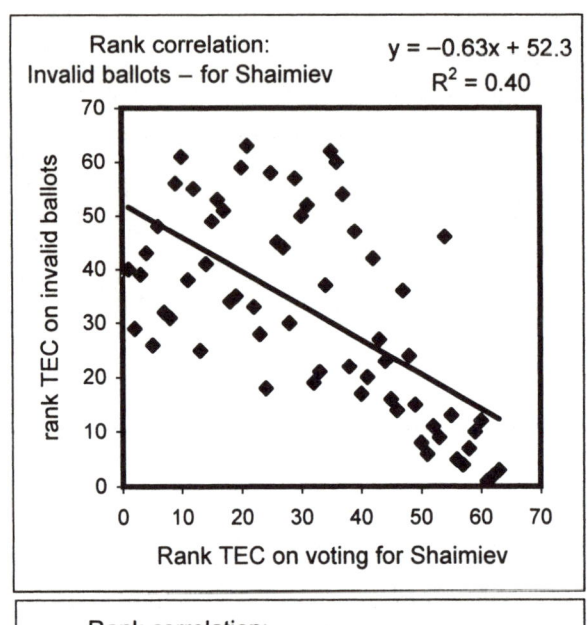

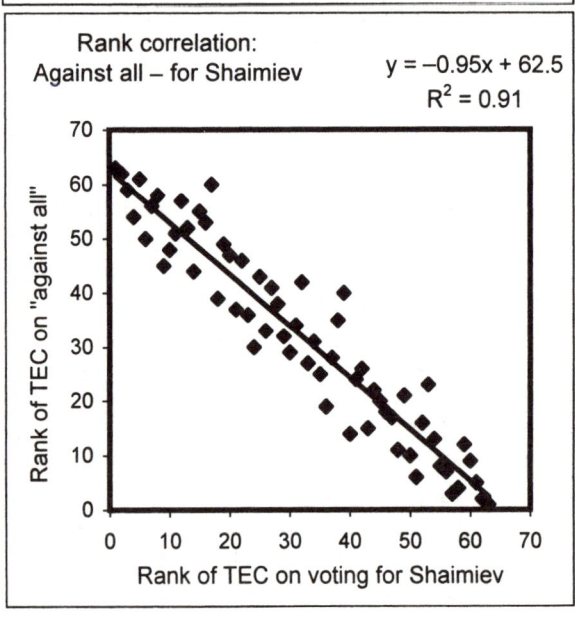

demonstrates a statistically meaningful correlation between the rank occupied by a TEC for invalid votes and the level of support for Shaimiev. If we consider only the 43 rural TECs, this correlation becomes even more meaningful: $Y = -0.76x + 38.7$; $R^2 = 0.58$. A very strong correlation can be seen in the bottom graph of Figure 11.12 which examines the correlation between a TEC's rank in the votes 'against all', and support for Shaimiev. The equation for the linear regression for the rural areas has similar coefficients: $Y = -0.90x + 42.0$; $R^2 = 0.82$.

My analysis also demonstrates that such powerful correlations cannot be explained away as simply the differences in the voting behaviour of urban and the rural populations. The correlation is uniform across the republic. It would also be naive to suggest that such a close correlation is the result of the greater popularity of the incumbent president. The decrease in the share of vote 'against all' cannot be explained by the almost universal support for Shaimiev in some districts. A more detailed analysis of election results at the level of PECs demonstrates important variations here. Some PECs have a normal share of votes 'against all', and the turnout in these PECs is lower than average. We find such results normally occur in district centres *(rayonnye tsentry)* and large villages (*poselki*) surrounding large industrial enterprises. However, in remote rural areas and in small villages, the official election results more often remind us of the ridiculously high turnout rates and support for the communist party which were common during the Soviet era.

In comparison to our graph for Tatarstan (Figure 11.12), there is a weak correlation between voting 'against all' and support for Titov in Samara Oblast confirming the observations we made in our analysis of Figure 11.9. $Y = -0.35x + 34$; $R^2 = 0.013$ (for Titov).

Similar equations for Shamanov and Goryachev also show that there are no correlations: $Y = -0.053x + 15.8$; $R^2 = 0.003$ (for Shamanov) and $Y = -0.16x + 17.4$; $R^2 = 0.026$ (for Goryachev).

The first competitive presidential elections in the Republic of Tatarstan were accompanied by anomalies that have not been found in the majority of other republics and regions. It is important to note that all these 'mysterious results' occurred in rural areas where the turnout is abnormally high (the average turnout was 94 per cent, while in 17 out of the 43 areas the turnout exceeded 98 per cent). The only other places in Russia where such turnout can be encountered are Kabardino-Balkariya and Ingushetiya. A similar, but rather weaker picture of voting can be encountered in Bashkortostan.

Conclusions

Our study of regional elections shows that deviations from the norm have been much greater in the republics, and especially Tatarstan and Bashkortostan Republics. However, other republics such as Dagestan, Kabardino-Balkariya and Mordoviya, also show deviations from statistic norms. In an earlier study carried out by this author these three republics alongside Bashkortostan and Tatarstan had the largest number of deviations.[13]

Of particular importance is the exaggerated electoral turnout in rural areas. As seen from Table 11.2, Tatarstan and Bashkortostan are undisputed leaders when it comes to high electoral turnouts. These exaggerated levels of turnout give the republican elites greater opportunities to falsify election results. Thus, for example, in the 1999 State Duma elections the average turnout was 97.4 per cent in 40 per cent of Tatarstan's rual TECs. In these rural TEC's FAR received the support of 83.2 per cent of the voters. In 60 per cent of TECs the average turnout was 86.2 per cent, and FAR was supported by 56.9 per cent of the voters. Thus, every additional percentage point of turnout can be seen to add 2.3 per cent to the total level of support for FAR. This means that in those areas where the authorities find it easy to manufacture maximum turnout, citizens also experience the maximum pressure to vote for FAR. Thus, turnout parameters can be considered to constitute one of the most important areas of electoral analysis.

From the many examples given above we can also demonstrate that the 'administrative management' of elections may be divided into two groups: (A) 'Influence' (illegal manipulation) in the *pre-election period* (through elite control over the mass media, electoral committees, etc.). This sort of influence is not very easy to detect through the kind of statistical analysis employed in this study. (B) Using illegal methods at the polling stations *during the elections* (e.g., putting pressure on voters, exercising administrative control over the electoral process) and *during the process of counting the votes* (e.g., putting pressure 'from above' on electoral committees in order to ensure the desired election results, appointing representatives of executive bodies as members of electoral committees).

The methods described in group B result in the worst violations of election rules and at the same time, they are very difficult to detect by observers at polling stations. However, as we have demonstrated they can be detected through statistical analysis. Many groups of election observers have reported that executive bodies have been able to gain control of electoral results before they were officially presented to the TECs[14] and there is widespread evidence of obstruction of election observers.[15] Such evidence confirms our conclusions about the unusual, and unrealistic, results uncovered in our statistical analysis. Election protocols have been doctored to satisfy the election organisers and have nothing to do with the free will of the voters. Thus, it is practically impossible to determine the real political preferences of voters in rural areas and particularly in the republics of Tatarstan, Bashkortostan, Dagestan, Ingushetiya, and Kabardino-Balkariya. Voters' preferences are simply removed from the final electoral protocols. For example, according to the voting results of elections over the period 1999 to 2001 the level of support for the CPRF in Tatarstan is among the lowest in Russia, and no higher than in St Petersburg or Moscow. In the most 'managed areas' of Tatarstan the level is three to four times lower than in the republic as a whole. It is notable, that the strength of the 'administrative resource' is unevenly distributed across the republic and even among rural areas. This suggests that there is resistance from the local population in some areas to 'administrative control', whilst in others such resistance is non-existent. In Dagestan citizens regularly vote in line with wishes of the heads of the district administrations. It would be wrong to conclude that these anomalies could be explained by the ethnic peculiarities of the republics. It is natural to expect that President Rakhimov (an ethnic Bashkir) should get more support in those areas where the Bashkirs constitute a majority of the population, while President Shaimiev (an ethnic Tatar) should have more support among the Tatars. However, the scope of falsifications in these two republics far exceeds our expectations. Administrative pressure and deception have no ethnic background, and their victims include both Russians and members of the titular population. In our view, any attempt to link the strength of administrative pressure and manipulation during elections with voters' ethnic make-up has no explanatory value. Our study has uncovered higher levels of falsification through widening our analysis to include not only TECs but also lower level PECs.[16] When shifting the level of analysis to PECs we can estimate deviations from the norm with a far greater degree of precision than when we simply study TECs However, according to the existing legislation, even the most clear-cut proof of falsification as we have demonstrated above, in the absence of written reports of observers or voters, is not sufficient grounds to organise a re-count. We believe that the law needs to be changed in order to take account of statistical analysis of falsification especially in those cases where it can be directly shown that falsification has taken place as we have seen in Table 11.1. It is important to create a system of efficient and speedy checks of all electoral documents in cases where statistical analysis leads us to believe infringements have been committed.

The development of authoritarian electoral systems arose in the Yeltsin era when regional elites were granted unbridled powers to organise their local economies and polities as they saw fit. After Putin announced an imminent reform of federal relations in 1999 and started to implement a radical reform of the federal system in May 2000, it was expected that federal authorities would begin to take a tougher line with infringements of electoral norms and violations of human rights in the regions but unfortunately such developments have failed to materialise.

The central authorities have tried to improve electoral laws since 1994. By the beginning of the new electoral cycle in 1999–2000 it looked as if federal law-making bodies had closed all the loops in the legislation that opened the way for falsification. In the summer of 2002 a new, federal law was adopted on citizens' electoral rights. However, the practice of implementing these laws at the level of TECs and PECs not only lags behind the level of these new and more sophisticated laws, but also demonstrates a considerable and painful regression in Russia's transition. Strengthening the democratic foundations of the state has not yet become a priority for the Kremlin administration. The practical steps, undertaken by President Putin from his very first days in office, demonstrate that his strategic vision for Russia include the development of a strong state and the promotion of a liberal economic policy. Enhancing democracy through the creation of free and fair elections is still very low down the president's list of priorities.

Notes

1 Translated by Elena Hore.
2 M. McFaul and N. Petrov, *Politicheskyi al'manakh Rossii*: *Vol. 1* (Moscow: Carnegie Centre, 1998), pp. 319–324.
3 M. McFaul 'Russia's 2000 presidential election: implications for Russian democracy and U.S.–Russian relations', *Johnston's Russia List*, 4247 (2000).
4 D. B. Oreshkin, 'Geografia elektoralnoi kultury i tselnost Rossii', *Polis*, 1 (2001), 73–93.
5 V. Mikhailov, 'Quantity of democracy (analysis of the Russian presidential elections of 1996 in the regions of the RF)', *Armageddon*, 3 (1999), 134–153.
6 V. Mikhailov, 'Demokratizatsiya Rossii: razlichnaya skorost' v regionakh (analiz vyborov 1996 i 2000: mesto Tatarstana sredi sub'ektov RF', in V. Mikhailov, V. Bazhanov and M. Farukhshin (eds.), *Osobaya Zona: Vybory v Tatarstane* (Ul'yanovsk: KOMPA, 2000), pp. 25–84. The results of the latter research largely correlate with the results of an extensive and thought provoking analysis by E. Borisova, a journalist from *The Moscow Times*. Although my research also contains a number of different and important conclusions. See Borisova, E., 'And the winner is?', *The Moscow Times* (9 September, 2000).
7 *Natsionalnyi Arkhiv Tatarstana*, Fond P-66, Opis' 8, Delo 89, 150, 97, 158, 107, 168.
8 Mikhailov, Bazhanov and Farukhshin, *Osobaya Zona*.
9 The latter is the only large region in this group of outliers. Tatarstan holds the ninth place in the Russian Federation according to the size of the electorate.
10 Author's calculations based on data from, *Putevoditel' Po Izbiratel'noi Sisteme Rossii* (Moscow: IEDS, 2001).
11 R. F. Turovsky 'Parlamentskie vybory 1999: regionalnye osobennosti', *Politiya*, 4:14 (Winter, 1999–2000), 111.
12 Mikhailov, 'Demokratizatsiya Rossii', pp. 59–60.
13 Mikhailov, 'Demokratizatsiya Rossii', Table 9, p. 70.
14 M. Lemieux, 'Long-term observer, November 21 to December 20, 1999', *OSCE Ufa*, Bashkortostan, RF. See also, *Osobaya Zona*, pp. 111, 197–199, 270–271.
15 See *Osobaya Zona*, pp. 103–108, 129, 133–139, 200, 225, 234, 249, 281, 288.
16 In this respect our study is more sophisticated than that carried out by Oreshkin whose research is based on a study of TECs.

V

Foreign policy and Chechnya

12

Russian foreign policy under Putin

Dmitry Polikanov and Graham Timmins

Introduction

Whatever else one may feel about Russia's status in contemporary world politics, there is no escaping the realisation that Moscow will continue to exercise considerable geopolitical importance within the European continent and will play an important role in the negotiation of a new international order in the post-Cold War world. The purpose of this chapter will be to consider developments and issues in Russian foreign policy under the Putin administration.

Vladimir Putin's political career began in 1990 when he left the KGB after fifteen years stationed mainly in East Germany to become head of external relations and later deputy mayor under Anatoly Sobchak, the mayor of St Petersburg. He was drafted in to the presidential administration in 1996 and following roles heading the Federal Security Bureau and the powerful Security Council he was in August 1999 appointed prime minister. When Boris Yeltsin stepped down as president on 31 December 1999, Putin was appointed acting president and following elections in March 2000, which he won with 53 per cent of the vote, took office in May 2000. This period during which Putin climbed the political ladder was one in which the European political landscape underwent a spectacular transformation following the collapse of Soviet power in Central and Eastern Europe in the autumn of 1989 and the eventual demise of the Soviet Union in 1991 and which has compelled Russia to construct a new international identity and role in the post-Cold War world.

It will be argued in this chapter that Putin's contribution to the evolution of Russian foreign policy can be detected in: (1) the receding ambivalence towards a pro-Western orientation, (2) the recognition of the importance of the 'soft' economic security dimension in international politics, (3) a subsequent shift in emphasis towards Russia's relations with the EU, and (4) the political prioritisation of a multipolar concept of the post-Cold War world

The evolution of Russian policy after the Cold War

One of the first major foreign policy statements by the emerging Russian state came in December 1991 when Yeltsin raised the possibility of Russia joining NATO. Whilst neither party saw this announcement as a firm statement of intent, it sent out a signal that the 'new Russia' was looking to a pro-Western strategy in the post-Cold War world. Russia's entry into the North Atlantic Co-operation Council in 1991which established a dialogue mechanism for the NATO and former Warsaw Pact states confirmed this as did Russia's first *Foreign Policy Concept* in 1993 which referred to a 'common understanding of the main values of world civilization and common interests with regard to key issues of the global situation'.[1]

The participation of Russia in NATO's Partnership for Peace (PfP) initiative and the signing of the Partnership and Co-operation Agreement (PCA) with the EU in 1994 seemed to establish a *modus vivendi* for Russian–Western relations. However, both events came at a time when President Yeltsin's Western policy was taking an increasingly erratic line. Russia's involvement in PfP was obstructed by Yeltsin's demands that Russia be granted special consultative status by NATO in return for its sanctioning of enlargement. NATO eventually acquiesced to Yeltsin's demands and in May 1997 the NATO–Russia Founding Act was signed which led to the creation of the 'Permanent Joint Council (PJC)' which provided a forum where NATO and Russia could meet and consult on a regular ongoing basis at various levels.[2] The PCA too was obstructed by a deterioration in Russian–Western relations. In this instance the first Chechen War which broke out in the course of 1994 led to a rupture in EU–Russian relations until early 1996 when Yeltsin announced a military withdrawal from Chechnya (see Chapter 14) and which facilitated eventual ratification of the PCA in December 1997. But far from heralding a new positive phase of Russia's relations with the West, 1998/99 proved to be the low point of the post-Cold War period. In the course of 1998 Russia suffered from a damaging collapse of the ruble and this was a crisis that came when the EU was launching its accession negotiations with ten Central and Eastern European candidate states in March 1998 and NATO was in the process of completing its negotiations for the entry of the Czech Republic, Hungary and Poland which took place in March 1999. It was, however, NATO's military intervention into Kosovo in the summer of 1999 in the guise of Operation Allied Force which was launched without prior consultation with Moscow that did most to damage Russian–Western relations. Russia responded with a temporary withdrawal from the PJC and it was not until February 2000 when NATO Secretary-

General, Lord Robertson, was invited to Moscow for talks were steps taken to rebuild the relationship.[3] What this move reflected was that despite Russia's unease with the manner in which NATO had responded to the Balkan crisis, the new administration under Putin was reluctant to move away from the 'western table'.[4]

This reluctance also indicated that growing priority was being afforded to the soft security agenda in the wake of the 1998 economic crisis and suggested a subtle yet important shift in emphasis away from the US relationship towards the European Union (see Chapter 13). Putin's keynote speech, 'Russia at the turn of millennium', issued on 31 December 1999 acknowledged the 'material and mental' damage of the Soviet-type system on Russian society and signalled a policy agenda of societal reconciliation, state reform and greater economic efficiency. In framing this agenda within the context of the need for deeper integration into the global economy and the specific objective of membership of the World Trade Organisation (WTO), Putin set Russia's future political direction clearly down the Westernising path.[5] In response to the European Union's Common Strategy on Russia which was announced at the Cologne European Council summit in June 1999, Moscow produced its own 'Russian Medium-Term Strategy for Development of Relations with the European Union' in October 1999. This document was instructive in so far that it provided the first clear statement that Russia had no aspiration to become a member of the EU (see Chapter 13). Russian strategic interest in its relations with the EU were identified as the development of a collaborative pan-European security defence identity which 'could counterbalance, *inter-alia*, the NATO-centrism in Europe', the strengthening of economic relations leading to 'a Russia–European Union free trade zone' and including an energy dialogue, the fostering of EU support for Russia's entry into the World Trade Organisation (WTO), increased political dialogue on a wide range of political, economic and technical issues and technological co-operation all of which would lead to 'a united Europe without dividing lines and the interrelated and balanced strengthening of the positions of Russia and the EU within an international community of the twenty-first century'.[6]

The Russian foreign policy line towards the EU was reaffirmed in June 2000 with the publication of Russia's 'Foreign Policy Concept of the Russian Federation' which highlighted Russian involvement in the developing European security architecture and broader recognition of the EU–Russian economic relationship.

> Of key importance are relations with the European Union (EU). The on going processes within the EU are having a growing impact on the dynamic of the situation in Europe. These are the EU expansion, transition to a common currency, the institutional reform, and emergence of a joint foreign policy and a policy in the area of security, as well as a defense identity. Regarding these processes as an objective component of European development, Russia will seek due respect for its interest, including in the sphere of bilateral relations

with individual EU member countries. The Russian Federation views the EU as one of its main political and economic partners and will strive to develop with it an intensive, stable and long-term co-operation devoid of expediency fluctuations.[7]

Where Russia's future relations with NATO were concerned, an element of pragmatism was exercised in stating that 'Russia proceeds from the importance of co-operation with [NATO] in the interests of maintaining security and stability in the continent and is open to constructive interaction'. However, it was also recognised that 'on a number of parameters, NATO's present-day political and military guidelines do not coincide with the security interests of the Russian Federation and occasionally contradict them'. The Kosovo experience had been a seminal point in the evolution of Russia's Western policy and the new foreign policy concept suggested that severe damage had been done to Russian–US relations. Russia reaffirmed its commitment to the United Nations arguing that it must remain 'the main centre for regulating international relations in the XXI century'. Of key importance to the Putin administration was the recognition of multipolarity and Russia's place in the post-Cold War order as a 'great power'. Russia criticised the 'growing trend towards the establishment of a unipolar structure of the world with the economic and power domination of the United States' and argued that 'the strategy of unilateral actions can destabilise the international situation, provoke tensions and the arms race, aggravate interstate contradictions, national and religious strife'. With the events of Kosovo in mind, the document concluded that 'substantive and constructive co-operation between Russia and NATO is only possible if it is based on the foundation of a due respect for the interests of the sides and an unconditional fulfilment of mutual obligations assumed'.

What the new foreign policy concept and the National Security Concept of the Russian Federation signed in January 2000 recognised was that little was to be gained by Russia taking a confrontational line towards the West as this would result in isolation and would undermine Moscow's preference for a multipolar concept of the world. However, a too co-operative line would increase Moscow's reliance upon the West and generate a course of path dependency.[8]

The events of the September 11 2001 in New York had a mixed impact on Russian foreign policy. The terrorist attack on the World Trade Centre strengthened George Bush Jnr's domestic position and provided an opportunity for the extension of US unilateral power first in Afghanistan and later in Iraq. In geopolitical terms it also led to the probable permanent stationing of US military forces in the former Soviet republics of Uzbekistan, Kyrgyzstan and Tajikistan. However, the events also afforded more room for manoeuvre in Chechnya when the West for the first time recognised that the use of force was a legitimate response to the threat of terrorism emanating from the region.[9]

Putin's first major speech following the 11 September coincided with his visit to Germany where on 25 September 2001 he addressed the German Parliament in German. Whilst condemning the attacks, he pointed to the lack of international co-operation between Russia and the West as a contributing factor to the rise of international terrorism.

> What do we lack nowadays for effective co-operation? Despite all the positive achievements of the past decades, we have not yet managed to work out an effective mechanism for co-operation. The co-ordinating agencies, established so far, do not give Russia any real opportunity to participate in the process of preparing and adopting decisions. Today, decisions are frequently taken essentially without our participation, and only afterwards are we insistently asked to approve them ... Not so long ago, it appeared that soon a truly common house would be built on the [European] continent, a house in which Europeans would not be divided into eastern and western, or northern and southern lines. Yet, these 'fault lines' will continue to exist. And this primarily because we have still not yet been able to free ourselves for good from many of the stereotypes and ideological clichés of the Cold War.[10]

Events since 2001 and until the US invasion of Iraq in 2003 revealed a commitment by both the EU and NATO to address Putin's agenda of greater inclusion. In May 2002 at the EU–Russia summit in Moscow the Russian proposed initiative of a European Security and Defence Policy (ESDP) Action Plan was agreed. However, until greater progress within the EU on the ESDP can be achieved, it is unlikely that any tangible progress will be made in this area. More likely is movement on proposals for the involvement of Russia in the European Economic Space or free trade area (see Chapter 13) as the accession of the Central and Eastern European states into the EU approaches in 2004.[11] Likewise in May 2002 Russia and NATO established a new partnership at the Reykjavik NATO summit although again it remains to be seen whether this will yield substantial change in the conduct of Russian–NATO relations.[12] But if the course of Russian foreign policy and Moscow's attitude towards the West has become clearer under Putin, the domestic context of Russian foreign policy formulation remains a contested arena and requires further consideration.

Russian foreign policy under the Putin administration

The Russian foreign policy under President Putin differs positively from the course of his predecessor and has a clear Western-oriented drive. From the dynamic multi-vector tossing of the early Putin years with all its mantras concerning the Commonwealth of Independent States (CIS) as the highest priority (see Chapter 15) and the need to restore the links with ex-Soviet satellites (like North Korea, Cuba or Vietnam), it is crystallising into a pragmatic policy with sound economic interests underpinning the process of decision-making. It is allegedly clear for Putin that Russia is bound to have partnership with the West in order to procure investments, management skills and exchange of high technologies. And this understanding makes Russia's drifting towards Europe and the United States inevitable, to a certain extent. Nonetheless, there are a number of significant constraints that may impede such rapprochement and the developments over Iraq have demonstrated once again how fragile Russia's 'normalisation' is and how far Moscow is from gaining its self-identity in the transforming system of international relations.

What are the key limitations of the Kremlin's course? First of all, one has to remember that the process of foreign policy decision-making is highly centralised in Russia. President Putin and a narrow circle of his colleagues shape the Russian course without any substantial effort to institutionalise this process or to involve a broader range of actors. A feeble attempt to do so was made by the State Council – a consultative club of governors around the president – in January 2003.[13] It mostly led to the loud approval of the presidential policy – 'the Putin doctrine' – while mentioning some regional dimension (e.g. the need for developing more frontier co-operation and strengthening ties with the CIS) and had no important intellectual breakthroughs. Moreover, some of Putin's fellows are not even able to keep pace with the president – a good example is Defence Minister Sergei Ivanov, whose tough statements (e.g. on American bases in Central Asia or the US military instructors in Georgia) the Kremlin has to moderate all the time.

This lack of human resources is one of the weak points of the administration. While Putin and his supporters comprise the top of the iceberg, myriads of bureaucrats form the invisible underwater part, which, in fact, determines its drifting through the cool waters of modern international politics. These people do not criticise the new course openly – moreover, they realise all the benefits of rapprochement with the West and have long ago accepted the advantages of the Western-style of life. Meanwhile, there are several reasons for their sabotage of radical foreign policy reforms. First of all, they are quite cautious in their approaches and prefer a wait-and-see attitude unless the economic situation in the EU and the USA improves and the transatlantic partners eventually come to some consensus about the future of their alliance. Second, many of these people with a Soviet background have spent most of their time condemning American imperialism and complaining about the aggressive character of NATO, so they still have to overcome some of the stereotypes in their mentality. Thirdly, it is quite profitable for them to build their careers on more conservative views, since their skills in counting nuclear warheads and heavy armoury in Europe can only be applicable in the situation of permanent tension with the West. Otherwise any serious reform of the diplomatic service or military institutions would make these experts obsolete. Finally, they assume in private talks that Russia's concessions to the West under President Putin outweigh the carrots, which

Moscow enjoys. The notorious Jackson–Vanick amendment is still under consideration in the US Congress, Washington develops missile defence and prepares for nuclear testing, the EU demands an increase in energy tariffs and takes a tough position on visas with respect to Kaliningrad. Moscow may well lose the chance to gain access to economic reconstruction in postwar Iraq, Russian corporations have not yet succeeded in the US oil market, intelligence sharing is not equal and balanced. All of these facts have enabled opponents of rapprochement to gain the support of key economic and political groups in their quest to block closer ties with the West.

As far as businesses are concerned, there is a certain contradiction as well. On the one hand, both large businesses with their desire for becoming real transnational corporations and small businesses with their eagerness to acquire management skills, technologies and money are supporting any rapprochement with the West. On the other hand, traditional tycoons, who make the pillars of the Russian economic success (military–industrial complex, nuclear-power machine building, energy sector), realise that Western hi-tech markets are closed to them. Small and medium-size enterprises also see that more openness with respect to stronger European and US economies would lead to growing competition, in which they may hardly survive. This accounts for the equivocal position of the business community towards Russia's accession to the WTO or towards the EU expansion.

As for public opinion, it is clear that foreign policy has always been a certain domain for the elite only. However, nowadays the Kremlin is more than ever dependent on domestic policy developments in its decisions. It is clear that Russian public opinion has changed for the better as far as its attitude to the West is concerned. But this process goes slowly and with some paradoxical trends. A key dilemma is that public opinion has becomes more nationalistic and assertive even during times of economic growth. Thus, by December 2002, 48 per cent still regarded NATO as an aggressive bloc, while 45 per cent assumed that its enlargement to the Baltic states would threaten Russia's security.[14] Moreover, it is quite easy to stir up anti-American sentiments – the most vivid examples are the Salt Lake City syndrome or the Russian public's response to the war in Iraq. In March 2003, 59 per cent of Russians believed that the United States was not a country friendly to Russia, while 41 per cent thought that Russia–US relations deteriorated in February–March.[15] Evidently, Russian public opinion with respect to foreign policy is mostly dominated by myths of the past and media coverage of the events,[16] but various forces on all sides of the political spectrum actively manipulate these feelings and not often to the benefit of the pro-Putin course. The only positive trend is that the young generation, those aged under thirty-five years, have a more balanced approach.

Another problem related to the lack of institutionalisation and appropriate human resources is the 'fire brigade approach'. A precise glance at current Russian foreign policy indicates that it reminds us of a grasshopper jumping from one crisis to another – from Kaliningrad to WTO, from the NATO–Russia Council to the Middle East, from North Korea to Iraq, etc. There is an obvious shortage of strategic vision, except the general guideline for rapprochement with the West set by Vladimir Putin. Most of the basic provisions of Russian foreign policy are still based on the Yalta–Potsdam understanding of reality reflected in the National Security Concept, or the Foreign Policy Concept. The documents were not amended in the aftermath of September 11 and still contain lots of anti-Western rhetoric. Presidential instructions to update the Military Doctrine and the National Security Concept, as well as strategic plans of the General Staff, given after the tragedy in the Moscow theatre in October 2002[17] and approval of the new US National Security Concept, have not yet been implemented – this process will take several months, if not years.

Besides, at the tactical level there are also serious problems with the implementation of the new course. As soon as the action requires something more than the personal involvement of the president or his foreign policy team, it frequently comes to stagnation or failure. The example of Kaliningrad showed that contradictions within the apparatus, confusion of domestic and foreign policy principles, and insufficient discipline in the implementation of the strategic decisions resulted in a gradual erosion of Russia's negotiating position.[18] Another factor making Russian foreign policy quite passive and reactive is the halt of domestic reforms, which it should service. Most of the reforms have stalled so far, partly due to the coming parliamentary elections in December 2003 and presidential ones in March 2004. Administrative reform and reform of the civil service are being postponed until post-March 2004; municipal reform and changes in the federal–regional relationship will not start sooner than 2005–6; the military reform is sporadic and chaotic;[19] deregulation of natural monopolies is only partially under way; experiments with the public utilities and communal sector have already provoked social unrest in many regions. The government has also failed to make structural adjustments and to overcome the striking imbalance between mining and manufacturing, thus, putting under risk further economic growth in Russia. Therefore, to a certain extent, there is no objective demand in active foreign policy with respect to the West, as the source of investments, skills, etc., since they will all disappear in vain in the cumbersome Soviet-like institutions. As a result, Moscow's external course turns more and more into a sit-on-the-fence policy. As the president has put it recently, 'Russia has lately – and there have been many crises lately – not afforded itself the luxury of being directly dragged into one of these crises. And I will do everything that depends on me in order to prevent Russia from being involved in the Iraqi crisis in any form.'[20]

There are some external constraints that impair Russia's attempts to forge an alliance with the West: (1) the West is not homogeneous and Russia will inevitably have to make a strategic choice between the United States and Europe; (2) the West itself, notably the EU, is not ready to accept Russia as a fully fledged member of the community of civilised countries.

As for the first impediment, the difference between Europe and America is not as striking as some Russian hard-liners would like to see it. Both parts of the Atlantic are quite keen on promoting the new system of global relationship. Its ultimate goal is to have as many democracies in the world, as possible, since allegedly liberal democracy and appropriate values would bring stability and predictability in international relations. This parade of democracy, however, is promoted by different methods: while the Anglo-American coalition is more assertive and is ready to make pre-emptive strikes against dictators of the 'axis of evil' or any other axis, the Europeans are more conservative in their approach (except for some distant periphery countries, as seen in French intervention in Ivory Coast or British involvement in Sierra Leone) and prefer economic means combined with multilateral engagement tactics. Meanwhile, it is clear that in the long run both sides will reach the same outcome – they will have to get rid of one of the obstacles of the past – the United Nations in its current form with the veto-paralysed Security Council and the General Assembly, more than half of which consists of non-democratic states, and which comprise the target of the Western quest for liberty.

Under these circumstances, Russia has no alternative in the new system. It can hardly make a strong and durable alliance with China (for demographic reasons) or India (New Delhi also became US-oriented quite a while ago), as Yevgeny Primakov claimed in the mid-1990s, and there are no reliable partners on the horizon, other than Western countries. Therefore, Moscow may get a unique chance to jump into this 'liberty armoured train' and fill the missing link in the 'northern belt' of stability, being formed against the unstable south. At the same time, this path will be long and not always straight, bearing in mind the Kremlin's desire to preserve its mythical defence self-sufficiency and diplomatic multi-vector manoeuvring, as well as bureaucratic inertia in protecting the ageing and inefficient system of the United Nations (instead of suggesting some new multilateral mechanisms).

Nowadays Moscow is balancing between Europe and America. In the early years of Putin's presidency he was always more inclined to develop partnership with the EU, since the latter is the largest trading partner and is closer to Russia in cultural terms. Even during the crisis over Iraq the Kremlin joined the Franco-German coalition, reminding many observers of the nineteenth-century reactionary post-Napoleon troika, which in this century desperately tries to save the 'corpse' of the Yalta–Potsdam system. Russia's rejection of any new UN resolution authorising the use of force was one of the crucial factors, which helped to block US endeavours within the Security Council.[21]

However, Moscow was happy to avoid the explicit clash with Washington and has repeatedly reaffirmed its commitment to good relations with the

United States.[22] In fact, for the Russian elite it is easier to find common language with the Americans on many matters (e.g. counter-terrorist activities, pre-emptive strikes, energy dialogue, WTO, etc.). And despite Russia's affiliation to Europe, Russia–EU relations (see Chapter 13) leave much to be desired – they are stuck in protracted negotiations on various issues and there is a clear willingness of the Europeans to impose on Moscow their vision of the future of Russia–EU relations. Moreover, as the Kaliningrad issue has demonstrated, Europe will tend to convert Russia to its values *à la acquis communataires*, regardless of Moscow's resistance to this process. Therefore, it is more agreeable for the Russian bureaucracy to work with the Americans, who are more flexible in their approach and can be quite 'discriminating' in their human rights criticism. Besides, the American economy is stronger than the European economy (which will further be weakened in the short run by EU enlargement) and inclusion in the US zone of economic interests (which now covers North America, Latin America and a significant part of Asia, let alone US investments in Europe) may be much more profitable to Russia in the distant future. Finally, Moscow with its post-imperial syndrome will still be more satisfied with the status of 'low equality' partner of a global leader, than with an alliance with the European 'beehive'.

Another reason for the possible choice of the United States as a partner is Russia's isolation within Europe. The enlargement of NATO and the EU inevitably leads to the erection of new dividing lines in Europe. Obviously, nobody seriously regards Russia as an adversary any more and the processes were not explicitly anti-Russian in their nature, but objectively they exclude Moscow from integration in the foreseeable future. To a large extent, this is the fault of the Kremlin, i.e. Russia's inability to meet or, at least, to seek compliance with the formal parameters required for joining the European Union. As we have mentioned above, Russian reforms are slow. The permanent recurrence of the crisis in Chechnya alienates Moscow from Europe, border and migration controls are yet to reach the appropriate levels, crime and corruption are thriving in spite of the Kremlin's efforts, etc. And it is obvious that Europe in this respect has no choice, but to prevent Russia from membership.

Besides, the Russia–EU and Russia–US agenda still bears the scars of the Yeltsin era. The economic agenda with Washington is extremely weak and even the emerging oil dialogue may become less useful after the war in Iraq, as the USA gains control over the second largest oil reserves in the world. Meanwhile, the importance of hard security matters of the past (national missile defence, strategic offensive arms and even non-proliferation as the regime is eroding, etc.) is diminishing. As for Europe, there is an evident stagnation in economic issues (low progress at the WTO negotiations, the unresolved economic future of the Kaliningrad area, lack of a clear vision of the Common European Economic Space initiative, contradictions over energy prices and the status of the market economy), which have always been the strongest aspects of the Russia–EU agenda. At the same time, due to the slow development of the European security and defence policy, there are no projects of specific co-operation in this area, except regular consultation mechanisms and some co-ordination of law enforcement and other 'soft security' activities. As Moscow tends to reduce substantially its peace-keeping presence in the Balkans, the chances of close military co-operation become even slimmer (see Chapter 15).

In this context, Russia's co-operation with NATO could play a cementing role in tying Moscow to Europe and the USA simultaneously. But after nearly a year of existence, the NATO–Russia Council with its numerous working groups does not demonstrate the miracles of efficiency either. Among the visible results so far are the joint emergency exercise 'Bogorodsk-02', the September 2002 agreement on a framework for the concept of peace support operations, the December 2002 conference on the role of the military in combating terrorism, the February 2003 rescue-at-sea framework agreement (to be further signed by Russia individually with each NATO member) and Moscow's accession to the NATO standardisation and classification system (which allegedly should open more arms markets to Russian manufacturers beginning in 2004). The recent appointment of General of the Army Konstantin Totsky, as Russia's permanent representative to the Alliance, will hardly improve the situation. An exborder guard, the General has little experience in this area as he has already admitted.[23] The negative attitude towards NATO among some Russian policy-makers also does little to strengthen the partnership. After the Prague summit, the NATO issue somehow vanished from political discourse and the US action in Afghanistan and then in Iraq only proves to many Russian politicians and military (even liberal and pro-NATO) that the Alliance is obsolete and that bilateral co-operation with the United States on various security issues is more preferable.

Paradoxically, the conclusions are quite optimistic with respect to a Russia–West rapprochement. In 2003 and early 2004 one could hardly expect any significant breakthrough in this area. The normalisation of relations is most likely but with some possible pre-electoral splashes similar to the Salt Lake City syndrome, the Kaliningrad hysteria or the outcry about the PACE resolution on the establishment of an international tribunal for war crimes in Chechnya. Most of these incidents were caused by the inability of the Russian bureaucracy to get used to the new culture of consensus building and decision-making within the European structures. However, the general pro-Western course persistently pursued by President Putin will not suffer a lot whilst he remains in power. Moscow will continue to run the razor blade of contradictions between Europe and the USA and the multi-vector approach of Russian diplomacy will not be substantially amended due to such institutional inertia.

Conclusions

The significance of Russia's reaction to the US invasion of Iraq in 2003 should not be underestimated. In refusing to support a second resolution in the UN and by backing the Franco-German position that the US arms inspection team should be given more time and that political rather than military means provided the most appropriate response to Iraq, Russia has cemented its preference for a long-term relationship with the EU and a pan-European security architecture. What this means for future relations between Russia and the US remains to be seen although it is unlikely that either party would seek an isolationist position from the other. The postwar reconstruction of Iraq and the continuation of a US military presence in the Middle East will be important test cases in determining the extent to which 'substantive and constructive co-operation' can be achieved. The key challenge for Russia in the foreseeable future will be to institutionalise its rapprochement with the West in order to make it truly irreversible. Firstly, the Kremlin will have to take more efforts to convert public opinion and to change the hidden sabotage of the elite – this process can only succeed if it is supported with some tangible incentives from the West and visible concessions (instead of the stubborn imposition of Western rules of behaviour). After all, when the public becomes more tolerant towards the idea of Russia as 'normal power' (vs. the concept of superpower), Russia will have to make a clear strategic choice of joining or abstaining from the 'northern belt' of stability, which is actually pre-determined. Secondly, to ensure deeper partnership with the West, Russia will have to concentrate on its domestic reforms, without which any co-operation with Europe or even the United States will remain superficial. Finally, Moscow should think about making its foreign policy more pro-active and should not hesitate in setting forth a new set of initiatives with the West.

Notes

1. S. Cross, *Russia and NATO toward the 21st Century: Conflicts and Peacekeeping in Bosnia-Herzegovina and Kosovo*, NATO–EAPC Research Fellowship Award Final Report, 1991, p. 31 (taken from NATO Academic Forum website at www.nato.int/acad/home.htm.
2. See M. A. Smith and G. Timmins, 'Russia, NATO and the EU in an era of enlargement: vulnerability or opportunity?, *Geopolitics*, 6:1 (2001), 69–90 for a more detailed discussion of NATO's relationship with Russia.
3. *Ibid.*, p. 79.
4. See M. A. Smith and G. Timmins, *The European Union, NATO and Russia* (London: Routledge, 2003) for further details on the pre-Putin period.
5. Vladimir Putin, 'Russia at the turn of the millennium', Speech, 31 December 1999. Available in translation at: www.government.gov.ru/english/statVP_engl_1.html.

6 *Ibid.*
7 *Foreign Policy Concept of the Russian Federation, 2000*. Available in translation at: www.bits.de/EURA/EURAMAIN.htm#RFpoldoc.
8 A. C. Lynch, 'The realism of Russia's foreign policy', *Europe–Asia Studies*, 53:1 (2001), 7–31.
9 See M. de Haas, 'The development of Russian security policy 1992–2002', in A. C. Aldis and R. N. McDermott (eds.), *Russian Military Reform 1992–2002* (London: Frank Cass, 2003) for a more detailed discussion of the military implications for Russia of 11 September 2001.
10 Vladimir Putin, speech to German Parliament on 25 September 2001. Available at: www.pegmusic.com/putin-in-germany.html.
11 G. Timmins 'Strategic or pragmatic partnership? The European Union's policy towards Russia since the end of the cold war', *European Security*, 2003.
12 *Financial Times* (15 May 2002).
13 Report of the Working Group on International Affairs of the State Council of the Russian Federation, 22 January 2003.
14 Results of the public opinion poll conducted by the Public Opinion Fund (*Fond Obzhestvennoye Mnenie* – FOM) on 30 November 2002. *FOM Weekly Bulletin*, 46: 444, (5 December 2002).
15 Forty per cent believed that there was no change in US–Russia relations and only 8 per cent presumed that they improved. FOM public opinion poll 03PEN12/22–03, 27 March 2003.
16 I. Zadorin and D. Konovalenko, 'Foreign policy principles in Russia: susceptibility and resistance to information influence', report presented at the seminar in the Carnegie Moscow Center, 28 January 2002.
17 *Vremya Novostei*, 29 October 2002.
18 I. Safranchuk, 'Metamorphosis of the Russian negotiation position on the Russia–EU–Kaliningrad Transit. Problems with Foreign Policy Tactics'. www.Polit.ru (12 November 2002).
19 According to Anatoly Kvashnin, Chief of the General Staff, 'It would not be ethical to refer to the changes carried out in the Armed Forces as to military reform. This is why the General Staff in its doctrinal documents prefers to avoid the terms "military reform" and "reforming". One can hardly expect radical changes even in the next 10 years.' www.Grani.ru, 10 February 2003.
20 Statement for the press on the Iraqi issue, April 3, 2003 (available at www.president.kremlin.ru).
21 www.Grani.ru (28 March 2003).
22 Statement for the press on the Iraqi issue, April 3, 2003 (available at www.president.kremlin.ru).
23 *Vremya Novostei* (12 March 2003).

13

Russian foreign policy towards the European Union

Jackie Gower

Introduction

For Russia to have a 'policy' towards the European Union is itself a new and significant development. In the days of the former Soviet Union official attitudes veered from indifference to mild hostility based on the perception that the European Economic Community was the economic wing of the Atlantic alliance, but it was rare to find any reference to it in foreign policy statements. There was no formal relationship until the conclusion of a Trade and Co-operation Agreement (TCA) in 1989 which facilitated the development of normal trading relations with their Western European neighbours but had little political content.[1] Under President Yeltsin the EC continued to be afforded a fairly low priority with NATO, the Organisation for Security and Co-operation in Europe (OSCE) and the Council of Europe seen as more important in terms of securing Russia's political interests in Europe and membership of the WTO the key to securing access to the global economy.[2]

Although the Maastricht Treaty had extended the scope of European integration, the Russians continued to view the newly created 'European Union' as essentially an economic institution and political and security relations were primarily conducted through bilateral relations with the United States and the major west European powers such as Germany, France and the UK. Russia's main policy objective in relation to the EU during the 1990s was to secure access to its single market on terms similar to those offered to the Central and East European states under the Europe Agreements.[3] The Partnership and Co-operation Agreement (PCA)[4] that replaced the TCA in December 1997 was in this respect a rather disappointing outcome to the protracted negotiations, containing only a rather weak commitment to the possible establishment of a free trade area in the future. However, the PCA did establish an institutional framework for regular dialogue between Russian and EU politicians and officials and over the next few years both the intensity and quality of the relationship gradually improved.

Since the late 1990s there has been considerable evidence that the Russian government has afforded a much higher priority to the development of its relationship with the EU. Of particular significance was the presentation by the then prime minister, Vladimir Putin, at the Russian–EU summit at Helsinki in October 1999 of a fairly lengthy document entitled 'Russia's Medium-term Strategy for the Development of Relations between the Russian Federation and the EU (2000–2010)'.[5] This was the Russian government's first comprehensive public policy statement on their objectives and vision of what they now refer to as the 'strategic partnership' they want to establish with the EU and reflected a reappraisal of the potential of the EU to be a valuable political as well as economic ally. The new status afforded the EU in Russia's foreign policy was confirmed in the new Foreign Policy Concept approved by the president in June 2000, where it is stated that 'The Russian Federation views the EU as one of its main political and economic partners and will strive to develop with it an intensive, stable and long-tern co-operation devoid of expediency fluctuations.'[6]

President Putin has steered Russian policy towards constructive engagement with the EU on a wide range of issues, including co-operation on the environment, scientific research, 'soft' security issues such as organised crime and illegal immigration and most recently more traditional security concerns. Since the September 11 terrorist attacks the more overtly political and security dimensions of the relationship have been afforded even greater prominence, as evidenced by the introduction of monthly meetings between Russia's Ambassador to the EU and members of the EU's Political and Security Committee. There are high-level discussions about the further development of the relationship, including proposals for the creation of a Common European Economic Space and for Russian involvement in actions under the EU's new Security and Defence Policy.

This chapter will consider why there has been this significant upgrading in the importance attached to the EU in foreign policy under President Putin and identify the main objectives in Russia's current policy. It will then examine policy developments in a number of key areas and assess the contribution they may make to the achievement of those objectives and the future prospects for Russia's relations with the EU.

Reasons for the new policy

Given the central position of the president in the formulation of Russian foreign policy, it is clear that Putin himself must have taken a lead in affording the EU a higher priority. He is a less ambiguous Westerniser than Yeltsin was, especially in his later years, and clearly believes that it is only through increased economic integration with western Europe that Russia can be modernised and growth sustained.[7] At his first EU–Russia summit after his election he also expressed 'a positive interest in the EU's evolving European Security and Defence Policy' and noted that 'there are possibilities for cooperation'.[8] Under his leadership, Russian policy towards the EU has become much more consistent and constructive, although he is regarded in Brussels as a tough negotiator.

In the aftermath of the September 11 attacks, Putin's decision to support the US's war against international terrorism decisively confirmed his Western foreign policy orientation and relations between Russia and the EU have become even more important for both parties. In his speech to the Bundestag in Berlin on 25 September 2001 he went out of his way to identify himself with a pro-European policy and called on Germany and Russia to work together to build a 'united Greater Europe'.[9] This led Dmitri Trenin at the Carnegie Moscow Centre to conclude that 'integration into Europe has been revealed as the main priority of Mr Putin's strategy' and 'the main track into Europe is, to Mr Putin, via the deepening of multi-lateral partnership with the EU'.[10] For their part, EU leaders went some way towards recognising Russia's case that the war in Chechnya is also a struggle against terrorism and thus one of the most persistent obstacles to good relations was at least temporarily removed.[11] The EU–Russia summit in Brussels in October 2001 gave a new impetus to upgrade the relationship on several fronts with a heightened sense of urgency injected into the discussions on the proposal to create a Common European Economic Space and the adoption of a 'Joint Declaration on stepping up dialogue and cooperation on political and security matters.'[12] The international war on terrorism also provided an impetus to greater co-operation between police and security authorities and the exchange of intelligence.

Putin's election and the September 11 atrocities have clearly played a significant part in ensuring that the EU is afforded a higher priority in Russian foreign policy in recent years. However, there are also a number of other objective factors that have contributed to the new focus of Russia's policy. One of the most important is the fact that the EU has become Russia's most important trading partner and it is widely assumed that this trend will continue. There was a major shift in the trade patterns of the whole of the Central and East European region in the 1990s as former CMEA states re-orientated their trade towards Western markets. Whereas in the 1980s less than 20 per cent of Russia's trade had been with the EU, by the mid-1990s it had increased to over 35 per cent.[13] Even under President Yeltsin, therefore, the EU was regarded as an important economic partner but two factors have served to reinforce this perception in recent years. Firstly, the expected enlargement of the EU to many of Russia's eastern neighbours will mean that the EU's share of Russia's trade is predicted to rise to over 50 per cent.[14] Secondly, under Putin the more outward-looking, entrepreneurial economic elite epitomised by the Round Table of Industrialists seem to be in the ascendancy and access to markets and investment are seen as essential to modernise the Russian economy. Relations with Russia's most important trading partner have therefore become increasingly central to its foreign policy, both with a view to protecting Russia's interests and to increasing the opportunities for closer co-operation.

A second significant factor is that Russia is taking the prospect of EU enlargement much more seriously now that it seems probable that up to eight of the Central and East European candidate states will become members in 2004–5. It already has a long common border with Finland which will be extended when Latvia and Estonia become EU members and one oblast, Kaliningrad, will become an enclave in the enlarged EU with borders with both Poland and Lithuania. Together with the accession of Slovakia, Hungary and the Czech Republic enlargement will inevitably therefore have the effect of making the EU seem much closer and more relevant to Russia. Generally, the official line on EU enlargement has been fairly positive and in marked contrast to the reaction to NATO's enlargement. However, the prospect of EU enlargement has raised a number of important issues such as the implications for Russia's own trade with the enlarged EU, the position of large Russian minorities in some future EU member states, the consequences of new members adopting the Schengen border procedures and transit rights from Kaliningrad across future EU territory.[15] These issues have increasingly dominated the agenda of Russia–EU meetings and transformed them from the rather formalistic exchanges of the 1990s into forums for negotiation on matters of real substance. There is also evidence that the Russian government is acutely conscious of the potential geopolitical consequences of enlargement, fearing that it could lead to a loss of Russian political influence in Europe if it finds itself 'excluded' or marginalised from this wider Europe. From the EU's perspective, one of the opportunities offered by enlargement is to be a much more significant regional, and indeed global, political actor and Russia is understandably anxious that it should not be at its expense. More positively, an enlarged EU will potentially be a much more important and valuable partner and therefore is seen to merit a higher priority in Russia's external relations.

Thirdly, it is also relevant that since the 1990s the EU has undergone a major transformation in its own character and role. It is not really surprising that the Russians saw the EU as primarily an *economic* organisation before the 1990s as it is only really since the Maastricht Treaty that it has tried to develop a major role in relation to foreign and security policy and the 'justice and home affairs' issues such as international crime, terrorism, asylum and immigration. It may be significant that these are policy areas that fall under the intergovernmental decision-making procedures of the so-called 'Pillars 2 and 3' of the EU which makes it easier for co-operation to include non-members. This is particularly relevant with respect to the EU's decision to develop a limited military capability to enable it to undertake peacekeeping and humanitarian rescue tasks independently of the United States. From Russia's perspective, therefore, the EU in 2002 is a much more interesting and potentially useful partner than it seemed a decade ago.

Russia's policy objectives

The most authoritative and comprehensive statement on Russia's foreign policy objectives is the 'Medium-term Strategy for Development of Relations between the Russian Federation and the European Union (2000–2010)'[16] adopted in 1999 in response to the EU's publication of its own Common Strategy on Russia.[17] Although prepared during the final months of Yeltsin's presidency, Putin was the prime minister and he personally presented it to the EU leaders at their summit in Helsinki. It remains the cornerstone of official Russian policy towards the EU, identifying a number of specific objectives as well as giving some indication of the overall shape and scope of the relationship Russia hopes to build with the EU.

Strategic partnership rather than membership

At a time when virtually all Russia's neighbours to the West are seeking EU membership, it is significant that the Medium-term Strategy explicitly excludes either accession to the EU or 'association' with it 'during the period under review', that is, before 2010.[18] It also gives the reasons behind this decision: 'As a world power situated on two continents, the Russian Federation should retain its freedom to determine and implement its domestic and foreign policies, its status and advantages of an Euro-Asia state and the largest member of the Commonwealth of Independent States, independence of its position and activities at international organizations.'[19]

The prospect of adopting the 80,000 pages of the EU's *acquis communautaire* and being bound by the constraints of the obligations arising from the common foreign and security policy has made EU membership unattractive to a political elite that continues to regard Russia as 'different' from other European states. Privately, Russian officials also concede that Russia is simply too large for the EU to welcome it as a member and also it comes nowhere near to meeting the EU's exacting criteria for opening accession negotiations.[20] For the rest of the decade, therefore, the expectation is that the PCA will continue to provide the legal framework for relations with the EU.

In place of the option of becoming a 'candidate member state' with all the inevitable implications of being a supplicant, the Strategy proposes that Russia should seek to develop a 'strategic partnership' with the EU, based on equality. The vision is of Russia and the EU as the two leading powers on the continent working together 'to achieve certain major objectives of mutual interest and to solve European and world problems'.[21] The core manifestations of this 'partnership' are envisaged to be the creation of 'an effective system of collective security in Europe' and 'progress towards the creation of the Russian Federation–European Union free trade zone',[22] (discussed in more detail below). But there is a long list of other areas identified where close co-operation with the EU is seen to have potential advantages for both parties. Indeed the whole concept of partnership is based on the assumption that the EU has as much to gain from the relationship as Russia and the goal is 'the interrelated and balanced strengthening of the positions of the Russian Federation and the European Union within an international community of the 21st century'.[23]

A pan-European security structure

One of Russia's key objectives since the end of the Cold War has been the development of a pan-European security system in which it will be an equal partner and therefore strengthening the OSCE has been its preferred option.[24] That remains its position but the decision by the EU to develop its own role in relation to the so-called 'Petersburg tasks' of humanitarian aid and rescue, peacekeeping and crisis management has led to interest in the contribution it might make to counterbalancing what the Russians continue to regard as the 'NATO-centrism' in Europe. When the Medium-term Strategy was being formulated, the EU was planning to use the Western European Union (WEU) as its 'defence identity' and so the Russians envisaged developing political and military relations with the WEU and exploring the possibility for joint actions. Now that the EU has decided to develop its own rapid reaction force and has become increasingly active on 'soft' security issues such as combating international crime, terrorism and illegal immigration, interest has shifted to a more direct relationship with the EU on security matters. The goal is 'to ensure pan-European security by the Europeans themselves without isolation of the USA, but also without their dominance on the continent'.[25]

A pan-European economic and legal infrastructure

One of the most serious practical implications for Russia of the EU's planned enlargement is that already it has resulted in the legal norms and technical standards governing its single market being extended to most of Central and Eastern Europe.[26] This is a much more serious obstacle to expanding economic relations between Russia and the rest of Europe than tariffs, and certainly after WTO membership has been secured will become the major focus for its external trade policy. Article 55 of the PCA recognised that 'the approximation of legislation' will be an important condition for strengthening the economic relationship and Russia committed itself 'to endeavour to ensure that its legislation shall be gradually made compatible with that of the Community' from banking and financial services to consumer protection, environmental standards and rules on public procurement and competition. The Medium-term Strategy reiterates this goal with the objective of creating a 'pan-European' system and the concept of a 'common European economic space' relies heavily on the idea of a single Europe-wide legal framework governing the European economy. However, the potential tension between 'preserving the independence of the Russian legal system' and 'preserving in the Russian Federation of its own standards and certification'[27] and the harmonisation of so much of its legislation with that of the EU is likely to make it controversial in the domestic political context.

A EU–Russia free trade area

Officially this has been one of Russia's most long-standing goals and was enshrined in the PCA as a commitment that 'the parties shall examine together in the year 1998 whether circumstances allow the beginning of negotiations on the establishment of a free trade area'.[28] The financial crisis in 1998 meant that the talks never got off the ground and there is considerable doubt in both Russia and the West about whether in fact a free trade area would be in the interests of its still quite vulnerable manufacturing industry. Membership of the WTO would remove most of the current obstacles to the expansion of Russia's trade and so the EU's active support for her application is particularly valued. The decision by the EU to recognise Russia's market economy status in May 2002 was especially welcome in Moscow and should remove many of the ongoing sources of trade tensions between them.[29] A free trade area with the EU remains the stated Russian goal as part of the elaboration of the Common European Economic Space initiative.

Creating a united Europe without dividing lines

This has been a recurring theme in Russian foreign policy for many years but has become increasingly salient as both NATO and EU enlargement threaten to cast Russia as an 'outsider' state on the continent.[30] The decision in May 2002 to create a Russia–NATO Council has gone some way to defusing the political tension surrounding NATO enlargement and attention has shifted to what the Medium-term Strategy sees as 'securing the interests of the Russian Federation during the expansion of the EU'. The specific economic and security objectives discussed above should therefore be understood as part of Russia's overall strategy to create what Putin and other Russian spokesmen frequently call 'big Europe', in other words one that is wider than the EU and includes Russia on equal terms.

Issues on the current Russia–EU agenda

Proposals for a common European economic space

There was a brief reference in the Joint Statement issued at the end of the EU–Russia summit held in Moscow in May 2001 to the decision 'to establish a joint high-level group within the framework of the PCA to elaborate the concept of a common European economic space' (CEES).[31] At the time it passed almost without comment in the press but in the context of the new momentum in EU–Russian relations after the September 11 atrocities, it has assumed a core position as one of the main initiatives for upgrading the relationship into a more 'strategic partnership'. The terms of reference of the membership and agenda for the high level group were agreed at the summit in Brussels on 3 October 2001 and it produced a report at the summit held in Moscow in May 2002. The importance both parties afford the proposal is demonstrated by the fact that it is jointly chaired by Chris Patten, EU Commissioner for External Relations, and Russian Deputy Prime Minister Victor Khristenko and their joint report can be assumed to reflect thinking on the subject at the highest level.

The first, and probably most difficult, task of the high-level group is 'to elaborate a concept for a closer economic relationship between Russia and the EU, based on the wider goal of bringing the EU and Russia closer together'.[32] In other words, they have to agree on what a common European economic space or area[33] might actually mean with regard to Russia's economic relationship with the EU. In the report to the May 2002 summit, they go some way towards outlining what the future goal is: 'Ultimately, economic agents should be able to operate subject to common rules and conditions in their respective fields of activity throughout the enlarged EU and Russia (a potential combined market of up to 600 million consumers).'[34]

The focus, therefore, is on what is described as 'regulatory and legislative convergence and the removal of barriers to trade and investment' in a long list of targeted sectors including standards, technical regulations, customs, financial services, accounting/auditing, transport, space launching services, public procurement, telecommunications and competition. Although the process is called 'convergence' or 'legislative approximation', realistically it is almost certain to mean in practice Russia bringing its legislation in line with the EU's *acquis communautaire*. It is also recognised that Russia will need to create 'appropriate institutional structures and strengthen enforcement and appeal procedures'. A detailed work plan was agreed which includes commissioning impact assessment studies to assess the economic benefits and costs of moving towards regulatory convergence in specific sectors and on the economies as a whole 'to allow Russia and the EU to better define the level of ambition of the CEES'.[35] To maintain the momentum, a 'detailed report' is to be presented at the summit in Copenhagen in November 2002.

It is clear that the CEES concept is still in the very early stages and a great deal of work needs to be done in defining 'the ultimate objectives of the CEES'.[36] However, the initiative is a reflection of the desire by both the Russian government and the EU to begin to think about the kind of medium to long-term relationship that they might develop. As has already been discussed, it is not current Russian policy to seek accession to the EU and it is certainly not on the agenda of the EU and yet both parties believe that it is desirable for Russia to be more fully integrated into the mainstream of European life, and in particular into the single market. The report of the high-level group specifically referred to the support it has received from the EU–Russia Round Table of Industrialists and pressure is coming from business people to take steps to ensure that they are not at a competitive disadvantage as a result of EU enlargement.

Some Russian officials and academics have therefore become interested in recent years in the relationship that certain West European states such as Switzerland, Norway and Iceland enjoy with the EU which seems to have enabled them to enjoy many of the economic advantages of EU membership while avoiding the political costs.[37] Obviously, the economic, and indeed political, social and legal, conditions in Russia today are enormously different from those operating in countries like Norway and Switzerland and many people in the EU are deeply sceptical about the viability of using their relations with the EU as a possible model for Russia. However, it is also believed that if Russia could be encouraged to become more like them, then that would be to the advantage of both her and the rest of the continent. Chris Patten in a speech at a European Business Club conference in Moscow suggested the CEES is 'absolutely central to Russia's decisions about what is sometimes called her "European choice"'.[38] He continued:

> At the heart of this idea lies the notion that Russia would use the present economic reform programme to make its own laws and regulations compatible with our own. How far this can be achieved will make a big difference in the attractiveness of Russia to EU investors and importers. The EU has already provided some €2.4 billion to support Russia's transition and we are willing to continue this support in future. However, we need to understand how far Russia is willing to go in this direction, how European does Russia really want to be?

Apart from the political will to meet the challenges posed by the CEES initiative, Timofei Bordachev has also argued strongly that Russia will need considerably to expand its pool of EU experts in the public administration and create a special government department for European integration affairs similar to those that the candidate countries have established.[39] As they have found, legal approximation involves a huge amount of immensely complex and detailed negotiations and requires a great deal of cross-ministerial co-ordination and at the moment the Russian government lacks the resources to undertake it successfully.

Strengthening dialogue and co-operation on political and security matters

The PCA established an institutional framework for regular political dialogue between Russia and the EU with twice yearly summits between the Russian president, the prime minister of the EU member state holding the Council Presidency, the president of the EU Commission and since 1999 also the EU's Secretary General/High Representative for the Common Foreign and Security Policy (CFSP). In addition the PCA established a Co-operation Council (ministerial level), Co-operation Committee (senior officials) and Parliamentary Co-operation Council. Regular meetings have also been introduced between Javier Solana, the EU's High Representative for CFSP, and Igor Ivanov, the Russian Foreign Minister and a dense network of consultation bodies exist at senior official and expert level. After the September 11 attacks it was agreed to step up the intensity of the dialogue by holding monthly meetings between the Russian Ambassador to the EU in Brussels and the EU Political and Security Committee troika where current international issues are discussed informally over lunch. The main objective of this political dialogue is 'to bring about an increasing convergence of positions on international issues of mutual concern thus increasing security and stability'[40] and the Joint Statements issued at the end of formal meetings include references to various current crises. The Russian authorities are generally positive about the value of political dialogue but have been somewhat frustrated by the absence of very much in the way of substantial joint action as opposed to joint statements.

The catalyst for potentially developing the political and security dimension of the EU–Russia relationship beyond discussions and declarations into the realm of practical co-operation and even joint action was the decision by the EU in 1999 to equip itself with a limited military capability in the form of a rapid reaction force. Russia's response has been largely positive and to a large extent the impetus to make co-operation on security matters a core part of the EU–Russia partnership is coming from the Russian side. At the May 2002 summit, for example, they proposed that there should be a 'Russia–EU Action Plan in the field of European Security and Defence Policy'.

There has been speculation that Russian policy-makers have seen co-operation with the EU on security issues 'as a means of driving a wedge between the European members of NATO and the United States'.[41] Put less crudely, Dmitri Danilov argues that they may be motivated by the belief that the development of an independent crisis management capacity will increase the EU's political weight and therefore further Russia's long-term goal of a multi-polar world order.[42] However, there are also other reasons for Russia welcoming the EU's potential engagement in regional security. Danilov also suggests that: 'paradoxically ... an EU with its own rapid reaction capability would be a factor of demilitarisation of international relations: the EU military dimension will take an auxiliary role in the broad security policy – in contrast with NATO, where military activities are the core of security management'.[43]

In other words, the very fact that the EU is only planning to have a maximum of 60,000 military personnel at its disposal and its decision-making procedures would make it very difficult in practice to deploy military forces means that it will rely as much as possible on alternative approaches to crisis management and peace-keeping tasks. This is a much more attractive option from Russia's perspective compared, for example, to NATO's aerial bombing in Kosovo. Furthermore, if the EU does have to resort to the deployment of troops, it might be grateful to take up Russia's offer of practical support, whether it be transport planes, satellite facilities or troops on the ground. Military co-operation is one of the few areas where Russia feels confident that its 'partnership' with the EU could be on more equal terms. Russia's objectives therefore in relation to political and security co-operation is to strengthen the institutional arrangements, perhaps by the establishment of a permanent Russia–EU Council and agree concrete measures for co-operation on a range of security issues, identified by Putin in May 2000 as covering 'notably early warning, conflict prevention, crisis management and post-conflict reconstruction'.[44]

Progress on the development of an effective EU–Russia partnership on security matters has been largely dependent on the EU's need first to put in place its own arrangements for the new European Security and Defence Policy.[45] At the European Council in Nice in December 2000 the EU member states agreed in principle that other states could be invited to participate in civilian and crisis management operations but it was not until June 2002 that the 'arrangements for consultation and co-operation between the EU and Russia on crisis management' were finally adopted.[46] During 'non-crisis periods' consultations will take place within the existing mechanisms with the Russian Ambassador to the EU and the Political and Security Committee troika playing the leading role. One important innovation, though, is the appointment by Russia of a contact person accredited to the EU Military Staff. The Chair of the EU Military Committee also met Russian military authorities in Moscow in May 2002. During the 'pre-operational phase' consultations will be intensified 'to ensure that Russia, as a potential contributor to an EU-led crisis management operation, is informed of the EU's intentions'.[47] This clearly falls below Russia's hope of securing a place in the initial decision-making forum. Only once the decision to adopt the military option has been taken will Russia formally be invited to participate and to discuss with the EU's Operation Commander what contribution it would like to make. However, at the actual operation stage, the proposals are more inclusive, specifying:

To the extent that Russia deploys significant military forces within the framework of a European Union-led operation, it will be invited to participate in the proceedings of the Committee of Contributors which will play a key role in the day-to-day management of the operation. In its capacity as a Contributing State, Russia will have the same rights and obligations in terms of day-to-day management of the operation as EU Member States participating in the operation.[48]

The EU has agreed to undertake its first crisis management operation in Bosnia and Herzegovina with a police mission from 1 January 2003 and has indicated its availability to take over from NATO in the Former Yugoslav Republic of Macedonia (FYROM). It is not yet known whether Russia will participate in either operation but it is following developments with great interest in the hope that they might pave the way for the creation of the pan-European security community that is its long-term goal.

The energy dialogue

This is much less of a headline-grabbing initiative than the CEES or cooperation on security matters but it has the potential to build the kind of economic interdependence and integrated infrastructure networks that would provide the concrete foundations for the EU–Russia strategic partnership. Russia already provides over 15 per cent of the EU's needs in imported energy and its share will rise when the countries of Central and Eastern Europe become members. The trade is also extremely important for Russia with 53 per cent of her oil exports going to the EU and 62 per cent of its gas exports.[49] In October 2000 therefore it was decided to develop an energy dialogue based on the recognition that Russia and the EU have a shared interest in ensuring their mutual energy security. The main areas of concern were identified as 'the stability of the energy market, the reliability and growth of imports and exports, the need to modernise the Russian energy sector, to improve energy savings and reduce greenhouse gas emissions from energy production and use'.[50]

A committee of experts jointly chaired by the Russian deputy prime minister and the European Commission Director General for Transport and Energy has identified a number of areas where it is believed progress could be achieved over the short and medium term to strengthen the energy relationship.[51] One of the most important is improving the legal framework and simplifying administrative and licensing procedures for energy production and transport in Russia to encourage greater Western investment in the sector. There is also a commitment to collaborate on improving the physical security of transport networks and infrastructure and reducing the incidence of gas leaks. A number of selected new infrastructure routes such as gas pipelines and electricity transmission networks have been identified as matters of 'common interest' and will receive support in mobilising private investment funding. There are also a number of ambitious projects for technical co-operation in improving energy efficiency and reducing environmental damage that will receive support under the EU's TACIS programme.

The energy dialogue has the potential to deliver tangible benefits to both Russia and the EU and therefore contribute positively to the strategic partnership and the development of a common European economic space. However, there are a number of sensitive issues that could lead to tensions. Chief among them is the long-standing complaint by Russia that its exports of nuclear materials are subject to unwarranted discrimination by the EU. There is also some concern in Russia that the EU's emphasis on the energy sector as the prime area for co-operation may have the effect of perpetuating the structural imbalance of Russia's trade with the EU with what they regard as its unhealthy preponderance of exports of raw materials. One of the objectives of Russian economic policy is to move away from what is regarded as its 'third world' trading position and expand its exports of high technology manufactured goods. The energy dialogue will therefore need to be balanced by evidence of encouragement of Russian trade with the EU in other sectors also.

Kaliningrad

As already noted, Russia has generally been quite positive about EU enlargement to include many of the Central and East European states, recognising its contribution to stability in the region. However, the prospect of their near neighbours introducing the EU's Schengen border controls governing movement of people and the common external tariff and customs regulations on the movement of goods has made ordinary Russian citizens fear that the old Cold War barriers are being resurrected. The Russian media has been very critical of the creation of this 'blue curtain' (so-called after the colour of the EU flag) and the special case of Kaliningrad has become the focal point for Russian anxieties giving rise to intense anti-EU comment.[52] President Putin has publicly identified himself with the issue and has said that he considers its resolution 'a qualitative test of our relations with the EU'.[53]

Kaliningrad has become a major issue by virtue of its unique position as an oblast dependent on transit agreements with Poland and Lithuania to provide road and rail access between itself and the rest of the Russian Federation. The EU insists that these bilateral agreements cannot continue once Lithuania and Poland have become members and their borders become the common external frontier for the Union. Lithuania and Poland are therefore obliged to introduce the EU's Schengen regime which would mean that anyone travelling through their countries between Kaliningrad and the rest of Russia would require a visa.[54] The EU had hoped to minimise the impact by improving the technical arrangements for issuing visas but from Russia's perspective the issue is more a matter of principle than practical inconvenience. Putin argued that 'they are making proposals to us which essentially mean only one thing: the right of Russians to free communication with relatives inside Russia will depend on the decisions of other states'.[55] The Federation Council has appealed to the European Parliament, the Parliamentary Assembly of the Council of Europe and the Polish and Lithuanian Parliaments about the 'violation of the constitutional rights and freedoms of Russian citizens' and the 'threat to the state sovereignty of the Russian Federation'.[56] The Russian representative also raised concerns about the visa issue at an OSCE meeting, arguing that 'unimpeded trips of our citizens from one region of Russia to another are a basic human right' guaranteed under international law and 'the processes of the European Union enlargement . . . lead ultimately to an infringement of the rights of Russians to freedom of movement'.[57]

Both Russian and EU officials have worked intensively to try to find an acceptable solution to a problem that both sides seem genuinely anxious to resolve before it poisons their otherwise promising relationship. At the Co-operation Committee held in Kaliningrad in May 2002 Russia presented detailed proposals that would avoid the emotive issue of visas but accept the introduction of very strict regulations governing transit through Poland and Lithuania. They proposed that special passes valid for twelve hours could be issued at border checkpoints allowing travel by private car along designated routes, with rest stops only permitted at specified locations. Rail and bus transit would be by a 'closed door' regime, with no stops and no embarkation while travelling through Poland and Lithuania.[58] The EU's response was that transit corridors across future member states are not a viable option and public concern about illegal immigration and terrorism make it politically impossible to make concessions on border security. No agreement was reached and the issue dominated the EU–Russia summit later in the month with Putin describing the discussions as 'very sharp'.[59] In August he tried to seize the moral high-ground by proposing a 'new integration initiative' for a general visa-free system arguing that 'it is becoming obvious today that a further development of this particular process calls for mutual freedom of travel by citizens of Russia and EU member-countries'.[60] In September the Commission proposed what it hoped would be a compromise arrangement involving 'a facilitated transit document' for frequent Russian travellers to and from Kaliningrad and an offer to investigate the technical feasibility of visa free non-stop trains after Poland and Lithuania have become members.[61] However, Prime Minister Kasyanov rejected the proposals as merely visas in another guise and said Russia and the EU still had to 'do a lot of work' to solve the problem.[62] There have been threats that unless the EU is prepared to back down on the visa issue, Russia may boycott the

EU–Russia summit scheduled for November 2002. Therefore, unless a satisfactory compromise can be found, Kaliningrad threatens to undermine the whole EU–Russia relationship and jeopardise progress on the other policy initiatives currently on the agenda.

The future prospects for Russia–EU relations

As has been shown in this chapter, under President Putin relations between Russia and the EU have become much more wide-ranging and ambitious in both their scope and objectives. There are a number of potentially very important new projects which if successful would go a long way towards creating the strategic partnership between Russia and the EU that is their shared goal. It is likely to be a partnership based more on pragmatic co-operation than a deep-rooted consensus on values but still offers significant potential gains for both sides. However, for this pragmatic co-operation to realise its full potential, it is essential that Russia continues its own reform programme and develops economic structures and legal and institutional frameworks that are compatible with those of EU member states. As Dmitri Trenin argues, 'Russia's rapprochement with Europe is only in the second instance a foreign policy exercise. Its success or failure will primarily depend on the pace and depth of Russia's economic, political and societal transformation. Russia's "entry into Europe" cannot be negotiated with Brussels. It has to be first "made in Russia" itself.'[63]

At the moment, President Putin's position seems secure and his domestic reform strategy is beginning to bring results. His EU policy is broadly supported by the political and economic elite, although evidence of the widespread ignorance about the EU still prevailing even at this level should make us cautious about assuming that support is very deep-rooted or secure.[64] Although foreign policy observers have commented on the major change in Russia's policy towards the EU under Putin, it has gone almost unnoticed by the general public and attracted little political debate. However, the question of transit to and from Kaliningrad threatens to become a major issue in the media and the Duma. If it is not resolved satisfactorily and quickly, Putin could find his EU policy held hostage by public opinion and his pragmatic co-operation may temporarily have to be suspended. However, given the importance that both the EU and Russian authorities attach to strengthening their relationship in the context of EU enlargement, a compromise does seem the most likely outcome. The challenge then will be to translate the currently rather vague aspirations for the creation of a common European political, economic, social and security space into specific policies so that Russia's vision of being a partner in a 'big Europe' can be realised.

Notes

1. 'Agreement between the EEC and Euratom and the USSR on Trade and Commercial and Economic Cooperation', *Official Journal of the EC*, L68 (15 March 1990). When the USSR disintegrated in 1991, the terms of the agreement were extended to all the individual successor states, including Russia, and continued to govern trade and economic relations until it was superseded by the Partnership and Cooperation Agreement.
2. For a more detailed discussion of this early period, see J. Gower, 'Russia and the European Union', in M. Webber (ed.), *Russia and Europe: Conflict or Cooperation?* (Basingstoke: Macmillan, 2000), pp. 66–98.
3. This is the name by which the Association Agreements concluded by the EU with ten central and East European states during this period are generally known. They provide for the progressive move to free trade in manufactured goods and the integration of their economies with the EU's single market.
4. Agreement on Partnership and Cooperation between the European Communities and their Member States and Russia, *Official Journal of the EC*, L327 (28 November 1997). It was agreed in 1994 but ratification was delayed by EU concerns about Russia's policy in Chechnya.
5. 'Medium-term Strategy for Development of Relations between the Russian Federation and the European Union (2000–2010)' available in English at http://europa.eu.int/comm/external_relations/russia/russian_medium_term_strategy/index.htm.
6. The text is available in English at www.great.britain.mid.ru/.
7. D. Trenin, 'Putin's "new course" is now firmly set: what's next?', *Carnegie Moscow Centre Briefing Paper*, 4:6 (June 2002).
8. EU–Russia Summit Joint Statement, 29 May 2000, available at www.europa.eu.int/comm/external_relations/russia/intro/summit.htm.
9. The full text can be found on the website of the Information and Press Department of the Ministry of Foreign Affairs of the Russian Federation, www.mid.ru.
10. Dmitri Trenin, 'Vladimir Putin's autumn marathon: toward the birth of a Russian foreign policy strategy', *Carnegie Moscow Centre Briefing Paper*, 3:11 (November 2001).
11. There were a number of reports that the reference to Chechnya in the *Joint Statement* issued at the end of the summit had been watered down in order not to alienate the Russians, for example see D. Cronin, 'EU caves in to Putin over Chechnya' in *European Voice*, 7:36 (4–10 October 2001).
12. EU–Russia Summit Joint Statement, Brussels, 3 October 2001, Annex 4. Available at www.europa.eu.int/comm/external_relations/russia/intro/summit.htm.
13. *Russia and the EU Member States Statistical Comparison, 1990–96* (Office for Official Publications of the European Communities, 1998), p. 152.
14. This figure is based on the assumption that the current levels of trade between Russia and the EU candidate states will be maintained so their 'share' of Russia's trade will be incorporated into the EU total. However, the impact of EU enlargement on trade between Russia and the central and East European states is difficult to predict. See J. Pinder and Y. Shishkov, *The EU and Russia: The Promise of Partnership* (London: The Federal Trust, 2002), pp. 93–95.

15 For a fuller discussion see J. Gower, 'EU–Russian relations and the eastern enlargement: integration or isolation?', in C. Ross (ed.), *Perspectives on the Enlargement of the European Union* (Leiden: Brill, 2002).
16 'Medium-term Strategy'.
17 The fact that the EU chose to make Russia the subject of its first use of the new policy instrument of the 'common strategy' introduced by the Amsterdam Treaty is a good indication of the importance it too now attaches to its relationship with Russia. See 'The European Union's common strategy on Russia', *Official Journal of the European Communities*, L157 (24 June 1999).
18 Belarus is the only state not to have indicated a wish to join the EU. 'Association Agreements' have generally been seen as 'stepping-stones' to full EU membership.
19 'Medium-term Strategy', paragraph 1.
20 The criteria were agreed at the Copenhagen European Council in June 1993 and require a state to have achieved stability of institutions guaranteeing democracy, the rule of law, human rights and respect for and protection of minorities, the existence of a market economy and the capacity to cope with competitive pressure.
21 'Medium-term Strategy', paragraph 2.
22 *Ibid.*, paragraph 1.
23 *Ibid.*, preamble.
24 'Russia as a key factor of security and stability in Europe', interview by Russian Deputy Foreign Minister Yevgeny Gusarov in *Diplomat*, 10:90 (October 2001).
25 'Medium-term Strategy', paragraph 5.
26 T. Bordachev, 'Russia and the "expanded Europe": new risks and new opportunities', *Moscow Carnegie Centre Briefing Paper*, 2:12 (December 2000).
27 'Medium-term Strategy', paragraphs. 52 and 53.
28 'Partnership and Cooperation Agreement', Article 3.
29 'EU announces formal recognition of Russia as "market economy" in major milestone on road to WTO membership', IP/02/775 Brussels (29 May 2002).
30 S. White, I. McAllister and M. Light, 'Enlargement and the new outsiders', *Journal of Common Market Studies*, 40:1 (March 2002), 135–153.
31 EU–Russia Summit: Joint Statement, Brussels and Moscow, 17/05/2001, available at www.europa.eu.int/comm/external_relations/russia/intro/summit.htm.
32 EU–Russia Summit: Joint Statement, Annex 2, para. 5, Brussels, 3/10/01.
33 Both 'space' and 'area' are used in the English translations although the Russian 'prostranstvo' is constant. The same linguistic confusion was noted at the time of the development of the European Economic Area in the early 1990s, although today the more frequent use of 'space' in relation to the initiative with Russia may be a deliberate attempt to avoid confusion with the EEA.
34 *Report to the EU–Russia Summit of 29 May 2002 of the High-Level Group on the common European economic space*, www.uropa.eu.int/comm/external_relations/russia/summit_05_02/rep.htm.
35 *Ibid.*
36 This is meant to be one of the objectives of the first stage of the work of the high level group but it seems unlikely that it will be possible to define the ultimate destination before the economic position in Russia is more settled.
37 In fact there is an important distinction between the three states in question, as Switzerland decided in a referendum in December 1992 not to join the European

Economic Area. However, subsequent agreements with the EU have in practice given it almost complete access to the EU's single market.

38 Speech by Chris Patten to European Business Club conference on 'Shaping Russian–European integration in the 21st century', Moscow, 28/05/02, European Commission SPEECH/02/235.
39 T. Bordachev, 'Russia and the European Union: a special department is needed', *Moscow Carnegie Centre Briefing Paper*, 4:3 (March 2002).
40 'Partnership and Coopeartion Agreement', Article 6.
41 M. Light, J. Löwenhardt and S. White, 'Russian perspectives on European security', *European Foreign Affairs Review*, 5: 4 (2000), 501. D. Gowan also suggests that one of the key objectives of Russia's Medium-term Strategy is 'to drive a wedge between Europe and America' in D. Gowan, *How the EU Can Help Russia* (London: Centre for European Reform, 2000), p. 11.
42 D. Danilov, 'The EU's rapid reaction capabilities: a Russian perspective', paper delivered at the IESS/CEPS European Security Forum (10 September 2001), 2.
43 *Ibid.*, 3.
44 'EU–Russia Summit Joint Statement', 29 May 2000.
45 This was acknowledged in the Joint Statement agreed at the Brussels summit in October 2001 which said 'in general, the dialogue on the ESDP will be conducted in the light of progress made by the EU'.
46 Council of the European Union, 'Presidency Report on European Security and Defence Policy', Brussels, 22 June 2002, 10160/2/02 REV COSDP 188, Annex IV.
47 *Ibid.*, paragraph, A.
48 *Ibid.*, paragraph, C.
49 EU Commission, *EU/Russia Energy Dialogue: an Overview* (Brussels, 1 June 2001).
50 'EU Russia–Summit Joint Statement' (3 October 2001), Annex 3.
51 'EU–Russia Energy Dialogue Second Report', Brussels/Moscow (May 2002).
52 Smirnyagin comments on 'the swiftness and intensity of this reaction, and the unanimity of opinion among all the mass media' to reports of the EU's rejection of Russia's proposals at the May 2002 summit in L. Smirnyagin, 'The Kaliningrad issue: the sensation that need not have been', *Carnegie Moscow Centre Briefing Papers*, 4:5 (May 2002). See also R. Burstein, 'Dropping the blue curtain' in *Transitions on Line* (3 June 2002).
53 Jack, A., 'Status of Baltic enclave overshadows summit', *Financial Times* (30 May 2002).
54 For a good discussion of the issues surrounding the whole Kaliningrad issue, see P. Joenniemi, S. Dewar and L. Fairlie, *The Kaliningrad Puzzle: A Russian Region within the European Union*, (The Baltic Institute of Sweden and the Åland Islands Peace Institute: Finland, 2000).
55 Taynor, I., 'Angry Putin warns against ending visa-free transit when Kaliningrad's neighbours join union', *Guardian* (30 May 2002).
56 'Appeal by the Federation Council of the Federal Assembly of Russia to the European Parliament, the Parliamentary Assembly of the Council of Europe, and the Parliaments of the Republic of Poland and the Republic of Lithuania Over the Necessity to ensure the Functioning and Development of the Kaliningrad Region as a Subject of the Russian Federation', 2002–06–014, Ministry of Foreign Affairs of the Russian Federation, Information and Press Department, *Daily News Bulletin* (26 June 2002).

57 'Statement by the Representative of Russia on the Theme "The Right to Freedom of Movement" at the seventh OSCE Human Dimension Implementation Meeting, Warsaw, September 12, 2002', 1868–19–09–2002, Ministry of Foreign Affairs of the Russian Federation, Information and Press Department, *Daily News Bulletin* (19 September 2002).
58 'Memorandum on possible solutions to the specific problems of Kaliningrad region concerning the movement of people', unofficial translation of an unpublished paper from the Russian Ministry of Foreign Affairs.
59 Burstein, 'Russia: dropping the blue Curtain'.
60 'Putin suggests EU heads of state consider Russia's new integration initiative', *On-line Pravda* at http://english.pravda.ru/politics/2002/08/27/35398.html.
61 'Communication from the Commission to the Council – Kaliningrad Transit', COM (2002) 510 final, 18.9.2002.
62 V. Mite, 'Russia: Kasyanov rejects EU's offer on Kaliningrad visas', *Radio Free Europe/Radio Liberty* (27 September 2002).
63 Trenin, 'A Russia-within-Europe', 1.
64 Light, Löwenhardt and White, 'Russian Perspectives on European Security', 9.

14

Conflict in Chechnya

Mike Bowker

Introduction

Boris Yeltsin's reputation both at home and abroad was badly affected by his handling of the war in Chechnya. Public opinion was consistently opposed to Russian military involvement in Chechnya,[1] and although he was successfully re-elected in 1996, his popularity never really recovered to pre-war levels. It was not only the public which was opposed to the war. Yeltsin's administration was divided on Chechnya, and parliament went as far as to seek his impeachment as president over the issue in early 1999. For Vladimir Putin, in contrast, Chechnya has helped to crystallise his public image as a tough and decisive leader. According to all the polls, Putin is a popular president and his uncompromising position on Chechnya is supported by the majority of the Russian people. But will 'the hammer of the Chechens' ultimately be brought low by Chechnya like his predecessor? For even a cursory look behind the image reveals that Putin has been no more effective than Yeltsin in his war with the Chechen rebels. Although Putin has claimed the war is over,[2] the Chechens are continuing a terrorist campaign against the Russians, and the siege at the Dubrovka Theatre in Moscow of October 2002 showed to the world that the dispute is far from resolved. In the immediate aftermath of the siege, it was scarcely surprising that the talk in Russia was of military retribution, but over time Putin's hardline stance may come to be seen as an obstacle to peace and stability. Ultimately, some kind of political solution would seem to be the only possible way out of the current impasse. Whether Putin is able to contemplate compromise with the Chechen rebels may well determine his place in Russian history.

The Yeltsin period

There was little support for the Chechens or their demand for independence amongst ordinary Russian people.[3] Yet from the start, Yeltsin handled the emerging crisis badly. In part, this may have stemmed from a curious insensitivity amongst the Russian political elite towards the issue of Chechen nationalism. Chechnya may be small with a population under a million, but it is economically important because of its oil resources, oil processing and the oil pipelines that traverse the republic.[4] The Chechens also have a well-documented history of resistance to Russian imperialism over a period of at least two hundred years. In their time, the Chechens have fought against absorption into both the Tsarist empire and Lenin's Soviet Union. Russian persecution climaxed in 1944 when virtually the whole Chechen population was herded into cattle trucks and deported to Central Asia for supposed support of the Nazis. A third died *en route* and many others who refused to travel were shot. A number of Chechens who emerged later as key figures in the subsequent independence movement, like Dzhokar Dudaev and Aslan Maskhadov, were brought up in exile in Kazakhstan.

Even though Khrushchev allowed Chechens to return to their homeland from 1957, ethnic Chechens were prevented from taking high political office in the republic until the Gorbachev era. Therefore, it was scarcely surprising that there was a demand for independence when the Soviet Union began to break up. Yeltsin even appeared to encourage it when in August 1990 he called on the regions of Russia to 'take as much sovereignty as you can swallow'.[5] When the sitting Communist president of Chechnya, Doku Zavgaev, was overthrown by Dudaev in September, Yeltsin seemed largely unconcerned. Zavgaev had alienated himself from the Yeltsin camp by remaining neutral during the August 1991 coup. Dudaev, on the other hand, had backed Yeltsin and looked a reasonably safe bet to Moscow.[6] Married to a Russian, Dudaev had fought against the mujahideen in Afghanistan as an officer in the Soviet air force, but importantly he had also been an eyewitness to the nationalist uprising in Estonia 1990–91. This latter experience clearly made an impression because when Dudaev returned to live in his homeland, he was determined to emulate the Estonian revolution and bring independence to Chechnya.

Elections were held in Chechnya in October, which seemed to ratify Dudaev's takeover of power. According to official Chechen figures, 85 per cent voted in favour of Dudaev with a turnout of 55 per cent.[7] Moscow, with some cause, described the elections as fraudulent and the Russian Congress declared them null and void.[8] Dudaev, however, chose to view the result as a vote for secession and in November proclaimed Chechnya independent from Russia. Moscow responded by declaring a state of emergency and dispatched a thousand troops to impose its decree. However, Dudaev's forces were waiting when the troops arrived and Gorbachev, who was still in the Kremlin at the time, ordered them to return home. For the first but not the last time, Yeltsin felt humiliated by the Chechens, and decided to place a partial economic blockade on the dissident republic.

Whilst Galina Starovoitova was Yeltsin's advisor on the nationalities, the administration adopted a relatively liberal line on Chechnya and attempted to prevent the further fragmentation of Russia through diplomacy and constitutional agreements. Thus, in March 1992, the Federation Treaty, which bound all the signatories to become subjects of the newly created Russian Federation, was signed by all constituent regions, except Tatarstan and Chechnya. Tatarstan, like Chechnya, was oil-rich and potentially very wealthy, but it was finally persuaded to sign a special bilateral treaty with Moscow in 1994 in return for a high level of autonomy over its own affairs. It was hoped in Moscow that Dudaev might be tempted to follow Tatarstan's lead, but he refused to compromise. Dudaev had already boycotted the December 1993 referendum on Yeltsin's new Constitution, which simply reaffirmed in his eyes the fact that Chechnya was a *de facto* independent state which was no longer bound by Russian law.

Initially, Dudaev was reasonably popular in Chechnya because of his defiance of Moscow. However, support soon fragmented as the Chechen economy collapsed, unemployment rose and Chechnya became a centre for drugs, gun-running and mafia operations. The Ingush people, incorporated into the Checheno-Ingush Republic in 1936, had become increasingly alienated by Dudaev's nationalist policies, and they seceded from the republic in July 1992 and rejoined the Russian Federation. The Russian minority left behind in Chechnya made up a quarter of the Chechen population according to the 1989 census and lived mainly in the cities (almost 50 per cent of the capital Grozny was ethnic Russian) and north of the Terek River (the Nadterechny Region).[9] These areas became centres of opposition to the Dudaev regime whilst support for Dudaev was centred on the poorer more rural and mountainous regions of the south. A problem for Dudaev, however, was that political loyalty amongst ethnic Chechens was often dependent on clan (or *teip*).

As conditions inside Chechnya worsened, Dudaev chose to act against his increasingly vocal opposition. He forcibly closed down parliament in June 1993, banned all opposition groups, and introduced direct presidential rule. When Dudaev's critics protested, police opened fire and killed up to fifty people.[10] At the same time as Dudaev was losing control in Chechnya, Yeltsin was consolidating his position back in Moscow. Yeltsin had finally defeated his parliamentary opponents in October 1993, but only after the military had come to his aid and agreed to shell the White House, which gave the power ministries and Yeltsin's hardline supporters greater influence in the Kremlin. The subsequent shift to a more assertive nationalist line was legitimised *post facto* by the strong performance in the December 1993 parliamentary elections of Zhirinovsky's proto-fascist party, the LDPR.

As a consequence of this power shift in the Kremlin, Galina Starovoitova was replaced as nationalities chief by Sergei Shakhrai (and then Nikolai Yegerov), and the policy of containment in Chechnya, advocated by Yeltsin's political advisor, Emil Pain, was abandoned in favour of a more interventionist line. Yeltsin was more easily persuaded by the hardliners when Ruslan Khasbulatov, one of the architects of the White House standoff, began to campaign for power in his native Chechnya after being granted an amnesty by the Duma in February 1994. Yeltsin became convinced that Dudaev was too weak politically to resist any challenge from his political rival. He thus ignored a number of approaches for negotiation from Dudaev in 1994 and cast around for an alternative leader.[11] After much hesitation, Yeltsin decided to back Umar Avturkhanov, whose main base of support was in the pro-Russian Nadterechny region. Yeltsin helped set up Avturkhanov's Provisional Council in June, donated a reported forty billion rubles, and supplied it with troops and military equipment.[12]

On 26 November, supporters of Avturkhanov marched on Grozny to overthrow Dudaev and take power in the name of the Provisional Council, but the attempted coup failed dismally. Avturkhanov underestimated his own support and the military capability of Dudaev's regime. During the battle for Grozny, Russian troops were killed and a further twenty-one were captured. Russian prisoners were paraded on television and Dudaev threatened to execute them all. Although this threat was quickly retracted, the failed coup was humiliation enough for Yeltsin. Surrounded by hardliners, Yegorov, Sergei Stepashin (intelligence chief), Oleg Lobov (Chair of the Security Council) and Pavel Grachev (Defence Minister), Yeltsin decided to intervene in Chechnya directly with military force. He was not prepared to allow Dudaev to continue his defiance of Moscow in an area of such economic and strategic importance to Russia. Yeltsin also anticipated, in the words of the Chair of the Security Council, a 'short victorious war' which would give a welcome boost to his ailing political fortunes at home.[13] After all, his Defence Minister had told him that Russian forces could take Grozny with just two paratroop regiments in two hours.[14]

The proposal for military intervention was presented to the Security Council on 29 November 1994, and according to Yeltsin the decision to use force was unanimous.[15] This was not entirely accurate. The Justice Minister, Yuri Kalmykov, was opposed to military action and resigned from Yeltsin's government after complaining about a lack of debate.[16] The decision in the country was controversial from the start, and led to a breach with many of Yeltsin's reformist colleagues, including Yegor Gaidar, his former prime minister. Both the Duma and Federation Council were opposed to the war and there were deep splits in the military too, with Boris Gromov and Alexander Lebed just two of the more notable figures to oppose intervention.[17]

After nine days of air strikes, the ground assault against Chechen rebels began on 11 December 1994. Despite complete mastery of the skies and an advantage on the ground of almost three to one (40,000 Russian troops faced, at most, 15,000 rebel forces), the first Russian attack on Grozny was easily repelled by the rebels. Poor planning and a lack of organisation led to a mounting casualty list on the Russian side, and many of the casualties were young conscripts who had been thrown untrained and unknowingly into the front line. Russian forces finally took Grozny in late January but the war continued until the last rebel stronghold, Samashky, was taken in April 1995. Thereafter, the rebels moved to the mountains in the south and prepared for guerilla warfare and a terrorist campaign against Russia.

Yeltsin revealed a mixture of deviousness and incompetence during the war in Chechnya. The day before the ground attack was launched, Yeltsin retired to hospital for what sounded like a minor operation on his nose. No doubt he hoped to reappear after the operation to declare a dramatic victory over the Chechen forces. Instead, the initial assault on Grozny was beaten back by the rebels and Yeltsin's silence began to look like an unwillingness to accept responsibility for the war. Yeltsin only appeared on TV to explain his decision on 27 December, some seventeen days after the launch of the ground war. Yeltsin's reputation as a democrat suffered. When the war came to an end in 1996, conservative estimates suggested that 30,000 had been killed, over two-thirds of whom were civilians.[18] Russian troops were also accused of a whole series of human rights violations, including torture and the deliberate targeting of civilian populations. Brutality, of course, was not all one-sided. Chechen rebels launched a series of terrorist attacks which outraged Russian public opinion. These included the capture of a hospital in Budennovsk near Stavropol in June 1995 when over a thousand patients and employees were taken hostage, resulting in the deaths of over a hundred people. The terrorists, led by the radical Shamil Basaev, were escorted home as part of the final agreement after two failed attempts by the authorities to end the siege by force.

As the war escalated, a poll taken in March 1996 indicated that the majority of the Russian population wanted an unconditional withdrawal from Chechnya.[19] With presidential elections approaching, Yeltsin's popularity fell to 5 per cent in the winter of 1995–96.[20] Pressure was mounting on Yeltsin to sue for peace. When Dudaev was killed by a Russian bomb in April, it finally opened up an opportunity for a settlement. A cease-fire was agreed in May and the Khasavyurt peace agreement followed in August, shortly after Yeltsin's re-election as president.[21] The agreement committed Russia to withdraw all its troops from Chechnya whilst local elections would be held in 1997. A formal decision over Chechnya's status, however, would be postponed until December 2001.

The former rebel leader, Aslan Maskhadov, was elected as Chechen president on 27 January 1997 with 64 per cent of the vote.[22] Although Moscow had doubts about the election (no anti-independence candidates were allowed to stand), it accepted the election result, believing Maskhadov to be more of a pragmatist than the other leading presidential candidates, Shamil Basaev and Zelimkhan Yandarbiev. Maskhadov promised Yeltsin at the time of the formal signing of the Khasavyurt agreement in May that 'there would be no place for terrorists and kidnappers in Chechnya'.[23] Yet Khasavyurt still represented a great military defeat for Moscow. As both Yeltsin and Putin later accepted, Chechnya had won *de facto* independence from Russia. The problem was that independence did not lead to peace and stability in the troubled republic.[24]

The Putin period

Only two years after Russian troops were withdrawn, Moscow launched a second war against Chechnya. Why? There were a number of reasons. First, there was little doubt that the Russian military and political elite had difficulty in coming to terms with the implications of the Khasavyurt agreement and the prospect of Chechen independence. A number of military officers, closely linked with the first war, including Kvashnin, the Chief of the General Staff, and Kazankov, the Commander of Russian Troops were eager for revenge.[25] Second, Chechnya offered an opportunity for Putin to stamp his authority on the country as whole. He was little known when he was appointed prime minister in August 1999, and his uncompromising stance on Chechnya certainly raised his profile. At the time, Putin's political advisers argued against him becoming too closely identified with Chechnya after the problems faced by Yeltsin. It is also reported that Putin himself believed Chechnya was a poisoned chalice which would end his career as prime minister.[26] However, Putin's conduct of the war won him considerable public support and, directly or indirectly depending on interpretation, led to his victory in the spring 2000 presidential elections.[27]

The third and most important explanation for Russian intervention in 1999, however, was the fact that the first war had left many issues unsettled. Chechnya remained politically weak, and potentially a destabilising presence in the North Caucasus region. As soon as Maskhadov was elected president in 1997, he faced determined internal opposition. The rift with the radical Basaev, his deputy prime minister, in spring 1998 destroyed the last chance of establishing some kind of basis for statehood. Chechnya descended into anarchy and became one of the most dangerous places in the world. It was estimated that as many as 1,300 people lost their lives in Chechnya between 1997 and 1999 and many thousands more fled the republic.[28] As the economy collapsed, kidnapping became an important source of revenue for the warlords, and many Westerners were amongst those kidnapped. One of the most brutal cases involved four telecommunication engineers from Britain and New Zealand who were brutally murdered in December 1998 and their severed heads were later shown on TV. The leader of this terrorist group was Arbi Baraev whose son, Movsar, led the Dubrovka theatre siege four years later. In March 1999, Maskhadov dissolved the legally elected parliament and introduced Shariah law. This may have been another attempt to rein in his opponents and restore order in Chechnya, but the actual effect was to alienate Moscow further and allow radical Wahhabists to operate openly in Chechnya.[29]

According to the former prime minister, Sergei Stepashin, plans to intervene in Chechnya were made in March 1999 after the kidnapping of the Russian General, Gennadi Shpigun.[30] However, action was taken only after a group of about 1,000 militant Chechens, led by Shamil Basaev, marched across the border into neighbouring Dagestan on 8 August in support of Dagestani Wahhabists who had taken over two villages in the Russian republic. The rebels called for an uprising and declared Dagestan to be an independent Islamic state.[31] In fact, the Wahhabists had little support in the republic and Russian and Dagestani forces were quick to expel the Islamic militants by force.

At this stage, there was no suggestion of pursuing the rebels across the border into Chechnya. This all changed in September, however, when a series of terrorist atrocities struck Russia. Apartment blocks were targeted in Moscow, Volgodonsk and Buinaksk in Dagestan, killing a total of three hundred civilians and Russian servicemen. Responsibility was never claimed by any group, but immediate suspicion fell on the Chechens since Basaev had openly threatened to unleash a wave of terror on Russia as his forces pulled out of Dagestan.[32] However, conspiracy theories circulated after FSB agents were discovered on 22 September 1999 in a Ryazan apartment block apparently planting explosives. Suspicions were fuelled when the FSB initially said the sacks were filled with sugar, but then claimed their agents were just involved in a training exercise. Many remained unconvinced, and believed that the authorities had used the terrorist attacks as a means to manipulate public opinion and legitimise renewed military action to finally destroy the Chechen militants.[33]

Putin vowed to defeat the Chechen terrorists within two weeks,[34] and initially, it appeared he might achieve his aim. The second campaign looked better planned and better organised than the first. To minimise Russian casualties (and learning the lessons of NATO's campaign in Kosovo), Moscow bombed Chechen targets extensively and over a prolonged three-week period from the air. Unlike NATO, however, Russia needed to introduce ground troops to take territory from the Chechens, but this time they went in with massive force. At the height of the campaign there were almost 100,000 Russian troops fighting in Chechnya.[35] The main assault on Grozny began on 25 December 1999, but the Russian troops again found it difficult to take the Chechen capital. Putin was anxious to take Grozny before the presidential election in March and he was prepared to act with considerable brutality to achieve his aim. Grozny was indeed captured in February, but it was turned into a 'slaughterhouse' and virtually 'razed to the ground' in the process.[36] Putin's reputation like Yeltsin's before him, suffered in the eyes of the West.

Putin, however, declared the war to be over in April. He imposed direct rule on the republic in June 2000, and the following March, announced that the Russian military would be withdrawn and replaced by a much smaller number of interior and specialist troops.[37] However, the terrorist campaign against Russian targets persisted. Russian forces continue to patrol the dangerous streets of Grozny and conduct regular sweeps (*zachistki*) to capture suspected Chechen terrorists. Moscow refers to a slow process of normalisation in Chechnya, although few perceive any major improvements. Indeed, the Moscow theatre siege of October 2002, in which 128 hostages and 41 kidnappers were killed, has further polarised opinion and set back the prospect of any new political initiatives in the near future.

Differences with the first war

There are clearly many similarities between the two wars. No doubt future commentators will be tempted to elide the two wars and speak of a prolonged conflict lasting more than a decade between the Chechens and the Russians. Certainly, the central cause of the conflict on both occasions was the Chechen struggle for independence. Nevertheless, there were important differences between the two conflicts. First, as already mentioned, there was general support for Putin's war amongst both the political elite and the public. Only Yavlinsky's reformist *Yabloko* party opposed the war, but it suffered as a result in the subsequent parliamentary elections in December 1999. There were differences amongst the military, but they were more about strategy than the war itself. Initially, the military simply sought to drive out the Chechen militants from Dagestan, but the subsequent terrorist atrocities across Russia convinced Moscow that Chechen militancy could not be contained within the republic itself. The second stage of the war was to destroy rebel bases in the Nadterechny region and to consolidate their position there. However, early successes seem to have emboldened the military to cross the Terek River in a bid to finally destroy the militants.[38]

The public also backs the war. The latest public opinion polls show that 46 per cent believe Putin's war should continue; and 35 per cent believe Russia's actions in Chechnya have not been 'severe enough'.[39] This represents a big shift in opinion since the first war which some commentators attribute almost entirely to the media.[40] For although Putin vetoed a bill after the Dubrovka theatre siege which would have banned news that could be interpreted as justifying 'extremist activities', journalists and media outlets still face considerable pressure to toe the government line.[41] Democrats have understandably become concerned, not only about government controls over the media, but also the apparent lack of public concern. One poll in 2001 found that only 18 per cent thought the government had too much control over the media, whilst 36 per cent claimed they knew nothing about human rights violations, had no opinion about them, or believed they should not be investigated.[42] Of course, the significance of such findings can easily be exaggerated. After all, even the US has shown itself willing to curtail traditional rights and liberties in George W. Bush's war against terrorism. In the case of Russia, however, democracy remains weak and there are understandable fears that restrictions on liberty are more likely to become permanent.

A second difference between the wars is the increasing role played by foreign militants in Chechnya. Curiously, the rebel links to al-Qaeda and other Islamic related groups is often played down in Western commentaries.[43] It is right to be cautious about Putin's statements when he seeks to link the Russian campaign in Chechnya with America's war against terrorism. It is also true that the so-called Arabs did not start the war in Chechnya, and the number of non-Chechens fighting in the war may be fairly limited, and the journalist Thomas de Waal may well be right in arguing that Russia's policies and conduct in the war are better explanations for the radicalisation of the conflict rather than foreign intervention.[44] Nevertheless, links with al-Qaeda and other extremist Islamic groups do exist and, at a minimum, their existence is making any future settlement more difficult to achieve. Outside funding and training has been important in the Chechen struggle. Russian intelligence estimated the radical group led by Basaev and Khattab received $30 million from Osama bin Laden alone,[45] and other sources claim that Baraev received as much as $600,000 from supporters in Saudi Arabia to carry out the Dubrovka theatre siege.[46] An estimated four thousand people from Chechnya and the North Caucasus, including Basaev, have been abroad to undergo 'intensive training in Wahhabism'.[47] Al-Qaeda camps have been set up in Chechnya, which Osama bin Laden visited on a number of occasions.[48] A leading figure amongst the foreign militants was the Jordanian ibn-ul Khattab who has a long history of fighting the Russians – in Afghanistan, Tajikistan and Chechnya. Khattab trained in al-Qaeda camps in Afghanistan and became close to Osama bin Laden.[49] He also forged links with Basaev, and together they planned the invasion of Dagestan in August 1999 which led again to war in Chechnya. They have also helped plan many terrorist attacks. Khattab, for his part, was rumoured to have organised the Buinaksk bombing in September 1999, whilst Basaev has claimed responsibility for planning the Dubrovka theatre siege.[50]

The extreme brand of Wahhabism represented by Khattab and Basaev is contrary to Chechen traditions, however, and the presence of the Arabs has led to resentment in certain quarters. The current leader, Maskhadov, has attempted, publicly at least, to distance himself from the actions of the extremists. Indeed, in March 2002, Khattab was killed by a poisoned letter, probably by, or on behalf of the Maskhadov government.[51] There may have been hope Khattab's death would lead to negotiations, but the Dubrovka theatre siege was designed, at least in part, to abort any possible moves in that particular direction. Abdul Waleed al-Ansari, from the Arabian Peninsula, and a member of the mujahideen who earlier fought against the Soviets in Afghanistan, has taken over as leader of the Arabs in Chechnya.

How to deal with terrorism

As of the winter of 2002, the prospects for peace in Chechnya look bleak. As Lord Judd, the rapporteur to the Council of Europe on Chechnya, wrote in the aftermath of the Dubrovka theatre siege, both sides appear more intransigent than ever.[52] Moscow will not consider independence, but it still seems prepared to accept autonomy for Chechnya. However, Putin will not negotiate with the internationally recognised leader of Chechnya, Maskhadov, because of his alleged terrorist connections. Moscow does not perceive Maskhadov as the moderate he is usually portrayed to be in the West. They argue that even if Maskhadov did not plan the invasion of Dagestan and the Dubrovka theatre siege, he was aware of both and did nothing to stop them.[53] But if the Russians do not negotiate with Maskhadov, whom can they negotiate with? There are some Chechens who would be willing to accept autonomy, like the current head of the pro-Russian administration, Akhmed Kadyrov (who incidentally fought against the Russians in the first war), but it is unclear how far he represents general opinion in Chechnya. Even if he does, he is not in a position to deliver on any such agreement. Many so-called moderates inside Chechnya believe that independence is the only option after all the suffering of recent years. Yet independence is not enough for the radicals who are still seeking a unified Islamic state in the North Caucasus, and are prepared to use terror to achieve it. Lord Judd is surely right to argue that no reasonable deal can ever be done with radicals like Basaev, but he urges the moderates to get together to negotiate a way forward.[54] Some commentators cite Northern Ireland as a possible exemplar, but the cases are too different to be particularly useful. The key to peace in Northern Ireland was inclusion, ensuring that all strands of opinion and all their representatives, including the IRA, were involved in negotiating the Good Friday Agreement. This inclusive policy was only possible because the main paramilitary groups in Northern Ireland were willing to abandon terrorism and moderate their absolutist demands. This has not happened in Chechnya. Furthermore, the level of killing and destruction is on a different scale altogether, making any such compromise less likely. In the circumstances, military containment appears to many in Moscow to be the least worst option.

The views of the West

Although it is commonly argued that the al-Qaeda attack of September 11 2001 changed Western policy towards Chechnya, this is greatly exaggerated. In fact, the West adopted what could be called 'an understanding attitude' towards Russian policy in Chechnya right from the start. The West refused to recognise Chechen independence and has accepted Russia's right to defend its territorial integrity. The only criticisms expressed publicly by Western leaders related to proportionality, with the EU, for example, describing Russia's actions in Chechnya as 'totally unacceptable'.[55] Since September 11, policy has not changed, but the tone and rhetoric has. President George W. Bush has simply asked the Russians to discriminate in their counter-terrorist activities more clearly between civilians and combatants.[56] But Russia was allowed to rejoin the Council of Europe, a body committed to human rights, after a year's suspension in 2001, whilst the UNHCR made no attempt to censure Moscow when the issue came up in April 2002. In return, Putin became an invaluable ally in Bush's war on terrorism. After September 11, Putin shared intelligence with the US on the Taliban and al-Qaeda operations in Afghanistan. More controversially, Putin permitted America to establish military bases in Central Asia, and allowed US military advisers to enter Georgia to train the Georgian forces in their struggle against al-Qaeda operatives and Chechen rebels hiding out in the Pankisi Gorge.[57] The American victory over the Taliban certainly weakened al-Qaeda, but it also had the effect of forcing more of their operatives out of Afghanistan and into other weak states and regions, like Chechnya and Georgia in the North Caucasus. The war against terrorism is still clearly not at an end, nor is Russia's struggle with Chechnya.

Conclusion

The cost of Putin's war has been rising all the time. Since 1999, an estimated 4,000 Russian soldiers and at least 20,000 Chechens (50,000 in all since 1994) have lost their lives, and the total bill to Russia's exchequer over the last three years has been estimated at $10 billion.[58] Yet, the political pressures on Putin to end the war are limited. This may serve Putin's interests, at least in the short term. For the war in Chechnya provides a convenient justification for his tough law and order policies – his 'dictatorship of the law'. However, the conflict is too intense and bloody to serve such political calculations for long. Before the Dubrovka Theatre siege, there were signs of growing unease over the war. This is likely to return when it becomes clear once again that there can be no obvious military solution to the crisis in Chechnya. The problem, however, is that there is no obvious political solution either. The Chechen government is too weak to negotiate effectively and it cannot control, even if it wanted to, the crime, terrorism and violence on its territory. The best hope for peace is to start rebuilding the shattered Chechen economy, but it is hard to see how this can begin before the violence, crime and corruption comes to an end. Russia's despair is understandable. However, Russia is also part of the problem. For whilst Maskhadov is currently *persona non grata* in Moscow, the Chechens have similar feelings about the 'hammer of Chechnya'. Putin's tough image may win support at home, but it looks rather different to those suffering in Chechnya. As gross violations of human rights continue to be perpetrated by Russian troops, it becomes increasingly difficult to see how any reasonable settlement can be achieved in the near future. But there will soon come a time for compromise and political flexibility. It is still unclear, however, whether Putin is the right man to provide those skills, but without them, it is hard to see how the conflict in Chechnya will ever end.

Notes

1. In a poll in early 1995, it was found that 66 per cent were opposed to the war in Chechnya, *Moscow News* (24 February–2 March 1995), p. 3.
2. For example, see his 'State of nation address', 18 April 2002 in *Rosinformtsentr* (8 May 2002), p. 1.
3. As few as 11 per cent backed the Chechens in a poll in *Moscow News* (24 February–2 March 1995) p. 3.
4. A pro-Russian website estimated that because of oil, Chechnya was worth as much as 10 per cent of Russia's GDP in 1991, see: www.Chechnyafree.ru (22 February 2002), p. 1.
5. *Pravda* (9 August 1990).
6. B. Yeltsin, *Midnight Diaries* (London: Weidenfeld and Nicolson, 2000), p. 51.
7. V. Bennett, *Crying Wolf: The Return of War to Chechnya* (London: Pan, 2000), p. 219.
8. See *Delovoi Mir* (25 February 1995) for an account of the election.
9. *RSFSR v Tsifrakh v 1989g* (Moscow: Finansy i statistika, 1990).
10. *Moscow News* (16–22 December 1994), pp. 1–2.
11. For details see Bennett, *Crying Wolf*, p. 313.
12. L. Shevtsova, *Yeltsin's Russia: Myths and Realities* (Washington, DC: Carnegie Endowment for International Peace, 1999), p. 111; and *Moscow News* (16–22 December 1994), pp. 1–2.
13. C. Gall and T. de Waal, *Chechnya: A Small Victorious War* (London: Pan Original, 1997), p. xii.
14. L. Aron, *Boris Yeltsin: A Revolutionary Life* (London: Harper Collins, 2000), p. 566.
15. Yeltsin, *Midnight Diaries*, p. 59.
16. Bennett, *Crying Wolf*, p. 326.
17. R. Seely, *Russo-Chechen Conflict, 1800–2000: A Deadly Embrace* (London and Portland: Frank Cass, 2001), pp. 223–236.
18. Aron, *Boris Yeltsin*, p. 566.
19. A. Lieven, *Chechnya: The Tombstone of Russian Power* (New Haven and London: Yale University Press, 1998), pp. 139–140.
20. S. White, *Russia's New Politics: The Management of a Postcommunist Society* (Cambridge: Cambridge University Press, 2000), pp. 95–96.
21. For the text of the agreement, see *Nezavisimaya gazeta* (3 September 1996), p. 3.
22. Lieven, *Chechnya*, p. 145.
23. Aron, *Boris Yeltsin*, p. 666.

24 For comments, see Yeltsin, *Midnight Diaries*, pp. 62–63; and an interview with Vladimir Putin online at www.infocentre.ru (15 December 2001).
25 Traynor, I., 'Russian general's personal war', *Guardian* (6 November 1999), p. 15.
26 T. M. Nichols, *The Russian Presidency: Society and Politics in the Second Russian Republic* (Houndmills, Basingstoke: 2nd eds., Palgrave, 2001), p. 164.
27 For an overview on this, see *ibid.*, pp. 164–165.
28 Seely, *Russo-Chechen*, p. 304.
29 G. Chufrin, 'Russia: separatism and conflicts in the north caucasus', *SIPRI Yearbook 2000: Armaments, Disarmament and International Security* (Oxford: Oxford University Press, 2000), p. 166.
30 Seely, *Russo-Chechen*, p. 309.
31 *Keesings: Record of World Events* (Bristol: Keesings Publications, 1999), p. 43119.
32 *Ibid.*, p. 43120.
33 Bennett, *Crying Wolf*, p. 547.
34 *Keesings*, p. 43119.
35 *SIPRI Yearbook 2000*, p. 44.
36 V. Petrov, 'Grozny taken', *Moscow News* (9–15 February 2001), p. 1.
37 *SIPRI Yearbook 2001*, pp. 43–44.
38 For details, see T. L. Thomas, 'A tale of two theaters: Russian actions in Chechnya in 1994 and 1999', *Analysis of Current Events*, 12:5–6 (September 2000), Foreign Military Studies Office, http://call.army.mil/fmso/fmsopubs/issues/chechtale.htm; and E. Pain, 'The second Chechen war: the information component', *Military Review* (July–August 2000), http://call.army.mil/fmso/fmsopubs/issues/secchech/secchech.htm, pp. 4–6.
39 Polls conducted by Nationwide *VCIOM* surveys, on the webpage: www.russiavotes.org/Mood_int_tre.htm, November 2002.
40 T. P. Gerber and S. E. Mandelson, 'The discontent in how Russians think about Chechnya', *CSIS Policy Memo 244: Programme on New Approaches to Russian Security, Centre for Strategic and International Studies* (Washington, DC: January 2002), pp. 8–9.
41 Glasser, S. B., 'NTV feeling Kremlin's wrath', *Washington Post* (22 November 2002), p. A35.
42 Gerber and Mandelson, 'The discontent', p. 8; and T. P. Gerber and S. E. Mandelson, 'How Russians think about Chechnya', *CSIS Policy Memo*, 243: *Programme on New Approaches to Russian Security, Centre for Strategic and International Studies* (Washington, DC: January 2002), p. 6. But also see a rather later poll which seems to give a rather different interpretation: *Nationwide VCIOM Surveys* (September 2002), http://russiavotes.org/Mood_int_tre.htm, p. 1. It found that 44 per cent believed human rights were definitely or probably being violated during the course of military action in Chechnya.
43 T. de Waal, 'Introduction', in Anna Politkovskaya, *A Dirty War* (London: Harvill, 2001), p xxviii.
44 *Ibid.*
45 Anonymous, *Chechnya: The White Paper: Part One* (Moscow: Novosti, 2000), p. 62.
46 S. Roy, 'Fighting Russia', *Moscow News* (30 October–5 November 2002), p. 3.
47 Chufrin, 'Russia: separatism', p. 166.

48 R. Gunaratna, *Inside Al Qaeda: Global Network of Terror* (London: Hurst Company, 2002), p. 5.
49 *Ibid.*, p. 135.
50 *Reuters* (23 November 2002); www.russia_chechnya_warning_dc_.
51 *Moscow News* (12–17 May 2002), p. 4.
52 *Guardian* (28 October 2002), p. 18. Lord Judd is much maligned in the Russian press along with many other Western commentators because of their 'concern' over the rights of terrorists rather than the victims of terrorism: e.g. S. Roy, 'Fighting Russia', *Moscow News* (30 October–5 November 2002), p. 3; and L. Chernoi, 'Business and blackmail', *Moscow News* (13–19 November 2002), p. 5.
53 For example, an editorial in *Moscow News* (30 October–5 November 2002), p. 3, cites Baraev's second-in-command at the Dubrovka theatre siege, Abu Said, as saying Maskhadov knew of the plot.
54 *Guardian* (28 October 2002), p. 18.
55 Quoted in Chufrin, 'Russia: separatism', p. 177.
56 'Russia: Bush urges respect for human rights in Chechnya', *Radio Free Europe/Radio Liberty* (24 May 2002), www.rferl.org/nca/features/2002/05/24052002104227.asp, p. 1.
57 For Russian views see *Moscow News* (4–10 September 2002), p. 4.
58 Statistics taken from, *Agence France-Presse* (27 June 2002), http://reliefweb.int/w/rwb.nsf/s/, p. 1; *Toronto Star* (21 November 2002), www.thestar.com, p. 2.

15

Russian foreign policy: the CIS and the Baltic states[1]

Ella Akerman and Graeme P. Herd

Introduction

September 11 challenged and questioned the scope and characteristics of post-Cold War security politics. It has highlighted, for example, the growing effectiveness of non-state transnational terrorist networks, demonstrated the extent to which failed states can act as incubators and then midwives of insecurity and underscored the rise of asymmetric warfare in the new century. September 11 turned the international focus on security politics in Afghanistan and instability in Central Asia, a region that is no longer considered as a backwater within the global security system. But more importantly, the events of September 11 and the subsequent 'global war against terrorism' clearly demonstrated the inability of the international community to provide for stability and peace on the global scale. More than ever international and regional co-operation among states appeared to be crucial for creating new conditions for a stable and peaceful environment. September 11 also appeared to radically transform Russia's relations towards the West, as witnessed most through an analysis of Russia's policy towards its near neighbours in the Baltic states and Central Asia.

Prior to September 11 Russia's desire to be viewed as an equal partner to the West, expressed in the new Foreign Policy Concept 2000, was patently unrealistic due to her systemic politico-economic weaknesses, Russia's dependence on Western aid and technology and the primacy of the US within a unipolar international system.[2] Russia's internal crisis was compounded by the reversal of President Clinton's 'enlargement and engagement' strategy following the election of President Bush to the US presidency in January 2000. The new Bush administration's rhetoric and discourse towards Russia became much harsher and more dismissive. Russia, it was noted by a range of prominent analysts, was deindustrialising, depopulating and barely managing the disintegration of federal authority and effectiveness. Although a nuclear and resource-rich state, with a veto in the UN Security Council and straddling the Eurasian landmass, it was by the end of the 1990s a weak, secondary power that demonstrably struggled to maintain regional influence and avoid slipping into developing-state status. Its interests could be largely ignored.[3] President Bush's promotion of a policy of 'going it alone' – evidenced by the promotion of National Missile Defence (NMD) and the scrapping of the Anti-Ballistic Missile (ABM) Treaty – reinforced this perception by highlighting the abysmal state of Russia's power relative to the US and suggested that Russo-US 'mutual ties will remain competitive for some time', with co-operation 'well nigh impossible in the not-too-distant future' on the issue of tackling transnational terrorism.[4]

For Russia and in particular President Putin, elected president in May 2000, September 11 2001 provided an unforeseen opportunity to undertake two interlinked foreign policy initiatives: to 'normalise' relations with the West (the US and major European powers), and to reassess its policy towards Central Asia, other CIS member states and the three Baltic countries. September 11 and the proclamation of a 'war against global terror' through the creation of a 'coalition of the willing' in which Russia was a key member, can either be considered the catalyst or pretext for initiating and then consolidating a fundamental strategic realignment of Russian foreign and security policy. Such realignment was, to its supporters, self-evident and easily demonstrable, not least through the signing of a new accord between NATO and Russia in May 2002 and Russia's participation in the 'global war against terror'.

September 11 – such an interpretation would hold – had facilitated fundamental foreign policy realignment between Russia and the West. But does this interpretation stand up to closer scrutiny? Russian policy towards the five Central Asian states and the three Baltic countries should provide a litmus test to the scope and nature of Russian foreign policy change under Putin and this in turn will clarify the quality and limitations of Russian strategic realignment with the West in the twenty-first century.

Russian foreign policy in the making: new actors, new challenges

The end of the Cold War and the disintegration of the Soviet Union in 1991 led to major changes in the international system. The Russo-Soviet empire had been transformed by Stalin during and after the Great Patriotic War through the 'annexation of the Baltic republics, Western Ukraine and Moldova in 1944–45'.[5] This empire was founded not simply on the incorporation of an 'inner empire' consisting of the Baltic states, Western Ukraine and Moldova, but also on the creation of an 'outer empire' through the installation of communist regimes in Central and Eastern Europe (CEE) between 1945 and 1948. The *Pax Sovieticus* collapsed in 1991, raising a series of new foreign and security challenges, obstacles and dilemmas for the

Russian Federation. Russia, having undergone a massive loss of territory, population, military assets and economic resources and infrastructure, had to redefine its role in the international community in line with its transformed political-ideological, socio-economic and military power. This in turn prompted debate and re-examination of Russian national interests and so the formation of a new approach to international relations and Russian foreign policy.

Russia's relations with its near neighbours was also complicated by the presence of 25 million Russians living beyond Russian borders (the diaspora issue), constitutional and political questions relating to state recognition and border delimitation, the presence of Soviet era military formations on the territories of the former republics, not least Soviet nuclear weapons in Belarus, Ukraine and Kazakhstan. In addition, Russia was itself unstable, its elite in psychological shock, with substantial ultra-nationalist and revanchist communist factions willing to undertake neo-imperialist policies to reintegrate former states into at worst a tighter commonwealth, at best a rejuvenated unitary state.[6]

Given the context of vanishing supremacies, diminished possibilities and a pervasive post-imperial identity crisis, it is hardly surprising that as a consequence Russian foreign policy strategy was lacking and elite opinion was divided over the basic orientation the new state should undertake. In the spring of 1992 the political chancellor to President Yeltsin, Sergei Stankevich and the Russian foreign minister Andrei Kozyrev, for example, almost simultaneously proposed two divergent foreign policy concepts for Russia, which reflected the opposing school of thought in Russian foreign policy and became known as 'Eurasianism' and 'Atlantism'.[7] Broadly speaking, three foreign policy schools emerged in the 1990s and dominated foreign and security policy debates within the Russian Federation.

The first – the liberal-Atlanticist school – rejected manifest destiny, the necessity of maintaining a militarised economy and the resurfacing pre-Soviet Russian Orthodox and communist-nationalist messianic strains in Russian political culture – the disparate and complex corner-stones of the second school, that of Eurasianist thought within Russia. Rather than integrating around a shared idea of Russian historical development that stressed the uniqueness of Russia as a distinct civilisation and perceived the West as 'denationalising Atlanticism', the liberal-Atlanticists wanted Russia to emerge as a prosperous – 'normal' – democratic country, to become (again) a pillar of Western culture and civilisation. They advocated the complete integration into the community of nations and the unconditional realignment with the West, not least because of Russia's urgent need for Western aid.[8]

Although Atlanticism appeared to be the underlying factor in Russian foreign policy, the deployment of Russian peacekeepers to Tajikistan in 1992 and the outbreak of the first Chechen War (1994–96), and an general undercurrent of dissatisfaction with the West's failure to provide the expected assistance, became a steady flow that caused a substantial shift in Moscow's foreign policy thinking. Eurasianist solutions to Russia's problems was a particularly attractive proposition for the Russian military, as arms exports to the Middle East, South and South East Asia became increasingly important sources of revenue for the Russian state and so a factor that rose in strategic importance as an object of Russian foreign policy.[9] This shift in Moscow's foreign policy thinking – from Atlanticist to Eurasianist perspectives – was underscored by the acknowledgement of the importance of post-soviet space for Russian security, leading to the proclamation that the 'Near Abroad' was Russia's 'zone of vital interests' in 1995.

The third orientation, the centrists, occupied a position – if not exactly between the Eurasianist and liberal-Atlanticist schools – then at least space that constituted the third corner of Russia's foreign and security policy-making triangle. Centrists perceived Russia's orientation as Western, lacking as it did natural allies in Asia. However, NATO 'expansion' would undermine good relations with the West, a process that avoided recognition of Russia as a great power with legitimate political, economic and diaspora-related state interests in its 'Near Abroad'.[10] It was to this camp that Putin is widely perceived to have located himself, with the result that Putin's government sought to normalise relations with the West, whilst at the same time placing the CIS member states on the top of Russian foreign policy agenda, regarding them as strategic partners and desiring integration of the CIS with Russia, in particular in the economic, security and military spheres.

Russia's Baltic and Central Asia policy prior to September 11 2001

The ongoing and contested debate on foreign policy approaches was largely reflected in Moscow's ambiguous policies towards the former Soviet republics. In Central Asia the main foreign policy issue concerned the nature and scope of Russian involvement in the region and a full spectrum of policy proposals were on display. Some analysts perceived Central Asia drifting out of Russia's geopolitical grasp gradually integrating into an extended Middle East. Others argued that Central Asia represented an unwelcome post-colonial economic and military burden that Russia should be unwilling to shoulder, proposing a complete withdrawal from the region, including the emigration of the Russian population. A further perspective advocated that Moscow must maintain its ability to exert control and influence in the region by all possible means and at whatever cost, in order to prevent the Central Asian states from becoming entangled in alliances hostile to Russia.[11]

The one core thread of continuity in Russia's Central Asian policy was the dominant and decisive role of the Russian military in formulating and applying Moscow's policy in Central Asia. This role is attributed not only to the presence of Russian troops deployed in the region, but also to the traditional influence of the Russian military complex on the decision-making apparatus in Moscow, particularly within former republics of the Soviet Union. The perspective of this military complex was reflected in Russia's Military Doctrine of 1993. This doctrine regarded local war and conflicts in the region as a serious threat to Russian national security. It acknowledged the necessity of deploying Russian troops outside Russia's territory, especially for the performance of peacekeeping operations. The need to establish an efficient security system in post-soviet space was underscored by the fact that the former republics only possessed military assets, infrastructure and troops that happened to be stationed on their territory when the Soviet Union collapsed. As a result they were determined, despite their lack of experience, to establish their own effective defence establishments and policies.

The tension between the real defence requirements of the former Soviet republics and their desire to remain independent in military matters was reached by the elaboration of a compromise – the Collective Security Treaty (now Organisation). Armenia, Kazakhstan, Kyrgystan, Russia, Tajikistan and Uzbekistan (and subsequently by Georgia, Azerbajian and Belarus) signed the Treaty in Tashkent on 15 May 1992. The Treaty made provision for the deployment of military observers and collective security forces and has been credited with helping to counter the proliferation of two specific sources of insecurity. Firstly, the threat that the conflict from Afghanistan spills over into Central Asia and, secondly, in ensuring that the conflict in Tajikistan remained localised. The CIS Charter of 1993 committed its member states to pursue a concerted policy in international security, to disarmament and arms control, the development of armed services and the consolidation of internal security and stability within the CIS.[12]

By the late 1990s, Russia's previously influential role as regional security provider was being eroded. In April 1999 the Collective Security Treaty (CST) was extended for the further period of five years. However, Uzbekistan along with Georgia and Azerbaijan withdrew from the Treaty in order to reduce Moscow's influence on their foreign and security policies and create a new sub-regional military–political–economic grouping with Georgia, Azerbaijan, Moldova and Ukraine and Uzbekistan (GUUAM). The last Russian border troops left Turkmenistan and Kyrgyztan in 1999, whilst they had never been deployed in Uzbekistan. On only one occasion, a limited number of Uzbek troops, one battalion, participated as peacekeeping troops in Tajikistan under the auspices of the United Nations. Kazakhstan is the one Central Asian state that accommodates a substantial number of Russian military personnel stationed on Kazakh territory in support of the Russian space programme. Hence, only Tajikistan remains a state within which Russian military assets and personnel can be deployed. According to a variety of different sources the number of Russian troops in Tajikistan is

22,000 to 25,000 strong, serving in the 201st motorised infantry division (garrisoned in Dushanbe, Kulyab and Kurgan-Tyube), the Russian Federal Border Troops and in an anti-aircraft unit. In line with the military agreement several dozen Russian military advisors work at the Ministry of Defence of Tajikistan.

At the same time, the Foreign Policy Concept of the Russian Federation June 2000 also prioritised the CIS member states in Russian foreign policy, viewing them as strategic partners and stressing the necessity for the full integration of the CIS with Russia, in particular in the economic and security spheres. President Putin underlined this objective in choosing the Central Asian states as the destination of his first foreign visits. Although Central Asian States took part in the joint military command-and-staff exercise, CIS Southern Shield-99, following the invasion of armed Islamic groups into Kyrgyzstan, prior to September 11 existing co-operative security structures were largely considered to be ineffective, Russian influence was waning despite its rhetoric of integration, whilst Western influence increased.

Despite geographical proximity and the shared experience of Soviet rule, however, substantial differences between Russia and Central Asian states in terms of disparate identities, different values and divergent visions for the future prevented successful co-operation. As a result of these underlying tensions and cleavages between the key signatories of the Treaty, the promotion of its ostensible and primary purpose – the integration of the security structures, policies and defence establishments and the shifting of the main military burden onto Russia – has been undermined from the outset.

When analysing Russia's foreign policy towards all former republics, analysts agreed that the geopolitical and geostrategic transformation of former Soviet space in the early 1990s hindered the formation of a clearly articulated Russian foreign policy towards its 'Near Abroad', the Baltic states included. In the mid-1990s, although the Russian Federation appeared to have adopted a policy of 'differentiated engagement' with each of the three Baltic States (with Lithuania highlighted as a co-operative neighbour), it had yet to define its 'State' interest in the Baltic region. However, in 1997 the rudiments of an emergent Russian–Baltic policy had become identifiable. But, just as Russia articulated a viable strategic framework through which to structure its Baltic relations – identifiable state interest balanced by the necessity of counter-engagement – Russia itself suffered the birth pangs of a renewed systemic transformation, felt most sharply by the August 1998 economic 'meltdown'.

In the early 1990s Russo-Baltic relations were dominated by a host of interrelated Soviet legacy-related disputes, particularly border demarcation, the rights of the Russian diaspora, and military troop withdrawal. Russia's border disputes between Estonia and Latvia, for example, were complicated by the linkage of the constitutional status of the two republics to their border delineation. In the post-Soviet period, Estonia and Latvia argued that their states were restorationist and that the Soviet occupations of 1940 and 1944 were illegal and that disputed border territories should be returned. The Russian Federation countered that to change federal borders would create a precedent within former Soviet space which invited chaos, and that the principles of the 1975 Helsinki Final Act should be upheld.[13] Border disputes clouded a subtler series of interconnected political issues – recognition that the Baltic states were illegally occupied, a desire by the Baltic states to internationalise inter-state disputes as a means of enhancing Western strategic reorientation, and a refusal by Russia to address the Baltic states as equal partners. For Russia, disputes with Lithuania were the most sensitive as they directly impinged access to the strategically important Kaliningrad, which became an object of rising strategic importance as NATO enlarged eastwards.[14]

Russian opposition to NATO 'enlargement' was initially characterised by a twin track approach. At first Russia adopted a policy of 'conditional enlargement'; former Warsaw Pact states could be integrated without strenuous Russian opposition, providing key conditions were met. These conditions included NATO signing a legally binding treaty to the effect that newly integrated NATO states would remain non-nuclear and only integrate according to an agreed and phased timetable of inclusion. Above all, neither the Baltic states nor any of the other former Soviet republics were to be integrated under any circumstances. The negative consequences of unconditional NATO enlargement were graphically posed at all diplomatic meetings and speeches – strident militarism within the 'Near Abroad', political instability within the Federation, a *veliki-derzhavost'* (great power or etatist) president at the 2000 elections, and closer Sino-Soviet relations were, it was claimed, just some of the likely negative consequences.

Russia proposed alternative 'non-NATO' mechanisms to oversee European security. In the spirit of post-Cold War East–West co-operation, Russia argued that new and more appropriate international organisations, such as the EU, OSCE or UN, should provide the context within which European security was guaranteed. Russia adopted a policy of 'opposition by proxy', that is, by illustrating that the aspirant Baltic states had not met the conditions for NATO integration it sought to halt that process. Secondly, a policy of constructive engagement emerged, characterised by a much more purposeful and co-ordinated Russian elaboration of hard and soft security initiatives in the region. The timing and nature of these initiatives appear designed to respond to the EU Amsterdam and NATO Madrid summits earlier in 1997, as well as the US–Baltic Charters (signed January 1998). Moreover, these Russian proposals directly complemented Finnish and Swedish 'sovereignty support' initiatives towards the Baltic states, and explicitly supported the preferred Russian policy of non-alignment (i.e. non-NATO Baltic integration) within the north Baltic region. The ultimate objective of this strategy was, as ever to retain the Baltic states within Russia's sphere of economic and social influence, and restrain Western military presence within the region.[15]

In February 1997 Yeltsin's presidential office published a document that elaborated Russia's long-term policy guidelines towards the Baltic states. The policy document outlined six interlinked issues that were central to Russo-Baltic relations. It began by reiterating Russian opposition to Baltic inclusion into NATO and stressed that until the protection of 'compatriot rights' was guaranteed, border ratification would be delayed. The document emphasised the necessity of Russia maintaining profitable economic ties to the Kaliningrad *oblast'* (region), whilst calling for Russo-Baltic co-operation to combat the threats posed by organised crime. Lastly, increased bi-lateral cultural co-operation between Russia and the Baltic states was encouraged.[16]

With the election of Vladimir Putin to Russian president in May 2000, Russia's policies towards the EU and NATO were clarified and less contingent on Russia's relations with her near neighbours. Russia's EU policy, for example, had already began to develop a more substantive profile following the elaboration of the EU's Northern Dimension, and Common Strategy for Russia' in 1999 (see Chapter 13).[17] By 2001 it was clear that President Putin's attitude towards NATO enlargement was softening. Even before September 11, for example, Putin stated in Helsinki that although Baltic integration into NATO would not increase stability in the Baltic region, such a decision was the sovereign right of any state within the region. Thus, on the eve of September 11 2001 there was a distinct warming in Russo-Baltic relations and a greater willingness for constructive dialogue than at any time since independence in 1991.

11 September 2001: a turning point in Russian foreign and security policy?

For many analysts, particularly for those from within the Russian Federation, September 11 has not produced fundamental foreign policy realignment, but rather the illusion of such a policy or 'virtual realignment'. These events provided a coincidence of interest, but co-operation was limited and the 'watershed' of September 11 was simply akin to détente in the Soviet period; it was easily reversible. According to this interpretation, rapprochement was temporary and conditional – tied as it was to Russia's desire to extract political payment or accrue political capital for the semblance of co-operation. Rather than exploiting anti-Americanism in the Moslem world, Russia could join the 'coalition of the willing' in return for a geopolitical quid pro quo of choice. It provided justification for the 'anti-terrorist operation' in Chechnya and gained Western support for Soviet era debt relief, Russian entry into the World Trade Organisation, or even a potential lever of influence within the NATO–Baltic integration debate.[18]

Moreover, some analysts (for example Andrei Ryabov and Andrei Nikolaev) also warned of the dangers of Putin moving too far ahead of the mainstream 'orthodox' objectives of his national security apparatus and political power base.[19] Here the danger of Putin being perceived as a Gorbachev-type figure of the late 1980s was raised; the 'Gorbachev syndrome' suggested that Putin, like Gorbachev, in return for being feted abroad might become extremely unpopular at home. The underlying implication of this comparison is that with Gorbachev the syndrome ended with the collapse of the Soviet Union – with Putin would it lead to Russia's abandonment of an independent foreign policy, a revolt by the power structures or a worse – a disintegration of the Russian Federation? Thus, strategic alignment was at best a rhetorical flourish generated by a shared aversion to the events of September 11, rather than a fundamental Russian reorientation forged by common foreign policy interests and objectives.

Such an interpretation is superficially compelling, but subject to an equally persuasive set of three key counter-arguments. These counter-arguments share a central contention, namely that the foreign policy of Putin's Russia – in particular the strategic orientation of Russia – exhibited the characteristics of greater continuity than change before and after September 11. The counter arguments also rest on the assumption that Putin had initiated a strategic reorientation, but only in so far as he consolidated existing influences, trends and tendencies in Russian foreign policy that were evident, though not dominant, in the first and second terms of Yeltsin's presidency during the 1990s. Prior to September 11 it is highly likely that President Putin had instigated a 'correlation of forces'-type analysis for Russia, identifying opportunities, constraints and key dynamic factors facing Russia in the new century. This approach constituted a pragmatic and strategic re-evaluation of Russia's future role within the international system.[20]

Firstly, it had become apparent prior to September 11 that Russia's domestic systemic drift was a source of growing pressure for strategic alignment with the West. It was clear at the end of the Yeltsin presidency that Russia was becoming dangerously decentralised, and that the federal centre was having greater difficulty in imposing legal, constitutional and economic order in the regions due to the internal structural and institutional weaknesses of state power. Putin was able to address the worst excesses and weaknesses of decentralisation, but at a cost to the emergence of civil society. The programme of federal reform – not least the creation of seven Federal Districts – appeared to insert police-state mechanisms into a delegative and declarative democratic state.[21] This trade-off between order and democracy was unlikely to integrate Russia into the global economy and suggested that Russia faced a more autocratic future.[22]

Indeed, Putin's evocative and stark warnings that Russia was in danger of falling from second-world to developing-state status caught the attention of analysts. Russia had been marginalised from the global economy in the

1990s and was unable to utilise its economic potential to generate a *pushek i masala* (guns and crude consumer goods) military-security orientated foreign policy.[23] Putin also appreciated the systemic impact of population dynamics on Russian internal security and international standing, arguing that Russia was in danger of becoming a 'drifting nation' as the demographic decline began to bite. As US Secretary Powell noted at a hearing of the Foreign Relations Committee on 25 October: 'it is clear that President Putin understands that Russia's future primarily lies to the West. That's the source of technology, it's the source of capital, it's the source of debt relief, it's the source of security'.[24]

Although isolation from the Euro-Atlantic security community would only deepen the impact of these systemic factors and integration ameliorates their worst effects, it had also become more apparent to the Russian political elite that there was no viable policy alternative to strategic realignment with the West. Putin's domestic critics, including the Cassandra's that warn of the emergence of a Gorbachev syndrome and those like Leonid Ivashov who have characterised Russian foreign policy post-September 11 in terms of 'geopolitical suicide' – have yet to elaborate meaningful and coherent foreign policy alternatives to strategic realignment for Russian in the twenty-first century. 'Russia first', 'great power' ideology, national-patriotic sentiment and neo-imperial or neo-communist revanchist visions of the early 1990s have been undone by the systemic drift and disintegration following the collapse of the Soviet Union. The articulation of Eurasianist 'third way' perspectives by Yevgenvy Primakov as foreign minister then prime minister did represent an attempt to create a multi-polar international order, but again such aspirations were undermined by the deepening Russian systemic weakness and the growth of US power that characterised the end of the 1990s.

Prior to September 11 President Putin had explored the multi-polar alternatives to the domination of the international system by the US – and recognised that none were viable – and Russian attempts to use NMD instrumentally to drive a wedge between European NATO members and the US also proved fruitless. Vehement Russian opposition to first-wave NATO enlargement had proved a failure and indeed counter-productive to Russian interests. As Putin himself noted at the Rome declaration on the creation of the NATO–Russia Council, the deepening of interaction with NATO on equal terms: 'is a real embodiment of a multi-vectoral approach, to which there is no alternative and which we intend to follow steadfastly'.[25]

Thirdly, it can be argued that strategic realignment did not just reflect the ability of Putin and supporters within the key power ministries (Ministry of Defence, Ministry of Foreign Affairs, Foreign Intelligence Service and Atomic Energy Ministry) to make a virtue out of necessity, but it also partly represented a policy of choice.[26] The three lobby groups that traditionally are credited with buttressing Putin in power – the security group, the

St Petersburg economists and presidential or 'family' group – all support strategic realignment to the extent that it creates a predictable framework of relations with the US, international stability and greater external legitimacy.[27] This in turn provides them with a benign environment within which to consolidate their power-bases within the Russian domestic landscape and address instabilities and sources of internal insecurities. Strategic realignment also recognised that foreign policy was a minority issue within Russia, one that could be depoliticised, and the minority split between Putin's supporters, non-aligned factions and those that opposed him.[28]

Case studies: Central Asia and the Baltic states

September 11 appeared to have had a profound impact on the nature of Russia–Baltic relations, but this perception was illusionary. When President Putin himself indicated at a meeting with Lord Robertson on 2 October 2001 that he would not invest political capital to oppose NATO integration of the Baltic States if NATO became primarily a political organisation, he echoed sentiments already expressed in April 2001 at the Helsinki Russo-Finnish Summit. Here Putin had articulated a variant of the official Finnish policy on NATO enlargement in the Baltic region: all states are sovereign and therefore free to choose their own foreign and security policies, and a non-alignment strategy enhance security in the region.

Two other inter-linked events have also shaped strategic realignment in this region. Firstly, the Reykjavik Summit of 14–15 May 2002 has provided stronger functional and political integration linkages between Russia and NATO. The creation of a NATO–Russia Council (NATO at 20) accord in Rome 28 May 2002 is integrating Russia deeply into NATO structures, institutions and policy and decision-making as fully as possible short of actual membership.[29] Secondly, the invitation to Baltic States to join NATO at the November 2002 Prague NATO Summit was achieved with hardly even a murmur of opposition or dissent from Moscow. As the Estonian Ambassador to the US, Sven Jurgenson, noted, the signing of the NRC accord 'lays the foundation for Russia to overcome' the hurdles that have 'made it reluctant to discuss really substantive maters'.[30]

In Central Asia Western influence has also been further strengthened and Russia's voice weakened following the events of September 11, as the region rose rapidly in strategic importance as a location for the staging of military and logistical operations.[31] Russia's desire to maintain its regional influence was clearly expressed at the Eleventh meeting of the Council of the Chiefs of Security Bodies and Secret Services of the CIS states that took place at the beginning of October 2001 in Dushanbe.[32] Russia attempted unsuccessfully to persuade the Central Asian leaders to act strictly in concert with Moscow to link as one Moscow-dominated echelon into the US-led operation;

Uzbekistan allowed the U.S. access to its air bases, transport facilities and military capabilities to launch offensive strikes on Afghanistan. In return, the US Congress passed a bill in September 2001 granting Uzbekistan $25 million for weapons and other military purchases. In January 2002, Washington announced that Uzbekistan would receive $100 million of the $4 billion that Congress has allocated for fighting terrorism. On 4 December 2001 the Tajik government officially allowed the coalition the use of its airbase at Kulob, about 40 km from the Afghan border. Similarly, in Kyrgyzstan the parliament approved allowing coalition forces use of Manas international airport, the only airfield suitable for US military aircraft.[33] As a result, Central Asian states 'have proven to be invaluable, particularly Tajikistan and Uzbekistan, to the United States and its allies in providing a location for the staging of military operations and for logistical operations'.[34]

In fact, some regional analysts have suggested that the arrival of the US troops in Central Asia would render a Russian-led CST irrelevant.[35] Indeed, it appears that despite Moscow's increased diplomatic activity in the region, the CST, as well as other existing co-operation structures failed to adequately respond to the new political realities in the region. Moscow has had to re-evaluate its Central Asia policy under the sustained pressure of a number of factors:

> the loss of the functions of a political arbiter and a security guarantor; degradation of the main instrument of military and political domination (the Collective Security Treaty – CST); transformation of the United States from an economic into a military–political force in the region; weaker positions of China's Russia's main strategic partner in Central Asia and a threat of the decline of the Shanghai Co-operation Organization (SCO) as a system of Russian–Chinese security in Central Asia; a real threat of new pipelines bypassing Russia; the growth of trade and economic contradictions between the Russian Federation and the Central Asian states, and the decreasing integration potential of the CIS.[36]

Moscow's determination to maintain its influence in Central Asia – despite these tactical retreats – was clearly expressed by President Putin's address to the Federal Meeting, where he pointed out that 'Russian policy [in Central Asia] will become more pragmatic and will take into account the interests of the post-Soviet states – allies in the anti-terrorism coalition.'[37] Moreover, the geo-economic realities of energy dependence and the dilemmas for US policy in subordinating support for democracy (and democratic civil–military relations) and human rights to the central strategic goal of defeating global terror might generate tensions which disrupt US influence in the region. Western aid for authoritarian regimes with poor human rights records cannot be balanced in the long term with the necessity of promoting democratic peace. This dilemma in Western and particularly US policy towards this unstable region will ultimately allow Russia a greater role in Central Asia.

Conclusions: a European anchor in an era of globalisation?

On September 11 Putin made a choice that was consistent with the orientation of Russian foreign policy since 2000: 'Russia's policy encompasses a blend of new thinking, globalism, Eurasian realism, and Euro-Atlantic economic internationalism.'[38] With regard to Russian relations with the Baltic States, September 11 has consolidated a prior shift in acceptance *of* full and unconditional Baltic strategic re-orientation westwards. Thus, strategic realignment can be understood in terms of Russia's two-phase adoption of NATO's normative agenda: constitutional and functional integration and growing compatibility, consistency and predictability is currently being realised; Russia's acceptance of NATO norms and values are likely to follow. This is not to suggest – as some have done – that Russia will receive full NATO membership in the near future.[39]

In Central Asia, however, September 11 has had the effect of rendering the erosion of Russian influence and power in the region more visible. The US-led 'coalition of the willing' has highlighted disparities, tensions and cleavages in Russia's Central Asia policy. However, as Central Asia is demonstrably unstable, a source of multiple insecurities which threaten to destabilise not just Russia's southern flank, but also the territorial integrity of Russia itself, Russia's strategic realignment is much more conditional here than in the Baltic region and this reflects the necessity of Russia maintaining a voice and a veto – where possible – on security issues in the region. When assessing Russia's policy towards the Baltic region and Central Asia during the Putin presidency, it appears that Russia has developed a policy of differentiated strategic realignment and engagement with the West.

This differentiation tells us as much about Russian foreign policy preferences as it does about the nature of power distribution, political will and state capability in the West. In essence, Putin's ability to undertake strategic realignment has been facilitated by fundamental and deep-seated disparities within the Euro-Atlantic security community. The gaps in technology, defence spending and the collective security capability of European NATO and US NATO have widened post-September 11 whilst NATO's command, committee and decision-making structures have never looked more obsolete.[40]

These differences allow Russia to draw closer to European NATO through adaptive acquiescence in the Baltic region with the growing importance of the Russia–EU agenda, whilst maintaining a semblance of strategic parity with the US through arms control negotiations and coalition partnership in Central Asia. A paradox emerges – the very weakness of the concept of a 'war against global terror' – becomes its greatest strength: the inherent ambiguities and ambivalence embodied by this 'war' provide Russia with an ideological pretext for foreign policy change through strategic realignment, whilst the disparities and fractures within the Euro-Atlantic security community allow the opportunity for President Putin to pick and choose which of the core values and interests of a divided transatlantic community Russia shares. Putin's Russia has thus through a combination of default and design, adopted a foreign policy at the start of the new century that can neither be characterised as pro-Western, nor Eurasianist in orientation, but rather pro-Russian. It is a foreign policy that is tied more than ever to challenges, obstacles and dilemmas posed by Russia's domestic agenda, and its contours and qualities can best be viewed through its relations to its near neighbours.

The decision by the US and its coalition partners to initiate Operation Iraqi Freedom to 'liberate' Iraq and force regime change in order to initiate a post-Saddam order drew reaction from Russia that has helped provide greater clarity to the question of the depth and strength of Russia's 'strategic realignment' westwards. The invasion of Iraq has posed choices that many governments would have preferred to evade and avoid, but Russia's response at least was clear and nuanced. On 20 March 2003 at a Security Council meeting in Moscow Putin in a keynote statement argued that the war was unjustified, that Iraq did not pose a threat to its neighbours and that military action represented a serious political mistake as it undermined the principle of state sovereignty and raised the spectre of an international order based on the principle of 'might is right' ('fist might', in Putin's words). Russia therefore joined France and Germany amongst the major European powers in opposing the war. This has resulted in the cooling of relations between the US and Russia. Other Russian politicians and political commentators have stressed that Operation Iraqi Freedom occurs in violation of the UN Charter and principles, that it weakens the anti-terrorist coalition, increases anti-Americanism and undermines the US's leadership of the democratic world.

However, the Iraqi invasion in the name of the 'global war against terror' has had the unintended effect of highlighting the key goals of Russian foreign policy in the twenty-first century. Firstly, Russia's advocacy of the need to negotiate a second resolution demonstrates its determination to maintain its status as a world power through the exercise of its seat on the UN Security Council. Secondly, the Putin government appears keen to reflect public opinion having in the eyes of many already made enough concessions to the US throughout the first-term presidency over, for example, the ABM Treaty, NATO enlargement, and the positioning of US troops in Central Asia and Georgia. Genuinely responding to public opinion is set to be an increasingly powerful dynamic in the context of presidential elections in 2004. Thirdly, Russia has successfully improved its relations with Berlin and Paris, moving its partnership to the strategic level and this trend is likely to have positive spillover effects on EU enlargement in the Baltic region in 2004 and 2005. Fifthly, reaction to the Iraq war and concern over the nature of reconstruction in the post-war phase reveals Russia's determination to protect its economic interests – particularly Iraqi debt repayment and a share of the oil concessions that will flow in the coming years. Sixthly and lastly, the Iraqi war also demonstrates Putin's interest in maintaining a good partnership with the US. Although Russia has opposed the war it has done so with far more flexibility and tactical élan than either Berlin or Paris. The major foreign policy achievement of Putin's first-term presidency has been to dramatically improve and consolidate relations with the US and this study of Russia's relations with the Baltic states and Central Asia demonstrates the extent to which this goal has been achieved. It is clear that the Iraqi war does not undermine this strategic realignment, but rather allows us to bring further focus onto this issue by placing such alignment within a context that although it lies outside the former Soviet bloc, serves only to delimit its extent and quality within it.

Notes

1 The opinions expressed in this chapter/volume are those of the authors, and do not necessarily reflect the official policy of the George C. Marshall European Centre for Security Studies or of the United States or German government.
2 S. G. Brooks and W. C. Wohlforth, 'American primacy in perspective', *Foreign Affairs*, 81:4 (July–August 2002), 20–33; Nodari Simonia, 'Russia's foreign policy and catch-up development', *International Affairs* (Moscow), 48:4 (2002), 34–45.
3 'How far can the west afford to ignore Russia?', *Conflict Studies Research Centre*, Occasional Briefing (July 1999), www.fas.org/nuke/guide/russia/agency/ob69-cjd.htm.
4 M. Ehsan Ahrari, 'Iran, China, and Russia: the emerging anti-US nexus', *Security Dialogue*, 32:4 (December 2001), 453–466.
5 D. Lieven, 'Russia as empire: a comparative perspective', in G. Hosking and R. Service, *Reinterpreting Russia* (London: Arnold, 1999), 15.
6 M. Webber, 'Russian policy towards the Soviet successor states', in M. Bowker and C. Ross (eds.), *Russia After the Cold War* (London: Longman, 2000), 243.
7 S. Gretsky, *Russia's Policy Towards Central Asia* (Lulea: Central Asia and the Caucasus, Centre for Social and Political Studies, 1997), available online at: www.ca-c.org/dataeng/GRETSKY.shtml.
8 A. P. Tsygankov, 'From international institutionalism to revolutionary expansionism', *Mershon International Studies Review*, 41 (November 1997), 247–268.
9 J. M. Godzimirski (ed.), *New and Old Actors in Russian Foreign Policy* (Oslo: Norwegian Institute of International Affairs, 2000).
10 I. Prizel, *National Identity and Foreign Policy: Nationalism and Leadership in Poland, Russia and Ukraine* (Cambridge: Cambridge University Press, 1998), pp. 239–299.
11 I. Zviagelskaya, *The Russian Policy Debate on Central Asia* (London: The Royal Institute of International Affairs, Chatham House, 1995).
12 R. Allison, 'Russia and the new states of Eurasia', in A. Brown (ed.), *Contemporary Russian Politics: A Reader* (Oxford: Oxford University Press, 2001), pp. 443–452.

13 Andrus Park, 'Ethnicity and independence: the case of Estonia in a comparative perspective', *Europe–Asia Studies*, 46:1 (1994), 69–87.
14 J. Berryman, 'Russian foreign policy: an overview', in Bowker and Ross, *Russia After*, p. 334.
15 P. Shearman, 'Russia and NATO enlargement: the case against', in Bowker and Ross, *Russia After*, pp. 299–318.
16 G. P. Herd, 'Baltic security politics', *Security Dialogue*, 28:2 (June 1997), 252–253; D. Trenin, 'Russia's Baltic concept', *Nezavisimaya Gazeta* (11 March 1997), p. 7.
17 D. Gowan, *How the EU Can Help Russia* (Centre for European Reform, December 2000), p. 48.
18 S. Kortunov, 'Russia–American partnership: a chance to open a new page', *International Affairs* (Moscow), 48:3 (2002), 23–39.
19 O. Antonenko, 'Putin's gamble', *Survival*, 43: 4 (winter 2001), 49–60.
20 V. Tretiakov, 'Putin's pragmatic foreign policy', *International Affairs* (Moscow), 48:3 (2002), 17–22.
21 N. Petrov, 'Seven faces of Putin's Russia: federal districts as the new level of state-territorial composition', *Security Dialogue*, 33:1 (2002), 73–91.
22 T. J. Colton and M. McFaul, 'Are Russians undemocratic', *Post-Soviet Affairs*, 18:2 (2002), 91–121.
23 M. M. Zadornov, 'Economic reforms: steady as she goes', *Washington Quarterly*, 25:1 (winter 2002), 105–116; S. Rosefielde, 'Back to the future? Prospects for Russia's military industrial revival', *Orbis* (summer 2002), 499–509.
24 Remarks by Colin Powell, US Secretary of State, *NATO Enlargement Daily Brief* (*Thursday* 25 October 2001).
25 *Interfax news agency* (28 May 2002).
26 V. Lukin, 'New century, greater concerns', *International Affairs*, 48:2 (2002), 46–53.
27 'Kremlin and the White House', *RFE/RL Russian Political Weekly*, 2:17 (22 May 2002); available at www.rferl.org/rpw/2002/05/17-220502.html.
28 V. Rukavishnikov, 'New threats and old phobias', paper presented at International Sociological Association Research Committee 01 (ISA RC01) on Armed Forces and Conflict Resolution, ISA World Congress, Brisbane, Australia, July 2002.
29 'NATO–Russia relations: a new quality' (declaration by Heads of State and Government of NATO member states and the Russian Federation) see, www.nato.int/docu/basictxt/b020528e.htm.
30 E. Woodward, 'Russia's neighbours affirm new NATO–Russia framework', DefenseNews.com (28 May 2002).
31 E. Ackerman, '11 September: implications for Russian foreign policy in Central Asia', *Review of International Affairs*, 2 (April 2002), 1–16.
32 N. Ulyanov, 'Kremlin is not going to lose influence on Central Asia', *The Russian Observer*, www.russianobserver.com/foreign/relations/2001/10/02/1002036251.html.
33 E. Ackerman, 'Wealth and politics in Central Asia: clan structures versus democratisation', *Conflict Studies Research Centre Paper*, K30 (May 2002), 1–11.
34 J. Stevenson, cited in B. Pannier, 'Central Asia: Tajikistan, Kyrgyzstan balancing relations with West, Russia', *Radio Liberty* (7 December 2001).
35 S. Blagov, 'Russia probes to bolster its authority in Central Asia', *Eurasia Insight,* 27 (March 2002), available online at: www.eurasiainsight.com.

36 M. Laumulin, 'Central Asia after 11 September', *Central Asia and the Caucasus*, 4:16 (2002), 32–33.
37 V. Panfilova and A. Chanbabian, 'Moscow and Washington again play the game of superpowers in Central Asia', *Nezavisimaya Gazeta* (25 April 2002).
38 C. A. Wallander, 'Lost and found: Gorbachev's "new thinking"', *Washington Quarterly*, 25:1 (winter 2002), 127.
39 J. A. Baker III, 'Russia in NATO?', *Washington Quarterly*, 25:1 (winter 2002), 95–103.
40 R. Kagan, 'Power and weakness', *Policy Review* (June–July 2002); available at www.policyreview.org/Jun02/kagan/html; J. Lindley-French, 'Terms of engagement: the paradox of American power and the transatlantic dilemma post 11-September', *Chaillot Papers*, 52 (May 2002); available at www.iss-eu.org/chaillot/chai52e.pdf.

Index

Abramovich, Roman 10, 11, 29, 141, 181
Alekperov, Vagit 128, 142
Almond, G and Verba, S. 77
al-Qaeda 263, 264, 265
Aslund, Anders 103, 107
Attlee, Clement 5
Avturkhanov, Umar 258

Babitskii Andrei 135
Baburin, Sergei 57
Bacon, Edwin 62
Badovskii, D. V. 162
Baltic states 269–85
Baraev, Arbi 260
Basayev, Shamil 8, 259, 260, 261, 263
Berezovsky, Boris 10, 28, 29, 30, 41, 128, 129, 135, 141
bilateral treaties 13
Blondel, J. 53
Boon, P. and Rodionov, D. 126
Bordachev, Timofei 244
Brezhnev, Leonid 5
Brudny, Y. M. 58
Buinaksk bombing 263
Burns, James MacGregor 3–4
Bush, George W. 263, 265, 269

Callaghan, Jim 5
capitalism
    competitive market-led 96, 97
    co-operative 109–10
    corporatist 110–11
    social democratic 109
    types of 95–6, 108
Central Asia 272–4
Chechnya 8–9, 30, 224, 255–68, 271
    comparison of two wars 262–4
    Khasavyurt peace agreement 259, 260
    media coverage 133–6
    under Putin 260–4
    support for war 262
    views of west 264–5
    Yeltsin period 255–60
Chernenko, Konstantin 5
Chernomyrdin, Viktor 6, 39, 58
Chubais, Anatoly 29, 96, 128, 144
Chukotka 11
Churchill, Winston 111
CIS 21, 269–85
    Charter 273
civil society 176, 183–5, 189, 192
Clinton, Bill 8, 269
Coalson, Robert 50
Common European Economic Space 243–4
Communist Party of France 55
Communist Party of Italy 55
Communist Party of the Russian Federation 45, 47, 53–75, 206–10, 218
    cowering of 69
    deal with *Edinstvo* 62
    Duma's largest faction 62

287

Index

electoral attraction 54–5
generational turnover 69
leadership in Duma 66
leadership style 56
loss of influence under Putin 69
mummified organisation 58
neo-Leninist colonisation of Duma 61
nomenklatura background 57
over-representation in Duma 63
parliamentarianism 61
portfolio purge 65–7
Constitution 20, 42, 76, 136, 156, 158, 159, 169, 171
   Bashkortostan 167–8
   infringements of 166–70
   Khakasiya 167
   Sakha 168–9
   Tatarstan 168
   Tyva 167
Constitutional Court 166
Constitutional Formalism 156
Corwin, J. A. 164
Cronin, Thomas 5

Dagestan 8
Dahl, Robert 178
Dahrendorf, Ralf 17
Danilov, Dmitri 245
democracy
   consolidation of 22–3, 176
   crypto- 24, 25
   delegative 18
   electoral 18
   and federal reforms 170–1
   guided 18, 32
   illiberal 18, 24
   managed 60
   manipulated 32
   regional 176–97
Deripaska, Oleg 10, 29
Diamond, Larry 18, 187
Dorenko, Sergei 141
Dubrovina, Elena 44
Dubrovka theatre siege 260, 263, 265
Dudaev, Dzhokar 256, 259
Duma 60, 63, 124, 125
   distribution of committee chairs 64
Dyachenko, Tatyana 20

economic reform 95–113, 114–32
economy 9–11
   August 1998 crisis 115, 117, 119, 121, 123–4
   bankruptcies 104
   capital flight 104
   Chaebolisation 126
   convergence 110–11
   extent of transformation 101
   financial crash 1998 10, 27
   fiscal performance 121
   GDP in Central and Eastern Europe 98
   legacy of communism 95
   macroeconomic management 119–23
   macroeconomic performance 117–19
   monetary policy 119–21
   oligarch management 127–30
   policy under Putin 115
   and politics 25, 127–30
   poverty 98–100
   predatory capitalism 10
   reasons for transition failure 103–8
   structural reform 100–3, 123–6
   tax reform 122
   see also capitalism; privatisation
Edinstvo see unity
Ekho Moskvy 134
Elazar, Daniel 156, 170
elections
   administrative control over 199–201, 218–20
   and democratisation 198–222
   falsification of official data 203
   gubernatorial elections 212–17
   invalid votes 203
   new law 219
   Presidential elections 199–206
   State Duma 206–12
electorate 76–92
   views in comparative perspective 85–9
   on current regime 83–4
   on elections 79
   freedoms 84–5
   parties 80–2
   satisfaction with democracy 90
   Soviet era 82–4
   trust in civic institutions 77–9

Index

ethnic diversity 177
ethnicity 191
Eurobarometer 89
European Union 225, 236–54, 231–3, 243, 276
   Common Strategy on Russia 225
   enlargement 229, 239, 241–2, 250, 282
   Medium-term Strategy 240
   Russia Summit 227
   trade with Russia 238–9, 242

FAR 44, 63, 64, 68, 137, 206–7, 208–11, 218
Farukshin, Midkhat 168
federal districts 13, 20, 158–62, 277
federal reforms 155–75
Federal Security Service (FSB) 6, 7
Federation 155, 156
Federation Council 157, 162–3
Federation Treaty 257
foreign policy 8, 20–1, 223–54, 269–85
   Baltic states 279
   Central Asia 272–4, 279–80
   and centrists 272
   concept 225, 230, 237, 269, 274
   evolution of 224–7, 270–2
   Eurasionist perceptions 272, 278
   liberal-Atlanticist school 271–2
   under Putin 227–34
   with USA 229, 232
Fridman, Mikhail 10
FSB 261

Gadzhiev, G. A. 156, 171
Gaidar, Yegor 258
Gazprom 129, 130, 139–43
Ghandi, Mahatma 4
Giddens, A. 19, 30
Glaz'ev, Sergei 28, 58, 65
Glushkov, Nikolai 141
Gorbachev, Mikhail 3, 4, 21, 277
Goryacheva, Svetlana 64
governors 157
   dismissal of 164–5
Grachev, Pavel 258
Gref, German 9
Gromov, Boris 258

Gubenko, Nikolai 64
Gusinsky, Vladimir 10, 29, 30, 41, 128, 129, 139–42

Hanson, Stephen E. 22
Hedlund, Stefan 10
Hellman, J. 114
Huntington, Samuel 22, 32, 192
Huskey, Eugine 59

Igrunov, Vyacheslav 7–8
Illarionov, Andrei 9, 118
Ilyumzhinov, Kirslan 165
IMF 111
Information Security Doctrine 136, 137
Iraq 234, 282
Ivanov, Sergei 13, 228, 245
Ivashov, Leonid 278

Johnson, Lyndon 5
Jowitt, Kenneth 32
Jurgenson, Sven 279

Kadyrov, Akhmed 264
Kahn, Jeffrey 12
Kaliningrad 239, 248–50, 276
Kalmykov, Yuri 258
Kas'yanov, Mikhail 14, 28, 123, 124, 129, 249
Kennedy, John F. 5
KGB 6, 7, 11, 13, 14
Khodorkovsky, Mikhail 10
Khristenko, Viktor 243
Khrushchev, Nikita 3, 21, 256
King, Preston 163
Kirienko, S. V. 158, 159, 160, 161
Kiselev, Yevgenii 29, 144
Kokov, Valerii 165
Kondratenko, Nikolai 180
Kostikov, Igor 9
Kozak, Dmitry 13, 14, 166, 169
Kozyrev, Andrei 271
Kruychkov, Vladimir 6
Kudrin, Aleksei 9, 123
Kulakov, Vladimir 180
Kuptsov, Valentin 56
Kursk nuclear submarine disaster 137
Kuvayev, Aleksandr 48

Index

Lakhova, Yekaterina 44
Latyshev, Petr 169
Lebed, Alexander 8, 258
Legal Dualism 157
legal reform 25
Lesin, Mikhail 136, 138, 143, 146
Liberal Democratic Party of Russia 42, 48, 58
Liberal Russia Party 50, 67
Linz, J. and Stepan, A. 22
Lobov, Oleg 258
LUKoil 11, 128, 141, 142
Lukyanov, A. 65
Luzhkov, Yurii 68, 138
Lysenko, Vladimir 170

Magomedov, Magomedali 165
Major, John 5
Mamut, Aleksandr 10, 29
Mandela, Nelson 4
Margelov, Mikhail 134
Markov, Sergei 32
Maskhadov, Aslan 135, 256, 259, 260, 263, 264, 265
Maslyukov, Yurii 65
Masyuk, Yelena 146
McFaul, Michael 199
McFaul, Michael and Petrov, Nikolai 181, 198
McMann, K. and Petrov, N. 182–3
measuring regional democratisation 176–8
media 29, 133–54
  confidence in 78
  under Putin 133–52
Media Ministry 135, 137, 143
Media-Most 134, 138–42
Mikhailov, Yevgeny 180
Military Doctrine 273
Mironov, Sergei 163

National Patriotic Union of Russia 58
National Security Concept 226
NATO 8, 224–7, 228, 229, 233, 236
  enlargement 8, 232, 239, 272, 275, 278
  Partnership for Peace 224
  Permanent Joint Council 224
  Russia–NATO Council 242, 278, 279

Nazdratenko, Alexander 29, 164
Nikolaev, Andrei 277
Nikolaev, Mikhail 169
Norilsk Nickel 128
NTV 10, 134, 135, 138–42, 144, 145, 146

O'Donnell, Guillermo 18
oligarchs 10, 29, 127–30
Oracheva, Oksana 158
Oreshkin, D. 199
ORT 134, 136, 138, 141, 144
Orttung, Robert 163
Orttung, Robert and Redaway, Peter 162, 165
Oslon, Aleksandr 136
Ostrow, J. M. 61
Our Home is Russia 39–40

Pain, Emil 258
parade of treaties 12
parties 39–75
  funding 47, 49
  key features of 43–4
  law on 39–52, 63, 66, 69
  multiplicity of 39, 47–8
  of power 42, 51
  registration of 45–6, 48, 50
  reorganisation of 25
  support for 44
  views of electorate 80–2
Partnership and Co-operation Agreement 236, 243, 245
party system 41–3
  floating party 59
Patten, Chris 243, 244
Pavlovsky, Gleb 22, 27, 65, 144
perestroika 6
Platov, Vladimir 178
Polish Democratic Left Alliance 55
political culture 76–94
political efficacy 80
political pluralism 12
Politkovskaya, Anna 136
polpredy 13, 158–62
Poltavchenko, Georgii 160
Potanin, Vladimir 128, 135
Potapov, Leonid 165

Powell, Colin 278
power-vertical 155
Precinct Electoral Commissions 198, 199, 201
Primakov, Yevgeny 6, 63, 144, 231, 278
Pristavkin, Anatolii 29
privatisation 115
Prokhanov, Alexander 28
Prusak, Mikhail 165
public opinion 26, 76–92
  see also elections
Pugachev, Sergei 10
Putin, Vladimir
  career 223
  centrist approach 18–19, 30
  comparison with Yeltsin 26–7
  consensual style 28, 59
  consolidation under 19, 26
  continuity with Yeltsin 32–3
  dictatorship of law 157
  economic policy 114–32
  elected monarchy 25
  electoral support 201–3
  elite and 30–1
  federal reforms 155–75
  leadership and regime change 3–16, 17–38
  Millennium Manifesto 21
  normalcy 18–21, 70
  normalisation 18–19
  normality 18–22, 24, 32
  patronage 25
  political process 27
  politics of stability 20
  press freedom 133–52
  relations to communists 60
  third way 30–1
  'vertical of power' 19
  war in Iraq 282
  Yeltsinism without Yeltsin 25

Rakhimov, Murtaza 165
Reddaway, P. and Glinski, D. 19
regional democratisation 176–97
regional elections 179–81, 198–222
regional index of democratisation 178–81
regional legislatures 164–5

Richter, Andrei 136, 143
Rigby, T. H. 23
robber baron privatisation 103
Robertson, George 225, 279
Roosevelt, Franklin D. 4
Rose, R. and Mackie, T. F. 54
Rose, R. and Mishler, W. 77
Ross, Cameron 177
Rossiya 68
RTR 134, 137, 140, 146
Russian Christian Democratic Party 50
Russia's Choice 40
Ryabov, Andrei 277
Rybkin, Ivan 39–40
Ryzhkov, Vladimir 48

Sakwa, Richard 58
Schumpeter, Joseph 18
Selezev, Gennadii 62, 64, 65, 68
Semigin, Gennadii 58
September 11 2001 26, 30, 226, 237, 238, 243, 264, 269, 270, 276, 277, 281
Seslavisnkii, Mikhail 135
Shabanov, Ivan 180
Shaimiev, Mintimer 165, 168, 206, 215, 216–17
Shakhrai, Sergei 257
Shamanov, Vladimir 214, 215
Sheinis, Viktor 30–1, 59
Shevtsova, Liliya 25, 58
Shoigu, Sergei 51
Shpigun, Gennadi 261
Shtyrov, Vyacheslav 179
Sibneft 11
Slavneft 10, 11
Smirnyagin, Leonid 171
Sobchak, Anatoly 6
social capital 176, 183–5
social democracy 68
Social Democratic Party of Russia 68
socio-economic development 185–8, 189
Solana, Javier 245
Stalin, Joseph 3, 4
Stankevich, Sergei 271
Starovoitova, Galina 257
START-II 63

Index

State Council 157, 164
Stepashin, Sergei 258, 261
Stiglitz, Joseph 103, 111
Stolypin, Peter 31
St Petersburg 11
Stroyev, Egor 165

Taliban 265
Tannahill, R. N. 55
Tarkhov, Viktor 212, 213, 215
Territorial Election Commissions 198–220
Titov, Konstantin 165, 212, 213, 215
Tkachev, Aleksandr 180
Tompson, William 13
transactional leaders 3–5
transforming leaders 3–5
Treaty of Tashkent 273
Trenin, Dmitri 238, 250
Troshkin, Nikolai 65
Tsipko, Aleksandr 28–9
Tsvetkovo, M. 163
Tuleev, A. 56, 68, 179
TV-Centre 134, 138
TV-6 141, 142, 144

unified legal space 166
Union of Journalists 135, 146
Union of Right Forces 47, 48, 49, 206–7
United Russia 51, 57, 64, 68
unity 50, 53, 56, 57, 65, 68, 157, 206–7

Urban, Michael 67
Ustinov, D. 143

Vanhanen, Tatu 178, 179
vertical chain of government 6
Veshnyakov, Vladimir 50
Voloshin, Aleksandr 11, 13, 28

Waal, Thomas de 263
Wahhabists 261
Washington Consensus 96
Watts, Ronald 155, 156
Weber, M. 95, 104
Wilson, Harold 5
Woodruff, D. 124
World Bank 111
World Trade Organisation 127, 225, 229, 230, 232, 236, 242, 276

Yabloko 45, 49, 68, 144
Yanderbiev, Zelimkhan 259
Yastrzhembskii, Sergei 134, 135, 146
Yavlinski, Grigorii 96, 144, 262
Yegorov, Nikolai 257
Yumahsov, Valentin 29

Zakaria, F. 18, 24
Zassoursky, Yassen 143
Zhirinovsky, V. 257
Zvyagintsev, Aleksandr 167
Zyuganov, Gennadii 55, 56, 60, 62, 65, 68, 199, 200, 201